Books by M. A. Stoneridge

A HORSE OF YOUR OWN, new, revised edition
A DOG OF YOUR OWN
GREAT HORSES OF OUR TIME

A HORSE OF YOUR OWN

M. A. STONERIDGE

A HORSE OF YOUR OWN

FOREWORD BY WILLIAM C. STEINKRAUS

DRAWINGS BY SAM SAVITT

OVER 250 PHOTOGRAPHS

New, Revised Edition

DOUBLEDAY & COMPANY, INC.
GARDEN CITY, NEW YORK
1980

Library of Congress Cataloging in Publication Data
Stoneridge, M A
A horse of your own.
Bibliography: p. 497
Includes index.
1. Horses. I. Title.
SF285.S88   1980   636.1
ISBN: 0-385-14617-5
Library of Congress Catalog Card Number 78–22369

Foreword

A good horse (to paraphrase Xenophon) will have sound feet, and be fast, strong, and willing. By contrast, the bad one will either be so lazy that you must beat him to make him go, or so highly strung that you must be constantly on guard to avoid upsetting him. So was it in Xenophon's time, a mere 2,400-odd years ago, and so it is today. That much has not changed, nor has most of the general advice proffered by Xenophon in his brief treatise *Hippike;* the horse has been with man for a very long time, and the basic anatomy of their relationship has long since been charted in elaborate detail from virtually every aspect.

Why, then, the need for yet another horse book, or indeed, a revised edition of an existing one? The answer is twofold. On the one hand, while *man's* relationship with the horse may not change very rapidly through the millennia, the relationship between individual men, women, and children and individual horses is commencing anew all the time. And since the horse can't very well read up on what he ought to know at the beginning of the relationship, it certainly behooves the human to obtain a bit of advance information, even if it's mostly the kind of stuff Xenophon already knew all those years ago.

The second reason is that while basics don't change very much, a lot of other things do, and with surprising rapidity. Hence those who happen to compare this revision with earlier editions of A HORSE OF YOUR OWN will find only occasional clarifications and amplifications of most general advice, but a considerable amount of space devoted to breeds and activities that have achieved significantly greater prominence in recent years. In addition, there are a great many changes in particular detail, mostly involving new personalities, products, styles and fashions, rules and technical requirements, and (sob) prices.

Many of the earlier illustrations have also been changed, not so much because they didn't show the right thing anymore as that they somehow looked old-fashioned. For example, virtually *nobody* wears "pegged" riding breeches in this day and age. The new stretch fabrics have noticeably changed the "look" of most formal riding attire, while the new informality has restricted its use more and more to the confines of the show ring and hunting field. For better or worse, plastics and other synthetics are doing dozens of jobs around stables that used to be done with leather, wood, rubber, or galvanized metal, and while mucking out is still mucking out, in many stables the bedding and the muck basket will be products that didn't exist when the first edition of this book was written.

As a long-time rules committee member, I am especially aware of the number of rules changes that had to be introduced into the present text, and join the rest of the world in deploring their constant proliferation. The earliest copy of the American Horse Shows Association rules I happen to have kept (1940) covers them all in a hundred pages, all the way from the front matter to the Bareback Comic Costume Class specifications. The 1978 tome takes three times the number of bigger pages with finer print to cover the same ground, and appends a couple hundred pages of lists and directory material. The International Equestrian Federation, however, has an even worse problem (from one slender pamphlet to seven portly volumes in four decades), and no doubt all the other alphabetic associations from the AAHA (American Andalusian Horse Association) to the WPSA (Welsh Pony Society of America) have struggled unsuccessfully with the same problem. In any case, only a small portion of this proliferation has had to find its way into the following pages, and if it is not exactly a good thing, at least it is arguably a necessary evil.

I am not enough of an economist to be able to say the same thing about the constant rising prices that have afflicted the horse world since the first edition of this book, and they still scare me witless. I am old enough to remember, along with nickel coffee, newspapers, and chewing gum, the days when you could board horses for a dollar a day, get riding lessons for five, and buy a darn nice horse for a few hundred, and I have to admit that I don't "relate well" to the concept of million-dollar yearlings and three-hundred-thousand-dollar show horses, even if they're jumpers. It's dangerous to be very specific about prices in writing books these days, and hence there's a strong tendency (in this one, too, I'm afraid) to discuss things more generally. Actual prices just don't mean very much after a year or two.

Spiraling prices and proliferating rules aside, most of the things that have happened in the horse world since the first edition of this book have been very much to the good. According to the American Horse Council (itself a new and valuable organization), more people in the United States ride and own horses than ever before, and there are many indications that the sport is continuing to grow in prestige as well as popularity.

Personally, I think that's not only marvelous but *right*—for I remain firmly persuaded that riding is one of the very best and most versatile of all sports. It can be enjoyed by almost all ages and temperaments of both sexes in forms that range from tranquil to breath-taking, and despite those rising costs, it remains one of the best values in the entire sports spectrum. There is nothing else quite like it.

There is also nothing else quite like owning your own horse. Riding, above all, is a relationship, and just as in human relationships, the finer grades of understanding require continuity. Admittedly, ownership brings added responsibilities along with its added pleasures, and this is truer than ever in this era of rising standards and rising ambitions. Owning a horse isn't *exactly* like being a parent—perhaps the horses aren't *quite* so good at staying a step ahead of you, and they tend to be a bit more forgiving of the mistakes you make with them—but there are certainly broad areas of similarity. And just as the parent can use all the sympathetic, sensible, and practical advice he/she can get in discharging the parental responsibility, so the horse owner who tries to depend entirely on trial and error is treading dangerous ground.

On the following pages, M. A. Stoneridge has sensibly, reliably, and, yes, charmingly too, provided the novice horse owner with all of the essential information it takes to cope with A Horse of Your Own. This book has done a great service for what are already several generations of horse lovers, and I am proud to have collaborated even in a small way (literally) in that achievement.

William C. Steinkraus

Acknowledgments

Just as it would be unreasonable to expect an individual horse to be adept at every equine activity from Gymkhana to Grand Prix Dressage, it is obvious that an author who attempts to furnish solid, basic information on a subject as vast as this one cannot rely entirely on personal experience. While the horse is generally obliged to limit his aspirations to a single specialty, an author fortunately has the possibility of augmenting his knowledge by benefiting from the experience of others—in other words, by research. This may consist of consulting existing literature, including official publications, rule books and manuals, current periodicals, and especially of personal contacts with eminent experts in the various phases of the subject involved. I have therefore sought the collaboration of many organizations and individuals in trying to make this book an interesting summary of "what every horseman ought to know," not only about horses in general, his own in particular, and his special field of equine interest, whatever it may be, but also all (or almost all) of the other breeds and activities.

It would be impossible to mention by name all those who have helped me to try to achieve this goal. But I would like to thank: the American Horse Shows Association; the United States Pony Clubs; the United States Equestrian Team, Inc.; the Professional Rodeo Cowboys Association; the United States Polo Association and *Polo Magazine;* the United States Trotting Association; the Jockey Club; the National Cutting Horse Association; the National Steeplechase and Hunt Association; the United States Combined Training Association; the American Quarter Horse Association; the Appaloosa Horse Club and the *Appaloosa News;* the Arabian Horse Registry of America; the International Arabian Horse Association; the American Connemara Pony Society; the American Paint Horse Association; the American Morgan Horse Association; the Pinto Horse Association of America; the Pony of the Americas Club; the American Saddle Horse Breeders and Exhibitors Association; the Trakehner Breed Association and Registry of America; and the Welsh Pony Society of America. And I would like to express special gratitude to the many horse men and women who have generously shared with the readers of this book their exceptional equestrian knowledge, in particular to:

Mr. Frank Chapot; Mr. Bertalan de Nemethy; Mr. Robert Freels; Mr. E. F. Leach; Mr. Arthur McCashin; Mr. George Morris; Dr. Joseph O'Dea, DVM; Mr. Kurt Rosenthal; Mr. Raymond Woolfe, Jr.; Mr. and Mrs. William C. Steinkraus; and Mr. and Mrs. W. Sheldon Winans.

Finally, a special word of thanks to Mrs. Ellin K. Roberts, whose original conception and painstaking preparation of this book have given constant proof not only of professional skill but also of a genuine love of horses.

M.A.S.

Contents

A HORSE OF YOUR OWN

1.   A Horse of Your Own

A horse of your own! It may be a sudden inspiration or a stubborn resolution. It may be an avowed ambition or a secret dream. But almost every horse lover sooner or later hopes to become a horse owner.

As in most dream projects, there is quite a difference between the dream and the reality. Owning a horse entails considerable responsibility, time, and expense. In return it provides an incalculable amount of pleasure and pride. You will give a lot, but you will receive even more, especially if you have taken the pains to select the most suitable horse for your particular circumstances, interests, and aptitudes.

Throughout the ages, nature and science have produced such a wide variety of equine breeds and types that every would-be horse owner has an excellent chance of finding the one that will fulfill his requirements. Just think. Your own horse might be a tiny, lovable Shetland pony, with its short legs and gentle disposition; a glamorous, hot-blooded Arabian with flowing mane and tail; a flashy, high-stepping American Saddle Bred; a dependable, sturdy Morgan. He might be that Rolls-Royce of horses, an aristocratic, sensitive Thoroughbred; or he might be a wise and kindly animal of indeterminate age and breeding who will teach you more about riding and horses than you could learn from any human instructor.

Obviously, the art of being a happy horse owner lies in acquiring the horse that is just right for you, one that is physically and temperamentally capable of performing the work that you expect of him, whether it is to jump an Olympic course or to promenade an elderly gentleman through the park. Despite their versatility, it would be unreasonable to expect any one horse to be equally adept at hunting, show jumping, cattle cutting, and in harness. So before you get down to the actual business of choosing a horse of your own, you might ask yourself some pertinent questions to make sure that you know exactly what you are looking for.

Remember that a horse is not just a decorative pet to have around the place, but an active, sporting animal. Therefore the first question might very well be: What is the principal equestrian activity in which you wish to indulge?

The two general categories of equine sport are riding and driving. If it is driving that interests you (and the amateur harness-driving sport is enjoying a marked revival at the moment), then you will be concerned with the types of horses especially suited to driving: Shetland and Hackney ponies, Standardbreds, and riding horses that can also be used for Fine Harness work such as Morgans and American Saddle Breds.

If you are happier in the saddle, you should ask yourself in which kind of saddle you feel most at home, because there are two principal riding styles: Eastern and Western. The main difference between them is that Western style employs split reins and involves more hand-riding, which accounts for all of those fancy bits; whereas Eastern riding involves closed reins, depends primarily on the legs and seat for communication and control, and utilizes far lighter, less cumbersome equipment. If the cowboy image gives you a thrill, you will find the right horse among the Western breeds, the American Quarter Horses, the Morgans, and the Arabs. But if you lean toward the classical refinement of the Eastern style, you must choose between the Saddle Seat and the Hunter Seat.

Should your talent and skill be most effective in the Saddle Seat, your ideal mount is likely to be either a Three-Gaited or Five-Gaited American Saddle Bred, a Tennessee Walking Horse, or perhaps an Arab. But for riding Hunter Seat, a Thoroughbred or Thoroughbred mixture, or a Western horse with some Thoroughbred blood will be most suitable.

Quite aside from the question of personal preference, your physical condition and age will have an influence in determining the type of horse that is best for you. And his quality within the type should be related to your degree of training as a horseman and to the extent of your showing ambitions—not to forget the size of your bank account.

It is also a good idea to consider the region in which you live, especially if you wish to show or to engage in organized activities with fellow horsemen. In many areas there is a distinct preference for certain types of horses, and if your own choice is too unusual you may find that competitions for your breed are limited or nonexistent. For instance, in the Middle Western states, horse shows include relatively few Hunter classes, the majority of prizes being reserved for the Saddle Horse and Fine Harness breeds, and horsemanship is usually judged in the Saddle Seat. In the celebrated hunting countries of Virginia, Pennsylvania, and Maryland, it's not surprising that the Hunting Seat is generally preferred.

If you live in the West, your choice is evident. Unless you have very definite leanings toward a special breed, a Western-type horse will be your most useful partner for taking part in the trail rides, Western horse shows, and horse-club activities that flourish in your part of the country. Even in the East, Western horses and Western riding have become increasingly popular. Many a Thoroughbred stable also houses a string of cutting horses, or a few well-bred Appaloosas or Palominos, and the most tradition-ridden Eastern horse shows include a Western Division. At the same time, Eastern riding has become more fashionable in the West, and a typical Colorado or Texas horse show now offers as many Eastern as Western classes.

Over a hundred recognized breeds of horses and an infinite number of crossbreeds have developed since the prehistoric five-toed Phenacodus and the four-toed Eohippus evolved into the handsome one-toed animal we call a horse. (The hoof, as you may know, is actually a form of toe.) Without going too far back in the family tree, it may be helpful for the prospective horse-owner to take a brief look at some of the leading breeds in America today, for in the veins of his own horse will probably flow the blood of one or several of these important strains.

THE ARABIAN HORSE

The most ancient of the modern breeds is the Arabian horse, who can trace his proud ancestry back at least three thousand years.

While horses in other lands were still roaming about in wild herds, he was being tenderly reared in the Bedouin tents by Arab women, caressed and taught tricks by their children, until he was of age to be trained by his Moslem master. To these desert nomads, often at war among themselves, a sound, fleet, and obedient mount could mean the difference between life and death, and a well-bred war-mare was a prized possession. Mohammed, who mounted his disciples on Arabians, decreed that it was the religious duty of all Moslems to love their horses, and the Koran is full of advice on horse care. It is undoubtedly due to these many centuries of controlled breeding and special attention that the Arabian horse developed its undeniable intelligence.

The Arab is a smallish animal (14–15 hands; 800–1,000 pounds), with an elegant appearance and a floating action. Among the marks that distinguish him from other breeds are his gazelle-shaped head with its "dish-faced" or concave profile, pointed ears, eyes set low and far apart, and a small soft muzzle that can fit in the palm of your hand. He has high withers, a high-set tail, a slim arched neck, and a well-knit, short back (the purebred Arab has twenty-three instead of twenty-four lumbar vertebrae, a peculiarity that endows him with unusual weight-carrying ability for his size). The bone structure of his legs is remarkably strong, with large joints, thick short cannon bones, and prominent leg tendons, making him less vulnerable to leg and hoof trouble than most other

An Arabian stallion. (*Photo by Budd*)

breeds. He is practically immune to respiratory ailments as well, possibly because his large throat and nostrils are capable of great distention. Among the leading families of Arabian horses the most highly prized is the "Kehailan," almost always bay in color and noted for speed.

As a riding horse, the Arabian has a flat-footed walk, a choppy trot (which some claim is not a natural gait to him, although it is quickly learned), a comfortable canter, and an excellent fast gallop. While he is too small to be a very good Jumper, the French have had success with modern Thoroughbred-Arab crosses (called Anglo-Arabs), especially in speed jumping contests where handiness is more important than power. The superbly trained Cadre Noir horses are by tradition Anglo-Arabs, as are perhaps the majority of high-class pleasure mounts abroad.

The only specialties in which the Arabian horse really excels are endurance trials and long-distance races, the all-breed world record having been set by Crabbet in 1920 for a distance of 300 miles, in 52 hours, 32 minutes, carrying 245 pounds. But the Arabian is outstanding for his versatility. He can do an amazing number of things reasonably well. Occasionally he makes a satisfactory Polo Pony and often a good rodeo, cutting, and roping horse. One Arab stallion, Farana, is said to have become so perfect as a reining show horse that he was finally withdrawn from competition in the state of California because nobody would ride against him. The Arab is an ideal Trail Horse, attractive on parade or in harness, and delightful as a pleasure mount, especially for a child or woman, because of his small size and his obedient, courageous nature.

However, the Arabian's greatest value still lies in his ability to improve other breeds, which is why a rather high percentage is kept whole as stallions. He is one of the founders of the English Thoroughbred; in Russia his blood helped to create the Orloff Trotter, in France the Percheron, in America the Morgan and, indirectly through the Thoroughbred, the Standardbred trotter and the American Saddle Bred Horse. Before the war there were world-renowned Arabian stud farms in Egypt and Arabia, and in Poland, where General George S. Patton managed to rescue some of the prize stallions from the retreating Germans and sent them to the United States as remount stallions. Today, many of the best modern Arabs are bred in America.

In recent years there has been a marked increase of interest in the Arabian horse in this country, particularly in the Western states, with an ever-growing number of active breeding farms, Arabian horse clubs, and more and more all-Arab shows and regular horse shows that offer Arabian classes in their programs.

An Arabian Western Pleasure Horse, Big Deal, owned by Van Jacobsen. (*Photo by Sparagowski, courtesy of the AHSA*)

THE THOROUGHBRED

A direct descendant of the Arabian horse is the aristocratic Thoroughbred—which is not merely a word denoting "purebred" as some people believe, but a name given to a deliberately created, distinct breed, developed in England in the eighteenth century. The Thoroughbred is the champion athlete among modern horses, which is as it should be, as he has been bred especially for speed and jumping ability.

Most horsemen are familiar with the names of the three desert stallions who were crossed with English mares and from whom all registered Thoroughbred horses are descended: the Godolphin Arabian (or "Barb") who came into the possession of the Earl of Godolphin in 1724 after a British horse-dealer supposedly spotted him pulling a water cart on a Paris street and recognized him to be an Arab stallion that had been presented to Louis XIV by the Sultan of Morocco; the Byerly Turk, imported into England by a certain Captain Byerly for use as a war charger during the Irish Wars; and the Darley Arabian, purchased in Syria in 1722 by the British consul there, who sent him as a gift to his brother, a Mr. Darley of Yorkshire.

Needless to say, each of these three foundation sires was extremely prepotent, but the most prolific was the Darley Arabian. One of his great-great-grandsons was the fabulous, unbeaten Eclipse, who is the ancestor of the great majority of modern race horses. The rest trace back either to Matchem, a grandson of the Godolphin Barb, or to Herod, great-grandson of the Byerly Turk (whose line was favored by the Aga Khan in his world-wide racing-stud operations), because all the other male branches have died out. Perhaps the most striking proof of prepotency in this extraordinary breed is the fact that almost every gray Thoroughbred descends from the Alcock Arabian, whose color has persisted for over 250 years! (The very few exceptions trace in an unbroken gray line to the Brownlow Turk.)

Due to his desert background and years of inbreeding, the Thoroughbred is not only the fastest and most beautiful of horses, but also the most spirited, sensitive, and excitable. Along with the Arab, he is considered to be "hot-blooded" as opposed to other "cold-blooded" strains. The average modern Thoroughbred measures 15–17 hands, considerably more than his distinguished ancestors, who were all under 14.2 hands. (For a complete explanation of the measurement of horses, see page 54.) He weighs between 900 and 1,200 pounds and is noted for his delicate head, long slender neck, sloping shoulders, a very fine skin showing the veins, and a general appearance of quality and refinement. He is a beautiful natural mover, with long, low, ground-covering strides originating from the shoulder, whereas common horses tend to move from the knees.

The exuberant courage of the Thoroughbred is legendary. Call it "heart" or "nerve" or what you will, it is part of the Thoroughbred character never to give up, and this generous quality has been exploited with remarkable results in jumping and racing. If he has suffered a bad fall during a race, for instance, a Thoroughbred will be up and off again even if it means hobbling along with a broken leg, whereas the common horse is apt to remain lying on the ground until forcibly pulled to his feet. A moving example of this Thoroughbred quality was Sandsablaze, a grandson of Count Fleet who became an outstanding show Jumper. A member of the Gold Medal U. S. Team in the Pan American Games in Mexico (1975) and again in Puerto Rico (1979), Sandsablaze fractured a cannon bone after clearing the last obstacle of the 1979 Garden State Grand Prix, yet managed to cross the finish line on three legs to win the

A superb Thoroughbred race horse, Secretariat, Triple Crown winner in 1973 and now a successful stud horse. (*Wide World photo*)

event. Unfortunately, the damage was irreparable and this gallant competitor had to be put down.

The adventures of the steeplechaser Moifaa, another particularly game Thoroughbred, have often been told—and probably embellished. Anyway, Moifaa, so the story goes, showed such promise on New Zealand tracks at the turn of the century that his owners decided to send him to England to try his luck in the formidable Aintree Grand National of 1904. In the middle of the voyage a terrible tempest arose and the ship that was transporting Moifaa was wrecked off the coast of a deserted island, its crew and cargo disappearing in the raging seas. That is, all except Moifaa! The race horse bravely swam to the nearest shore and several weeks later a rescue party discovered him, alive and well. Resuming his interrupted route, Moifaa arrived in England shortly before the Grand National. Despite his harrowing experience, he appeared in splendid form at the starting gate—and won the race. (To make the fairy-tale ending even better, he was subsequently purchased by the Prince of Wales and lived happily ever after in royal splendor.)

Most modern Thoroughbreds are bred and raised primarily as race horses and are registered with the American or British Jockey Clubs, which exercise so rigid a control over the breed that the great Man O' War (who was, of course, 100 per cent Thoroughbred) was refused for registration in England because part of his breeding record had disappeared during the Civil War. The American Jockey Club is no less strict, one of its numerous regulations requiring that the name of imported

Thoroughbred stallions and brood mares be preceded by an asterisk, to show that they were bred abroad.

In order to simplify racing classifications, another Jockey Club ruling gives all Thoroughbred horses the same birthday, January 1, even though most colts are born between February and June. Thus, a colt born in June is officially one year old on the following first of January. There have been recurrent movements to change this arbitrary birth date, because some racing colts are imported from other hemispheres where the seasons are the reverse of ours (notably Argentina), and the present rule obliges them to race against American-bred animals who may be as much as six months older. So far, however, the proposed revision has always been voted down.

Racing foals start their training at the age of one, much earlier than other breeds, and colts who turn out to be unsuitable for the track, as well as older horses with mediocre racing records and unpromising stud prospects, often make excellent riding horses. Thoroughbreds possess superior ability for jumping, hunting, and dressage. The U. S. Olympic Equestrian Teams are mounted mostly on Thoroughbred horses. The Thoroughbred has also invaded the rodeo arena in recent years, and an ever-increasing number is being trained to become outstanding stock horses. In the right hands, a Thoroughbred can be amazingly versatile. For example, Rock Pocket, who was purchased by two professional polo players, Bobby Rawlings and Vincent Rizzo, retired after his ninth race

A famous Thoroughbred Conformation Hunter Champion, Cap and Gown, owned by Mr. and Mrs. A. E. Cunningham. (*Photo by Marshall Hawkins*)

The Thoroughbred Bally Cor, ridden by Tad Coffin, is shown above during the Dressage test of the 1975 Pan American Games, and below during the cross-country phase of the 1976 Olympic Games. The pair won both Gold Medals. (*Photo above by Gamecock; photo below by Sue Maynard*)

The renowned Thoroughbred Olympic Three-Day Event horse, Laurenson, with rider Michael Plumb, made this fantastic jump over the "coffin" at the Ledyard Horse Trials. (*Photo by Sue Maynard*)

track victory to become Mrs. Rizzo's personal riding horse. As Field Master of the Potomac Hunt, Mrs. Rizzo was soon riding him regularly to hounds, had won a Combined Training Event with him, and was even winning ribbons in Dressage competitions.

A part-bred Thoroughbred with one-half or three-quarters Thoroughbred blood is one of the most useful and versatile riding horses that can be found, for he may be ridden in Eastern or Western rig and share with his owner the varied pleasures of hunting, jumping, polo, learning rodeo specialties, or merely hacking across country or through the city park. The best U. S. Cavalry horses were most often one-half or more Thoroughbred, while most of the top Hunters today have at least three-quarters Thoroughbred blood.

Although the full Thoroughbred is not usually considered to be a child's or a beginner's horse, since he can be more easily spoiled by rough handling than other breeds, some of them with suitable temperaments fill the role admirably. At any rate, almost all modern light-horse

Harry Gill's famous Thoroughbred, Idle Dice, the top money-winning Open Jumper of all time, ridden by Rodney Jenkins. (*Photo by Sue Maynard*)

breeds owe much of their quality, intelligence, and performing ability to their Thoroughbred blood.

THE WESTERN HORSE

One of the breeds that has been most improved in recent years by Thoroughbred crosses is the Western horse, a name that denotes a type of horse rather than a specific registered breed. The vast majority of the equine population of the United States at the present time is Westernbred, and dealers' barns and riding stables from coast to coast probably have more Westerns in their stalls than any other single kind of horse.

Western horses come in almost all colors and a wide variety of shapes and sizes. For show purposes, their height has been limited to 14.2–16 hands, although many working cowboys consider an animal over 15.2 to be too big for practical ranch work. All of them share the same principal qualities of smallness, liveliness, hardiness, and versatility.

While it may be romantic to think of him as descending from the wild ponies that once ranged the Western prairies, the Western horse actually traces his origins back to the perfectly domesticated Spanish horses brought to the New World by the conquistadors. (Domesticated animals that have thus reverted to wild life are described as "feral" rather than "wild.") Cortez is known to have taken seventeen horses of Arabian and Barb blood on his expedition to Mexico in 1519, and a few years later Coronado set forth with his companions on 260 Spanish steeds to explore what is now the state of Kansas and, incidentally, to discover the Mississippi River.

The American Indians were quick to adopt this strange new animal; in fact, the "adoption" sometimes took place on dark nights in an unguarded mission corral. The agile redskins were among the most gifted equestrians who ever lived, but they were hopeless as breeders. Preferring to use the most handsome stallions as war steeds, they allowed the others to propagate in a semi-wild state, living off the land and migrating from one grazing plain to another. This hardy life produced a sturdy, lively, intelligent animal, somewhat limited in size and lacking in refinement. He has been given many different names, including Cayuse, Mustang, and Bronco, which is a Spanish word for "wild."

The superb Thoroughbred stallions of the U. S. Army Remount Service and modern breeding methods have added greater quality to the Western horse, without altering his natural character. Today he is most often part-Thoroughbred, part-Quarter Horse, part-Morgan, part-Arab, or merely of undetermined mixed blood, the present trend being to breed predominantly Thoroughbred and Quarter Horse types.

Another trend has been to create separate registries for different types of Western horses, based on their breeding, color, and markings, in order to perpetuate and improve such breeds as the Appaloosa, Palomino, Albino, Buckskin, Paint Horse, Pinto, Spanish Mustang, and Spanish Barb.

However, the ordinary Western we are talking about is at the same time the typical pleasure horse and the typical working stock horse, for he can be ridden Eastern or Western style with equal ease. He may also be trained as a Parade horse, a rodeo performer, and for jumping or hunting. But most often, he is seen as an agreeable riding partner on trails and bridle paths, from West to East.

THE AMERICAN SADDLE BRED HORSE

The most popular show horse in the United States is the American Saddle Bred, a strictly American creation developed on the vast plantations of Kentucky, Tennessee, and Missouri as a comfortable and elegant means of transportation either under saddle or in light harness.

Although the official foundation sire, Denmark, was of Thoroughbred and Arabian descent and a race horse besides, the modern Saddle Horse has been bred for show and is quite different from the modern Thoroughbred. About the same size (15–16 hands; 900–1,200 pounds), his hind legs are not as straight as the Thoroughbred's; he is shorter backed and holds his head high on a long, tapering neck. While the Thoroughbred attains fantastic speed with an extended action, the Saddle Bred picks his feet up high off the ground, his back scarcely seeming to move, offering a picture of proud elegance to the observer and a sensation of easy comfort to the rider.

The Three-Gaited Saddle Horse, who wears his mane "roached" and the top of his tail clipped too, produces the three natural gaits (walk, trot, and canter) with a high degree of animation and refinement. The Five-Gaited, usually of heavier build and with his tail and mane left long and flowing, acquires two additional artificial gaits: a "slow gait" which is almost always a syncopated four-beat running gait called the stepping

A Three-Gaited Saddle Horse Champion, Barbados Exit, ridden by Helen Crabtree. (*Photo by Lois Rappaport*)

The peerless Five-Gaited Saddle Horse Champion, Wing Commander, ridden by Earl Teater. (*Photo courtesy of the American Saddle Horse Breeders Association*)

pace; and a fast gait, the "rack," which is the rider's pride and joy, being speedy, flashy, and comfortable—but tiring for the horse. During the rack, each foot strikes the ground separately at equal intervals, marking four distinct beats. It is the most strenuous of all gaits and is seldom well performed by any other breed.

The Saddle Bred also excels as a harness horse, the Three-Gaited (familiarly referred to as a "Walk-Trot" horse) and the Five-Gaited (a "Gaited horse" to the experts) being shown to a buggy as well as under saddle in Combination classes, while others are trained to perform exclusively in the Fine Harness division.

The Saddle Horse has often been called an equine peacock; but you mustn't be disappointed if the gentle and trustworthy riding hack you may be considering seems plain compared to the Saddle Bred champion you so admired at the Kansas City Royal Horse Show. The fact is that the show Saddle Horse is usually so highly bred and schooled and so artificially groomed that he can be used for nothing but showing. His feet, which are permitted to grow long and then are weighed down with special shoes to increase his high action, would not stay sound very long

A Champion Saddle Bred Fine Harness Horse, Glenview Radiance, owned by Mr. F. D. Sinclair. (*Photo by Jack Holvoet*)

A Saddle Bred Horse ridden in Western style, Genius Ebony Lady. (*Photo by Joan S. Byrne, courtesy of the American Saddle Horse Breeders Association*)

during a rocky trail ride, and his glamorous high tail is the result of cutting the depressor muscles and the horse spending most of his time in a tail set. His show-ring appearance is often further enhanced by such artifices as a dyed mane and tail and even a tail wig.

The riding-type Saddle Bred, on the other hand, is an ideal hack and makes an excellent Combination pleasure horse, being equally amenable to riding under saddle and to driving in light harness. Although their gaits are largely a matter of skillful training, Saddle Breds seem to have an inborn aptitude for learning more gaits more quickly than most other breeds. In fact, they are quick and willing to develop a variety of different skills, and a number of superior Jumpers and Dressage horses have been registered Saddle Breds. Some of them are ridden Western style and taught to neck-rein; others are trained for practical ranch work and become quite competent as cutting horses, although they lack the speed necessary for winning arena competitions.

Today their popularity still remains largely concentrated in the Middle Western states where the breed originated. But because they are quick and willing to learn, pleasant and comfortable to ride, usually of a gentle and tractable nature, Saddle Bred horses can be the ideal mounts for horsemen, even very young ones, who seek more pleasure than thrills from their riding hours.

THE MORGAN HORSE

The oldest of the American breeds is the Morgan horse, developed quite unwittingly in New England by a Vermont schoolteacher-farmer, Justin Morgan. In 1795 he brought back from Massachusetts in part payment of a debt a two-year-old bay colt, who became known as "the Justin Morgan horse," the only horse to found a breed which bears his name.

He was a small animal, 14 hands high, very sturdily built and with amazing stamina. The thirty-two years of his life were filled with hard work. He toiled as a farm horse, as a race horse, trotting and running short distances under saddle and in harness; he pulled out stumps and hauled timber, always with extraordinary willingness and terrific energy. He had such remarkable ability to pass on his physical and temperamental qualities to his offspring that he became in great demand as a stud. In fact, every Morgan horse is descended from this one stallion.

First appreciated as trotting horses, the Morgans were mostly used for general light utility work until recent years, when the emphasis has been placed on the saddle and show type, with a more refined head and legs. As a matter of fact, Morgan breeders have been criticized for adding so much Thoroughbred and Saddle Horse blood for the sake of refinement that today true Morgans are very rare. There was even a government-sponsored project some years ago to "Save the Morgan," for although his uncontested superiority as a roadster is of little interest any more, the original Morgan blood is of inestimable value to breeders.

He has remained a relatively small horse (14–15.2 hands; 900–1,200 pounds), with a short back and legs, a naturally high head carriage, extremely heavy sloping shoulders, a deep-barreled chest, and sturdy quarters. A typical Morgan head is instantly recognizable, with its straight or slightly dished face, big eyes set wide apart, small ears set wide and carried alertly, a small muzzle with firm lips and large nostrils and a prominent jaw. His gaits are quick and "trappy," with brisk, short steps, and he still inherits the unusual endurance, longevity, and gentle disposition of his ancestor, the Justin Morgan horse.

A Morgan horse in a Junior Saddle Seat class. (*Photo by Judy Frederick*)

Furthermore, the modern Morgan is just as versatile as was the Justin Morgan horse in his day. He can, in fact, do almost anything honorably well, from harness driving and pleasure hacking to hunting, jumping, and elementary dressage. Westerners have discovered that he has considerable cow sense, and nowadays he is apt to be seen almost as often in Western rig as in Eastern tack. All-Morgan shows invariably feature a unique Justin Morgan Performance event, in which the entrants first race a half-mile in harness at the trot, then race a half-mile galloping under saddle; they next compete in the show ring at a walk, trot, and canter, and finally crown the display by hauling a 500-pound weight. Is it any wonder that the admirable little Morgan horse, on the brink of extinction fifty years ago, has been steadily gaining in popularity?

The Morgan horse, or a mixture of Morgan blood with some other breed such as Western, Saddle Bred, or Standardbred, produces a very good all-round riding-driving horse, and for pleasure hacking he is as reliable in city traffic as he is sure-footed on mountain trails. Justly appreciated by riding academies, schools, camps, and dude ranches, he excels wherever stamina and dependability are required. A Morgan strain can often be found in small horses especially bred for children; a cross between a Morgan horse and a Welsh pony, for example, produces one of the best possible mounts for a young child who is just learning how to ride.

The Morgan horse Gallant Shamrock, owned by Morningside Stables, pulling the "stone boat" in a Morgan Versatility competition. (*Photo by J. D. Symer, courtesy of the Morgan Horse Club*)

THE STANDARDBRED

While the fame of the little Morgan horse has spread far beyond the boundaries of his New England birthplace, the entire world recognizes the American Standardbred as one of the best racing trotters and pacers that exists. Our most successful contribution to the horse family has required over 150 years of selective breeding based more on performance than on conformation, and the result is an assortment of different types of horses, but all of them fast. Originally, in order to qualify for registration as a Standardbred, a horse had to produce a certain "standard" of speed per mile: 2'30" for a trotter, and 2'25" for a pacer (fairly modest by today's standards.) But now that the breed has been established, any foal of a registered dam and sire is eligible for registration.

The official founder was a gray Thoroughbred stallion called Messenger, who was imported to Philadelphia in 1788 from England, where he had enjoyed only mild success as a race horse, despite a distinguished pedigree which traced back in a straight male line through Mambrino, Engineer, Sampson, Blaze, and Flying Childers, to the Darley Arabian; on his dam's side, he was distantly related to both the Godolphin Arabian and the Byerly Turk. But the speed that Messenger didn't show himself, he delivered generously to his offspring, who include many of the greatest trotting and pacing champions as well as such flat-racing stars as Whirlaway and Equipoise.

One of Messenger's great-grandsons, Rysdyk's Hambletonian, was even more successful as a stallion—he fathered no less than 1,335 foals! —so that to many people "Hambletonian" is practically synonymous with "Standardbred." There have been other renowned trotting families, including the Morgans, Mambrinos, Black Hawks, and Clays, but it is true that most of the leading trotting and pacing champions are predominantly of Hambletonian blood.

The greatest of all was Greyhound, who held more world records than any horse in history. His trotting time for the mile in 1:55¼, set in 1938, was unequaled during his lifetime. He passed away in 1965 at the age of thirty-three, snow white by then. In 1969, Nevele Pride at last succeeded in breaking his long-time record by trotting a mile in 1:54⅘.

Standardbred breeders, like their Thoroughbred colleagues, attempt to produce outstanding racers by a judicious combination of bloodlines and sell their training drop-outs for nonracing purposes. Among the lead-

The American Standardbred trotter Greyhound, one of the great horses of all time. (*Photo courtesy of the U. S. Trotting Association*)

ing Standardbred sires, such as Bye Bye Bird, Most Happy Fella, Star's Pride, Rodney, and Tar Heel, the greatest was certainly Adios, who died in 1965 at the age of twenty-five, having sired 589 foals of which 500 became racers, winning more than 5,200 races and almost twenty million dollars in purse money. His gifted progeny included three top sires in their own right: Adios Harry, Adios Butler, and the sensational Bret Hanover, who was perhaps the best pacer in history. In 68 starts he was never out of the money, and retired to stud at the end of his record-setting four-year old season bearing the title of Harness Horse of the Year for the third successive year.

While they may vary in appearance, almost all Standardbred horses have powerful haunches, with the hind legs placed behind rather than under the croup, to give the pistonlike action necessary for trotting or pacing speed. Conformation is more important than size in harness racing. Small horses like Billy Direct and Good Time, and big ones like Greyhound and Speedy Scot, were all great champions. Standardbreds are longer-bodied and shorter-legged than Thoroughbreds as well as somewhat smaller, measuring from 15 to 16 hands and weighing between 900 and 1,100 pounds. Their principal qualities are speed, endurance, and soundness of feet and legs, although they are often cow-hocked.

An American Standardbred pacer, Bret Hanover, driven by Frank Ervin. (*Photo courtesy of the U. S. Trotting Association*)

As with all horses, their natural gaits are the walk, trot, and canter. But some Standardbreds inherit a tendency to pace, which is a two-beat gait with the lateral legs moving simultaneously and which has proven to be slightly faster than the racing trot. It is unusual for a Standardbred to be equally adept at trotting and pacing; ordinarily, as soon as his natural gaits can be judged at about the age of two, he is given specialized training in either one or the other.

The 3,000-year history of harness racing has had its ups and downs, but it seems to be entering a Golden Age. There are over 470 annual Harness Racing meetings licensed by the United States Trotting Association, and they range from those at the famous Roosevelt Raceway in New York and Meadowlands in New Jersey, where extremely valuable trotters and pacers are driven by skilled professionals before thirty or forty thousand excited onlookers, to the small country tracks, where more and more amateurs of all ages are experiencing the unique thrill of driving a horse they may have bred and trained themselves. Amateur Standardbred drivers can also display their skill in some of the larger horse shows, which sometimes feature classes for Roadsters hitched to a bike or wagon, and for Roadsters Under Saddle, a Combination class.

While his main mission in life may be to break harness-racing records, the Standardbred lends his blood (considered "cold" as opposed to the "hot-blooded" Thoroughbred) to other breeds. A full Standardbred is not a very good riding horse because of his carriage and gaits, but a Standardbred mare crossed with a Thoroughbred stallion was a favorite breeding formula of the U. S. Cavalry and this cross has produced some good Hunters too. Anyone who has seen a Saddle Bred horse in action can recognize the Standardbred influence, and the Standardbred is also half responsible for a more recent American creation, the Tennessee Walking Horse.

THE TENNESSEE WALKING HORSE

From the late nineteenth century, plantation owners in the Tennessee region were developing a breed of horse that would provide a comfortable mount on which to survey their estates: a horse possessing an easy, ambling gait and a straight canter to enable them to ride between the rows of crops, as well as sufficient strength and stamina to do light work around the farm. But it was only as recently as 1947 that the U. S. Department of Agriculture officially recognized as a distinct breed the Tennessee Walking Horse, sometimes called the Plantation Walker or, more colloquially, a "turn-row" horse or "nodder," because of his characteristic movement of the head.

A remarkably prepotent stallion of Hambletonian and Morgan ancestry, Allen F1, who was a double-gaited trotter and pacer, is credited with being the official founder horse, although the modern breed probably includes additional strains of Thoroughbred, Saddle Bred, and Narragansett and Canadian Pacer.

The Walking Horse inherits a little bit from each of his ancestors. In head and soundness of legs he resembles the Standardbred; he has the excellent disposition, longevity, and balanced conformation of the Morgan; he has the short back, sloping croup, and long, flexible shoulders of the Saddle Horse, always a sign of comfort to the rider; he has very strong legs and is larger-boned in the knees and hocks than most other riding breeds, which some horsemen consider as evidence of an additional Quarter Horse strain. There are no official restrictions as to color and markings, although some are more fashionable than others. Since the success of the great breeding stallions Midnight Sun and Merry Go Boy, black and solid colors have become most popular, whereas roan and sorrel with flaxen mane and tail were most in favor in the forties and fifties.

A Champion Tennessee Walking Horse. (*Photo courtesy of J. Glenn Turner and the Tennessee Walking Horse Breeders and Exhibitors Association*)

Of comfortable riding size (15–16 hands; 1,000–1,250 pounds), the Walking Horse is ridden with long stirrups in three distinctive high-stepping gaits: a flat-footed walk accompanied by a cadenced head motion, a slow rolling canter, and the running walk, which is his most important feature. This is an inherited gait, smooth and gliding and very fast, covering up to nine miles per hour. Frequently it is performed quite naturally, including the rhythmic nodding of the head, by newborn foals running in the pasture alongside their dams. The famous stallion Roan Allen is said to have possessed no fewer than seven natural gaits: a flat walk, canter, square trot, fox trot, pace, and rock, in addition to the running walk.

The running walk cannot be taught, but it is improved by schooling. In fact, in order to increase the all-important overstepping by the hind legs (which is normally twelve to eighteen inches, but may be considerably exaggerated for showing), trainers have employed so many artificial devices that present show regulations require the horses' boots to be removed during a ring inspection to make sure that the gaits have been produced without the aid of pain-inflicting contrivances. And even though his feet may not be tampered with, the show Walker is still decked out with such adornments as mane and tail wigs (or, if he wears his own, they may be dyed or bleached) and a rigid tail brace.

When these artificial practices began to cause a decline in the breed's popularity (and some of them were outlawed by the Horse Protection Act of 1970), Walking Horse fanciers took steps to curb abuses and to show their mounts in a more natural condition, as Arabian and Morgan breeders, faced with the same problem, had done. The result has been renewed interest and a promising future for this pleasant and useful breed.

However, only a small portion of the Walking Horse population is trained for show. The vast majority is used for pleasure, trail, and endurance riding, Eastern or Western style (although most owners prefer an English saddle). And you don't have to own a plantation in order to pass many enjoyable hours astride a Plantation Walker or behind him in the driver's seat, because he makes a very agreeable Combination horse.

His unique running walk, much less tiring for covering territory than the trot and just as rapid, is highly appreciated in cattle country, where many hours are spent in the saddle every day. He takes to schooling readily and has an even, docile disposition, making him a fine choice for a child or novice rider. The exceptional comfort of his gaits is of great appeal to elderly horsemen, so much so that the national breed show features a class for riders fifty years old or over. Another specialty is the "Water Glass Class," in which the riders hold a full glass of water in one hand while performing the flat walk and the running walk, with the canter as a tie-breaking gait if necessary.

Although unsuitable as a Hunter, the Walker makes an excellent shooting pony and is often seen on shooting plantations and at Field Trials. In fact, his usefulness on the ranch or farm is practically unlimited, since the good-natured Walking Horse is willing and able to do anything from hacking and trail riding to light draft work.

THE AMERICAN QUARTER HORSE

Every cattleman can describe the admirable qualities of the American Quarter Horse. Developed originally in the early days of the American colonies as a quarter-mile sprinter (which explains his name), he is an ideal working ranch horse, with a sureness of foot and sudden bursts of speed that have helped many a cowboy win a cutting contest.

As you may have guessed, it is still another breed to descend from a Thoroughbred stallion; in this case Janus, a small, heavy horse imported into Virginia in the late eighteenth century. One famous early Quarter Horse sprinter, Steeldust, was sent to Texas, where many Quarter Horses are still called "Steeldusts" in his honor. In some other areas they are known as "Billy horses," after the sire Billy, a descendant of Steeldust, or "Copperbottoms," after the favorite stallion of Sam Houston, who was an early Quarter Horse fancier.

As a matter of fact, until recent years the term "Quarter Horse" referred more to a conformation type and racing standard than to definite bloodlines, so that even Thoroughbreds were also registered as Quarter Horses, sometimes under different names. But with the creation of the American Quarter Horse Association in 1940 the regulations were reformed in order to control the introduction of outside strains and to improve the homogeneity of the breed. Since then its popularity has been growing at a phenomenal rate, almost four times as fast as any other registered breed in the world. After doubling in size in just five years, the registered Quarter Horse population today is well over one million, according to the current AQHA "book," which is the largest registry of horses in the world. No other breed is used by so many people for so many different things. While the greatest concentration is still in Texas, California, and Oklahoma, there are Quarter Horses stabled in every one of the states, including Alaska, and in 52 foreign countries. Over a third of them live in the city or suburbs rather than on the range, and many are "performance" as well as pleasure horses, participating in an unusually wide range of competitive activities.

The modern Quarter Horse is a smallish (14.3–15.1 hands; 1,100–1,300 pounds), stocky, deep-muscled animal, whose sturdy legs give him great maneuverability. He is extremely heavy in front of the saddle, which accounts for his lightning-fast getaway at the post or on the prairie. His forelegs are short and heavy-boned to withstand the concussion of his spectacular sliding stop, while powerful hindquarters are so characteristic of the breed that it is customary to draw attention to them by photographing Quarter Horses from the rear. They have a lower center of gravity than most other horses, with a broad chest, low-set, heavily muscled hocks (both inside and outside), a thick neck, and a broad, short head, their heavy muscles extending even to cheeks and jowls.

The present tendency is to breed for a finer head and less bunchy muscles, while the so-called "mutton withers" of the early Quarter Horses

A Champion American Quarter Horse shown at Halter, Snipper's Sarah, owned by Chris Marting. (*Photo courtesy of the American Quarter Horse Association*)

are considered undesirable today. But even the more refined modern types are still extremely hardy and can practically live off the land, sometimes to the age of twenty-five or thirty years.

In spite of the stimulating work he does, the Quarter Horse is noted for his even disposition. He is said to be the only breed of horse who, when not working, will naturally stand quite still and calm, no matter how great the commotion around him may be. Almost always ridden with loose reins and under Western saddle, he has three natural gaits of moderate height and free action: the walk, trot, and lope (the last is a medium-fast uncollected canter).

Originally used for practical ranch work, and especially for cutting calves from a herd in order to be sold or branded, more and more Quarter Horses are being bred and trained as pleasure mounts and for arena competitions. Some two thousand AQHA-approved shows are held each

Skipper Chock, a Champion Amateur Western Pleasure Quarter Horse, owned by Richard Kogat. (*Photo by Doug Leahy, courtesy of the American Quarter Horse Association*)

year, featuring a wide variety of events designed to test and display the breed's intelligence and ability, such as Reining, Working Cowhorse, Western Riding, Barrel Racing, Pole Bending, Cutting, Chariot Racing, Trail Horse, Pleasure Driving, Calf and Steer Roping, Dally Team Roping, Bridle Path Hacking in Hunter Seat, and Jumping. As a matter of fact, a number of successful Open Jumpers bear a strain of Quarter Horse blood. Fire One, of the U. S. Equestrian Team, for example, was a registered Quarter Horse although he looked like the 100 per cent Thoroughbred he also was. The Canadian Team had an outstanding Quarter Horse jumper in Texas, whom John Simpson rode to victory in the Grand Prix of Rotterdam, The Grand Prix in New York, and The President's Cup in Washington, D.C., against top international competition.

Some Quarter Horses are bred especially for racing the quarter-mile sprints which often end in thrilling neck-and-neck finishes. (The actual distances range from 220 to 870 yards.) Those that have proven to be outstanding sires as well as Champion racers, like Go Man Go (three times Quarter Horse of the Year and the first of his breed to be syndicated for one million dollars), Jet Deck, Three Bars, and Top Moon, bring as much prestige to a pedigree as do illustrious Thoroughbred names. A more recent Quarter Horse celebrity is Dash for Cash, who is holder of the Quarter Horse speed record and was retired to stud at the end of his 1977 season as Horse of the Year. The Quarter Horse's sprinting gallop is more energy-consuming than the Thoroughbred racing gait, but it seems to be far safer in terms of stress, so that Quarter Horses are apt to be less prone to injury and to enjoy longer careers than most Thoroughbreds. Incidentally, the richest horse race in the world does not involve the "Sport of Kings." It is the Million Dollar Quarter Horse Futurity at Ruidoso Downs, New Mexico.

Most of the top rodeo performers are Quarter Horses, and that represents some very valuable horseflesh indeed! One of the most famous was Baby Doll, who earned for her owner, Willard Combs, and fellow bulldoggers who rented her services, a record-setting $400,000 during her long career. The rodeo cowboys had such confidence in Baby Doll that one year in Fort Worth she carried forty-seven out of the eighty bulldogging entrants into the arena.

Fire One, ridden by Bill Steinkraus in many international jumping events, was a registered Quarter Horse as well as a registered Thoroughbred. (*Photo courtesy of the USET*)

The exciting finish of an American Quarter Horse race. (*Photo courtesy of the American Quarter Horse Association*)

Despite their domination of rodeo contests and their recent invasion of the polo field, the vast majority of today's Quarter Horses can be found in riding stables and on cattle ranches, where their cow sense, agility, and steady temperament make them perfect Western pleasure horses for riders of all ages, as well as ideal cow ponies.

THE PALOMINO

Quite a number of registered Quarter Horses are listed in a second stud book as Palominos, which is not as contradictory as it may seem, since the Palomino is not so much a breed as a color. And what a lovely color! A coat of gleaming gold like a newly minted coin (or five shades lighter or darker), with a flowing silver (or ivory, or white) tail and mane. Often he has white socks or stockings and a blaze, and preferably a black skin and dark eyes.

The earliest Palomino breeding took place in Spain, where they are called Isabellas in honor of Columbus' patroness, Queen Isabella, whose personal troops were mounted entirely on these golden steeds. But the modern American Palomino may be a good riding horse of any of the recognized breeds, with the exception of draft and Shetland types, as long as he conforms in color. Many registered Palominos are full or half Saddle Bred, Tennessee Walker, Morgan, Standardbred, or Quarter Horse, but there never has been a purebred Arab or Thoroughbred that was a Palomino, although light chestnut-colored horses of both these breeds are often crossed with Palominos in order to improve their color and quality.

Controlled Palomino breeding is too new a science to have solved the mystery of color determination, and the Palomino hue is not yet entirely inbred. When two Palominos are mated together, there is only a 50 per cent chance of producing a Palomino foal; 25 per cent of the time the foal is chestnut, and 25 per cent of the time light cream or white. When a Palomino is mated to a colored horse, there is still only one chance out of two that the foal will be a Palomino. It seems to be proven that at least one parent must possess color genes for buckskin in order to perpetuate the golden coat.

The Palomino Jumper Nautical, ridden by Hugh Wiley. (*Photo by Jean Bridel/l'Année Hippique*)

A Champion Palomino Hunter, Lemon Springs, owned by Mrs. E. R. Johnson, ridden by Sandra Caldwell. (*Photo by Budd*)

The large and showy Palominos are in great demand as Parade horses, while the smaller, less spectacular individuals are often put to work on cattle ranches. More and more are being bred as Park Hacks and for general pleasure riding, and they are seen ever more frequently in the show ring, in Jumping, Harness, and Saddle classes. One of the most sensational international show Jumpers of the fifties was the Palomino Nautical, of Thoroughbred and Quarter Horse blood, whose achievements for the U. S. Olympic Equestrian Team won him world-wide fame and a Motion Picture Academy Award as Walt Disney's "Horse with the Flying Tail."

THE APPALOOSA

The Appaloosa is another breed that is readily identified by its distinctive appearance—in this case, a white or roan coat with black or brown spots scattered mostly on the quarters. Mares are usually less colorfully marked than males, and no two coat patterns are exactly alike. The skin is mottled, the tail and mane are short and wispy, and the hoofs are very often vertically striped in black and white, a trait which, according to fanciers, endows the Appaloosa's feet with unusual resiliency and resistance to unsoundness. An essential breed characteristic is the white sclera encircling the eye.

The Nez Percé Indians of the Palouse country in Idaho are credited with developing this striking breed, although horses of similar appearance can be seen in ancient Chinese art and even in prehistoric cave paintings. At any rate, the Indians exploited the camouflage value of the Appaloosa's coat by using him as a war steed and a hunter. At leisure moments, they also raced him.

Today the Appaloosa horse is fashionable, and the vogue for him has spread abroad as well. In America, there are over 200 regional breed clubs and some 250,000 registered Appaloosas, a figure that is topped only by that of the American Quarter Horse and the Thoroughbred.

He may be as small as 14.2 hands (even 14 hands, if he is over five years old). There is no maximum height limit, although the majority are of a compact size most practical for cattle work, which is their principal activity. Ideally, they should be deep-chested, with well-defined, prominent withers and good length and slope to the pastern, shoulder, and hip. Some Appaloosas bear Arab, Quarter Horse, or Thoroughbred blood, which produces splendid cutting horses, tireless trail horses, adept stock horses, and fine all-round Western pleasure mounts. Secretariat sired an Appaloosa son called First Secretary, the result of a test breeding to an Appaloosa mare. One of the most widespread breeding formulas combines an Appaloosa sire with a chestnut Quarter Horse mare. Standardbred, Saddle Horse, and Morgan crosses are also permitted under certain conditions, but Albino, Pinto, Paint, draft and pony breeding and markings are strictly prohibited.

Versatility is one of the hallmarks of the Appaloosa, who can be seen almost everywhere horses gather: on the range, in the jumping arena, in the show ring, on endurance trails, in the hunting field, and on the race track.

Appaloosa parimutuel racing has been organized in eleven states, and horse shows all over the country offer Appaloosa events. In addition to the usual Western classes (and often Eastern as well), these may include Appaloosa games, such as a Stump Race (rather like Barrel Racing, with two contestants racing against each other in opposite directions) and a Rope Race (a variation of Musical Chairs). Under the "saddle log program" of the Appaloosa Horse Club, riders can win awards for hours spent riding, no matter what the equestrian activity. The supreme achievement is the "Chief Joseph Commemorative Award" for completing 1,000 saddle log hours, 10 competitive Trail Rides, and 10 Endurance Rides.

An Appaloosa competing in a Junior Western Pleasure Horse event. (*Photo by Johnny Johnston, courtesy of the* Appaloosa News)

Last but not least, the Appaloosa is often seen as a Parade Horse and on dude ranches—perhaps because he looks just like what an Eastern dude thinks a Western horse should look like.

THE PINTO

The formation of a breed association and official registry has done much to improve and standardize this striking spotted horse (who is bred in pony size, under 14 hands, as well). It is their coat patterns that distinguish Pintos from other horses, and there are two of them: "*Tobiano,*" with color on the head, chest, flanks, and some on the tail, generally white legs and smoothly edged white markings extending over the back; and "*Overo,*" in which the white markings are lacy and jagged, located mostly on the midsection of the body and the neck, in a wide variety of shapes, usually accompanied by solid-colored legs. Because equine markings continue to develop until maturity, permanent registration is accorded only after a reinspection at the age of two.

These Pinto patterns were introduced to the United States by the

A Pinto Horse with a "Tobiano" coat pattern. (*Photo by Judy Frederick*)

A Pinto Horse with an "Overo" coat pattern. (*Photo by Judy Frederick*)

Spanish Barbs and Hispano-Arabian horses brought here by the Spanish conquistadors, although the same markings appear in ancient art of China and the Middle East. The Tobiano pattern is, oddly enough, common in Shetland ponies and in wild Russian steppe horses, as well as in Indian ponies.

Far greater latitude is permitted in bloodlines than in coat patterns for a registered Pinto who, like the Palomino and the Appaloosa, may qualify for double registration in certain books. You will see Pintos of Quarter Horse conformation and breeding used as cutting and reining horses, for barrel racing and trail riding. The pleasure horse Pinto is usually part Arabian or Morgan, and is ridden either Eastern or Western style. A strong dose of Thoroughbred blood produces a Hunter type that is bound to attract attention in the field, while Saddle Bred breeding and conformation are practically essential if a Pinto is to compete successfully as a Parade, Fiesta, or Western Show Horse.

The Pinto Horse Division of the American Horse Shows Association offers a wide range of classes, Eastern and Western, driving and riding, including an Indian Costume Class, and even elementary Dressage. The Pinto Horse Association also sponsors many Youth activities.

PONY BREEDS

For very young children, even up to thirteen or fourteen years old, a pony may be a better mount than a small horse. In the first place, a small child hasn't often the length of leg or the strength necessary to ride properly on a horse, and then a fall is apt to be more dangerous, and certainly more frightening. A well-trained pony, on the other hand, is less sensitive and excitable than a horse and is often wiser, more affectionate, easier to care for, and more likely to develop a young rider's confidence. A pony can even become a project for the entire family, when parents take an active interest in driving and in pony trotting races. An increasing number of adults are finding that a large pony can offer more pleasure and versatility with easier upkeep than a horse. A Thoroughbred-Connemara cross, for example, or a Thoroughbred crossed with a large Welsh pony can carry a lightweight adult in the Hunting field, in a driving vehicle, over a jumping course, and even around the Dressage arena.

One of the best-known pony breeds is the SHETLAND, originating in the Shetland Islands about two hundred miles north of Scotland, whose rocky land and hardy, humid climate are probably responsible for the pony's unusually small size, his long, shaggy coat and heavy mane. The American-bred Shetland is a definite improvement on the English type, however, being more slender, longer-legged, and better gaited than the English, with a more tractable character as well. As a matter of fact, the American Shetland Pony Society will no longer register animals imported from the Shetland Islands.

The Shetland's sturdy body adds up to an average of merely 10 hands or so, and his height is usually given in inches, making him 40–46 inches high, and only 250–500 pounds in weight. But he has extraordinary strength for his size. He is considered a colt until he is three years old, and his adult life is unusually long; there was a Shetland mare in Wyoming who was said to be still spry at fifty!

Today the Shetland pony in America is often bred for showing in Fine Harness classes, singly, in pairs, or in teams; and he seems very proud indeed of his well-clipped coat and impeccable grooming as he trots around the ring with high, smart steps. But he is perhaps happiest of all with a child on his back or behind him in a cart, for his loving, intelligent, quiet but spirited nature makes him a wonderful riding partner for a tiny beginner.

The most beautiful of the pony breeds is probably the WELSH PONY, who resembles a miniature Arab in appearance, with the same delicate head, fine coat, and graceful limbs. According to popular belief, a Thoroughbred stallion let loose in a field of native Welsh mares in 1825 was the father of the modern breed, increasing its quality and substance so that most modern Welsh ponies measure between 12 and 14 hands. In America they are divided into two size groups: the original Mountain Pony type under 12.2 hands; and the larger riding pony up to 14 hands.

Docile but spirited, most often gray in color, the charming Welsh ponies are not inclined to be as mischievous or spoiled as some Shetlands, or as nervous as many Hackney ponies. They are frequently chosen as hunting ponies by children and even by some small adults, since they possess prodigious strength and endurance considering their size, and often exceptional jumping ability. They may be trained for show—in hand, in harness, or under saddle—and are in ever greater demand as Parade ponies, for hunting, dressage, open jumping, and all-round pleasure riding.

Among the other English pony breeds are the NEW FOREST, a very gentle, biggish, short-legged, all-round riding pony; the tough and hardy little EXMOOR, with its characteristic "mealy" nose and rim

A Shetland Pony can be a child's best friend. (*Photo by Judy Frederick*)

A Shetland Pony Roadster. (*Photo by Judy Frederick*)

around the eyes and light-colored belly; the versatile FELL, the elegant DARTMOOR, and the larger Irish CONNEMARA, a Hunter-type pony who measures up to 15 hands and shows strong evidence of his Arab blood. Interest in the Connemara is on the increase in this country, perhaps because he may be ridden either under saddle or in harness and is often an excellent Jumper. A Connemara-Thoroughbred cross has produced some truly sensational performers, including Little Squire, an amazing 13.2 hand pony who won the National Open Jumper Championship in 1939 ridden by Mickey Walsh; Tommy Wade's Dundrum, the Jumper Champion of the London International in 1961; Grasshopper, the Three-Day Gold Medal winner at the Pan-American Games in Chicago; Little Model, an outstanding British Dressage performer; the Event horse St. Finnbarr (the result of a test breeding to Native Dancer); and the hero of them all, Marion Coakes' brave, cocky little Stroller, who soared over the imposing obstacles of the 1968 Individual Jumping course in Mexico City to win an Olympic Silver Medal at the age of fifteen, the only genuine pony ever to have appeared in an Olympic arena.

The CHINCOTEAGUE pony, a regional American breed originating in the Chincoteague Islands off the coast of Virginia, and made

A Welsh Pony Hunter, Snow Goose, ridden by Gregory Best, owned by Millbrook Farm. (*Photo by Budd*)

A Connemara Pony, Whitewood Muffin. (*Photo by Marshall P. Hawkins, courtesy of Mrs. M. Dent, Jr., and the American Connemara Pony Society*)

famous by Margaret Henry's children's book *Misty of Chincoteague* and its sequels, has been gaining nation-wide popularity, undoubtedly because he is a bright and lively riding pony for small children and at the same time a delightful family pet.

The PONY OF THE AMERICAS is one of the youngest registered pony breeds, dating only from 1956, when Black Hand No. 1, foaled out of an Appaloosa mare by a Shetland Pony stallion, was officially designated founder sire. The present breed standard calls for a conformation between that of the Quarter Horse and Arabian, with Appaloosa color and characteristics, including the typical sclera or white around the eyes. At maturity, the POA must measure between 46 and 54 inches in height. Since the minimum height of an Appaloosa is 56 inches, the principal thing that distinguishes the Pony from the Horse is that 2-inch margin. POA breeders strive to produce an ideal riding pony for children aged 8 to 18, with emphasis on tractability and versatility. Their success can be measured by the fact that there are over 21,000 registered Ponies of the Americas, and well over 200 annual POA shows throughout the country which feature events ranging from halter and carting classes to jumping, calf daubing, Western and English Pleasure, Trail Riding, and numerous Gymkhana competitions.

While all of these strains and many others can be found in the United States, the majority of our pony population consists of mixed breeds and undersized horses. (Horses must be over 14.2 hands, except for Registered Appaloosas, Arabians, Morgans, Palominos, Pintos, Paints, and Quarter Horses, who may measure a little less; but any animal under 14.2 hands may quite correctly be called a pony.) Our outstanding national type is the INDIAN PONY, which is nothing more than a small Western horse, with all of its qualities of hardiness, stamina, intelligence, and speed.

The HACKNEY PONY is rather a special case, since he is bred today almost exclusively for showing in light harness, and showing Hackneys is one of the most expensive of the equine sports. He is a pocket

A Pony of the Americas. (*Photo courtesy of the Pony of the Americas Club*)

version of the Hackney horse, a high-class harness horse of Arab, Thoroughbred, and Norfolk Trotter blood that is hardly ever seen any more. But years ago his popularity was widespread, and the founder sire, Shales 699, was the most famous trotter of his day.

Fór those who enjoy examining family trees, it may be interesting to note that Shales was the son of the Thoroughbred Blaze, who was himself a grandson of the Darley Arabian. Blaze's great-grandsons included Messenger, founder of the Standardbreds, and among his grandsons was Herod, the famous racing sire. So you see, many quite different present-day breeds of horses share the same ancestors.

But to get back to the Hackney, he varies in size more than any other breed, if the horses are included with the ponies—from 12 to 16 hands. Show ponies, however, are limited to a maximum height of 14.2 hands, and most present-day Hackney breeding in this country is being done within that limit.

The Hackney pony is a high-spirited and dainty animal, presenting in harness an unforgettable picture of sporting refinement, with his short muzzle and arching neck, a natural high knee action (accentuated for show purposes with long toes and special shoes), and a brilliant allure, but little speed. A born showman, his light, bold movements are practically impossible to imitate artificially.

While he is a delight to the eye, he is a bit rough in the saddle, and consequently purebred Hackneys are seldom suitable as riding ponies. However, some of the Hackney horses inherit a surprising talent for jumping. One of them who had an unusual record was Sir Gilbert, a large-sized stallion whose show-driving days came to an end when he was blinded in one eye, whereupon he turned to open jumping with considerable success. Another outstanding Hackney horse was Revelation, one of the most famous show horses in history, whose owner-driver, Loula Long Combs, became a legendary figure in the show ring during a career that spanned some sixty years.

Our inventory of the horse and pony treasures of America could go on indefinitely, for there are many other kinds, each with its own characteristics and working specialties. To name just a few more, there is the PAINT HORSE (a small stock-horse type with Quarter Horse or Thoroughbred conformation and Pinto markings); the pure white ALBINO; the SPANISH BARB and SPANISH MUSTANG; the COLORADO RANGER; the MISSOURI (or AMERICAN) FOX TROTTER, which is bred and used by the U. S. Forest Service, and is characterized by its

A Hackney Pony, Terry Jean's Souvenir, five-time World Champion in the division, driven by Elric S. Pinckney, owned by Mr. and Mrs. Kenneth Wheeler. (*Photo by Jack Holvoet, courtesy of Mr. Pinckney*)

medium size, slightly crested neck, and small, foxy ears that flop in time to his distinctive Fox Trot gait, which gives the impression of walking with the front feet and trotting behind in an easy gliding movement; the HARNESS SHOW PONY, a graceful cross between a Hackney or Welsh and a Shetland pony, which is a specialty of the Middle West; and the CLEVELAND BAY, a harness breed noted for its uniformity of color and its ability to produce top heavyweight Hunters when crossed with Thoroughbreds. Several British Olympic horses have borne Cleveland Bay blood, including Cornishman IV, Madison Time, North Riding, North Flight, Sumatra, and Sir Harry Llewellyn's unforgettable Foxhunter. The PERCHERON, a relatively refined draft horse of French origin, which is the traditional mount of circus bareback riders, also produces attractive heavyweight Hunters when it is crossed with Thoroughbreds for two generations, thus resulting in a 3/4 Thoroughbred with Percheron stamina, steadiness, and weight-carrying ability.

From time to time, there is a flurry of popularity for an imported breed, such as:

All registered German horses bear a distinctive brand that indicates their breed. From left to right, top row: Trakehner, Hanoverian, Holsteiner, Oldenburger; bottom row: East Friesian, Westphalian, Wurttenberger.

—the German HOLSTEINER, a powerful, warm-blooded breed which has collected many international jumping prizes for the German team, including two Olympic Gold Medals won by Fritz Thiedemann and Meteor (in addition to an Olympic Bronze, a European Jumper Championship, and the German Grand Prix at the age of seventeen). Retina, Godewind, and Torphy were also Holsteiners, as is Granat, Christine Stueckelberger's Olympic and World Champion Dressage horse. The Holsteiner carries a lot of Thoroughbred blood. Two of its three foundation sires, Owstwick and Brillant, were full Thoroughbreds, and the third, the Burlington Turk, was a half-blood. However, it is Brillant's line that is prevalent today, his bay coat and athletic ability having been perpetuated by intense inbreeding.

—the HANOVERIAN, the leading riding breed in Germany, which aroused interest in America due to its numerous successes in the 1972 and 1976 Olympics in Jumping, Three-Day, and Dressage events. Alwin Shockemoehle's Individual Gold Medal Olympic horse at Montreal, Warwick Rex, was a Hanoverian gelding. Caroline Bradley of Great Britain, the world's leading lady rider, has scored many of her triumphs on her Hanoverian Tigre. Considered a warm-blooded breed due to his high proportion of Arabian and Thoroughbred blood, the Hanoverian was originally developed as a Cavalry mount in what is now West Germany, then as a refined but sturdy performance horse in every major equestrian discipline, and also as a high-class Hunter. The versatility of the breed is exemplified by Djaccomo, the left lead horse of Emil-Bernhard Jung, a prominent German breeder and Grand Prix driver, who has also won in Three-Day Events, in Show Jumping, and in Intermediate Dressage. Among the top four Grand Prix Dressage horses in Germany in 1978, the first three were Hanoverians (and the fourth, a Trakehner). Our own U. S. Equestrian Teams have utilized Hanoverians in recent years with considerable success.

—the TRAKEHNER, also of German origin, which was developed especially to be a superior Dressage and Combined Training mount. Of medium size (15.2 to 16 hands), he has a rectangular frame as opposed to the "square" Thoroughbred, with a longer back and neck, shorter legs, heavier bones and joints, strong hocks, and large quarters, giving tremendous impulsion. His neck is also set on a little higher, which facilitates collected movements. He has a floating, ground-covering action, especially at the trot, and his disposition is usually very amenable. Nevertheless, he carries a lot of Arabian and Thoroughbred blood, and is gen-

Trakehner Stallion, a Morgenglanz. (*Photos courtesy of Edith Kosteska*)

erally lighter, more sensitive, and more hot-blooded than either the Hanoverian or the Holsteiner. The Trakehner barely avoided extinction during World War II, when devotees managed to smuggle breeding stock out of East Prussia to safety in West Germany in a historic "trek." Breed control is rigid, thanks to a strict inspection and testing program. In Germany, full-blooded foals are branded on the left haunch; mares and stallions that are accepted in the stud book as adults are branded on the offside crest. Although there are as yet very few approved Trakehner stallions in the United States, the demand is increasing and the population will undoubtedly rise to meet it.

—the ANDALUSIAN horse, an ancient Spanish breed which has contributed its blood to the Appaloosa, Pinto, Palomino, and the Mustang and, in greater measure, to the Lippizaner. Saved from extinction by the Carthusian monks of Jerez, Spain (where sherry wine is made), the breed is rare in America, where it is attracting attention as a flashy, strong pleasure mount and as a Parade horse. Born dark and gradually turning gray or white around the age of ten, like the Lippizaner, he is rather large, short-backed, high-stepping, with a full wavy mane and tail and an arched neck. He has so calm a temperament that he appears in bullfights in his native land, and is also used as a pleasure horse, a cutting horse, and for Dressage and Jumping.

The Andalusian is not the only Spanish breed to be introduced (or, more accurately, reintroduced) to the United States. There is also the GALICENO, another flashy high-stepper, and the PASO FINO, a smooth, striking, versatile riding horse with pronounced aptitudes for Dressage, who was first brought to the New World, and especially to Peru, by the Spanish conquistadors.

All of these imported breeds are rather like collector's items, however. A registered Trakehner, for example, would cost at least $10,000, while fanciers pay two or three times as much for a good young Dressage prospect. So the average horseman is more likely to select his horse from one of the more readily available American breeds.

And now that we have had a glimpse of the most important ones, you must be getting very impatient to find among these equine riches a horse of your own!

2. Choosing a Horse of Your Own

Where should you look for your horse? Perhaps the very best start-
ing-place is also the most obvious: at the riding academy where you have
been taking lessons or renting a riding horse. Most stable-owners and riding teachers do some horse-dealing on the side, and nobody is better
qualified than they to help decide what type of a mount will be most
suitable for you. In choosing your horse this way, you have two built-in
guarantees of satisfaction: a chance to get really well acquainted with
your horse before you buy him, and the experienced advice of a professional horseman whose own interest is to have *your* interest at heart.

Quite often, after a rider has tried out a number of different horses from the stable string, he hits upon one with whom he gets along particularly well. If you should be lucky enough to have this happen to you, it will frequently be possible to reach an agreement with the owner either to rent the horse for a certain period of time or to buy him outright. Moreover, in most riding establishments there is a steady turnover of horses. If the owner or instructor knows that you are looking for a horse of your own, he can keep your needs in mind when he is replenishing his string and sooner or later he may find one that is exactly what you've been dreaming of. This simple and safe procedure is especially recommended for children and novices; in fact, the majority of the United States Olympic Team riders acquired their first horse in just this way.

Another tried and true method of looking for a horse is to contact a reliable dealer. The fly-by-night itinerant who inspired all of those horse-dealing stories has pretty much disappeared, and most well-established dealers recognize that they can only stay in business by making satisfied customers. You can learn the names of the leading horse-dealers in your locality from your riding instructor or stable-owner, from other horsemen, or from advertisements in the specialized horse publications such as *The Chronicle of the Horse, The Western Horseman,* etc. (Ken Kimbel, Plant City, Florida, has a complete listing and can supply you with subscriptions.) You will also find horse-dealers at most horse shows and fairs, which serve as showcases for their wares. Countless horses have changed hands as a result of a casual conversation with a dealer at the show-ring In Gate.

The customary procedure with a dealer is to tell him exactly what you are looking for, and, if he believes he has a suitable animal in his stable, to make an appointment for a visit. One word of advice (which may sound a bit like reversing the roles): Be honest with the dealer. That is to say, don't try to impress him by pretending to be a much more advanced horseman than you really are. It will only lead to disappointment in the end, because one of the worst mistakes a novice can make in choosing a horse is to "overmount" himself.

It is highly advisable to have your teacher or an experienced horseman accompany you when you visit the dealer's horse. You will have a reasonable opportunity to examine him, of course, and to ride him long enough to observe his degree of training, general behavior, and way of going, as well as any outstanding physical flaws or virtues. But an hour or two is a short acquaintance compared to the months of friendship you may have shared with your riding-academy mount, and it takes an experienced eye to evaluate the character and quality of a horse in so brief a time.

Working Hunters can sometimes be actually tried out in the hunting field before making up your mind; and some dealers will deliver a horse to a prospective buyer for a trial period of a week or two. But this practice is more often reserved for the horsemen they know well and in whom they have complete confidence. A sensitive young horse can be spoiled in far less time than a week, and it is only natural that a dealer may be unwilling to entrust an animal he prizes to an unknown rider. More often, it is possible to reach an agreement whereby the dealer promises to buy back a horse if it proves to be unsatisfactory after a reasonable period of time. However, in this case the original sale and an eventual resale are considered to be two entirely separate transactions and the price will not necessarily be the same. Not that the dealer is trying to take advantage of you, but, like any other merchant, he may consider his wares to have been returned in a deteriorated condition.

You can and should trust the reputable dealer. The profit that is included in his price represents a perfectly legitimate fee for the training and conditioning he may have given your horse, and for his judicious selection at the auction sale or breeding farm.

Of course, you too can go directly to a breeding farm to look for your horse. It is a fascinating and instructive experience. For some specialized breeds, in fact, a breeding farm may be the best shopping center. However, it requires much skill and experience to evaluate the young stock that is usually for sale, and while "green broke" horses may already have been "backed" (mounted) a few times by a rider, most of them are by no means fully trained.

Qualified horsemen prefer to buy their horses as untrained colts, but it is hardly recommended to the rider for whom horses are a pleasure rather than a career. Of course, every time you ride him you are (or should be) training your horse. But training a colt is an entirely different matter, requiring generous amounts of time, technique, and talent. While you may be utterly charmed by a breeder's lovely little filly, some rapid calculation will prove that buying an immature animal is not sound economics for the average horseman. First of all, you will have to put her in the hands of a competent trainer, and the abler he is the higher will be his fee. You must add the cost of boarding for a year at least, plus the time you'll lose while waiting for her to grow up, not to mention the danger of some unforeseen unsoundness or training accident. By the

Mares and foals on a Thoroughbred breeding farm in Virginia. (*Photo by Bert Clark Thayer*)

time you actually mount on her back, the filly's original price will have more than doubled, and you will probaby agree that it is more sensible for an amateur to buy a horse that is fully grown and already trained.

There are breeding farms that also train and sell "finished" horses, and if you are lucky enough to live within traveling distance, a visit to one of these establishments may be worthwhile. You should try to get an experienced horseman friend to go with you, and examine the animal who may appeal to you just as thoroughly as if you were inspecting him in a dealer's barn.

Horses are also proposed to eventual buyers at sales and auctions, which range from the famous Yearling Thoroughbred Sales at Saratoga Springs or the Tattersalls Sale of Saddle Bred horses at Lexington, Kentucky, to the dispersion of a dealer's boxcarload, or of a summer-camp stable.

Thoroughbred yearling sales have become very international. Today most of the best bred foals are offered at auction to buyers from all over the world at one of these famous Thoroughbred markets: Keeneland, Saratoga, Del Mar, Hialeah, Deauville (France), Ballsbridge

(Ireland), Newmarket (England), and, more recently, Ocala (Florida). But there are also numerous regional auctions of high quality foals and older horses throughout the United States. Knowledgeable buyers can find bargains in such Western states as Nebraska, North and South Dakota, Oklahoma, and Texas, although these range-raised animals need a lot of conditioning and training to convert them into riding horses.

Generally speaking, the small country sales are best avoided by the inexperienced, but the larger ones do offer certain guarantees. Most of these are organized by professional concerns that specialize in public horse auctions. The sales are extensively advertised in advance in the horse publications and usually a catalogue is available beforehand, with full descriptions of the horses, including their past history and breeding, and a "hip number" (sales number).

Many Thoroughbreds at auction are also given a family number, according to an intriguing if disputed theory devised in 1895 by an Australian, Bruce Lowe. Believing that the maternal line was more im-

Majestic Native, a son of Raise A Native, being sold at the Saratoga Yearling Sales for $125,000. (*Photo courtesy of the Fasig-Tipton Company*)

portant than the sire line, Lowe studied the pedigree of every winner of the three leading English stakes races and found that all of them traced back to one of forty-three foundation mares. To each of these mares and their descendants he attributed a number. The first five families produced the most winners; these he called the "running families," and their numbers are printed in sales catalogues in italics. Certain other female lines, which produced throughout the years the most successful stallions, are known as the "sire families," and their numbers are printed in bold type.

Fabulous bargains may occasionally occur in the auction ring, as in the case of Seattle Slew, a $17,500 yearling who became the first undefeated Triple Crown winner and was syndicated as a breeding stallion for $12 million. Alsab cost a mere $700 at the Saratoga Yearling sales and earned over $350,000 during his racing career, while the famous pacer Adios Butler, a $6,000 bargain from the Harrisburg sales, was later purchased by a breeding syndicate for $600,000—one hundred times his original price! But such long shots are very rare, and are far more likely to be to the profit of a shrewd professional than a lucky amateur. Besides, the average Saratoga selling price has risen to over $75,000.

Sometimes there are sales of horses and ponies especially selected for pleasure riding, and it would surely be an interesting experience for you to study the catalogues and attend one of these auctions, even if you never actually put in a bid. But it is safer to leave the others to the experts, or to reserve them for later on in your horse-owning career.

Many horses are bought and sold through classified advertisements in horse publications. Mary Anne Tauskey, member of the Gold Medal-winning U. S. Olympic Three-Day Team in Montreal, discovered her remarkable bargain pony Marcus Aurelius through an advertisement in *Horse and Hound*. Other lucky owners have found their dream horse as a result of contacts made through breed organizations or the inevitable grapevine that exists among blacksmiths, veterinarians, and farmers. In all of these cases a thorough trial and examination by yourself, by an experienced horseman, and by a qualified veterinarian is essential, because the results of these more personal transactions range from perfect to perfectly dreadful. The horse that was Pegasus himself to one of your riding friends may be quite unsuitable for you. And no advertiser has ever been obliged to point out the flaws in his merchandise—it is up to the buyer to beware!

However optimistic you may be by nature, don't expect to find your horse immediately. It is far better to be prepared for a lengthy search

Mary Anne Tauskey and Marcus Aurelius, the Three-Day Event horse that she found through a horse magazine advertisement. (*Photo by Sue Maynard*)

and then to be agreeably surprised, than to make a hasty horse-deal that ends in disillusion. And don't be too determined to pick up a bargain. With horses, you are apt to get just about what you pay for in terms of soundness, breeding, disposition, and training. Sometimes, it is true, the expert dealer or experienced horseman will decide that an animal whose price is low because of a minor conformation fault or temperamental vice may be straightened out by proper training and conditioning. But this sort of a gamble is strictly for the person whose business is horses. It would be a pity for the amateur horseman to start his career as a horse-owner with more problems than he knows how to handle. Besides, a good horse will help improve your riding as well as win ribbons, whereas a poor horse or an unsuitable one will hinder your riding progress and may discourage you from competition.

All horses that are offered for sale will be described to you not only as to breed origin, but also as to height, sex, age, and color. Perhaps you have wondered about the significance of these points in choosing a horse.

As far as the horse's height is concerned, the only way you can judge its suitability for you is to get up on the horse's back and "try him on for size." If you're looking for a pony, you should take along the child for whom it is intended. Horses are always measured from the highest point of the withers to the ground in "hands" of four inches, with the figure following the decimal point representing inches. Thus a 15.2 horse would be 62 inches high at the withers (which is an average size, well suited to a rider of medium height and weight).

While there is no definite rule to follow, your horse should not be so small that it is an effort for him to carry your weight; neither should he be so big and powerful that you cannot control him effectively with the use of your hands and legs. It may be vastly amusing to see a tiny child perched on the back of a great big horse, but it can be awkward and dangerous for the child (who, besides, will probably never learn to ride correctly until he has been given a more suitable mount). On the other hand, heavily built horsemen should not necessarily limit their choice to colossal mounts. A horse's weight-carrying ability depends more upon his conformation than his size. The Cavalry specifications were 15 to 16 hands for mounted use, since Army tests had proved that a horse's strength ceases to increase in proportion to his size, and may even decrease slightly, beyond the height of 16 hands. An animal of 17 hands becomes less agile and sure of foot and much more difficult to balance because of his high center of gravity. He is more prone to respiratory troubles too. An incidental point to bear in mind is that a horse's growth is not usually completed before the age of five (though many ponies reach their full growth by the time they are three), with geldings being particularly slow to mature.

Stallions (whom the British call "entire horses" in contrast to geldings, who are castrated males) are most often seen at the race track and on stud farms. In fact, the Russian Olympic Equestrian Team caused something of a sensation when it appeared in Helsinki for the 1952

Games with an all-stallion string. In this country, most male horses are gelded in the spring of their second year unless they are of special breeding value, as, for example, successful Thoroughbred race horses, Saddle Bred show horses, Arabians (whose blood is valuable in crossbreeding), and Morgans (because of the danger of the breed's dying out). Stallion Dressage horses are esteemed for their brilliance of movement. But due to their somewhat aggressive nature, stallions considerably complicate stabling and pasture arrangements and they are barred from many show-ring events. Many boarding stables will not accept them.

Mares are generally believed to be more sensitive than geldings, which can be both an advantage and a drawback. One undeniable advantage of mares is that they can be used for breeding if some minor accident makes them unsound for work. Their heat periods may sometimes cause a slight inconvenience; they occur every eighteen to twenty-one days or so and last an average of four to six days, although they are generally most noticeable only twice a year, in the spring and fall. The owners of international show and jumping mares sometimes have their veterinarian induce or suppress the heats artificially in order to avoid interference with important competitions, but this is a delicate procedure and is forbidden by the American Horse Shows Association.

Geldings are usually considered to be more stable in character and to have greater endurance but less resistance to disease than either mares or stallions. Occasionally you may come across a ridgeling or "rig," which is the equine equivalent of a monorchid, only one of whose testicles had descended properly into the scrotum. It is not always possible to geld a ridgeling successfully; neither is his future as a stud very brilliant. Generally he will resemble a stallion in appearance and temperament, but lack the stallion's breeding value.

Although in normal practice you will most likely be seeking your horse among the mares and geldings, the wisest course is to judge each animal on its own physical and temperamental merits, regardless of sex.

And what about age? To digress a bit and deal first with the age of the rider, many children have started out on ponies at five or six, and there seems to be no maximum age limit at all for confirmed horse-lovers. Mrs. Brenda Williams represented Great Britain in the Dressage event of the Rome Olympics when she was sixty-five years old, while in America Mrs. Leila Havens was driving her own Shetland and Hackney ponies in the show ring at the age of eighty-six. Driver Bi Shively won one of Harness Racing's most prestigious contests, the historic Hambletonian, when he was in his seventies. In England there was a veteran trotting driver who was still winning races at eighty-two, while his horses were groomed and exercised by his son, aged sixty-four!

The age range of the horse is, however, much more limited. One year of a horse's life may be said to equal about three years of a man's. It is a foal until weaned and then is called a colt or filly until the age of four, at which point it is identified as a mare, gelding, or stallion. (A male horse that has produced offspring is a sire as well as a stallion, regardless of age.) It starts to go to school at one, if it is to be trained as a race horse, while riding horses are usually broken at two years at the earliest, and heavy breeds at three. A horse is generally considered to be mature at the age of six, although horse show regulations have him reach maturity at four. From ten years until the end of his life (usually between twenty and thirty) he may be described as "aged," which to horsemen means "fully mature" rather than "senile."

The horse is very generous with man, lending him the service of his heart and limbs until his early twenties, when he is usually retired. Thoroughbred race horses are obliged to retire at the age of fourteen and Standardbreds at fifteen. But modern veterinary techniques and improved feeding and stabling methods seem to have prolonged the active career of many horses. For example, the Lippizaners of the Spanish Riding School frequently perform in public until the age of twenty-four or even thirty. The great show Jumper Democrat crowned a strenuous year of Olympic campaigning by winning eight consecutive international competitions when he was nineteen years old, and Goldsmith Maid, a famous trotting mare, set her fastest time at the same rather advanced age. When Alan Oliver won a White City jumping class in London on Silver Mint, the horse was twenty-eight—almost twice as old as the rider! And then there was Tom Hal, a Canadian stallion of Morgan blood, who lived to be forty and was active as a stud until his death; in fact, he foaled his best son at thirty-five.

Notwithstanding these exceptional examples, the best age at which to buy a horse is between four and twelve years. If younger, his physical structure has not yet been fully formed, and beyond twelve his years of usefulness are limited. Needless to say, the four-year-old is still really an adolescent and requires a more delicate and skillful hand than the well-trained, experienced older animal. One might even invent a formula: the less experienced the horse, the more experienced should be the rider. Often an inexperienced rider can learn more from his horse than his horse can learn from him. A wise and sound fourteen-year-old pony may be an excellent buy for a very young beginner, who will probably graduate to a horse well before the pony has reached the end of its active life. But the more advanced rider, who looks forward to difficult jumping and strenuous equestrian exercise, would be happier with a horse who is, like himself, at the peak of his physical development.

Age can be a factor in judging conformation and soundness. A horse that is six years old or older has already achieved his adult stature and appearance, but you can only guess how a two-year-old colt is going to turn out. A sound eight- or nine-year-old is apt to remain sound under normal conditions, but a perfectly sound three- or four-year-old may not be able to stand up to the work demanded of him as an adult. There is also a relationship between age and training. Unbroken horses offered for sale are usually under three years old; "green-broke" horses between three and five or older; while fully trained horses are generally eight or nine, occasionally somewhat younger.

The traditional method of determining a horse's age is to examine his teeth. The horse's dentition develops in a special way and at a systematic rate until the age of eight, when there appears a brownish-colored groove on the corner incisors called "Galvayne's mark," which gradually runs down the tooth until it finally disappears at about the age of twenty. Thanks to these well-tabulated indications, it is not very difficult to learn to tell how old a horse may be. But it is even simpler to ask the veterinarian who examines your horse for soundness to estimate its age for you.

If your horse is a Thoroughbred who has been to the race track, he will have a number tattooed inside his upper lip with a letter indicating the year of his birth (it began again with A in 1971) and the last four numbers of his registration certificate. Today it would be impossible for a four-year-old race horse to win the Epsom Derby, although this actually occurred some years ago when Maccabeus was "rung in" (dishonestly substituted) for a three-year-old called Running Rein. Even then, the deceit was later discovered and the horse disqualified. A more recent alleged horse-switching attempt that involved two Uruguayan imports, an excellent racer named Cinzano and a mediocre one called Lebon, was quickly spotted by an alert groom at the Belmont Race Track, and the individuals involved were immediately suspended from racing pending an investigation. The lip tattoo and the nighteye identification system have virtually eliminated any chance of such an incident occurring undetected on the flat tracks, and the U. S. Trotting Association as well as the American Quarter Horse Association have adopted the same system. Registered Arabians and Appaloosas are freeze-branded on the neck with a graphic code corresponding to their registration number.

Color should be of no importance at all in choosing horses—unless you are buying them for the New York Mounted Police (in which case you'll be interested exclusively in bays), or for the Royal Canadian Mounted Police (who only accept blacks or browns—and need very few of them, now that the legendary Mounties "get their man" by more scientific methods and maintain a string of 500 horses only in order to perpetuate their traditional "Musical Ride").

"If he's a good horse, he's got a good color." Many horsemen dismiss the subject with this succinct statement. In other words, the quality of a horse is shown in his conformation and soundness, never in the shade of his coat. While an unattractive, washed-out color may sometimes be a sign of a poorly-bred animal, its inferior quality is bound to be even more evident in a badly constructed body. The ancient belief of the Arabs that bays have the most endurance and chestnuts the most speed has never been scientifically proved.

It is true that certain breeds are apt to be found mainly in certain colors. Pure white or black Arabians are comparatively rare, for instance, and there never has been a piebald Thoroughbred. And then some breed classifications, as we have seen, are based entirely or partially on color restrictions, such as the golden Palomino, the spotted Appaloosa, and the snow-white Albino.

Equine colors are described as black, brown (often mixed with black), chestnut (golden yellow to reddish brown, with a mane and tail of similar shade), sorrel (a light chestnut), bay (reddish tan to dark mahogany, always with black "points," that is, black manes, tails and, usually, lower legs), and gray (which is black at birth and grows gradually lighter, often turning completely white at the age of five or later). A buckskin horse has a dull light-brown coat with a black stripe along the back, black points, mane, and tail; a dun is similar but of a yellow-gray shade. Grullo Quarter Horses are smoky or mouse-colored with black points. The word "roan" is used to describe white hairs mixed into a solid coat (chestnut roan, gray roan, etc.), while the spotted Western ponies called Pintos or Paints may be either piebald (black spots on a white coat) or skewbald (spots of any color other than black). Fanciers classify as "Tobiano" horses whose coats have large, colored markings on a white base, and as "Overo" horses with irregular white markings on a colored coat. A horse's true color, incidentally, is shown on his muzzle, and if you look closely you'll see why many horses that seem black are really dark brown.

White markings can attractively brighten a dark coat. You may find very pleasing the effect of a star (a white mark on the forehead), a stripe (a narrow line down the face), a snip (a small mark between the nostrils), or a blaze (covering the entire nasal bone). Many well-bred horses carry a bit of white on the feet, coronet, heel, pastern, or fetlock, and one or two white socks or stockings. There is a somewhat superstitious prejudice against a horse with four white feet, although some outstanding horses have had them, one who comes to mind being the late great racing sire Hyperion.

But instead of lingering on a subject that may be aesthetic but is of little interest to the serious horseman, let's get on with the business of choosing your horse.

Whatever his breed and purpose in life, every good horse should rate a passing score when examined for temperament, conformation, and soundness.

Temperament is perhaps the most important of all. A horse with a good temperament is confident, obedient, courageous, intelligent, willing to learn, and free from major vices such as refusing to be handled, habitual kicking or rearing, and excessive shyness. Except for the congenital rogue, who is extremely rare, all horses are born with a natural generosity that is often disarming even to the most hardened professional. But alas, not all horses manage to conserve their kindliness toward humanity, especially if they have had the misfortune to undergo rough or inconsiderate treatment. That is why it is advisable to inquire into the background of the horse you are considering buying. If he has frequently passed from hand to hand, study his disposition with special care, for it may have been completely ruined in the process. Many experienced riders therefore prefer to buy a youngish horse, who has not yet had an opportunity to be spoiled.

The principal qualities to look for are a special sort of willingness and amiability that are peculiar to the equine race. Of course, courage and intelligence are important in all horses, and particularly if you are seeking a show Jumper or a Hunter. In a child's or novice's horse a gentle and obedient nature will be most desirable. And here a word of warning might be useful. Don't mistake sluggishness for docility. A lively pony can also be a gentle one. But a sluggish animal, which too many parents are tempted to buy out of safety considerations, will only force a child into bad riding habits and perhaps even make him lose interest entirely.

You should also look for a certain compatibility of temperament between yourself and your mount, and strangely enough, it may be a case of opposites attracting. The placid animal may get just the stimulation it needs from a rider of a nervous disposition, while the excitable horse will be more effectively controlled by a calm and imperturbable master.

Horses vary in temperament just as humans do, and it can be even more difficult to get to know and understand their true character. According to many experts, a lump between the eyes indicates meanness or stupidity, while wide-set eyes are supposed to leave plenty of brain-room and thus be a sign of intelligence. Short, deeply arched ears are believed to be evidence of sensitivity and ability to learn; tiny ones, pricked inward, are said to signify a strong will and a hot temper, while large ears flopping sideways often go with a sluggish disposition or, it is sometimes claimed, with jumping ability.

A horse's moods are usually reflected in the expression of his eyes, the carriage of his head and ears. You should look for a kindly eye as opposed to a shifty, nervous one that shows a lot of white; and normally mobile ears, rather than ears habitually held flat back on the head, which is a danger signal, typical of the horse who is getting ready to kick.

Finally, if you are in doubt about a horse's disposition, ask the previous owner, or the breeder, or the dealer—or, better still, all three. It is a question much too important to pass over lightly, for the most beautiful horse in the world won't give you much satisfaction if he has an ugly character.

It is true that a few famous horses have been noted for their bad dispositions. The great Eclipse was so bad-tempered that his owner considered gelding him, which would have deprived Thoroughbred racing of many of its finest performers. Count Fleet was considered dangerously vicious too, while Ribot became so intractable that it was impossible to ship him home to Italy at the end of his stud lease in America. Another talented rogue was Billy Barton, whose continual outbursts at the starting post caused him to be barred from the race track. Sold for a modest sum as a Hunter prospect to the Master of the Elkridge Hounds, it was decided to try him out as a Hunt racer. On three successive Saturdays Billy Barton won the Maryland Grand National Steeplechase, the Maryland Hunt Cup, and the Virginia Gold Cup—a fantastic feat—and then crossed the Atlantic to place second in the Aintree Grand National of 1928. Nevertheless, such exceptional horses require exceptionally experienced horsemen, and the person who rides for pleasure should put a good disposition at the top of his list of requirements when seeking a horse of his own.

The next step in judging a horse is to examine him for conformation. Good conformation is of interest not only for show horses. A well-built horse is usually healthier, sounder, easier to train, and more comfortable to ride than a poorly built one, quite aside from being more pleasing to look at. Of course, some breeds have special points of conformation, like the heavy hips and low-set neck of the Quarter Horse, and the short back of the Arab. But in general the basic principles hold true for all horses.

Your first impression of a good horse is that he is well-proportioned all over, with every part of his body fitting together harmoniously. If the general picture your horse presents is well-balanced and attractive, you should begin to study him in greater detail.

You can judge a horseman very quickly by the way he looks at a horse. The novice usually starts with the horse's head and then goes on to the neck, chest, and so forth, in the order in which they meet his eye. Sometimes he is so taken in by a pretty face that he never does get around to a thorough examination of the legs and feet! The experienced horseman, on the other hand, studies the different parts of the horse in the order of their importance. If he finds out that the animal's feet or legs are badly constructed, there really isn't any point in going farther.

First of all, he seeks a general symmetry and balance in the horse's body, with no glaring disproportions. He has a simple way of visualizing the ideal shape of a horse: Looking at a horse from the front, an imaginary line drawn from the point of the shoulders to the ground should just about bisect the front legs and feet. Looking at the horse from the side, you should be able to draw a vertical line from the point of the breast-bone to the front of the forefoot, and from the stifle through the point of the hind toe. Viewed from the rear, the hind feet should be placed closer together than the front feet, and the point of the hock and the thighs should touch the same vertical line.

Next, the experienced horseman studies the horse's top-line, from the poll of the head to the root of the tail, which should be fairly straight just as the underline of a well-built horse is more or less horizontal. The head should be in proportion to the neck, neither too heavy nor too small. The neck should be long, muscular, and flexible, appearing slender and graceful when seen from the side, with a straight underline, but thick and firm when seen from behind. The length of the neck is important for balance and also influences a horse's stride, in that a horse with a short, thick neck will often have a short stride and rather choppy paces. A long neck usually means comfort to the rider, but if it is too long, it will be too weak for the weight of the head and the horse will tire easily. The two principal conformation faults of the neck are the "ewe neck" (a concave neck, put on "upside down") and the "swan neck" (excessively arched and pliable); both may be somewhat improved by training but neither of them is desirable.

The withers, at the base of the neck, should be well-defined, prominent but not exaggerated or surrounded by fatty tissue. If they are too high, the saddle tends to slip backward; too low, the saddle may slide toward the horse's head. But the main reason for the desirability of fairly high withers has nothing to do with the saddle. The withers are a prolongation of the vertebral processes of the spine, and the muscles running to the shoulder are attached to them; consequently, if the withers are suitably high without exaggeration, these important muscles will be of a suitable length, and as you probably know, longer muscles permit greater contraction than short ones and produce more vigorous, elastic movements with far less strain.

The back, well-knit and neither too long nor too short, should dip slightly toward the quarters. A real sag in the middle comes only with old age. There is a difference of opinion as to the best length of back in a riding horse. Short backs may be stronger, but longer ones are often considered more comfortable. Your own preference will depend upon the type of activity you wish your horse to engage in.

The loins (the space between the last rib and the point of the hip) should be short and strong, exaggerated length being a sign of weakness. Good hindquarters are level and nicely rounded, appearing wide, muscular, and symmetrical when seen from behind. Sloping rumps are eyed with disfavor, but they may denote jumping ability; in fact, the high point just before the slope is often referred to as a "jumping bump."

The most detailed examination is reserved for the horse's legs and feet. On the horse's forehand, it might be prefaced by a glance at the shoulder blades on either side of the withers. These are not joined to the skeleton (since the horse has no collarbone), but float in a cushion of muscle so that the front of the body is suspended on the forelegs more or less like a car on its chassis. This peculiar construction is part of an ingenious shock-absorbing system that nature has invented for the horse. The shoulder blades should be long and slope at an angle of about forty-five degrees. The greater the slope, the more efficiently the shock will be absorbed from the forelegs. Oblique shoulders give working freedom to the forehand muscles and tendons, better balance to the horse, and more comfortable gaits to the rider; straight shoulders give short strides and rough rides, and limit the degree to which a horse can extend his fore-legs.

In order to allow him freedom of leg action, the point of the horse's elbow should be at least a finger's breadth away from his sides.

The forearms and thighs should be long and well-muscled, the knee joints large and flat, and the cannon bone, below the knee, thick from front to back and relatively short, giving the impression that the horse's knees are close to the ground. Incidentally, when one speaks of "bone" in a horse, it is the circumference of the hollow-cored cannon bone that is being considered. To give you a standard of comparison, a circumference of eight and a half inches is just about ideal for a 16-hand horse. How-ever, the quality of the bone is as important as its measurement. Arabian and Thoroughbred bone, being denser and harder than that of common breeds is relatively much stronger for its size.

Behind the cannon lie the tendons, which should form a straight line from the back of the knee to the fetlock joint and be well separated from the bone, not "tied in" below the knee.

The forearm and the cannon bone should form a straight line when seen from the front or side, but this is not always the case. Some horses "stand over at the knee," that is, their foreleg knees are permanently bent, which may not be attractive but is not necessarily a weakness if it is inherited rather than a result of work. In fact, some racing trainers consider them more likely to stand up under hard training than straight forelegs, as in the case of the eminent English racing sires St. Simon and Galopin. However, being "back at the knees," with the forelegs forming a concave line between the forearm and the fetlock, is a serious defect.

The "knee" of the hind leg is called the hock. (Actually, the horse's stifle corresponds to the human knee joint, the hock to our ankle, the fetlock joint to the human knuckle, and the pasterns to our fingers and toes, so that the horse is really walking on his tiptoes.) The hocks should be identical, large, low, and free from thickness, while the inside angle should be wide, especially in Jumpers and gallopers. Straight hocks are, however, fairly frequent. In fact, some famous families of Thoroughbreds have been noted for them. Certain strains of horses also tend to be "cowhocked," with the hocks turned in when viewed from the rear, and this is usually considered a sign of weakness. The opposite extreme—hocks turned out—gives the horse a bowlegged appearance which is quite common in Quarter Horses and may even be a sign of strength.

At the base of the cannon bone is the fetlock joint (the fetlock being the tuft of hair behind the joint), and below that the pastern, a vital part of the shock-absorbing system. The two small bones that form the pastern should break the straight line from the elbow and hocks to the fetlock by sloping gently forward, the ideal angle of slope being about forty-five to fifty-five degrees from the vertical. If the pastern is straight, much of its shock-absorbing value is lost; if it is exaggeratedly sloping, the ride may be comfortable but there will be a much greater strain placed on the ligaments and tendons, which can lead to trouble. In any case, the pastern should be long rather than short.

Inside each of the horse's legs you will notice a sort of horny excrescence called Chestnuts or Night Eyes, which are vestigial toes (remember, prehistoric horses had four or five of them). Night Eyes vary in form, with no two alike; they are as individual as human fingerprints and are recorded as part of the identification system for Thoroughbred race horses and registered trotters.

The horse's feet should slope gently forward as a continuation of the pastern. The horny, insensitive outside of the hoof should be hard and smooth, free from ridges and dryness. White horn is generally believed to be weaker than blue or black, and Appaloosa fanciers say that the striped hoofs so frequent in their breed possess unusual elasticity. Whatever the truth of these claims, it is a fact that most horsemen seem to prefer dark hoofs.

The expert always picks up the horse's feet one by one to examine the soles. The forefeet should be round and flat, the hind ones slightly elliptical, all with a well-marked outer rim and a moderately concave sole, free from signs of past or present foot ailments. The frog, the soft rubbery wedge jutting out from the heel, which is the first point of shock absorption, should be large and well developed, healthy to the eye, and firm to the touch. "No feet, no horse" is an equestrian adage; and, in fact, feet and legs are the most vital points in the horse's entire body.

When he is standing still, all four feet should be planted squarely under the horse's body, pointing straight ahead. If his toes turn in, it is not too serious a flaw; but if they turn out, you may have to treat a lot of bruises caused by "brushing" or furnish your horse with special brushing boots. If a horse's feet are small and round like a donkey's, or too flat and heavy, you may have trouble with lameness or chronic stumbling.

When you get into the saddle, your first impression should be that there is "a lot of horse in front of you." His mouth should feel light and sensitive and he should react promptly and willingly to the demands of your hands and legs. Try to find out how much he knows by putting him through all of his paces, without neglecting turns, stops, and backing. And try also to find out what he *doesn't* know. Keep in mind that it is the horse who is being judged, and not your own riding form. As any dealer can tell you, usually with a wry smile, many of the young riders who come to see a horse seem much more interested in impressing the dealer with their own equestrian skill than they are in discovering the qualities and weaknesses of the animal they are supposed to be testing.

One shrewd dealer says: "Any fool can spot the obvious faults of a horse, but it takes a real horseman to recognize the good points." So when you are trying out a new horse, be just as much on the lookout for good points that may be exploited as you are for faults. And when you find the flaws, try to evaluate them fairly and to distinguish between the inherent defects and those that may be improved or even completely corrected.

If a horse has passed inspection reasonably well on these major points, now is the time to check the rest of his conformation.

It is desirable for all horses to have a deep broad chest and well-sprung ribs. The horse's rib cage, consisting of nine pairs of true ribs attached to the breastbone and nine pairs of false ribs attached to each other, form a barrel that should be wide, and the deeper the better to make plenty of room for his heart and lungs. Many horsemen say that the measurement around the girth should be greater than the horse's height. In racing circles, a massive chest is considered to be the attribute of a "sprinter," while a "stayer" is expected to be lighter, longer-bodied and leggier.

Finally, the experienced judge gets around to looking at the horse's head. While the profile may vary according to the breed, it is preferable for his eyes to be large and well set, neither too high nor too close together, and the ears should be delicately arched and mobile, of medium size. The nostrils should be large and sensitive, standing well open, since the horse can only breathe through his nose. The jaws should be strong and wide if the horse is going to learn to flex his neck properly, and his mouth should be undamaged outside and in.

An examination of the mouth is important not only in determining a horse's age (by the teeth) but also in determining his bite. A horse with a faulty bite will have difficulty in grinding his feed properly and some grain will pass through his system undigested. Moreover, it may be difficult to bit him properly, especially if he has a "parrot mouth" (an overshot upper jaw).

Having studied the horse from head to tail (by a roundabout route), our expert may already have formed a rough opinion of the animal, but he hasn't yet completed his examination. A horse may present a lovely picture when he is cleverly posed, and then show all kinds of defects in action.

The horse's movements should be straight, natural, and effortless. One of the most useful warnings one can give to the prospective horseowner is to avoid buying a horse that doesn't go straight.

Your experienced horseman friend or your teacher can be of great help in evaluating the horse's action and in judging whether an apparent flaw is due to poor training, bad condition, or faulty conformation. The first two causes may possibly be removed by patience and care.

Before mounting the animal yourself, do as the experts do and have him led up and down so that you can study his natural gaits from every angle. If a horse stands square and walks well, with free, even, and "frank" movements, the odds are that all of his gaits will be good. If possible, have him walked on a level, hard surface and listen for the even cadence of four distinct walking steps. It is often easier to hear than it is to see that a horse is favoring one leg because of lameness.

Some of the most common action defects are:

Trappy action (short quick, choppy strides, often a result of straight shoulders and straight pasterns)

Brushing or *Interfering* (hitting one leg with the opposite foot)

Forging or *Overreach* (striking the forefoot with the toe of the hind foot)

Paddling or *Dishing* (throwing the front feet outward as they are picked up)

Winging (exaggerated paddling)

Rolling (excessive lateral shoulder motion)

Speedy Cutting (a bruising contact of the diagonal fore and hind pasterns, most often affecting fast trotters)

Stringhalt (picking up one or both of the hind legs excessively high in a spasmodic movement. This is an action defect of nervous origin and is most apparent when a horse is not yet warmed up.)

If your horse has passed the test for conformation and action, you will now want to have him examined for soundness. By all means have his soundness certified by a qualified veterinarian—one who is experienced with horses, and not the local doctor who treats your dog for mange.

Most horse sales are, in fact, made "subject to" a satisfactory veterinary report. If you haven't a vet of your own, you can ask your riding instructor or an experienced horseman friend to arrange for the veterinary examination and a discussion of his findings. There is usually plenty to discuss! Very few horses are completely unblemished, and very few vets give a horse a perfectly clean bill of health. (Very few doctors, for that matter, fail to find something wrong with their human patients during a complete check-up.) If you obtain a written veterinary report on the horse you are considering buying, you will at least be making your purchase with open eyes, knowing what you are getting and aware of the risks you are taking. The cost of this report is one of the cheapest insurance policies you can buy.

Certain defects of soundness will automatically rule out any horse for you, even though he may seem absolutely perfect in every other respect. One of these is bone spavin, especially inside the hock, which frequently leads to trouble; another is any sign of navicular disease, a foot ailment that is usually incurable; and yet another is evidence of laminitis. Roarers, or horses with broken wind, should be avoided. But certain bony enlargements called curb, ringbone, and sidebone may or may not lead to chronic lameness, depending upon where they are formed and whether or not they interfere with the action of the muscles and tendons. If around the horse's knees, cannons, hocks, or fetlock joints there are tiny pricking scars covered with lighter-colored hair or perhaps no hair at all, it is very possible that he has suffered in the past from one of these or some other limb ailment, since the flecks and scars are telltale signs of a treatment known as pin-firing. You should ask the veterinarian for his advice (and read Chapter 9, "Your Horse's Health," for a detailed description of these and other unsoundnesses).

It is not uncommon for a horse to be marked by certain blemishes such as scars from badly treated wounds or wire cuts (over which the new coat usually grows in completely white), rope burns, or capped hocks. These superficial defects may detract from his appearance, but they do not necessarily diminish the value of a horse.

Other flaws may come to light which are more important but still may not affect the horse's ability to perform the particular job you have in mind for him. For example, you would immediately rule out a horse who shows evidence of bowed tendons or periodic ophthalmia (a serious eye infection); and yet many race horses are running despite a history of bowed tendons, and some years ago there was a successful international Jumper on the U. S. Olympic Equestrian Team named Belair, whose blindness in one eye never seemed to bother him. This is not a recommendation that you should knowingly buy an unsound horse. Only a few of the most expert trainers and veterinarians are equipped to handle such a risky project, like Hirsch Jacobs, who seemed to have a special gift for patching up and rehabilitating unsound race horses. But amateur horsemen should take pains to ensure that the horse on whom they choose to lavish their affection, time, and care is in the best of condition both physically and mentally. Although a few less than perfectly sound horses have performed on the U. S. Equestrian Team (including Bill Steinkraus' Olympic Gold Medal winner Snowbound, a race track discard who suffered from recurrent leg trouble), the USET has found that, generally speaking, the best prospects for the demanding competitions in which it is involved are Thoroughbred geldings, physically sound, of good temperament, between five and ten years of age, and at least 16 hands in height.

Despite the efforts of man and nature and the claims of some effusive breeders, the perfect horse has not yet been born. You will be lucky indeed if the first horse you examine is the answer to your dreams. As a general rule, every horse purchase is a kind of compromise, and that is why it is so important for you to know not only what you are looking for, but what you are looking for *most* in a horse. Once you have a clear picture in your mind, you can give in on the points that are unlikely to affect the horse's ability to do the work you expect of him, while you remain adamant in seeking the qualities you consider indispensable. There is no reason to feel dishonored by your horse's minor physical imperfections. Any observing eye could see that the great show Jumper Nautical was ewe-necked, that the Olympic Champion Halla was over at the knees, and that the legendary British race horse Brown Jack was afflicted with the opposite defect (according to his portrait by Munnings.) Certainly, some of the most outstanding performers in racing and jumping history have been very unprepossessing-looking individuals.

Having evaluated objectively what the horse you are considering can do for you, give a thought to what you can offer him. Some breeds require more care, better feed and stabling conditions, and more expert training methods than others. So do not make the mistake of choosing a horse whose purchase price you may be able to afford, but who is beyond your means in terms of daily care and training.

Michael Matz and Jet Run, Individual and Team Gold Medal Winners at the 1979 Pan American Games in Puerto Rico. (*Photo by Sue Maynard*)

At last we have come to the inevitable final question: How much does it cost to buy a good horse?

This is difficult to answer, because the value of a horse depends upon so many different factors. Prices vary from year to year, from breed to breed, and from one part of the country to another. In general, however, you will get just about what you pay for.

The Saddle Horse Champion at the National Horse Show is usually considered to be worth in the neighborhood of $100,000, and F. Eugene Dixon is rumored to have paid over twice that sum for the show Jumper Jet Run. At the other end of the scale, many a farmer in rural districts is delighted to get $500 for a nondescript horse suitable for general utility work.

Quality is, of course, the principal factor that determines the price of a horse, and quality is usually a direct result of breeding. When discussing an equine pedigree, a horse's father is called his "sire," the mother his "dam," and it is correct to say that an animal is "by" a certain stallion, "out of" a certain mare, the stallion's offspring being termed his "get" and the mare's her "produce." In Thoroughbred circles two horses of exactly the same breeding are said to be "full" or "own" brother or sister; half-brothers and half-sisters are out of the same dam but by different sires. Oddly enough, having the same sire does not make two horses half-brothers; they are merely described as being "by the same sire."

The law of supply and demand has an influence too, and in fact explains the notable increase in price in recent years of promising Eventing, Dressage, and Quarter Horse performers, of Arabian show horses, and, to a lesser extent, of well-bred children's riding ponies.

Then there is the question of registration. A horse who "has his papers," that is to say, who is listed in an official breed stud book, is relatively more valuable than a crossbred (whose sire and dam are purebred, but of different breeds) a grade horse (who has one purebred parent and the other of mixed or unknown breeding, and takes his name from the purebred, being called, for example, a "grade Thoroughbred"), or a Half-Bred (who has only one registered Thoroughbred parent, even though he may carry as much as 31/32, or even 63/64 Thoroughbred blood). A horse possessing some Thoroughbred blood along with that of another registered breed may be called an Anglo-Arab, Anglo-Cleveland, etc., as the case may be, with the word "Anglo" referring to the Thoroughbred heritage. While registration generally means a higher price, this is, however, true only of the well-established breeds, for some of the newly created "books" that have been springing up, based mostly on color or markings, are not yet widely enough recognized to enhance the value of the animals they list.

Training, on the other hand, definitely adds value to a horse, and this is reflected in his price. But while it is advisable for a novice rider to buy a well-trained horse, it is possible for an animal to be *too* highly trained for him. A Five-Gaited Saddle Bred show horse would rapidly deteriorate in the hands of an unskilled rider, and a Quarter Horse cutting champion would be quite unsuitable for ordinary pleasure hacking. Bear in mind, too, that the purchase price of a horse represents only a fraction of the sum you will spend on him during the coming years. For example, a Thoroughbred or a Saddle Bred show horse is generally more expensive to keep than a Quarter Horse or a Morgan.

All other things being equal, mares and stallions are more expensive than geldings, because of their breeding possibilities (which is also one reason for the comparatively high prices of Arabian horses). In general, the value of a young horse increases with age and maturity, reaching its maximum at six to ten years, and then declines very slightly until about twelve, from which point the depreciation becomes more rapid.

Among the registered breeds, Thoroughbreds are on the whole the most expensive. You might consider $2,500 the minimum base price for a young, sound horse, and increase it by $1,000 for every additional asset such as size, training, manners, and show winnings. A green four-year-old costs from $4,000 to $8,000. A Thoroughbred Working Hunter that has won at local shows might be worth $7,000 or more; a winner at an A show at least $10,000; and a Conformation Hunter winner $20,000 and up. (Just for the record, at the top of the Thoroughbred scale, a yearling by Secretariat would bear a price tag of at least $750,000.)

Quarter Horses suitable for pleasure riding range from $1,500 up, although the average Quarter Horse price at the 1977 King Ranch auction sale was $7,650, and the top-priced colt brought $20,000. Prices at a recent Appaloosa sale averaged $1,584, but a good show model would fetch around $5,000—which is still a lot less than the $100,000 recently paid for an outstanding Arabian show champion.

The greatest range of all is found in the prices of Jumpers: starting with the $80 that Harry de Leyer paid some years ago for his famous Snowman (today's inflated equivalent would be closer to $800), going up to several thousand for a consistent winner at small shows to well over $50,000 for an established star. Norman Dello Joio made a real bargain when he purchased Allegro for $7,500, and got almost all of it back by winning the 1978 American Invitational Jumping prize in Tampa, Florida.

By comparison the pony breeds represent a more modest outlay: about $2,500 for a well-bred pony, for example, a Shetland or a Welsh, and as little as $1,000 for a nice crossbred. Show ponies, however, are far more expensive.

While it is the dream of all horse-lovers to own a purebred horse, the fact remains that most pleasure riding horses and ponies are of mixed breeding. Only a small percentage of the estimated 8.5 million horses in the United States is registered with a breed association. Untrained grade horses bred in the West are frequently bought by dealers for about $450 (this minimum price depending on the price offered by horse-meat dealers, which is currently around 45¢ a pound). They are then resold after a period of conditioning and training for two or three times the purchase price. A grade horse suitable for a novice owner—that is, a nicely bred animal that is neither too young nor too old, neither too green nor too highly trained—should cost no more than $1,500 or $2,000, except for grade Thoroughbreds, who are more likely to be priced from $2,500 up.

But whatever you pay for your horse, if you choose him wisely, you will find that you have acquired a lot more than appears on the bill of sale.

3. Where to Keep Your Horse

Nothing brings richer rewards to the real horse-lover than taking care of his horse himself.

While struggling out of bed on a cold winter morning to dash to the barn and muck out a stall may not be exactly your idea of fun, if you have a genuine love of horses, you will find many compensations for your efforts. A special kind of friendship will develop between you and your horse, along with a mutual understanding that is bound to improve your riding partnership. You'll find that your horse's schooling is apt to come along faster too, because you will be perfectly familiar with all of his quirks and foibles and with his individual psychology.

Being able to control every influence that affects a horse is a great advantage to a trainer. Just as educators maintain that a child's home environment is as important in forming his character as the hours spent in school, the kind of life your horse leads in the stable has as much to do with his physical and mental development as does his actual training program—even more, perhaps, because he can be such a sensitive and impressionable creature. Professional trainers usually insist on boarding in their own barns the young animals they are schooling and the ones they are preparing for the show ring. They know that the confidence and sensitivity they work so hard to build up in the training ring wouldn't develop very quickly if, at the same time, their pupil was being handled carelessly or roughly in the stable.

Where young horsemen are concerned, taking care of a pony can be a wonderful education. A child who looks after his own horse will learn more about the animal's mental and physical characteristics in a few weeks than during an entire year of riding lessons, and the knowledge he acquires in the barn is certain to improve his skill in the saddle. Thanks to modern methods and labor-saving devices, many jobs that used to be backbreakers have become literally child's play, so that even quite young children are perfectly capable of handling many simple stable chores. It is no longer at all unusual to see women and girls running their own stables single-handed; in fact, some of the best professional grooms are young women, even at the race track and on stud farms.

With the correct equipment and a bit of method, the tiresome work involved in running a stable can now be reduced to a minimum. And even this is soon forgotten, when you experience that special feeling of satisfaction as you lock the barn door for the night, knowing that your well-fed horse is snug and comfortable in a nice clean bed, or when his happy and expectant nicker greets your footsteps in the morning.

To be perfectly honest, however, there is another side to this pretty picture. A horse is as helpless as a child when it comes to looking after himself. He will depend upon you for everything: water and food, proper clothing and exercise, keeping warm, dry, and clean—not to mention getting him out of trouble. You will sometimes feel that he spends all of his spare time figuring out new and ingenious ways of getting into difficulty! What is most important of all is that he needs this attention not just once in a while or when you happen to be in the mood, but several times a day, every single day, every single week and month of the year. On the average, an owner-groom should expect to devote about an hour and a half a day, not counting the time spent riding, plus another half-day or so each week, in order to give his horse the best of care. Furthermore, he must count on spending at least $50 or $60 per month for the top quality of feed and bedding and miscellaneous stable expenses.

It is only truthful to add that many owners spend less money and far less time on their family horse. (On the other hand, perfectionists with an important investment to protect may spend even more. It has been estimated that 3.2 million horse-owners in the United States, 80 per cent of whom own horses purely for pleasure, spend no less than $7 billion a year for tack, food, and veterinary services.) Let us say that these estimates represent a rather high average, and that it is better to be well aware of the expense and responsibility involved than to be unpleasantly surprised by the recurrent feed bills and grooming chores. The point is that you should be very sure your love of horses is genuine and lasting, and not just a passing fancy, before you decide to keep a horse at home. Growing children and some adults as well are often somewhat fickle in their interests, even though their waves of enthusiasm may seem to be perfectly sincere—while they last. Then too, there is a definite distinction between the horsemen who love horses, and those whose real love is riding. In the latter case, you should weigh the matter very carefully indeed before deciding to set up your own stable, because nothing is more pitiful than the horse who suffers helplessly from the neglect of disinterested children or the indifference of busy adults. Finally, a certain amount of physical and moral strength is necessary in handling horses. A smart horse is quick to recognize weakness and timidity and will not hesitate to take advantage of it.

BOARDING STABLES

If you come to the conclusion that it isn't practical for you to keep your horse in your own barn, that doesn't mean that you must deprive yourself of the joy of owning a horse. In every part of the country there are Hunt clubs, riding academies, and private or commercial stables that offer boarding facilities for horses. Sometimes a breeder, a professional horseman, or a neighboring horse-owner will have an empty stall that he would be delighted to rent. In any case, arrange for the very best accommodations you can find, and make sure that there is sufficient personnel in the stable of your choice to give your horse the regular care and attention he needs.

The cost of boarding varies a good deal, according to the location and the quality of stabling facilities and the amount of care given. But it is always expensive, usually at least twice as much as it would cost to feed and look after your horse yourself. In city and suburban areas, it will be about $150 to $250 per month, with a supplementary charge if you wish your horse to receive daily exercise in addition to the routine care. In rural and farming areas, boarding charges are somewhat lower, but seldom less than $80 or $100 per month.

This fee normally covers everything but the cost of shoeing and veterinary services (an added minimum expense of about $250 to $300 per year). The owner is expected to supply all the necessary tack and clothing for his horse, including blankets, bandages, and halters, while the stable provides the usual grooming supplies, water buckets, and other stable equipment. Also included in the boarding price is a routine daily grooming and care of tack. In actual practice, the rider who can find the time to spare is often well advised to take care of the latter chores himself, not only because he will probably do a more thorough job but also because grooming, like training, is a bond-forming activity. Horses form firmer attachments to those who ride and groom them regularly than to the people who feed them, muck out, or pay the bills.

A special consideration for parents who are choosing a boarding stable for their child's pony should be the quality of riding instruction available. Many young riders have failed to develop their natural riding talent because of inferior teaching methods. No matter how great the temptation may be, don't succumb to the lure of a boarding stable just because it is so conveniently close to where you live. You should inspect not only the stable, but the competence of the riding instructor as well. Parents who are themselves horsemen accept without hesitation an extra hour or more of chauffeuring a day, if necessary, in order to deliver their offspring into the hands of the very best riding teacher they can find.

If boarding stables seem too expensive and maintaining a stable of your own too complicated, there is another way of keeping your horse, which in certain cases and under certain conditions can be quite satisfactory, and that is

KEEPING YOUR HORSE IN A PASTURE

In his natural state, of course, the horse lives in the open. Long ago, nature provided him with a hardy constitution and a coat that sheds or grows according to the season, to keep him healthy and comfortable under all sorts of weather conditions. Some rugged pony breeds and Western types of horses have retained a remarkable resistance to outdoor living, and they will be quite happy living in a pasture all year round in temperate regions of the West, South, and Southwest, where the thermometer never falls very far below freezing.

Many Western horses used for ordinary pleasure riding are turned out in the winter and rounded up again in the spring and they seem to suffer no ill effects, except perhaps for an unsightly shaggy growth of coat. Even in the severe New England states, some thriving Quarter Horses don't know what it's like to spend a night in a barn. However, Thoroughbreds or any well-bred riding horse being worked regularly or doing hard work such as hunting, jumping, or advanced training—and, needless to add, all horses used for showing—should definitely be kept in a comfortable stable.

Even if you don't have a suitable pasture of your own, you can sometimes rent a field from a neighboring farmer or rancher. If it is a large one, and your horse or pony shares it with other animals such as goats or cows, he will be all the happier for it. Horses are gregarious souls and love company; besides, they bite off the short, fine grasses that the other animals dislike. Intergrazing horses and cattle alternately is even better, but you should never put a horse in a field that has been artificially seeded to fatten beef cattle, because the grazing will be much too rich for the horse's more delicate digestive system.

The ideal size for a small pasture is five or six acres, the minimum being two acres, since you need at least one acre per horse and he should be free to graze in only half of the pasture at a time, while the other half is harrowed and allowed to rest.

The most important considerations are the nature of the land (which must be well-drained and never damp or marshy) and the quality of the grass. It is not a mere coincidence that many of the most famous horse breeds in the world have been raised in Kentucky, Virginia, Ireland, and Normandy, regions which are all noted for their luxuriant meadows. If yours isn't a very good natural pasture, you might contact your county agricultural agent, whose services are free and who can recommend pasture preparation suitable to your region and to your type of soil. You will also need to plant some excellent grass, and he can help you to select a nourishing variety most likely to flourish on your land.

In general, horses do best on a limestone subsoil, which provides the calcium and lime essential to their growth and health. If necessary, the lime supply should be renewed every two or three years in the fall or

A well-kept horse in a pleasant paddock. (*Photo by James Deutschmann*)

early spring, and the field must be mowed and chain-harrowed, fertilized and seeded at regular intervals. The presence of buttercups in your pasture may make a lovely picture, but it is a sign of soil acidity or lime deficiency, both of which are bad for horses. An absence of clover indicates a lack of phosphates. Live oak trees are said to indicate fertile soil and fine pasture.

Like some children, horses seem to be irresistibly attracted to danger, so inspect your field carefully to make sure that it is free from holes, obstructions, and litter, and from poisonous plants such as toadstools, laurel, and especially poison ivy, which horses carry on their hair and pass on to anyone who touches them. They cannot be relied upon to avoid toxic food themselves, nor can they resist drinking the polluted water from a stagnant pond if they happen to be thirsty. The mysterious death of a group of Welsh Mountain ponies in Pennsylvania a few years ago was discovered to have been caused by eating wild-cherry-tree leaves that had withered on the ground.

On the other hand, a patch of wild garlic and male fern will be wonderful for your horse's health, since both of these plants are natural worm remedies and field-kept horses are easier prey to parasites than stabled animals. If the pasture is a small one, you can limit both parasite infection and flies by removing the droppings as often as possible. Besides, horses are naturally clean feeders who hate to graze off land that has been soiled.

The entire pasture should be enclosed by a fence, with rounded rather than sharp corners, and a wide, firmly-closing gate. The best type of fencing, as well as one of the most attractive, is post-and-rails, with sturdy rails at least two inches thick. Heavy wire mesh also makes an effective enclosure, but a board should be run all the way around the top to prevent accidents. Whatever you do, avoid barbed wire, which is very dangerous for horses and certain to cause unsightly scars, if not serious infection. Picket fences and gates are invitations to disaster for obvious reasons; even smooth wire can catch in a horse's shoe and cause him injury. X-braced fences are another potential source of trouble, for the horse can easily get his foot caught in them.

You will want to furnish the field with shade, water, and shelter—in fact, some local laws require that shelter be provided. The shelter can be a quite simple structure. Three walls about ten feet high and a pitched roof, open to the south and offering protection from the prevailing winds, from rain, sun, and flies, make quite an adequate shelter for a field-kept horse or pony. You can install a feedbox in a corner for giving him sup-

A Pennsylvania pasture scene. (*Photo by Ray Woolfe, Jr.*)

plementary hay or grain whenever you're working him very much, and for the winter when the grazing becomes poor and the weather cold. Even though he may need no extra feed, always leave a big lump of rock salt in a handy place for your horse or pony to lick.

If a running stream meanders through your pasture, you are fortunate indeed. Otherwise, you will have to make arrangements for a constant supply of clean, fresh water. It may be a piped water supply running to a trough. There exists a self-filling model which requires little supervision other than cleaning out the trough from time to time and checking against freezing in cold weather. Another type has a built-in thermostat and heater that is automatically set into action when the temperature drops below the freezing point. Whatever method you choose, remember that water is absolutely vital to a horse, so make sure that he gets plenty of it even if you have to carry out a fresh tub to him twice a day.

While a field-kept horse or pony doesn't need as much care as if he were living in the stable, he won't do very well if he is completely neglected either. Nature has given him a practical all-weather coat, but it's up to you to pick out his feet every day and to inspect him for cuts and scratches or other signs of injury, which you should treat at once. During your daily visit you should also give him a light grooming, only not as thoroughly as you would for a stabled horse, because he needs the natural grease of his coat to protect him from dampness and cold.

Frequent friendly visits serve another purpose. If you drop by often to pet him or to bring him a tasty apple or a couple of carrots, your pony will get in the habit of coming to you readily and eagerly when you call him. And anybody who has undergone the annoying experience of wasting half the time he hoped to spend riding in trying to catch a stubborn pony, can tell you that this is a very desirable habit to instill!

Many riding ponies and horses are permanently kept in fields in England and Ireland, but the practice has never been as widespread in the United States, perhaps because we consider the disadvantages to outweigh the advantages.

On the positive side of the ledger might be noted:

There is considerably less grooming and stable work to be done every day;

A field-kept horse is less likely to develop stable vices or bad habits resulting from boredom; and

Feed bills are somewhat less expensive.

But on the negative side, it must be admitted that:

Some horses will get terribly out of condition in a pasture, since too much grass in the diet is not good for all of them;

Keeping your pasture in a clean and nourishing condition entails a certain amount of regular farm labor;

It is not always a quick and simple matter to catch and saddle a stubborn field-kept pony; and finally,

A horse kept out-of-doors will grow a heavier coat and never look as smart as a well-clipped, well-groomed stabled animal.

COMBINATION METHOD

Should the pros and cons seem to form a perfect balance in your mind, there is a compromise method that might be just the thing for you. In the winter, you may leave your horse in the pasture by day and take him into the stable at night, especially when the nights are very cold. In summer, you may bring him into the stable during the hottest part of the day and when the flies are bad, letting him loose in the pasture the rest of the time.

4. Your Own Stable

From the simple shed that is home to many a cow pony to the palatial edifice designed to house a string of Thoroughbred race horses, all good stables have in common certain fundamental characteristics.

A good stable is built on high, dry land to ensure proper drainage and to avoid dampness; it is light and airy but free from drafts, and faces south if possible; it is fireproof and well insulated against cold and excessive heat; and it is screened against flies, but open to human and animal sights and sounds.

You may already have a stable on your property. If so, before you blithely bed down your horse in a stall that possibly hasn't been occupied for years, it is a good idea to inspect the building in the light of modern principles of stable management, because new methods and materials have been developed which facilitate the job of running a stable and are beneficial to the horse's health and comfort.

You will very likely want to enlarge the stalls, change the flooring, improve the lighting and ventilation, and install water pipes. If it is an old barn, you will certainly want to lower the iron hayracks that used to be placed high in the corner of the stalls, or even remove them entirely. You may also have a hayloft in your barn, especially if it is a large one, because a loft is really practical only when there are many animals consuming huge quantities of hay and straw. You wouldn't bother to build one in a new riding stable; and even if one already exists, you will probably find that it is easier and less tiring to store your hay and straw in an empty stall than to clamber up into a hayloft and wield a heavy pitchfork several times a day.

Perhaps you own a garage or outbuilding that can be converted into a riding-horse stable. If the building is easily adapted to horses, you may be able to reduce somewhat the amount of your initial investment. But be sure to make a detailed estimate first. When the bills begin to come in for installing proper drainage, raising the roof, enlarging the doors, adding windows, and changing the flooring, you may find that you would have been better off if you'd started building your barn from scratch.

Before designing the plans of your dream stable, you will have to select an appropriate site on high, dry land, not too far away from the house and road. One hundred feet is a good average distance from the house. But it is wise to check the local zoning laws before you start digging the foundations, because most zoning boards have their own regulations concerning separation between horse stables and the nearest habitation, and sometimes there are restrictions as to the type of construction materials or drainage system you can use.

The size of your stable will depend upon how many horses you wish to accommodate. If you do your own work (and have plenty of free time), you should be able to look after as many as four horses all alone. One full-time groom can be expected to handle four to six, with show horses, of course, requiring more time and attention than pleasure-riding mounts.

Even if you intend to start out with just one horse, you'll find it most agreeable to have plenty of space in your stable and you'll appreciate the convenience of an extra stall or two for storing bedding and hay, for placing your horse when his own stall is being disinfected, for taking in a boarder, or—who knows?—for one day adding another horse or pony to your string. So you should plan on at least two roomy box stalls, or even three if you can manage it.

The interior arrangement of a stable hasn't changed very much over the centuries: it is basically a series of stalls on one or both sides of a long, large passageway, with wide doors at each end to provide cross-ventilation without causing a direct draft in the stalls. If you cannot find a builder experienced in constructing riding-horse stables, you may be interested in the conventional plans for small horse barns that are often advertised for sale for a few dollars in the horse magazines. The U. S. Department of Agriculture has also prepared a standard plan for a small two-horse stable which can be easily adapted to almost any region and includes within its compact dimensions (thirty-four feet by twenty-two feet) a tack room, a feed room, two box stalls, and a covered way. An excellent plan for a somewhat larger stable consists of an indoor ring with box stalls on both long sides.

The outer construction may be of almost any material in keeping with the architecture of your house, as long as you bear in mind the importance of protection from heat, cold, dampness, and fire. No heating system is necessary, but the building should be well insulated. Asphalt shingle or slate are suitable roofing materials. Wooden roofs should be well fire-proofed. Corrugated iron should be avoided entirely, as it can get infernally hot in sunny climates and frigid in cold ones unless it is very carefully insulated. You may wish to investigate plastic or fiber glass roofing as an economical possibility. In any case, the roof should provide for the drainage of rain water and melted snow so that it runs off well away from the stable foundations.

A small, inexpensive do-it-yourself stable. (*Photo by Ray Woolfe, Jr.*)

An attractive small stable in Connecticut. (*Photo by James Deutschmann*)

Low ceilings are dangerous for horses, who always seem to be looking for something to bang their heads or hips against. You won't have to worry if the inside height is at least ten feet. For the same reason, the dimensions of doors must be generous: at least eight feet high and four or four and a half feet wide. Sliding doors are excellent, and Dutch-type doors in two parts (the bottom part measuring four feet six inches in height) are the most popular of all, since they offer maximum safety with maximum ventilation.

Moisture is another danger to combat in housing horses—not only the moisture in the environment but also that which the horse produces at the same time that he produces heat (which causes condensation) and a certain amount of odor. The best prevention for all of these inconveniences, which are also menaces to his health, is proper ventilation. An exhaust fan in the roof helps to combat moisture by improving ventilation and at the same time helps to keep the stable cool in hot weather.

Some horse-owners like to install Dutch doors in place of windows in the stalls, especially if they are exposed to the south, pointing out how entertaining it is for the horse to be able to stick his head outside whenever he feels like seeing what's going on, and how it reduces the development of stable vices that so often are caused by sheer boredom. Furthermore, if the Dutch door leads directly onto an enclosed paddock, it may be kept completely open for part of the time, leaving the horse free to come inside or go outdoors as he pleases.

Other horsemen believe that the danger of boredom is much less than the danger of a horse's catching cold when a chill breeze suddenly

Horses enjoy keeping an eye on what is going on around the stable. (*Photo by Ray Woolfe, Jr.*)

blows down his neck, and that a horse will soon get out of condition if he is allowed to run about loose much of the time. Perhaps the real truth of the matter is that it all depends upon the individual animal—his breed, temperament, and the work he does—and also, of course, on the time you can devote to exercising him every day.

Stable flooring should be of concrete, the only surface that is hard-wearing, non-porous, and smooth enough to be cleaned easily and still not so smooth as to become dangerously slippery. However, concrete is too hard and cold for the flooring in the stalls, where clay or asphalt or special paving bricks of a cork composition are your best choices. Dirt floors are still seen in many old barns, although they are prohibited by some zoning laws. Besides, dirt retains dampness, so harmful to a horse's health, and wooden floors are slippery, difficult to clean, and retain not only dampness but odors as well.

Whatever its material may be, the stall floor should slope very gently toward a drain, and the foundations should have been conceived to offer the best possible drainage and the least possible hospitality to rats and mice.

All of the materials used to build your stable must be very strong, right down to the smallest piece of hardware, such as the hinges and handles on doors and the hooks to hold them open. You'll need much more solidity than for normal habitation use, as it is astounding how destructive some horses can be.

Special care should be taken in planning the installation of your water and electricity. A rational, well-thought-out arrangement can save you hours of time and spare you many a backache during your horse-owning career. You must consider security as well as convenience by protecting all electric wiring from moisture, the gnawing of rodents, and the horse's curiosity. Some areas have strict rules concerning barn wiring. Your local Fire Department may be able to provide useful advice—including, perhaps, a reminder to install a lightning rod.

There should be a light in every stall, placed high enough to be out of the horse's reach and enclosed in a wire cage or screened recess, with the light switches safely located outside the stalls. You will also want to have several electric outlets in convenient places: in the passageway, for attaching clippers or an electric groomer, and in the feed or tack room, where you may wish to use a small electric stove for heating water or cooking mashes. (It should be pointed out, however, that many horsemen are adamantly opposed to any cooking in a stable because of the fire hazard involved.) Finally, don't forget to install a light outside the stable, and another one if necessary between the house and the barn, controlled by a switch near or inside the house. You'll be thankful that you thought of it when you have to pay an emergency visit to your horse in the middle of a pitch-black, moonless night.

Running water is essential in a modern riding-horse stable. The basic minimum installation consists of a water faucet located in a convenient place inside the stable and another one outside, both of them adapted to fitting a hose. It is not uncommon to have a water connection in each stall, right in the corner where the drinking pail is fixed, making the watering chore a very simple matter indeed.

Many stables have adopted the system of a self-filling water fountain in every stall, whereby the water supply is automatically renewed when the horse's nose touches a sort of paddle near the bottom of a removable stainless-steel bowl. This is, of course, a great time-saver and horses learn to use it very quickly. On the other hand, there is no way of knowing how much water a horse is consuming. Most really solicitous owners therefore prefer to water their horses in the traditional way by giving them a fresh bucket of water several times a day.

In any case, you'll find it convenient to have running water—both hot and cold, if possible—in the tack room, to simplify the job of cleaning muddy tack—not to mention washing your own hands. And you'll want to make very sure that all the water pipes are well insulated against freezing.

Some form of effective fly and insect control is essential in a well-run stable, because horses seem to attract flies the way honey attracts bees. The stable doors and windows should be screened during the summer months. In warm climates, screens are necessary all year round. The most modern insecticide systems consist of battery or electrically operated spray devices installed in vulnerable areas, which emit a fine mist of insecticide at the flick of a switch or by a programmed automatic timer.

Having passed in review the basic points to look for in stable construction, now let's go on a tour of a typical well-planned and well-furnished small riding barn. Without lingering for the moment in the passageway, we'll first of all take a look inside the most important part of the entire stable, that is to say, the

STALLS

Although horses, like other grazing creatures, are a wakeful species and need only two or three hours of sleep each day, they enjoy being able to lie down when they feel like it and many of them love to roll—except perhaps for very old or clumsy ones, who are sometimes afraid that they won't be able to get up again (called "getting cast" in horsemen's language).

Today, straight or "tie" stalls are considered somewhat Spartan for riding horses and are rarely seen in private riding stables, except occasionally for head-shy horses or confirmed kickers, or animals being treated for certain ailments. It is possible to equip a box stall with a removable partition so that it can be converted into two straight stalls. But the only satisfactory permanent arrangement is to provide for each horse a roomy, individual box stall, where he will be free to move about as he pleases.

The standard measurements of a box stall have long been 12 feet square for horses and 10 feet square for ponies; but the trend is toward more spacious dimensions and most new barns are built with stalls 14 feet square. Stallion and brood mare boxes are usually 16 feet square.

The partitions between adjoining stalls are made of very heavy two-inch planks up to a height of 5 feet or so, the edges reinforced with angle iron so that the horse won't nibble them away. The partition is usually extended above the solid wood by an additional 2 feet of vertical iron grill; in order to protect the horses from each other without isolating them, and also to improve the ventilation.

Each stall should have a window high in the wall, opening outward from the top, screened against flies and protected by a grill if it is within the horse's reach. And it is amazing how far a horse's reach can extend. The Olympic Jumper Night Owl amused himself one idle afternoon by kicking the panes out of a stall window over 6 feet high!

The less you put in the stall, the better. Every piece of indispensable equipment should be securely fastened and include nothing that is sharp, pointed, or of potential danger.

You should take the trouble of fitting absolutely horse-proof bolts on the stall doors, because some of these guileless-looking creatures are as clever as Houdini when it comes to opening locks. One of the master equine escape artists of all time was probably a British Army Jumper called Gnome, who was active in international competitions right after World War II. His favorite sport, however, took place not in the jumping arena but in the stable of the Royal Scot Greys, where he would steal out of his stall in the middle of the night and make the rounds of the barn, letting all the other horses out of their boxes too.

The first essential item of furnishing is a manger or feed bowl, placed at a convenient height of about 3½ feet, according to the natural position of the horse when he lowers his head. It may be made of various sturdy materials, such as galvanized iron, hard rubber, or plastic, the latter two being particularly practical since they are removable, easy to clean, and unlikely to injure the most careless animal.

The old Cavalry method of watering a horse four or five times a day is now completely obsolete. Modern owners give their horses a constant supply of fresh water and control their drinking only when they bring them in hot from work. So every stall will contain either an automatic water fountain or a water bucket, placed in a corner opposite the feed bowl. The bucket may be a twelve-quart one of galvanized iron, or it may be made of the same hard rubber as the feed bowl. It will be attached by a snap hook fastened to a screw eye, making it easy to remove for cleaning but still firmly fixed to the wall, with the additional security of a wooden or metal brace around the bottom of the bucket to prevent the horse from knocking it over in playfulness or by accident.

Next to the feed bowl, or in another corner, there may be an iron hayrack. The old-fashioned kind used to be placed high on the wall, obliging the horse to eat from an unnatural position with his head stretched high, and also causing unnecessary eye irritation from falling dust or seed. In modern stables the hayrack is lowered to a more natural height or even eliminated entirely and the hay served right on the floor. The U. S. Olympic Team favors this more natural method of feeding hay, but some stable-owners believe that it can cause a certain amount of waste from soiled hay and may lead a horse into the disagreeable habit of eating his bedding.

The final essential item of furnishing is a good strong tying-up ring, firmly anchored to the wall about four or five feet high.

And now, all that remains to be done in order to make the stall comfortable and inviting to your horse is to provide it with a generous supply of appropriate

BEDDING

A well-cared-for horse runs through a considerable quantity of bedding during the year. Experiments have been made with many different materials, including dried pine needles, sugar cane, recycled paper, and peanut shells, in an attempt to find one that is cheap and plentiful as well as comfortable, clean, dry, and odorless. However, nothing yet has been found superior to the traditional stable-bedding classics, which are:

STRAW. In the Northern states wheat straw used to be the most common of all bedding materials and it is probably the best, being light, dry, elastic, and absorbent. However, it tends to retain stable odors, and so soiled straw must be removed frequently if the stable is to be a pleasant place to stay in. Straw is easily available through your regular feed man and the cost, which may run from $65 to $200 per ton when baled, is somewhat offset by the fact that the soiled bedding can be readily sold as fertilizer or used in your own garden. If your horse has the habit of eating his bedding, you can try rye straw, which is quite satisfactory, even though slightly less absorbent than wheat or oat straw, unless it has been chopped up. To be perfectly safe, you should check all straw for mold before you place it in the stalls. Moist clumps that are hard to separate probably contain fungi and bacteria and should never be used as bedding.

WOODSHAVINGS. This is very common bedding in the South and has become popular throughout the rest of the country since straw is so expensive. Shavings are clean and comfortable and so unpalatable that even the most gluttonous horse won't be tempted to make a meal of them. If there is a sawmill in your vicinity, you may be able to buy fine dry wood shavings prepared in small convenient bales that cost between $2 and $4; sometimes you can even get them free. But be sure to check carefully for stray nails and splinters before you spread it in the stalls, and make certain that the wood has not been treated with chemicals or insecticides which might cause hoof disorders such as founder. Pine or cedar shavings are particularly agreeable because of their pleasant odor, but oak should be avoided as it contains tannic acid, which has a heating effect on horses' feet. All shavings are somewhat drying to the hoofs.

SAWDUST is cheap and has many of the same advantages as shavings, with two major disadvantages: it clogs the stall drains and gets caked in the horses' feet, necessitating blocking the drains before you spread it, and frequent sessions with the hoof pick afterward. Sawdust is also harder to handle and more messy than most other beddings, and will probably prolong the time it takes you to clean a stall.

PEAT MOSS, so widely used in Great Britain, used to be popular in this country too, especially with horsemen who did their own stable chores. It is very easy and quick to handle, highly absorbent, increases the value of the manure, has a deodorant effect on stable smells, and needs to be renewed less frequently than either straw or shavings. However, it is now much more expensive than other types of bedding (over $8 a bale) and is practically unavailable here because it must be imported from abroad. One other criticism of peat moss is that it leaves dust in the stable drains and on the horse's coat.

STAZDRY (or similar commercial materials), is a specially prepared bedding made from dried sugar cane; it may be the ideal solution for a small stable and wherever economy is no major preoccupation. It is as absorbent as peat moss, horses won't eat it, and it is simple to store and handle as it is delivered in conveniently portioned bales.

Whatever bedding you select, the important thing is for it to be clean and dry and of sufficient quantity. You will need two to three bales of bedding per week to maintain a clean and comfortable bed in a 12-foot square box stall, if your horse spends most of his time in it. In well-run stables the stalls are cleaned at least twice a day—in the morning and at bedtime—the soiled material being replaced with fresh. Once a week the bedding is changed completely. As a matter of fact, it is a good idea to remove manure and dirty bedding from the stalls at any spare moment during the day, because dirty, damp straw provides the most favorable environment for the development of the nasty fungus disease of the foot called thrush. Your horse's health is closely related to the quality of your stable management.

While there is no great mystery to the art of making a good bed, you wouldn't see so many horses around with bruised knees and elbows if they were always bedded down correctly. And so it may not be out of place to review the proper procedure for

MAKING A BED

First of all, remove the horse from his stall and put him in crossties in the passageway, or place him in an empty stall.

Collect all the soiled and damp bedding in a dung basket, wheelbarrow, or cart, to be removed later to the manure pile.

Push the clean bedding to one side of the stall; pour a little disinfectant on the soiled places on the floor and sweep dry. (Once a week, remove all of the old bedding, wash and lime the floor, and make an entirely new bed, using two full bales for a large stall if you want to be really generous.)

Bring into the stall enough fresh bedding to replace what you have removed, and with the rake or pitchfork push and toss it all together until it is well mixed; in the case of straw, the individual straws should be lying crisscross. Bank the bedding well up around the sides and in the corners of the stall, covering the floor with a nice thick layer so that the horse will be standing in it almost up to his shins.

A good way to test whether or not you have used sufficient bedding is to walk around the stall. Wherever you can feel the floor with your feet, you haven't used enough.

Needless to add, you wouldn't want to lead a dirty horse back into

When making a bed, be sure to bank the bedding (in this case, wood shavings) generously along the sides of the stall walls. (*Photo by James Deutschmann*)

such a clean, fresh bed. So pick out his feet and give him a light brushing before bringing him back to his stall.

And now, to resume our tour of the stable, let's look into

THE FEED ROOM

It is very practical to have a separate room set aside for grain storage and feed preparation, quite apart from the living quarters of the stable. Otherwise, you will have to fix up an empty stall, making sure to add a door that locks. (A greedy horse can quite literally eat himself to death if he wanders into an unguarded store of grain.)

A good feed room is about 12 feet square in size, completely free from dampness, ratproof, and well ventilated. Hay has been known to catch fire from spontaneous combustion when stored in a small, airless space.

It need not be a large room, but there should be enough space for storing bales of hay and for installing metal-lined wooden bins to contain each kind of grain, which should never be kept in the original sacks.

Large-sized metal garbage cans with tight-fitting lids make very satisfactory grain containers where there are no built-in storage bins.

In every stable you will probably find the following useful items of

Feed-Room Equipment

A Table or Shelf for mixing feed

Feed Buckets. One for each horse (Paint them in your stable
colors with your initials.)

A Quart Measure; a dry Gallon Measure, marked in quarts

A couple of big wooden Spoons

A Knife for chopping carrots and apples

A Wire-cutter for opening bales

A three-tined Pitchfork for handling hay

A Saucepan or Kettle for boiling water; a Double Boiler for
cooking mashes; and a small Electric Stove (but only if the
barn is absolutely fireproof. Otherwise, all cooking should be
done in your own kitchen.)

A Blackboard for noting diet requirements

The principal menaces to a stable's store of feed are: (1) the vora-
cious horse who mysteriously gets loose and wanders into the feed room;
and (2) rats and mice.

Fortunately it is quite a simple matter to defend your grain supply
by putting a good strong horseproof bolt on the feed-room door; by lining the feed bins with sheet metal, and by keeping a stable cat!

THE TACK ROOM

If you are building your own stable, you should plan to have another separate room devoted to tack, as simple or as luxurious as you
care to make it. It may be merely a well-organized storage space, or an
attractive den complete with a desk and chairs, hot and cold running
water, with maybe an electric heater to make it snug and cozy in winter.
But even unheated, the tack room should be just as free from dampness
as the feed room, for cold and moisture soon cause leather to mildew.

You will need a saddle rack for each saddle you own, either a standing wooden frame or the wall-bracket type. Although you may prefer to
hang your saddle racks from the wall, it is still useful to have at least
one standing saddle rack for cleaning.

Bridles are hung on special circular wall brackets—never on hooks

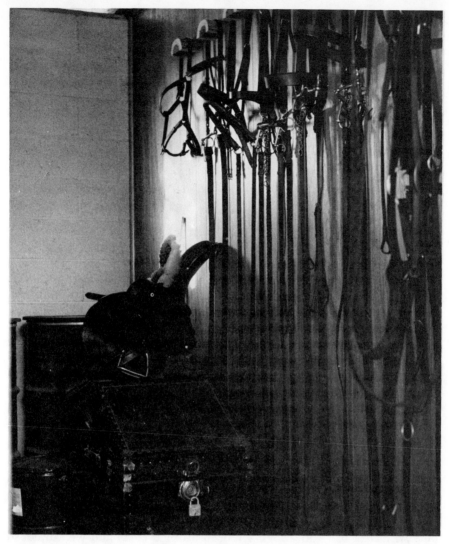

A corner of the tack room showing a bridle rack, a tack trunk, and the correct way to put a saddle down temporarily. (*Photo by Ray Woolfe, Jr.*)

or nails, which weaken the leather. You can, in a pinch, improvise one from an empty cat food or tuna fish can, cleaned, painted, and nailed to the wall. But hooks and nails conveniently placed in pairs are quite all right for holding extra metal bits. A cleaning hook, suspended from the ceiling, is practically indispensable if you want to do a thorough job of cleaning a bridle.

Where there isn't enough space for a table and a chair or two, you might build storage bins along one side of the room with flat, hinged covers to be used in place of a table for cleaning tack, while the insides furnish an ideal storage place for sheets and blankets and other items of

A saddle rack. (*Photo by James Deutschmann*)

tack or clothing. Of course, horse blankets and sheets should never be put away after use until they have been brushed clean and well dried, so it is a good idea to install a sheet or blanket rack, which is nothing more than a smooth round pole attached to the wall about waist high, for hanging up the horse's clothing that you may not wish to fold up and store right away.

The tack room is a logical place for your first-aid cabinet, and you will also want plenty of separate cupboard space or open shelves for keeping tack-cleaning equipment, grooming supplies, the ordinary tools you need for simple stable repairs, as well as the different products you use for your stable housekeeping chores, such as lime, disinfectant, and fly spray.

Saddle Horse stables require a separate shelter or "buggy room" for storing their breaking and training carts and show buggies.

THE PASSAGEWAY

A nice wide aisle is one of the most practical features of a well-designed riding barn. The standard width is 8 to 10 feet, a space in which a horse can be easily turned around. With a width of 14 feet, two horses can pass each other safely. You'll always find the aisles of well-run stables absolutely clear, because it is here that the horses are usually placed in crossties while the stalls are being cleaned, or for grooming, shoeing, and saddling. But this doesn't mean that you cannot make use of the passage walls for storing some of the less cumbersome stable gear. As a matter of fact, a hook next to each stall door is standard equipment for hanging up each horse's ordinary stable halter when he isn't wearing it, and a blanket rack is often fixed to the outside of the door itself for hanging up his stable sheet. If the stall doors are the sliding kind, not an inch of aisle space will be lost.

In the passageway near the stable entrance is perhaps the most convenient place to hang up brooms and rakes, a flashlight for emergencies,

Essential stable tools, safely stored: a rake; a ten-tined fork for removing droppings; a three-tined fork for bedding; a sweeping broom; and a shovel for removing soiled bedding. (*Photo by James Deutschmann*)

A manure cart. (*Photo by James Deutschmann*)

and a fire extinguisher—the last item being an absolute necessity, as your insurance company will no doubt agree.

Somewhere along the aisle, in the spot that is most convenient for grooming and saddling your horse, you should firmly anchor an iron ring to each side of the passage or in the ceiling, for attaching crossties. These may be either of ordinary rope or of metal chain with leather shanks; you'll know they are of the proper length if they hang fairly taut when attached to each side of the horse's halter. And you will save yourself many steps if you leave the crossties permanently in place.

It won't take you very many days of stable housekeeping to discover the most practical places for putting away your different tools so that they are always near at hand when you need them, without being under foot the rest of the time. In even the smallest barn you will find nooks and corners for storing the following items of

Stable Equipment

A Sweeping Broom
A Broom for scrubbing the floor
A Dung Basket for collecting manure (As this is rather awkward to carry, you may prefer some kind of a cart on wheels that is easier to move about and not as heavy as a wheelbarrow.)

A lightweight Pitchfork for straw bedding; or a Rake for shavings
A ten-tined Manure Fork
A lightweight Shovel
A long length of plastic Hose, with fittings
A couple of extra Stable Buckets
A Tool Kit containing a hammer, pliers, nails, etc. for taking care of simple stable repairs
Cleaning Supplies: disinfectant, lime, detergent
A Spray Gun and a nontoxic Fly Repellent
A Flashlight
A Fire Extinguisher
(Especially for women: several pairs of work Gloves, including one of rubber)

THE PADDOCK

The living space in which the stabled horse spends the greater part of his time is only about twelve feet square, and you can enlarge his diminutive universe considerably by installing a pleasant paddock, directly adjoining the stable.

Although it may be quite modest in size—as small as twenty-five feet square in many cases, or as large as fifty by two hundred feet—any paddock at all is of great benefit to a horse. For the owner who is his own groom, or who hasn't always the time to give his horse the regular daily exercise that is essential to his circulation and digestion, a paddock is an absolute necessity.

You can turn your horse out in the paddock while you are cleaning his stall or whenever you want him to have an hour or two of fresh air and sunshine without running about too much. You'll use it for cooling out your horse before returning him to his stall after a ride, or for taking the edge off a frisky animal before you ride him. Judiciously exploited, your paddock will cut down your stall-cleaning chores to a remarkable degree.

Needless to say, the paddock should be completely enclosed with a strong fence such as post and rails, furnished with a wide gate that has a horseproof bolt or lock. It should contain a water trough if your horse is to spend very much time in it, and it is also nice to have some shade, either from trees, from a lean-to attached to the stable, or from the stable's

A horse in crossties in the stable aisle. (*Photo by Ray Woolfe, Jr.*)

natural overhanging roof. Some thoughtful owners spread a ton of sand in one corner. Most horses love to roll in it.

The paddock should always be kept clean and free from litter, and the droppings picked up as often as possible in order to reduce parasite infestation. Unfortunately, no system has yet been invented to eliminate this endless stable chore!

Two horses may quite safely be kept in the paddock at the same time if they get along well together, especially if they are unshod; but there is always some chance of a quarrel, which may lead to kicking and result in injury, so many owners prefer to keep each horse in an individual paddock. Others are even more cautious and separate adjacent paddocks by a narrow lane in order to avoid playful or malicious nipping over the fence. Where space is no problem, as on large breeding farms, the horses are assigned paddocks according to their sex, size, and age. Big strong horses and little weak ones rarely get along well together, while playful young horses tend to irritate or tire older ones. Although they may look quite innocent, colts should not be trusted around fillies from the time they are one year old, and full-grown stallions must always be separated from other horses and supervised closely.

THE SCHOOLING RING

If your principal riding activity takes place on nearby roads and trails, a comfortable stable and a small paddock are the only facilities you'll need to prepare for your horse. But if you plan to school him seriously, or if your area is too built-up to permit cross-country riding, you'll also want to fix up some kind of an outdoor riding ring.

It may be round or oval or square (square corners are very useful for training), depending upon the kind of schooling you have in mind. It may be very large, or really quite small. A good average size for normal riding use is 100 by 200 feet, and for a small ring, 60 by 160 feet.

The fencing need not be especially strong, for your horse will be (it is to be hoped!) under your control, either under saddle or on the longe, during the time he spends in it, and the main purpose of the fence is simply to limit the dimensions of the ring.

Your major preoccupation will be the condition of the ground, since hard work on hard ground is probably responsible for more lameness in horses than any other single cause. You should make sure that the riding ring is free from stones and that the footing is level and springy. You may have to spread a ton or so of sand, sawdust, fine wood shavings, tanbark, or "grit," which is somewhat coarser than ordinary sand. Frozen ground is very bad for horses' feet and legs, and most horsemen find it necessary to add rock salt or calcium chloride to their riding ring to prevent freezing in the winter and to keep the dust down by retaining moisture the rest of the year. Or you can cover the frozen track with a thick layer of straw (which may be soiled bedding).

THE MANURE PIT

If you have been wondering what happens to the soiled bedding and droppings that you have been advised to pick up throughout this chapter, it won't come as much of a surprise to find that the last spot we visit on our stable tour is devoted to this unavoidable byproduct.

Every stable should have some kind of permanent installation for collecting manure, located not too close to the buildings and definitely out of sight, but still where trucks can approach it easily to cart the manure away. It can accumulate at an amazing rate, since a mature horse on normal rations is estimated to produced from 33 to 50 pounds of dung each day. The ideal arrangement is a small concrete platform, sloping toward a center drain, with concrete walls three or four feet high on three sides. Some sort of cover or simple roof will help to ward off flies, and you should also treat it with a fly repellent of a type that won't effect the value of the manure as fertilizer.

If you have no use for manure in your own garden, it is always possible to arrange for it to be carted away regularly (and sometimes even purchased) by a local nursery, farmer, or a commercial fertilizer company. Mushroom growers are excellent prospective customers, for they require great quantities of manure. Whatever you do, your property will be a much more pleasant place if you hose down and disinfect the pit occasionally, if you keep the manure pile always as neat as possible, and if you arrange for it to be removed weekly (or at least once a month) before it accumulates in too great a heap and becomes a rendezvous for flies and rodents.

5.   Stable Management

The most luxuriously appointed stable in the world won't be a very happy home for your horse unless it is well managed.

Stable management is in one sense a skilled profession and those who practice it take enormous pride in their work and earn respectable salaries for it too. But for the amateur horseman, managing a stable is not too different from running a home, and there is more method than mystery involved in doing it successfully.

The efficient owner-groom can get an astonishing number of things done in a day by organizing his stable routine so as to obtain the maximum results from a minimum of time and effort. With judicious planning it is not impossible for a horseman to do all of his own work while holding down a full-time job—and still find leisure hours for riding.

A typical daily schedule of an owner-groom might be something like this:

Before breakfast: Feed horse; remove him from stall and clean stall, renewing water and hay; pick out feet, brush horse lightly, and return him to stall.

After breakfast: Ride. Groom horse and clean tack. Return horse to stall.

Noon: Feed. Put horse in paddock, or leave in stall if he's getting plenty of daily exercise.

Evening: Feed. Clean stall, arrange bedding for the night, and bed down horse, making sure that he has fresh water and sufficient hay to last until morning.

An owner who has a full-time job might prefer to do his riding in the evening when he gets home from work, in which case his daily program might be:

Early morning: Feed horse. Remove him from stall and clean stall. Pick out feet. If horse is being ridden every day he may be returned to stall until evening. Otherwise he may spend the morning in the paddock, being returned to stable and fed at noon by another person or by owner if he returns home for lunch.

After work: Remove horse from stall and clean stall. Ride. Groom horse and care for tack. Return clean horse to stall and feed.

Evening: Renew water and hay supply for the night.

Of course, you can relieve yourself of much of the tiresome toil by hiring a full- or part-time stable employee, but that is easier said than done these days, especially if you happen to live in a suburban area. And even should you be fortunate enough to find any, competent stable help is an expensive luxury. A full-time groom earns $400 per month or more, with top-notch show grooms getting as much as $700 per month plus room and board, the "room" perhaps meaning a house big enough for a wife and children! Needless to say, the present situation makes employing a first-class professional groom out of the question for the one- or two-horse owner, who must look elsewhere for willing hands to help him with the daily stable chores.

Sometimes he will find them right in his own family; or perhaps there is a neighboring schoolboy or schoolgirl who is interested in horses and who could be taught to handle the simple routine stable jobs such as changing water, distributing feed, cleaning the stalls, and leading your horse to the paddock or returning him to his stall. But you wouldn't want to let a child attempt such work as grooming or exercising your horse, unless you are very sure of his ability—and of your horse's good manners.

Quite a few owners of small stables outfit an extra stall with the express purpose of letting it out as boarding space in return for stable services from the boarder's owner. Others, who already have some permanent employees, arrange for one of them—the gardener, for instance—to take care of certain routine stable chores in addition to his normal duties. When the work is shared by two or more members of the family, keeping a horse becomes a very light burden indeed.

However, even in the largest establishments where personnel presents no problem, the real horseman always supervises his stable personally. After all, one of the greatest pleasures of having your own stable is getting to know your horse more intimately and following his development day by day.

Besides, even though you may already be quite an accomplished rider, you will be astonished to find how much you will learn about horses when you look after one of your own. Perhaps the first thing you'll discover is that your horse is completely reliant upon you for his

SAFETY IN THE STABLE

Most horses are incapable of protecting themselves from even the most apparent dangers, and you must get into the habit of thinking about them defensively all of the time.

You should never take unnecessary chances around the barn. The string removed from a bale of hay and left carelessly in the stall is bound to be gobbled up, and because of the horse's inability to regurgitate what he has swallowed, complications may ensue. A hay net that is hung too low, a loose wallboard, or a stray bucket are invitations to a horse to catch his foot in them, whereupon he will probably become panicky and possibly injure himself badly in his frantic struggle to get free. You will eliminate many trying incidents if you keep your stable equipment always in perfect working order and in its proper place when not in use, and if you attend to necessary stable repairs without delay.

Too many horsemen, especially very young ones, succumb to the temptation of treating a horse like an oversized pet dog, a foolish error not only from the training point of view but also as concerns the horse's personal safety. If, for example, you allow your horse to roam freely about the stable because it seems to amuse him, you can be sure that one day he will get into trouble, and you will have only yourself to blame.

The horse's size and strength, essential to your riding partnership, are more of a handicap to him around the barn. A great many horses tend to forget their rear ends, especially when going through doorways, which is why you see so many of them with "dropped hips," resulting from repeated knocks and bruises. Some of them will lie down against the wall and get "cast," that is, be unable to get up again without help.

Remember too that a horse's principal defense when confronted by danger is in flight. Since the natural position of his potential enemy is therefore behind him, he is particularly apt to become frightened or "spooked," to use the current expression, by unexpected noises or sudden movements to his rear. And so, in order to avoid unpleasant scenes or injury, you will be wise to acquire the habit of taking special precautions every time you execute the simplest stable maneuver.

When entering a stall for watering, feeding, or for any other reason, you should never fail to speak to the horse before approaching, since many horses doze while standing in their stalls. You should always let your horse know by voice or gesture exactly where you are whenever you are working around him. If you approach him from the rear, pat him on the thigh after speaking to him and move your hand up along his back to the shoulder, gently pushing him aside. When you wish to pass from one side to another behind him, place your hand well forward on his back, slide it along to the top of his hips and keep it there as you walk around his hindquarters.

When removing a horse from his stall, you should first turn him, if necessary, by gently but firmly pushing around his quarters so that he is facing in the direction of the stall door. Then lead him quietly through, keeping his body straight. You mustn't start to turn him again until you are certain that his hips have passed through the doorway.

When returning a horse to his stall, you should always precede him, leading him in a straight line and turning only after having checked to make sure that his rear end is well inside the stall. Then turn him around to face the front of the stall before removing his bridle.

Sometimes you may be obliged to leave your horse in his stall for a few minutes with his bridle on, in which case you should remember to run the reins up underneath the stirrup irons so he won't get caught up in them, and take the added precaution of tying him up.

When leading a horse, you should always walk slightly ahead of him and on his near (left) side. Never face him, or he is apt to refuse to go forward. A gentle tug and a voice command, which you never vary,

Leading a horse. (*Photo by James Deutschmann*)

will make your intentions perfectly clear. If your horse shows signs of balking when being led, try above all to keep him moving by pulling his head around and turning to one side or the other; once you have him in motion, you can eventually resume your original direction. If he simply won't budge, don't waste your time in a tug of war with the odds against you. The only thing to do is to have another person come behind him and urge him from the rear by tapping or shoving on his quarters.

When leading a horse by the halter, most horsemen attach the lead shank to the halter ring under the horse's chin, which is ordinarily satisfactory (although he can catch his foot in it if it is held too slack). When leading a nervous or fractious animal, it is better to pass the end of the lead through the near side ring of the halter, make one or two twists over the noseband, and clip it to the ring on the far side. This is common practice at the race track. Another simple safety measure is to tie a simple knot in the loose end of the lead so that it cannot slip through your fingers.

When leading a horse by the bridle, you should usually pull the reins forward over his head, holding the loose ends in your left hand (but

1   2

never wound around your hand) to keep them from dragging and possibly getting entangled in the horse's feet. With your right hand, hold the reins together firmly about six inches from the bit.

In actual practice, you should lead your horse by the bridle as little as possible, especially if you are trying to teach him the meaning of proper communication with the bit. It is much better to slip a grooming halter right over the bridle and to lead him by that.

Leading a horse without a halter is best avoided entirely. But if you find yourself in a situation where it is absolutely necessary, you can slip a short length of rope or your own belt around his neck behind the ears and grasp the ends closely together at the throat. If neither a belt nor a rope is available, your best recourse is to grab one of the horse's ears with your right hand and hold your left hand over his nose. In this position you will be able to exercise at least some slight control over his behavior.

When tying up your horse, you should snap one end of the tie rope to the halter and attach the other to a ring firmly fixed to the wall, slightly higher than the horse's head, by means of a slip knot that is perfectly secure and yet easy to unfasten quickly. The length of rope between the halter and the tying-up ring should be neither too long (your horse can catch his foot in it if it hangs too low) nor too short (preventing freedom of the head).

3

4

5

Opposite, tying up a horse correctly means making a secure knot that can be released quickly in an emergency and that a playful horse cannot untie. Among the many ways of tying a halter rope, one of the best is the U. S. Cavalry method. Start by taking the standing part of the rope in the left hand and the free end in the right hand. Bring the free end underneath and make a loop as shown in picture 2. Next push part of the right hand rope through the loop to make a second loop, as shown in picture 3. Then push the free end through the second loop, as shown in picture 4. You can release this knot quickly, but your horse's efforts to undo it will only make it tighter. (*Photos by James Deutschmann*)

When you put your horse in crossties, the ties should be somewhat taut rather than hanging loose when they are attached to either side of the horse's halter. Never fix the crossties to the bit rings of a bridle, because a horse is always liable to make a sudden movement of the head which may break the bridle or injure his mouth, or both.

When you groom your horse, think of your own safety too. Always warn your horse of what you are going to do. Talk to him often, and work from a position where you are least likely to receive a playful (or a warning) kick. (The safest spot is near his shoulder.) Make your movements slow and gentle, but businesslike. Watch for any symptoms of irritation or nervousness, and never disregard a warning signal.

Since riding horses spend the greater part of their lives in their stalls, it is not surprising that many of them suffer from boredom, which often leads to the development of certain disagreeable practices that are commonly referred to as

STABLE VICES

The most widespread of these bad habits are:

WEAVING. Some horses have a nervous habit of swaying from side to side when standing in a stall, shifting their weight from one pair of legs to the other. It seems to be a natural instinct with many animals, as you may have noticed when observing caged bears or lions at the zoo. If your horse is afflicted with this annoying habit, he will expend a lot of nervous energy needlessly and it will be very difficult to keep him in condition. He has probably picked it up from a stable companion at one time or another and there really isn't much that you can do about it at this late date. However, if there are other horses in your barn, by all means keep the "weaver" out of sight, because the habit is highly contagious and can spread through a stable like wildfire.

CRIBBING and WIND-SUCKING. A "cribber" nibbles on the edge of his manger, the stall compartments, or on any other exposed wooden edge. Actually, it is a perfectly natural teething tendency, comparable to thumb-sucking in children, and the longer it is allowed to continue, the more difficult it will be to stop.

Cribbing becomes really harmful when the horse throws his head back, arches his neck, and swallows air (wind-sucking), getting a grip on the manger or partition edge with his teeth before performing this strange ritual. All of that air in his stomach can bring on a bad colic, and may even lead to chronic digestive disorders if it becomes habitual—in addition to causing excessive wear and tear on the horse's teeth. So the earliest signs of cribbing should never be ignored.

The best preventive measure is to protect all of the exposed edges in his stall with a metal rim. In some barns a wire is strung a few inches above the edge of the stall partitions and charged from a small battery with a feeble electric current—not enough to harm the horse, but sufficient to give him a mild and disagreeable shock whenever he reaches for the wooden edge. Horses develop an immediate respect for the wire and will soon avoid it even though it may no longer be charged.

There is also a special leather strap designed to be fastened around the horse's throat snugly enough to make it painful for him to swell his neck preparatory to swallowing air, but comfortable if he behaves himself. A less severe version can be improvised by using an ordinary stirrup leather. Nevertheless, you may as well know that it will be a long time, if ever, before a cribber is cured completely so that you can discard the cribbing strap and remove the electric wire.

KICKING at the stall partitions may be merely a sign of boredom or of too many oats and not enough work, or it may stem from deeper causes that only a psychiatrist could analyze. A little bit of kicking when eating grain seems to be a natural instinct with many horses, and a few playful kicks when starting out to ride should not be taken too seriously. But if a sharp word won't stop it, and if the kicking becomes prolonged or habitual, you should protect your horse from injury to his legs and hocks by lining the walls of his stall with padding. Often it is the noise they like, and the padding, by removing the noise, also removes the reason for kicking.

A horse who habitually kicks at other horses or at people from sheer malice should never be in a private riding stable in the first place, for he will give you lots of trouble and little pleasure. If you take him hunting, he must wear a red ribbon in his tail and stay to the rear of the Field. However, these traditional precautions do not absolve you of responsibility in the eventuality that your horse kicks another rider's mount or —the impardonable crime!—if he should kick a hound while hunting.

Some of the corrective devices that have proved effective with stable kickers consist of a ball attached by an elastic to the horse's fetlock, or a heavy knotted rope attached to his tail, either of which will hit him sharply every time he kicks up his hind legs. There are also heavy felt kicking-boots, designed to take the sting out of the most energetic kick. But if you have a confirmed kicker in your stable, the wisest thing that you can do is to find some way of moving him and his problems into some other horseman's barn.

While mares and geldings kick, stallions may strike (with the front hoofs). Even experienced horsemen consider it a dangerous business to keep a striker in the stable, and the risk is even greater around novices or children.

NIPPING is most often the direct responsibility of the horse's owner. If you treat your horse like a house pet, with frequent lumps of sugar and much hand-feeding, you cannot really blame him for nosing in your hand or pocket every time you come within reach. The trouble is that what starts out as a more or less gentle nuzzle may soon become an unpleasant nip, and eventually a greedy bite, violent enough to rip your coat sleeve. The only remedy is a preventive one. Always place tidbits for your horse in his feed bowl, and give him sugar from your hand only very occasionally, if he shows any tendency toward overeagerness.

TAIL-RUBBING against the stall partitions is particularly frequent among Saddle Bred horses wearing a tail set, and consequently all Saddle Horse show stables equip their stalls with a "tail board," which is a wooden shelf twelve to eighteen inches wide running all the way around the stall at a height just below the point of the horse's buttock, about four feet from the floor, making it impossible for him to get his tail close enough to the wall to rub it. During vanning, all horses should have their tails bandaged or, better still, wear a leather tail guard in order to prevent involuntary rubbing, taking care not to wrap it too tightly.

If you notice this problem suddenly appearing in your own horse, you should first of all check under his tail for possible skin irritation and have his droppings examined for the presence of parasites. And if you find either of them, you should immediately resolve to be more thorough with your daily grooming care and more regular with your horse's worming treatments.

BOLTING is the specialty of the greedy horse. He gulps down his grains without bothering to chew them and as a result they pass through his system whole, leading to frequent indigestion and eventually to chronic digestive disorders. First of all, check your horse's teeth. If they are in good grinding condition, the bolting is a vice and you must take immediate measures to stop it. Fortunately, the remedies are numerous. You can feed a bolter a bit of hay to take the edge off his appetite before giving him his grain. You can add "chop" (chopped hay) to the oat ration in order to induce proper mastication, or you can put large stones the size of your fist in his feed bowl, which will prevent him from getting more than a suitable amount of grain in his mouth at a time. Man O' War, a noted glutton, always had stones in his manger. You can also invest in a "slow-feeder" feed tub especially designed to outwit bolters. Finally, you might review your stable management to make sure that your horse is being fed on a regular schedule. A horse fed at irregular times may understandably wonder whether each meal is going to be his last and so may bolt it down; whereas an animal on a regular feeding schedule will have the confidence to chew his oats in a leisurely manner.

SHYING, REARING, REFUSING TO BE SADDLED OR GROOMED are forms of bad behavior that can make a horseman's life perfectly miserable. As they are all probably caused by bad handling in the past, permanent rehabilitation can be long and is sometimes impossible. The best advice to an amateur horse-owner is to resist buying a horse who is addicted to any of these exasperating vices, no matter how attractive his appearance may be, nor how tempting his price.

PAWING THE GROUND is not really a vice, but more of an instinctive gesture that can become obsessive. It may be allied to the act of pawing through snow for forage, since many horses paw the ground while another one is being fed. In some circumstances, it may be merely an expression of frustration. In any case, it is a harmless habit and because of its atavistic nature little can be done about it.

As you can see, some stable vices may have been acquired long before you ever got your horse, but others are the direct result of bad stable management. An animal who is getting sufficient work and proper exercise will not normally develop any of these unpleasant habits. Besides, if your stable supervision is what it should be, you will be able to spot the first signs of abnormal behavior and take immediate preventive measures.

In order to avoid boredom, the origin of many stable vices, you

Horses often become very fond of their stable companions. (*Photo by Sue Maynard*)

should keep your horse busy enough and vary his program sufficiently so that he doesn't settle down in a rut and feel the need to seek relief from the monotony of his daily life. You might also follow the example of the many stables that are equipped with speakers in the stall area, as well as in the indoor ring, to provide continual background music. Racing stables often go a step further by playing tapes from time to time of crowd noises. A radio, at least, is an essential item of stable equipment.

There is another simple means of combating boredom in a stabled animal, especially if you have only one horse in your barn, and that is to provide him with a stable companion. It is a racing tradition to give race horses a pet to keep them company. Exterminator's best friend was a pony named Peanuts; Seabiscuit had a goat and Brown Jack a cat, while War Admiral's famous rabbit accompanied him from track to track and later into retirement. The temperamental trotter Goldsmith Maid refused

A happy trio. (*Photo by Ray Woolfe, Jr.*)

to race unless her stablemate, a yellow mongrel dog, was present; and the European trotting champion Krakovie never made a move without his pet lamb, Brigitte. Riding stables have made delightful mascots of dogs (especially coach dogs and the terrier breeds), roosters, cats, deodorized skunks (they are great ratters), and many other animals. Goats are favored by many old-time grooms due to the popular superstition that the presence of a goat in a stable protects the horses from distemper.

Cats are particularly satisfactory, because good mousers are always welcome around a barn, and horses get along with them famously. One of the founders of the Thoroughbred breed, the Godolphin Arabian, was noted for his extreme attachment to his favorite stable cat. Unfortunately, one day quite by accident he kicked up his heels and struck his furry friend a mortal blow. So great was his remorse that the aged stallion refused all feed and water and, according to legend, died shortly thereafter of a broken heart.

In the long run, experience will be your best teacher of stable management—or, to be more exact, experience and your horse. You will find that the essence of good stable management is simply attention to details, maintaining a good balance in the amount and timing of feed, exercise, and watering, and adhering to a well-planned regular schedule. However, to facilitate your very first steps, there are a number of dependable sources of guidance.

Pony Clubs and 4-H groups give wonderful training to children in horse care. Many of the state universities and agricultural schools hold clinics in horse management from time to time as well as regular extension courses, where adults can receive excellent, up-to-date instruction. Some colleges and universities give college credits for equestrian training programs, and Pennsylvania State University even offers a correspondence course in the care of riding horses. The various equestrian publications often print articles devoted to the different phases of installing and running a good stable. They also print advertisements of the stable management schools that are cropping up all over the country. Perhaps the best way of all to learn how to manage a stable is to take a summer job or a part-time one as an apprentice in a first-class establishment and carefully observe the methods of the top professionals. If this is impossible, you can always seize every opportunity of talking with experienced horse-owners, who have already found the answers to the very problems with which you may be struggling.

6. Feeding Your Horse

Your own idea of a nourishing meal may be a juicy sirloin steak with plenty of French fries, but if you are to give your horse a well-balanced diet, you will have to follow an entirely different set of nutritional principles.

The horse's digestive system is somewhat special. First of all, his stomach is quite tiny in relation to his size, with an average capacity of only about three and a half gallons, and it must fill and empty itself two or three times during every normal feeding. To complicate matters, a horse cannot vomit or even eliminate gases by burping; his digestive juices are rather weak and he has no gall bladder at all; his stomach and intestines are very sensitive to toxic or hard-to-digest foods; indigestion and constipation have more serious consequences for horses than for most other animals.

The actual digestive process begins in the horse's mouth, where the flat, broad surfaces of his teeth are used for grinding. Needless to say, this causes considerable wear and tear, and so the horse's teeth, unlike our own, continue to grow throughout his life; however, like ours, they must be in good condition if mastication is to be perfect. In fact, one of the first things an experienced horseman checks in cases of chronic indigestion is the state of his horse's teeth.

During mastication the food mixes with the horse's frothy saliva. It has long been considered preferable to give a horse dry feed in order to increase the saliva flow, except in the case of windy or coughing horses or dusty hay, when it may be slightly dampened (the simplest way is to sprinkle it with a watering can). Nevertheless, with healthy normal eaters, dry or damp feed is merely a matter of taste or convenience. Many horses like to dunk their feed and hay in the water bucket, and while this may lead to messy stalls and dirty pails, it doesn't seem to do the horses any harm.

Digestion lasts about an hour and a half and takes place in the stomach and in the intestines, which are very long. A horse's food must travel at least a hundred feet before it is finally eliminated.

Horses need quiet as well as time in order to digest properly, and so they should never be asked to do hard work within at least an hour after a heavy meal. They digest less well when tired too, which is why the traditional evening meal of Hunters after a hard day's run is a warm steamed mash. Creatures of habit, some horses will get upset or angry if their meals aren't served on time, and this might be kept in mind when dealing with nervous animals, since their digestion is bound to suffer if they have to throw a tantrum in order to get fed. It may even cause them to run transient temperatures, sometimes as high as 107 degrees.

The horse's natural diet is, of course, grazing, which provides ample nourishment for an animal who has nothing more to do all day long than to roam lazily about a meadow munching clover. But the civilized horse leads quite a different life. He is subjected not only to long periods of confinement in a stable, but also to periods of activity much more violent than he would voluntarily undertake if left to himself. He has no feeding instinct, as do so many cats and dogs, which tells him how much to eat and what is best for him. And so he must rely on man to provide him with a nourishing and balanced diet.

The horse's solid food consists of roughage (hay and grazing) and concentrates (various grains). The hay provides bulk, while the grains are essential for building muscle, furnishing energy, and for growth. Mature horses doing slow work, as well as many ponies, can often get by on hay alone; but those being ridden regularly also need a certain amount of grain each day, the ration being increased as more effort is demanded of them.

Once you have a general idea of the special nature of the horse's digestive system and nutritional needs, the art of feeding him becomes merely a matter of common sense. The principal rules to remember are:

1. Get a good feed man and have him supply you with clean, nourishing hay and grains of the best quality possible.
2. Feed your horse frequently, in small amounts and at regular intervals.
3. Serve the hay ration first of all and then the oats, the former being more quickly digested. (Besides, a bit of hay will take the edge off a horse's appetite and prevent him from bolting his oats.)
4. Never feed a hot, tired horse. You may give him a handful or two of hay to play with, but wait for at least an hour after hard work before feeding the grain ration. Afterward, give him an hour or more of rest and quiet before exercising him again.
5. Never impose upon your horse a sudden change of diet. Introduce new feed little by little, always making a very gradual transition over several days from a grazing regime to a stable diet.

HAY

Although it may all look alike to the uninitiated, hay can vary a great deal in quality and nutritional value according to when it was cut, how it was cured, and what kinds of grasses it contains. The important thing is to provide your horse with the very best hay that you can find.

Many horsemen believe that the most satisfactory kind for horses is *clover* or *timothy*, or a mixture of the two, with perhaps a small proportion of *alfalfa*. The latter, called lucerne abroad, is a "legume hay" (as are clover and lespedeza), the sweetest and most nourishing of all. Being high in protein, calcium, lime, and Vitamin A, it may even be *too* rich for some horses (it is also somewhat laxative and stimulates the kidneys); so it is best to give alfalfa only in small amounts to horses who are working hard or in need of conditioning.

Even if you order hay by telephone from a feed-supply house, you should learn how to recognize good hay from bad. The best is blue-green in color, rather than pale and bleached; sweet-smelling and clean; free from irritating dust or toxic mold; and crisp enough to feel dry to the touch and to rattle on the pitchfork. You cannot be too particular about the quality of hay you feed your horse. Smell it and shake it up as you dole it out. An especially heavy flake probably contains mold and should be discarded. Legume hay requires careful checking because it molds most easily. Hay with excessive moisture is also likely to heat, mold, and ferment in storage, creating the risk of fire by spontaneous combustion. So you should keep your hay reserve dry and well ventilated, and check the temperature of the reserve bales from time to time. Bales of new hay should be stored at least a month before feeding, in order to complete the curing process.

Hay not older than six months is generally preferred, since beyond that age it loses much of its food value and is harder to digest, becoming unfit to feed after two years. Toward the end of summer, *green hay* is available; it is nourishing, appetizing, and somewhat richer than cured hay.

The modern method of feeding hay—and the most natural—is right on the stall floor, although some owners still cling to the hayrack system. Another much slower way is to suspend a hay net at nose height in the horse's stall, but there is danger that the horse will catch his foot in the net, which naturally hangs lower and lower as it is gradually emptied of its contents. In this country, hay nets are most often used only when one wishes to divert a horse by letting him munch just a little bit of hay at a time—while traveling, for example, or during horse shows.

Today most riding horses are given a constant supply of hay and allowed to eat as much as they like. The usual schedule is to distribute the hay in the morning, at noon, and in the evening, with the bulk at the last feeding in order to see them through the night. Since hay is usually prepared in compressed sections or "flakes" that are wired into bales, you should shake it up well with your hands after carrying it into your horse's stall, to make a nice loose pile and at the same time to settle the dust.

Many large stables grow and cure their own hay, but the small-scale horse-owner usually calls upon the services of a feed man. Prices vary with the season and the region, and bargains in hay can turn out to be very costly indeed. Unless you are a knowledgeable buyer, it is less risky to trade with a well-established feed man than to make a deal with a local farmer who offers you a special rate. You may pay more—about $80 to $110 per ton for the top quality—but you will have the advantage of an expert selection from many different farmers' crops. Even so, you should inspect the bales upon delivery and send back any sections that are damp or moldy.

An average horse will munch his way each year through three or four tons of hay or even more, according to the amount of grazing he does. It is probably most practical to order it by the ton, if you can find a convenient dry storage space for this amount in your stable. Too great a quantity of hay in storage will become dusty; but don't wait until the old hay is all used up before reordering. Horses can be very fussy about their feed and dislike sudden changes in their diet. You can be sure that they will notice the unexpected appearance of a new mixture and perhaps turn up their noses at it. The best practice is to make a gradual transition from one lot of hay to another by mixing the two together, adding more and more of the new variety until your horse's system has become accustomed to the change.

GRASSES

Green food is the horse's only nourishment in his natural state and it is not surprising that civilized horses love it too. But it is laxative and their bellies will swell if they get too much of it. Besides, while some kinds of grasses are quite nourishing, none of them has enough food value to keep a horse in condition for work without supplementary concentrates.

In some parts of Australia there used to be races for grass-fed horses, and the results were interesting. While the horses retained a reasonable amount of speed, their stamina suffered greatly and they could run only for about three furlongs (three-eighths of a mile).

Horses always enjoy grazing after exercise, and there is no reason why they shouldn't be allowed to do so after they have been walked on a lead shank for a few minutes and are no longer hot. However, a wise general rule is never to permit a horse to graze when he has a bit in his mouth. You can give a stabled horse fresh lawn mowings if you happen to have them and he will be delighted. Make sure, though, that the grass is freshly cut, for it ferments very rapidly. And be certain that it has not been sprayed with weed-killers or insecticides that may be poisonous to horses.

Grasses are merely extra delicacies in the diet of a stabled horse, but sometimes they can be of real value. A grass diet is said to help reduce

fever and promote the healing of wounds, while chronic coughs may disappear completely.

OATS

The best grain of all for horses is undeniably oats. In fact, oats are absolutely essential for horses doing fast work, as well as for building up colts into strong and healthy adult horses.

You will soon learn to recognize good oats by their appearance, weight, and feeling. They should be heavy, plump, sweet-tasting (and never bitter), hard, smooth, short, clean, free from mold and dust, and should weigh about forty to forty-five pounds to the bushel. New oats should be fed no sooner than one month after threshing, while many horsemen like them to be one year old. The top grade will cost between $10 and $11 for a hundred-pound sack, which is generally the most practical buying quantity.

Your horse's oat ration will depend upon his condition and the amount of work he is doing, for oats are his prime source of energy. They may be served whole, which is the most usual form; or they can be crushed or crimped (only slightly broken up). Crimped oats are perhaps preferable, since crushing causes a loss of flour and unnecessary dust in the feed tubs. Both crushing and crimping increase the digestibility of oats and may be advisable in the case of old horses, animals with defective teeth, those getting very little exercise, or confirmed bolters who gobble up their grain at such a rate that whole oats pass through their intestines undigested. Mixing either whole or crimped oats with chopped hay is another way of inducing a horse to chew his food more thoroughly, and it is also effective in outwitting bolters.

Horses are gourmets in their own fashion. One of their favorite winter dishes is:

Steamed Oats

The simplest method of preparation is to take 1 or 2 Tablespoonfuls of Salt, a ration of crushed or crimped Oats, with perhaps a few cut-up Carrots, a Cup of Blackstrap Molasses, or 2 Tablespoonfuls of Linseed Meal for extra tastiness. Mix with a suitable quantity of boiling water (which should be entirely soaked up by the oats), cover, and leave to steam until cool enough to eat (thirty minutes to an hour). Another method is to cook the mixture in a double boiler until it is the consistency of breakfast porridge, and cool before serving.

Because of the high cost of oats nowadays, cheaper substitutes have been devised and modern feed methods tend to put less emphasis on oats. A typical example of this new style of feeding would be a combination of ear corn, soybean meal, mineral supplements, salt, and hay. Nevertheless, an owner who asks a lot of his horse in the way of performance or who has an expensive investment to protect would never dream of eliminating oats entirely from his horse's diet.

CORN

Corn is heat-producing, fattening, and highly nourishing, and may be added to the grain ration in cold regions or in wintertime, for it is cheap, plentiful, and simple to store. But because of its heatening effect, you should never feed corn to a horse doing fast work during warm weather, as this may lead to a serious ailment called founder (laminitis). Furthermore, some horses tend to be allergic to corn. It can upset many of them until they get used to it.

In normal cases and in cold climates, three or four ears of corn on the cob added to his regular grain mixture will benefit a healthy horse. If he is doing very light work, his cold-weather rations might even consist of one third oats, one third bran, and one third freshly cracked corn.

BRAN

As all readers of breakfast-cereal advertisements know, bran adds bulk to the diet, is very digestible and gently laxative. Where horses are concerned, wheat bran is a useful addition to the diet, ensuring good elimination for horses who are not getting very much exercise, and being easily digested by those who have put in a hard day's work. As always, you should be particular about quality. Good bran has large, flat, sweet flakes; poor bran is floury.

Bran may be served dry, or mixed in a small proportion with the oat ration (one part bran to four to eight parts oats), in which case it loses its laxative properties and may even have the opposite effect; or you can cook it into a mash, the traditional Saturday-night supper of Hunters, who rest on Sundays.

Bran Mash

Place about 2 pounds (4 quarts) of Wheat Bran in the horse's feed bucket; add a large pinch of Salt, a handful of Linseed Meal. Wet with boiling water, cover, and let steam until cool enough to feed but still slightly warm. The mash mixture may also be cooked slowly for an hour in a double boiler. (Because of its laxative effect, it is best to serve a bran mash only as the last meal of the day and to give the horse only light work the day after.) You can also follow the above method using one third crushed oats, two thirds bran, and salt.

Another Bran Mash recipe calls for 2 parts of sweet feed and 1 part bran. Add boiling water to form a rather dry paste, then cover and allow to steam for fifteen minutes, until all the water has been absorbed. Serve warm.

LINSEED (FLAXSEED)

To add a shine to a horse's coat, to put weight on a skinny horse, or to hasten the convalescence of an animal who has been ill, nothing is more effective than a bit of linseed meal, dampened slightly and added to the grain ration. Because its hard outer shell makes assimilation impossible, linseed must always be ground into a meal or steamed in a mash.

Linseed Mash

Boil 1 quart of ground Linseed Meal in water for three hours. Add 2 quarts of Bran, which should soak up all of the remaining water. Stir, cover, and cool to feeding temperature.

PREPARED HORSE FEED

Most of the large feed concerns sell a mixture of their own, especially composed for riding horses, and this may be the most practical feeding solution for a small stable, since it requires no preparation and little storage space. Consisting of corn, oats, and molasses and fortified with alfalfa, linseed, salt, minerals, and vitamins, it is ordinarily referred to as "sweet feed" and often appeals to horses who are otherwise finicky eaters. The same, or a similar, mixture may be bought in small dry pellet form, called "crunch," which is a complete feed that most horses find delicious and delightfully crisp to chew. It costs slightly less than sweet feed—about $8.50 for a hundred-pound sack. All horses may welcome one of these preparations as a change from their habitual feed from time to time. However, if you wish to try it, you should introduce it to your horse gradually. Start by mixing a little with his regular oats, and make sure that it agrees with him before serving sweet feed as the basis of his diet. Furthermore, for psychological as well as digestive reasons, it is never advisable to eliminate hay from a horse's feeding program. Munching hay keeps him occupied as well as nourished, and if you deprive him of this distraction, he may start nibbling away at the stall door . . . or his neighbor's tail.

MISCELLANEOUS FOODS

The most succulent dish in the world would soon lose its appeal if you had to eat it three times a day, every day of the year. The horse's appetite can become jaded too if he is always fed the same old grains. Sometimes a horse will go off his feed completely and his worried owner will seek all sorts of physical explanations for the sudden lack of appetite, when just plain boredom is the cause of it all.

It is quite a simple matter to vary your horse's diet. For example, he loves apples and they are good for him. Cut in pieces so they won't get

The only safe way to feed a horse by hand.

stuck in his throat, an apple or two will be a welcome addition to his usual grain ration. Raw carrots are excellent for his nerves and eyesight because of the Vitamin A they contain. You can feed them sliced lengthwise or chopped up in a mash; either way your horse will relish them. Raw turnips can be cut up just like carrots to give a slightly different flavor to his oats. Perhaps your horse has some special *gourmandise*, like the French trotting champion Jamin, who could not get his fill of artichokes; or Ramon, Gerd Wiltfang's World Champion Jumper, who eats six pounds of pumpernickel a day when in hard training or competition.

You can vary the trimmings as much as you like, but the horse's diet should always be based on wholesome hay, oats, and bran. It may be true that horses in other parts of the world manage to get by on some very bizarre feed, such as crushed beans or peas, sugar cane, pumpkin, and even boiled potatoes. Many Arabian horses have been raised in the desert on dates alone, and wild Shetland ponies in their natural habitat have been known to survive hard winters eating nothing but seaweed. However, it is obvious that these foods—even including barley and wheat—are vastly inferior to oats in nutritional value and are quite incapable of maintaining a well-bred riding horse in good health and working condition.

SALT AND MINERALS

Salt is essential to the horse's organism and should never be omitted from his diet. It is, oddly enough, the one instance where he seems to have an instinct that warns him of his body's needs, and many stables simply place a large piece of rock salt in each stall, or a brick of salt in a special wall dispenser for the horse to lick whenever he feels like it. Other horsemen want to be absolutely sure of the amount of salt their horses are getting, and so they add a tablespoonful of iodized salt to the noon grain, increasing the amount to two tablespoonfuls a day during very hot weather or when the animal is perspiring a great deal from hard work or schooling.

If you decide on the wall-dispenser method, you might as well order the kind with two compartments: one for salt, and the other for a block of mineral supplements specially prepared for horses, consisting mostly of lime, calcium, and phosphorus, with vitamins A and D. The same formula exists in powdered form, and many owners add a dose to the daily feed as a matter of course during the winter months, and for conditioning horses who have been out of training. Another popular dietary supplement for stabled horses in winter is an ounce of tasteless cod-liver oil mixed with the grain once a day, to compensate for the Vitamin D that is provided by sunshine in other seasons.

A glance at the advertising columns in the horse publications will give you an idea of the wide range of patent vitamin compounds and conditioning concentrates that have been developed in recent years. If a mature riding horse is doing well on a normal, balanced diet, he shouldn't really need any of these products unless the veterinarian prescribes them for some special purpose. However, all show horses are given vitamin and mineral supplements as a matter of course, and the few cents cost per day is very cheap insurance against a deficiency.

There is much talk nowadays of *electrolytes*, which are the essential basic minerals (including calcium, sodium, chlorine, potassium, phosphorus, and magnesium) that are dissolved in the horse's body fluids and are lost through perspiration. When sweating is intense during stress and physical exertion in hot, humid conditions, electrolyte depletion can reach a dangerous level and these chemical elements must be supplied if the horse is to continue his efforts. Electrolyte supplements exist in solution, powder, and tablet form and can be given by mouth or by injection.

It has become customary to give them during and after stressful competitions such as Endurance and Trail Rides and Combined Training Events. But there is no point in administering electrolytes unnecessarily. Horses cannot store these elements in their bodies but must eliminate the surplus, which can put a strain on their kidneys and thus cause more harm than good.

FEEDING PROGRAMS

The precise quantity of food a horse requires to stay in condition is a highly individual matter, depending upon his size, age, type, metabolism, and temperament, as well as on his state of health and the amount and kind of exercise he is getting.

Nevertheless, there are certain standard feeding rations and the usual practice when starting out with a new horse is to observe his reaction to an average feeding program and to adjust the amounts accordingly. You can judge the suitability of the diet you are giving your horse by noting his eating habits, the condition of his coat and droppings, and any changes of weight. (If he seems to be getting too fat or too thin, you can spot it best along the backbone, rather than the belly, which may swell from other causes.)

Proper feeding is important not only for maintaining a horse's shape and condition but also for keeping him healthy. Overfeeding is certain to result in obesity and may also lead to such ailments as azoturia and laminitis (founder). An unbalanced diet is bound to result in eventual vitamin deficiencies and may also cause such disorders as chronic colic or heaves.

In modern stables, riding horses are given all the hay they care to eat, which usually amounts to fifteen to twenty pounds, or about three or four "sections" per day. The grain ration is more variable and must be carefully adjusted to each individual case. Since horses often go off their feed for a few days after moving into a strange home, new owners frequently start them off with four quarts of oats a day, building up the amount gradually as the horse's appetite returns to normal.

Conformation provides a clue to the most satisfactory quantity. Compact, short-barreled horses stay in condition with comparatively little feed, while some narrow-chested, lanky ones never get fat no matter how much grain you give them. But a normal eater who suddenly starts losing weight on his regular diet may be suffering from parasites, tooth trouble, or a more serious ailment.

As a "rule of thumb," you can expect a pleasure horse who does one hour of hacking a day to stay in condition on one pound of concentrates and one and a half pounds of roughage for every hundred pounds of body weight. To find the weight per quart of your oats, ask your feed man for the test weight per bushel of the quality he supplies you, and divide the figure by thirty-two. Thus, with oats weighing forty pounds to a bushel, a quart will weigh one and a quarter pounds; a quart of bran weighs about one-half pound.

Generally speaking, an average horse being ridden every day will get along well on eight to ten quarts of oats; you will give him less when he is idle (because overfeeding is just as dangerous to his health as underfeeding), and somewhat more when you ask him to do extra hard or fast work. Whenever you wish to feed him a more generous grain ration after a long day of hunting, for example, it is better to add an extra meal than to increase the size of his normal ones. Remember, the horse's stomach is really quite small.

During the hunting season a 16-hand Hunter may be fed as much as sixteen quarts of grain, while eight quarts should be an adequate ration if he is merely used for hacking. Jumpers can consume great quantities of grain when in training, and some race-horse trainers feed promising colts as much as twenty-two quarts a day. At the opposite extreme, Arabians, Morgans, Quarter Horses, and Western breeds do very well, even when in competition, on four quarts a day or less. In fact, they will soon get fat and out of condition if they are fed too much.

Saddle Bred horses, unless they are very highly bred, are usually easy feeders; eight quarts of grain a day should fill their normal daily requirements, although the amount may be increased and the feed enriched with vitamin conditioners in order to produce the fire and animation expected of them in the show ring. On the other hand, Thoroughbreds are often fussy eaters, particularly sensitive to changes in their diet and susceptible to the various disorders that can arise from imperfect feeding methods. It is essential to provide them with a digestible, nourishing diet based on top-quality hay and oats, to ensure regular elimination by adding a few quarts of bran to the oat ration, and to serve cooked mashes after exceptionally hard work.

It is not surprising that the trotting and racing stables have developed some of the most skillful feed experts in the country. In a field where speed is all-important and every pound of useless weight an unnecessary handicap, feeding can make or break a racing career. Horses doing this demanding work need a diet rich in protein (oats and legume hay) to keep their muscles hard and their nervous system resistant.

The small pony breeds are the easiest of all to feed. Often they get along best on hay alone. While you may give three or four quarts of oats a day to a large pony doing fast work such as jumping or hunting, it is wise to be very cautious, even stingy, with the grain, for oats can go to a pony's head in much the same way that alcohol affects human beings. Many field-kept ponies thrive on grazing alone, or with a little supplementary hay. But in the winter, natural grazing is not very nourishing and must be almost entirely replaced by hay.

Because his digestive system has been conditioned to receive small amounts of food at frequent intervals, the horse's daily feed should be divided into several separate meals. Some horse-owners can manage only two: the first around 7 or 8 A.M., and the second at 5 or 6 P.M. Two daily meals are customary on breeding farms, where the animals spend most of their time at pasture. Most riding-horse stables like to serve three meals a day: at about 7 A.M., 12 noon, and 7 P.M. Four daily feedings are even better, with the addition of a late supper at 10 or 11 P.M. The Cavalry used to feed its mounts no less than five times a day.

If you follow the most usual program of three meals a day, you might divide your horse's feed like this:

Morning: One third of the grain ration, plus a little less than half the hay
Noon: One third of the grain ration, plus a few handfuls of hay
Evening: One third of the grain ration, and somewhat more than half the hay

WATER

Watering a horse properly is just as vital to his health as feeding him intelligently—perhaps even more so, since his body chemistry is composed of 80 per cent water. The average horse drinks from six to twelve gallons of water a day, and even more when in hard work and during very hot weather. He needs about half a gallon of water for every pound of dry food he consumes.

If water is always available, a horse will not normally drink to excess. In fact, modern horsemen are inclined to believe that the old Cavalry system of watering the horses four or five times a day was designed less to satisfy thirsty animals than to give the enlisted men something to do! Today you will find a permanent water supply in the stall of every well-tended riding horse, either an automatic fountain or a water bucket. The latter should be kept clean and be refilled the first thing in the morning, the last thing at night, and before each meal, so that it is never empty. Water fountains fill themselves automatically, but it's still up to you to keep them clean and to check them regularly to make sure they are always in good working condition.

There is only one occasion when you have to control your horse's drinking and that is when you bring him in hot from work. Allowing a sweating horse to drink his fill and then to stand around, is a sure way to bring on founder, one of the most troublesome ailments that can afflict a horse. That is why race horses are allowed just a few swallows from time to time as they are being walked after a race; and during some competitive trail rides, the veterinary committee advises when and how much each horse should be permitted to drink after the day's run.

EXERCISE

Exercise is inseparable from feeding, because the amount of one depends upon the amount of the other. It is an unfortunate fact that most pleasure horses don't get enough regular work. If you were to calculate the time many of them spend in their stalls, you might reach a total of twenty or twenty-two hours a day.

And yet daily exercise is the only means of keeping a horse fit and of ensuring good circulation, sound feet, and efficient digestion. The absolute minimum for a stabled riding horse is a half-hour of walking and trotting every day; a full hour of work is far better, with ten or fifteen minutes of walking both at the beginning, to warm him up, and at the end, to cool him off.

In addition to his daily ride, your horse will benefit immensely if you give him an opportunity to stretch his legs every day. For example, if you ride him in the morning, you might also let him loose in the paddock for an hour or two in the late afternoon.

If you cannot exercise him yourself every day, or at least five days a week—in other words, if you are just a "weekend rider"—it will probably be kinder to your horse to board him where he will have the daily services of an exercise boy (more likely an "exercise girl") rather than to keep him confined all day long in a stable of your own. Otherwise, you must arrange with somebody to exercise him for you. You can, of course, simply put him in the paddock for part of the time; it will at least be good for his circulation. But most mature horses are easygoing, even lazy creatures, and the kind of exercise they give themselves is not an adequate permanent substitute for supervised work.

There is, however, one way of exercising your horse that is just as effective as actually riding him, and that is to work him on a longe line. It takes practice to become skillful with the longe and to control the horse's gaits and speed as you keep him moving around you in a circle. But it is extremely worthwhile to master the technique. Longeing is an essential part of the training of many kinds of horses, and it is also an excellent way to keep a pleasure horse in fit condition.

CONDITIONING

Once a year, preferably in the early springtime, most hard-working horses need a vacation in a nice green pasture with their shoes off. Hunters and Polo Ponies are often "roughed" (turned out unshod) for two or three months after a hard season. If you haven't a pasture, you can give your horse a rest right in the stable by gradually feeding him a lighter diet and cutting down his exercise to a half-hour's or an hour's daily walk. After a few weeks' holiday your horse will be relaxed and rested but somewhat let down. The process of hardening him up again for normal work is called "conditioning."

It may take a month or more to bring back into condition a horse who has spent six or eight weeks leisurely grazing in a field. He may have gained as much as two hundred pounds and will certainly have lost much muscle tone. That is why older horses, over fourteen or fifteen years, are never allowed to get completely out of condition, as it is practically impossible to bring them in again. Show horses are never taken completely out of training either; even if they should be turned out to pasture, their condition is maintained by exercise and the grazing is supplemented with four or five quarts of oats a day.

To make a horse fit again, you will need to follow a regular program of gradually increased work to "muscle him up." Starting with a half-hour daily walk, you must add enough work each week so that his muscles and wind become strong enough to sustain him during a full normal exercise period. Walking uphill and down is an excellent conditioning exercise. When possible, race horses and Jumpers in training are ridden along a sandy ocean beach, because of the beneficial effect of salt-water leg baths. (The going is best for this purpose right after the tide has receded.) At the same time you'll gradually increase the amount of oats you give your horse, until he is back on his usual rations. And this is one occasion when it may be worthwhile to investigate the virtues of the various patent conditioners and vitamin compounds, especially if you are preparing him for a season of competition. Vitamin B complex and E are especially recommended, as well as electrolyte supplements (minerals) during heavy work. Some trainers have concocted unusual personal recipes for conditioning their horses before an important race or jumping event. For example, the continental trotter Krakovie prepared for his 1961 American debut by drinking a daily eggnog composed of milk, eggs, and honey; a chocolate sundae was reported to be Kelso's favorite treat and the best means of calming his racing nerves before an important event; and a member of Mexico's victorious Olympic Jumping Team in 1948 revealed to the London press that each horse was given half a bucketful of brown sugar before going into the ring. Notwithstanding the apparent success of these novel formulas, the average horseman is better advised to restrict himself to conditioners recommended by his veterinarian.

Conditioning a horse for competition is an art as well as a science, in which a sense of timing is all-important in order to bring the horse to his peak of condition at just the crucial date. You must exercise your judgment every step of the way, guided by your observation of your horse's weight and appetite, his coat and eye, his enthusiasm or boredom. Grooming and shoeing are also essential elements of conditioning, in addition to feed and exercise. Every horse is individual in this regard, but all of them will suffer from overtraining. The basic idea is to make a gradual transition from a life of leisure to one of strenuous activity. You can break down a good horse in no time by demanding too much, too soon. But if his conditioning program has been sensibly planned and if you've followed it faithfully, you will recognize the unmistakable signs of a horse who is in excellent form. His wind will be sound, even after fast work; his endurance will have developed so that he shows no sign of excessive fatigue at the end of a long ride or schooling period; his muscles will be strong and hard, and when you touch his neck muscles, they will feel like iron.

Conditioning a horse is easier than it may seem, since most of them are endowed with remarkable physical resiliency. For example, there was once a California-bred Thoroughbred named Rubio who was hopefully trained for a racing career. But he started to break down, and since there seemed to be no better future for him, he was shipped to England, where he was sold for fifty dollars and sent to work pulling a bus. At the end of three long, weary years as a draft horse, it was discovered that Rubio could jump. He was put back into training and given a final chance to prove himself in the Grand National of 1908. The skeptical public, aware of his past history, let him go to the starting-post as a long-shot of sixty-six to one. But only the fittest of horses could have won that strenuous steeplechase, as did Rubio, by ten full lengths.

7. Grooming Your Horse

Smart women know the importance of good grooming, and so do experienced horsemen. In fact, grooming is even more necessary for horses than it is for pretty girls; not only can it improve the looks of an animal whose conformation may be imperfect, but it is essential to his health and hygiene. With horses, as with other animals and birds, grooming is also a bond-forming ritual. So your daily grooming session is of psychological value too.

A daily grooming is the only way to remove the dust, grease, scurf, and dead cells from a horse's skin; the accompanying massage is necessary for stimulating the circulation of an animal who spends so much of his time confined in a barn. Odd as it may seem, the less work a horse does, the more grooming he should have. Furthermore, regular attention to his feet will avoid a score of tiresome, unpleasant foot ailments. Remember the saying, "No foot, no horse"? Well, it would be just as true to say, "No care, no foot"!

Well-bred riding horses are usually groomed for the first time soon after they are born. And this is not a bit too early to accustom them to being handled, especially around the head, and to allow their feet to be picked up. By the time they are grown horses, some of them will simply love to be fussed over and will stand quietly during grooming if they are merely tied up by the halter. Others are more sensitive, due to previous rough handling or a naturally nervous nature, and they are more easily groomed in crossties. The most high-strung horse should soon get used to his daily grooming session if treated with tact and gentleness, particularly when handling parts of the body where the skin is thin and the nerves touchy, such as under the belly, inside the legs, and around the head and ears. Even caresses irritate some horses until they have learned to accept them as an expression of friendship.

A stabled horse needs to be groomed once a day. Half an hour or even less should give you ample time to do a good job once you have acquired a certain expertise. The horse should be brushed lightly to remove the straw and dust from his coat every time you take him from his stall, especially if you intend to saddle him; and he should always be put away clean. The most practical grooming program is to brush your horse lightly and to clean out his feet the first thing in the morning and the last thing at night, and to give him a complete grooming after his daily ride, whenever that may be.

A horse kept in a pasture needs less grooming than a stabled animal because his diet is lighter and produces less waste matter through the sweat glands. Besides, he needs the grease in his coat to keep him weatherproof. But even horses who live outdoors should be given a light going-over with the brush every day, with special attention to the feet. Dirty feet can lead to thrush, and wet feet eventually cause cracked heels, which are similar to chapped hands in humans and are very painful and slow to heal. Mud packed in a horse's foot is harmless—in fact, it helps to prevent dried-out hoofs. But manure or sawdust packed in can lead to trouble.

PICKING OUT A HORSE'S FEET

You should hold the hoof pick in the hand opposite to the side on which you are working and stand facing the horse's rear, pushing your shoulder against *his* shoulder to get him to shift his weight to the opposite foot. Support the toe of the foot with one hand, using the pick with the other.

The usual method is to start with the near front foot, do the near hind, and then move over to the far side to clean the fore and hind foot there. But before you pick up his foot at all, warn your horse of what you are going to do by gently running your hand down his leg. Most beginners get off to a bad start by wrenching the poor horse's foot as they turn it back, so be sure to bend it at its natural angle. Remove all of the foreign matter that has become packed into the foot cavity, moving the pick from the front of the hoof to the back as you work, in order to avoid scratching the sensitive frog.

Clean feet are essential to your horse's working condition. It is even a good idea to carry a folding hoof pick in your pocket when you take him for long rides, or if you work him over terrain where he is apt to pick up a stone in his foot. A hoof pick slipped into the pocket of a pink coat has saved many a day's hunting that might otherwise have been spoiled.

A THOROUGH GROOMING

A show grooming can take hours and a *very* thorough grooming an hour or more. But you can do a perfectly adequate daily job in twenty or thirty minutes, by practicing the following procedure:

1. Put your horse in crossties, or tie him up by the halter.

2. Pick out his feet.

3. Go over the horse's entire body with a rub rag to make sure he is completely dry. Start on the near side, at the neck behind the ears, and work toward the tail. Then repeat on the far side.

4. Now go over the body in the same way with a stiff "dandy brush," working with short deep strokes to remove mud, dust, and scurf. (For horses with very sensitive skins, the dandy brush may be too stiff, and the softer body brush should be used.) Brush in the direction the hair

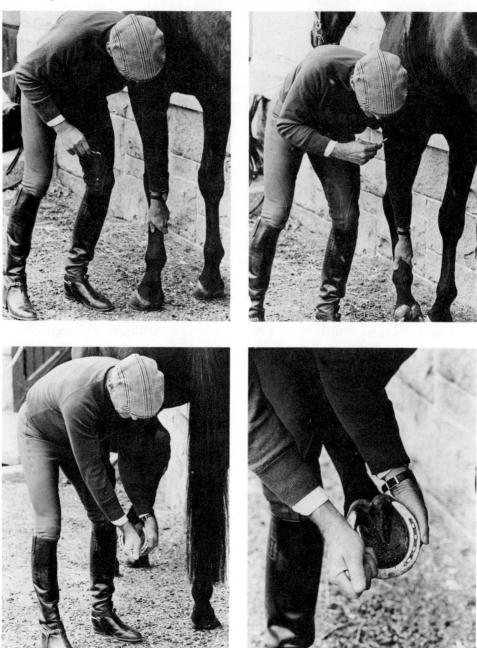

Picking out a horse's feet. (*Photos by James Deutschmann*)

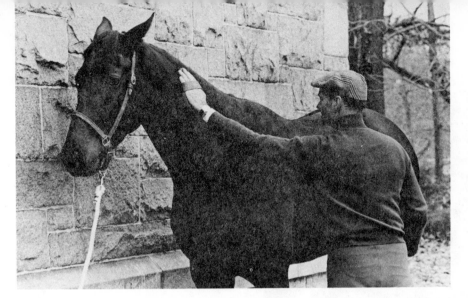

The soft body brush is used in the hand toward the horse's head and cleaned in the currycomb held in the other hand.

lies, cleaning the brush after every few strokes by running it over the currycomb, which you hold in your other hand, and cleaning the currycomb by tapping it against your heel or on the floor. You will sometimes have to brush with special care to remove the girth and saddle marks, if you have not (as you should have) cleaned them right after riding when they are still wet, using a damp sponge and then a rub rag.

5. Having cleaned the body, go over each leg in turn with the body brush.

6. Then go over the face and head very gently with the body brush, without neglecting difficult places such as behind the ears.

7. Brush the forelock, mane, and tail with a slightly dampened water brush, taking care not to pull out the hairs. It is better not to use a metal comb on the mane and tail unless they are extremely matted, because it can easily break off the long hairs. For the same reason, you should avoid combing skimpy manes and tales, but encourage growth by gentle brushing.

8. With a damp sponge, wipe your horse's eyes, then inside his ears and nostrils, and around the mouth. Clean under the tail and at least once a week wipe off the sheath (or the teats and udders of mares)—a detail that is all too often neglected.

9. With a soft rag, a slightly damp sponge, or your own bare hand, give a final polish all over, ending with a good brisk body and leg massage. (When grooming for show, some horsemen rub a bit of olive oil,

The stiffer dandy brush can be used on
the horse's legs.

Only a soft rub rag or sponge should be used to clean the horse's eyes and nostrils.

A damp water brush is used to "lay the mane," working from the opposite side. (*Photos by James Deutschmann*)

baby oil, hair tonic, or a silicone preparation onto the horse's coat, and Vaseline around the eyes and muzzle. But the horse must immediately be covered with a stable sheet, or dust and straw will cling to the grease and make him messier than when he started. A final polish is given just before entering the ring.)

10. Paint the hoofs with a hoof dressing, both inside and outside, in order to replace the natural hoof polish and prevent the horn from drying out by evaporation.

And now, stand back and admire your horse. He may never win a blue ribbon in a Conformation Class, but at the moment he will probably seem to you to be the handsomest horse in the world. (However, to make sure that he is perfectly clean, run your fingers against the hair of his coat; if gray traces are left on them, it means that your horse is still dirty and you must get busy with the brush again.)

A final word of advice: while you are grooming, keep an eye open for any signs of cuts and bruises, any discharge, any soreness or cracking in the hoofs, and any puffiness or heat in the legs or feet, as these may all be indications of trouble. (The easiest way to detect heat or swelling in the limbs is to compare one leg with the other matching one.) Notice

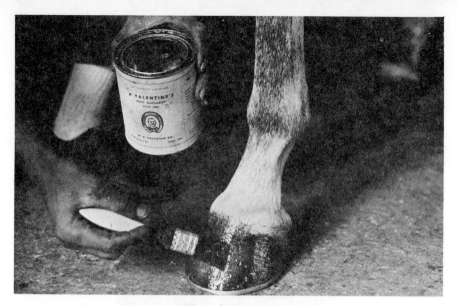

Painting the hoofs. (*Photo by Ray Woolfe, Jr.*)

also any change in the condition of your horse's coat. A dull or staring coat may be a sign of an unsuitable feeding program or of illness.

While this is the standard grooming procedure in many stables, quite a number of horsemen invest in an *electric groomer,* which is a marvelous invention for overworked owner-grooms, since it does a very thorough cleaning job in record time. It operates on the principle of a lightweight vacuum cleaner, and most horses take to it at once. The only disadvantages are its price (about $200), which may make it an extravagance for a small stable, and the fact that electric grooming doesn't stimulate a horse's circulation the way vigorous hand-rubbing does. However, where there are many horses to groom every day, it can be a great timesaver.

Even though you may groom your horse in this relatively effortless way, you will still need to have on hand the standard tools for minor touch-ups between regular groomings. Most saddleries can furnish you with the following basic items of

Grooming Equipment

A Hoof Pick

A Dandy Brush (made of stiff rice root or fiber)

A Body Brush (softer than the first, made of natural bristles or of nylon)

Some grooming equipment. Top row, l. to r.: hoof pick; a rubber grooming mitt (useful for sensitive horses); sponge; rub rag: bottom row, l. to r.: water brush; dandy brush; body brush; rubber currycomb. (*Photo by James Deutschmann*)

A Water Brush (the hardest of all, with bristles cut in a concave form. It is used to dampen and dress the mane, forelock, and tail)

A Currycomb (a hard-rubber or plastic currycomb is more practical than a metal one because it may also be used—but only exceptionally—to remove caked mud from the horse's coat, always with a circular motion and never over bony areas. Its normal purpose, however, is to clean the *brush* and not the horse!)

Several Sponges

Several Rub Rags (special linen grooming towels are not expensive, but terry cloth towels are just as practical and even cheaper.)

A Sweat Scraper

A Brush for applying Hoof Oil, and a supply of Hoof Dressing (there are many good brands on sale)

A Mane-pulling Comb

Scissors (for trimming whiskers and eyebrows)

Electric Clippers

A Grooming Kit, to hold all of this equipment (the handiest model has a flat, wide wooden carrying handle that can also be used as a stool to stand on when grooming around the horse's head or braiding a mane)

COOLING OUT A HORSE

As we have seen, the most logical time to give your horse his daily grooming is when you bring him in from work. But before you can start to groom at all, he must be thoroughly cool and perfectly dry. Brushing a wet coat is simply a waste of time.

To use their own expression, experienced horsemen "cool out" their horses, and generally do it the same way: they end the exercise period with ten or fifteen minutes of walking, so that the horse is no longer sweating when they return to the stable.

Formerly, horses used to remain saddled while they were walked about until their coats were dry and their skin temperature normal. But nowadays the more common practice is to remove the saddle as soon as the horse has finished working. On hot summer days he will find it most refreshing to be sponged all over with warm water to which a bit of brace (an astringent lotion) has been added; the excess water is then removed with a sweat scraper and a lightweight cooler thrown over his back to prevent chills. In cold weather the horse is covered with a woolen cooler as soon as the saddle has been removed, and the cooler is folded back just enough to expose each part of his body while it is rubbed dry. You should work from the neck backward and rub against the lay of the hair.

Now the horse is slowly walked on a lead shank in an undrafty place for fifteen or twenty minutes. He may be allowed to graze if he likes, as you occasionally rub the damp spots on his coat; and he may be given a few sips of water from time to time to help him cool off from the inside, too. You can tell when his skin temperature has returned to normal by feeling the skin on his chest between his legs. When he is dry and cool, he should be given a thorough grooming before being led back to his stall.

Incidentally, quite a few horses like to flop down and roll while they are cooling out, and you shouldn't let yourself be taken by surprise so that you drop the lead shank. As your horse starts to go down, it is best to move in front of his head and follow his movements with the lead shank, rather than to stand at his side where you might get rolled on or struck by a hoof.

If all of this seems like a lot of bother, you must remember that it can be really dangerous to let a hot horse stand around unattended, even with a cooler on, or to let a wet horse dry off by evaporation, or—an even greater crime—to put a hot, damp horse back in his stall without proper grooming care. Founder is only one of the serious ailments that can result from this kind of negligence, and as you probably know, a foundered horse will be unfit to be ridden during many months and may never "come right."

Race horses are sometimes allowed a full hour for cooling out after a hard race, while many trainers insist that their charges be walked for forty minutes by the clock after each exercise period, no matter how cool and dry they may appear to be.

BATHING A HORSE

Some horsemen believe that a horse should never be bathed, on the theory that it removes too much natural oil from his coat and that there is too great risk of his catching cold. However, this is another one of the rather old-fashioned ideas that have been discarded by most modern stable-owners. In fact, it is a racing-stable tradition, as well as the practice of the U. S. Equestrian teams, to give a horse a warm bath after every workout.

If proper precautions are taken, there is no reason why your own horse cannot have an occasional bath. You will need a sponge, soap, and warm water for a cleansing bath, and just warm water with a little brace added for a cooling one. A brace bath may be given as often as every day during very hot weather—it is sometimes the only way of cooling out a horse on torrid days. But cleansing baths should be relatively infrequent because they do remove from the horse's coat much of the grease that protects him during cool, damp weather. In winter it is better to remove stains (from urine, for example) by spot-cleaning.

You should choose a warm, sunny day for your horse's bath. Work up a lather in warm water with a gentle liquid soap or an ordinary shampoo, starting at the neck behind the ears and working backward. Then rinse well with clear water, just as if you were washing your own hair. Use only a wrung-out sponge on his face, and don't neglect to wash thoroughly under the tail, especially in hot weather when a horse perspires a lot, because if this area is not kept clean he may develop a scabby skin irritation. You must also take care to avoid getting water in his ears, for it is very difficult to get the water out again and the sensation is most distressing to him, apparently affecting his equilibrium.

Now, scrape off the excess water with a sweat scraper and finish by using a squeezed-out sponge on the head, legs, and feet. If the sun is shining brightly, your horse will be dry in a very short time. A few brisk brush-strokes to make the hairs of his coat lie flat and to untangle his mane and tail, a final burnishing with a soft cloth, and your horse should truly gleam.

CLIPPING

Twice a year, in the springtime and the fall, the horse sheds his coat and nature replaces it with a growth more suitable to the season. That is why horses are most sleek and attractive in the summer, when their coats are short and they are in between shedding periods.

If his coat were always left in its natural state, your horse would look rather disreputable during much of the year. His shaggy winter growth would make it almost impossible to cool him out after a long ride

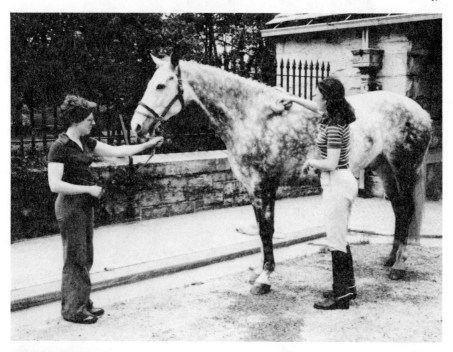

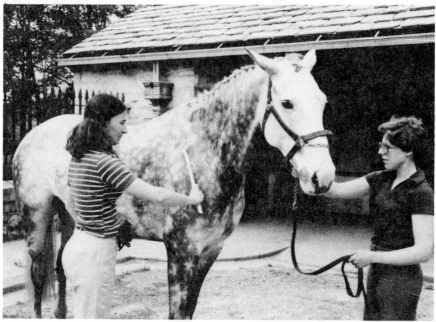

Bathing a horse.

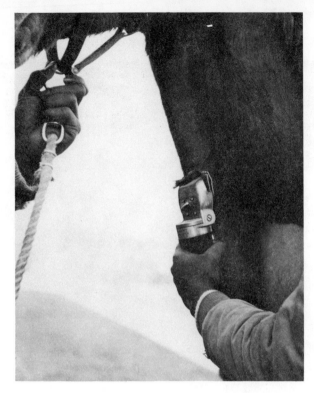

Using an electric clipper. (*Photo by Ray Woolfe, Jr.*)

because it would stay soaking wet for a very long time. Besides, a heavy coat would overheat him, causing him to perspire profusely, which is very weakening for an animal who is doing fast or difficult work.

Field-kept horses and ponies are quite often left unclipped throughout the winter, but even they will look better, feel better, and be easier to groom if their bodies are clipped with only the legs left untouched. You must in this case replace the warmth of their natural coat by covering them with a fitted woolen blanket when they are in the pasture.

All stabled horses should definitely be clipped, as well as horses used for hunting, showing, or regular riding. Veterinary judges of endurance trail rides have observed that unclipped horses are far more apt to develop sore backs and saddle bruises than are horses that have been clipped. And so it is more than likely that you will have to add the art of clipping to your rapidly growing repertory of stable techniques.

A well-bred horse with a fine coat will usually need only two clippings: the first in the fall, about November or so, when his winter coat has already come in; and the second some time in January, to finish off the job. But do not clip after a horse has already started to shed; it will be detrimental to his new coat. Horses with much cold blood and particularly heavy coats will need more frequent clipping, but a monthly trim around the face and the edges of the ears is sufficient for the others.

It takes some practice to do a professional-looking job. You will need an excellent pair of electric clippers with correctly adjusted blades, a perfectly dry coat to work on, and at least an hour of time—with perhaps an assistant to steady the horse while you work. It will help to have an experienced groom show you how to go about your very first attempt.

After you have finished with the clippers, you will probably have to use a pair of sharp scissors to snip off any stray long hairs that are left, especially around the coronet, the fetlock joints, the pasterns, and the ears. When your horse's coat is short and smooth, you will be surprised by the amount of grease that is on his skin and you will want to go over him with a sponge and brush. Immediately afterward you should throw a warm blanket over his back so that he won't catch cold. In fact, you must *always* remember with clipped horses that you have to replace the natural protection you have removed by giving them clothing suitable to the prevailing weather conditions.

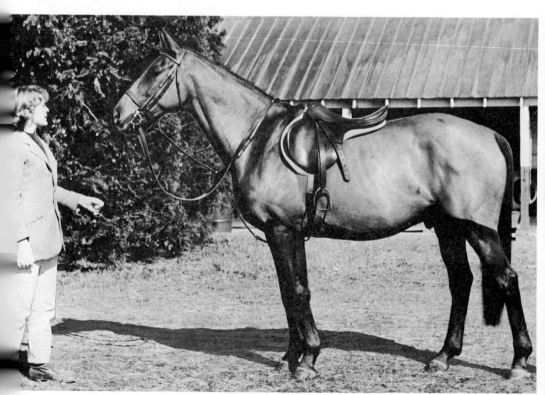

The field Hunter's legs are usually left unclipped. (*Photo by Ray Woolfe, Jr.*)

There are different styles of equine haircuts. You can clip your horse all over; you can leave the legs untouched, with the dividing line between the clipped and unclipped portions curved rather than straight and slanting slightly downward from front to rear (this is recommended for protecting the limbs of trail horses, stock horses, and working Hunters); or you can leave the legs plus a saddle patch (the "Hunter Clip") or only the saddle patch. Some horsemen like to clip all over the first time and to leave the legs and saddle patch unclipped the second time. However, those who do a lot of showing or much fast work such as jumping and galloping prefer to clip all over both times. They believe that a saddle pad protects the horse's back from sores even better than his natural coat, and it doesn't prolong the cooling-out process as does a shaggy saddle patch. Show Saddle Horses are always clipped all over.

GROOMING THE MANE AND TAIL

Many horses who wear a natural mane and tail still need special grooming if they are to look their best—like the women who spend hours at the hairdresser's in order to achieve a "naturally wind-blown effect." In the horse's case the hairdressing technique is called "pulling," and it is exactly what it sounds like: pulling out the long underhairs of the mane and tail so that the mane lies flat in an even length of five or six inches (if it is too short, it will be impossible to braid), and so that the tail is flat and smooth rather than bushy at the root, and fans out into a natural flourish toward the tip.

Tails and manes should never be cut with scissors, except at the very bottom where the tail may be "banged," that is, cut straight across at the height of the hocks in a line that is horizontal to the ground when the tail is carried in a normal position. You must remove the hairs a few at a time either with the fingers, wearing a leather glove dipped in resin to get a good grip and using a rapid plucking movement, or with a mane comb, winding a few strands of hair around the comb and pulling sharply. In either case you'll have to repeat the thinning about once a month.

To be perfectly correct, a well-dressed horse wears his mane on the right side of the neck, although the fashion is sometimes just the opposite abroad, as it is with working stock horses, who may wear their manes on the near side to keep them from interfering with the cowboy's rope. It is not always a simple matter to induce a mane to lie flat on the correct side, especially if it has ever been clipped. You must train the hairs to lie the way you wish by wetting and brushing or by putting them up in braids, or even by attaching small weights like fishing sinkers to the ends of the hairs to set the mane flat. The trouble is that any of these methods may cause the hairs to break, and the result is likely to be a flat mane, but also a wispy one.

Thoroughbred Hunters and well-bred Jumpers are shown with braided manes, particularly if the latter are somewhat short-necked, because many small braids give the impression that a horse's neck is longer than it really is; conversely, a few thicker braids tend to shorten a horse's neck. According to tradition, a mare wears an even number of braids, a gelding an odd number. Neck braids also help train a mane to lie on one side of the horse's neck instead of parting in the middle, which is the natural tendency of a great many manes.

To braid a mane, you should first dampen it and start behind the ears with a well-combed strand of hair about three inches thick, divided in three. The ends of the braids are fastened with an elastic band or wound around with yarn or heavy thread (*never* with adhesive tape!), then folded underneath to the root of the mane at an even length and fastened in place by knotting or sewing with a long blunt needle. The forelock is braided in just the same way. It is fashionable to use heavy thread of the same color as a Hunter's coat, reserving the brightly hued wool for ponies' manes and tails. A gray pony and bright-green yarn is one of the most popular equine color schemes.

Five-Gaited Saddle Horses and Tennessee Walking Horses, as well as Fine Harness Horses and Ponies, display their stable colors when showing by wearing a ribbon braided in the forelock and three long ribbons in the first upper lock of the mane, the rest of the mane remaining loose and flowing except for a small top portion that is clipped. These braids are very fine, and instead of being folded underneath they are left long, to fall well down on the horse's neck. The show-ring tradition is to repeat the stable colors in the horse's browband.

Clipping the mane close to the roots is called "hogging" or "roaching." It is the current fashion with many stock horses and is required of Three-Gaited Saddle Horses in order to distinguish them from the Five-Gaited, who wear their manes as long as possible. To be perfectly exact, a clipped mane is "hogged," while a "roached" mane has a fine line of hair left standing up straight in the middle, called a "herringbone." But the latter style is rarely seen nowadays and the terms are used interchangeably.

Wetting the hair.

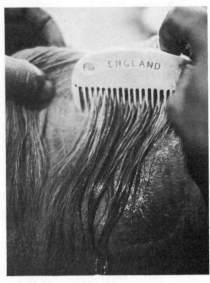

Combing.

Separating the strands.

Starting to braid.

Braiding.

Reaching the end.

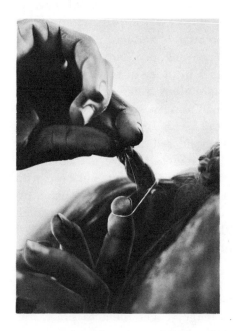

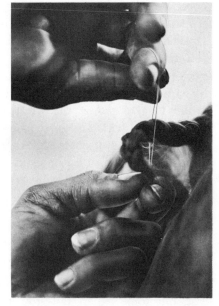

Fastening with a rubber band.

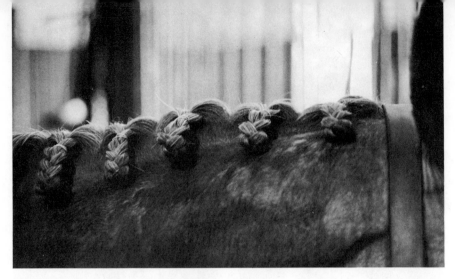

The finished job. (*Photos by Ray Woolfe, Jr.*)

You should be quite sure that your young trainee isn't going to develop into a Five-Gaited horse before you clip his mane. It can be quite difficult to get it to grow out again, and even though it may eventually be coaxed to lie down flat, it will never be as full as it was before being clipped. The first time you clip a horse's mane, you must cut it short with scissors before using the clippers. Afterward, you will have to repeat the clipping every two or three weeks if you want it always to look smart, for hogged manes grow out as straight and bushy as a crew cut.

Thoroughbreds rarely wear their manes clipped, but it is very common to clip the manes of Quarter Horses in order to refine the appearance of their heavily muscled necks. Quite often, a lock of hair is left on the withers to make these seem less broad and flat, and the forelock may be left long to reduce the width of the head. In other breeds a long forelock worn with a hogged mane is considered incorrect. Many grade horses with short or coarse necks will be more attractive if their manes are closely clipped. It is a question of taste and judgment. But even with long-maned horses, perfectionists clip a narrow portion of the mane exactly where the bridle crownpiece goes, so that it will lie flat and smooth on the horse's neck. Likewise, if just the underpart of a bushy forelock is clipped, the hairs will lie flatter and avoid an unattractive "topknot" effect.

Thoroughbred show grooms take great pride in growing the longest, fullest tails they can. Ideally, a horse's tail should reach the hocks at least, but some expert tail-growers manage to get them to practically trail on the ground. Arabian horses' tails are naturally long and flowing and they should never be touched except for brushing and washing. On the other hand, Quarter Horses' tails are often shortened by pulling (plucking the long hairs to leave a shorter length) in order to show off the width and muscles of the hindquarters that are so desirable a feature of the breed. The Three-Gaited Saddle Horse has his tail clipped closely about a foot from the root, while the Five-Gaited's is worn full, fanning out in a flourish at the bottom, embellished for show by the addition of an artificial switch. Both of them have their tails "cut," which requires a surgical incision and a healing period of at least six weeks, during which the tail is set in the desired shape by wearing a tail-set. It is essential that the entire operation be performed by an expert, because the danger of infection is great. Besides, a miscalculation in the angle of the tail-set (which should conform to the natural angle at which the root of the tail is set on the body) will create an effect that is more grotesque than elegant.

A bushy effect at the top of the tail is unattractive in all horses, so in addition to being pulled, many horses' tails are placed overnight in "tail wraps" (the foam rubber, Velcro-closed kind have completely supplanted the old-fashioned bandages that were laborious to wind and very apt to cause pressure points under the ties). Care must still be taken, however, to make sure that the tail wrap is not too tight and that the closing is perfectly smooth. You still sometimes see a horse with white hairs in an otherwise colored tail, the result of damage to the hair roots by too tight a tail wrap or bandage. Even direr consequences occurred when a group of Polish Thoroughbreds were recently shipped by train to

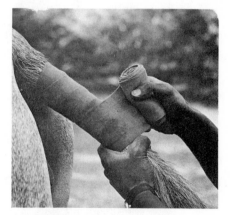

Bandaging a tail. (*Photos by Ray Woolfe, Jr.*)

Braiding a tail. (*Photos by Ray Woolfe, Jr.*)

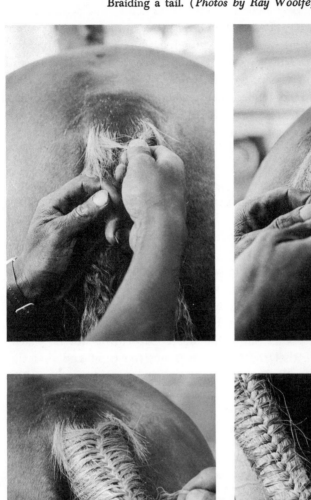
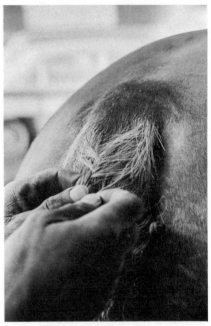
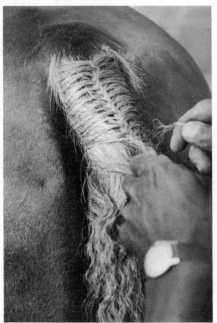

England. When their tight bandages were at last removed after the five-day trip, several of the horses literally lost their tails, for gangrene had set in and the dead tails dropped off. A scary story, and an unusual one. But let it serve as a warning.

When a Hunter's mane is braided, his tail is usually braided too. A clever groom can take advantage of this tradition to improve the appearance of the horse's entire hindquarters, since just a few thick braids along the upper part of the tail tend to widen narrow quarters, while fine braids right down to the tip refine a rear end that is too big and coarse.

Tail braids are somewhat more difficult to make than mane braids. You should start at the root. Take a strand of hair from underneath each side of the tail and cross them. Now add a strand from the middle and braid these three strands together. After each twist you must add another strand from each side and from the middle and continue in this way until you have reached the desired length. The last braid should be tucked up underneath the others, and the entire work of art held in place by sewing with a long blunt needle and heavy thread.

On rainy hunting days, fussy grooms prepare their horses in "mud tails," a rather lengthy process of firmly braiding, tucking up, and sewing all of the long tail hairs to make a compact stub. Mud tails may not be as pretty as flowing ones, but they are highly practical for bad-weather Meets and stormy outdoor horse shows where the best-groomed horses invariably wear them.

The next time you go to a horse show, wander around the area where the horses are stabled and watch the grooms at work. Every show groom has his own secrets and some are past masters in the art of beautifying horses. The best way to learn such techniques as tail- or mane-braiding is to watch an expert do it, and you are sure to pick up a number of other useful tricks besides.

For example, show stables often use blueing on white legs and markings—a very diluted solution (you don't want a pale-blue horse!) of a product that is guaranteed safe for human skin. Another professional showman's trick to brighten white coats is to rub white rice powder in the hair while it is slightly damp, or cornstarch on a dry coat, working it in well and brushing out the excess only just before the horse enters the show ring. Ordinary hoof dressing is never used for show grooming, since the grease it contains will pick up dust and dirt before a horse has taken more than a stride or two in the arena. Instead, show grooms beautify the horn by using black liquid shoe polish on dark hoofs; another simple way to put a shine on either light or dark horn is to rub the outer wall of the hoof with a cut onion.

Stable supplies catalogues devote pages to products that are best described as equine cosmetics. There is no harm in trying them if you enjoy fussing over your horse. If you don't, you can still turn out quite a splendid-looking show horse by using the traditional conditioning and grooming methods.

Show horses of different breeds are usually required to be presented groomed in a certain manner, as described in the *Rule Book* of the American Horse Shows Association. Before you take your horse to a show, you must make sure that his grooming corresponds to the official requirements, for any irregularity may cause you to be penalized or eliminated entirely from a Conformation Class.

Even if you never intend to show, it can be interesting and lots of fun to experiment with different appropriate grooming styles, until you find the one that does the most for your horse.

8.   Shoeing

In a nation where Smith is such a common name that the average American citizen is identified as "John Q. Smith," it is sad to say that the honorable profession presumably practiced by the founders of this profuse clan has practically disappeared.

It is true that there are still a few expert blacksmiths to be found, especially around the trotting tracks, since skilled shoeing can cut seconds off a Standardbred's racing time; and in Saddle Bred country you may be able to find a few specialists who are veritable wizards in perfecting a horse's gaits and action by cleverly forged shoes. But unfortunately, many modern horse-owners must deal with a busy traveling farrier who has neither the time nor the interest to make a detailed study of the foot problems of each individual horse. In fact, many blacksmiths, if you don't keep an eye on them, would rather shape the horse's hoof to fit their ready-made shoes than go to the bother of shaping the shoes to fit the feet, which is the Number One rule of correct horse-shoeing.

Under the circumstances, every rider should understand at least the rudiments of this ancient art so that he will know how shoeing ought to be done, even though he'll probably never have to attempt it himself. Some ranchers and farmers do shoe their horses themselves, but it is too technical a job for an amateur, who should deal with the very best blacksmith he can find, preferably one who specializes in his particular breed of horse.

In order to appreciate the principles of correct shoeing, it will be helpful to first make a more thorough examination of your horse's feet.

Starting at the coronet (that soft ring of cartilage you see at the top of the hoof), the horse's foot is encased in a hard, horny wall, which is similar to our own fingernails in that it is insensitive and grows at a regular rate of about a quarter to a half an inch per month. It takes almost a year for new horn to grow out from the coronet to the toe, so you can understand the importance of keeping the hoof in a healthy condition. A daily painting with a good hoof dressing will prevent it from becoming brittle. If the horn seems very dry, you can use a pair of wet felt "swabs," which are first soaked in water and then buckled around the hoofs, where they remain moist for as long as twelve hours and can easily be remoistened. You may prefer to pack the feet with clay once or twice a week, or to stand your horse in moist clay or water; after the moisture has been absorbed, you should finish off the treatment by brushing on a hoof dressing, as usual.

When you lift your horse's feet to inspect the soles, you will see an outside rim formed by the bearing surface of the edge of the hoof wall, which turns forward at the rear into two wedges, called the "bars." The space between the wall and the bars is the most common seat of corns. Joined to the edge of the horny wall is the tough outer sole. There is no visible joint between the horn and the sole on the surface, but when the blacksmith is rasping the horn before shoeing, a fine white line will appear; this marks the division and is also the sign to stop rasping.

At the back of the foot above the heel is a large pad which is the "cushion of the heels." Jutting into the rear of the sole is the "frog," which prevents slipping and is the first and most important part of the equine shock-absorbing mechanism. When a horse is unshod, the resilient frog is the first part of his body to come in contact with the ground, and it absorbs a considerable amount of concussion—especially in the front feet—thereby sparing the leg joints and tendons, but causing much wear and tear of its own substance. While this rubbery material grows out and renews itself constantly, one of the purposes of shoeing is to re-duce the impact on the frog by slightly raising the rest of the foot.

A healthy frog is never dried out or withered-looking, but large and firm and well defined. When a good blacksmith prepares the foot for shoeing, he will trim off any rough, ragged edges around the frog where dirt may gather, but only a careless one will pare away any substantial part of the frog itself.

While the elements described above are all that appear to the naked eye, there is concealed inside the foot a complex mechanism built around three bones: the bottom part of the short pastern bone, the boat-shaped navicular, and the coffin or pedal bone. All of them are joined together by elastic cartilage and surrounded by myriad tiny blood vessels and nerves and hundreds of microscopic fleshy leaves called "laminae," which dovetail into the horny laminae of the outer covering. The fleshy laminae are similar to the quick of the nail and just as sensitive. Every good blacksmith is extremely careful to avoid driving nails deep enough to prick the laminae, for such pricks can cause a horse intense pain and re-sult in lameness even after the nail has been withdrawn.

At the bottom of the pedal bone there is a tender, fleshy sole which supplies new tissue to the outer horny one; in the same way, the rubbery frog grows out of a softer, sensitive inner frog.

The relatively rapid growth of horn means that your horse's feet need to be reshod every four or five weeks. The hind feet don't get as much wear as the forefeet because they undergo less intense concussion, but they will need to be rasped and trimmed every month or so just the same. In fact, even if none of his shoes shows wear, your horse should still keep his date with the blacksmith, though the blacksmith may merely trim the feet and reset the same shoes afterward. A number of troublesome ailments, including corns and contracted heels, can result from too long a delay between the blacksmith's visits.

The first thing a blacksmith does after removing the old shoes is to inspect the horse's feet for signs of injury and the development of condi-tions which may need treatment and corrective shoeing. He then trims off any dead material of the frog or outer sole, without, however, cutting into the healthy tissue. Next, he carefully rasps the edge of the wall abso-lutely level, with the inside and outside exactly the same length from the ground, so that the concussion will be evenly distributed on the weight-bearing surface of the foot, and the elastic frog will maintain a light con-tact with the ground. For greater accuracy in preparing the feet, the con-scientious shoer uses an instrument called a foot gauge or hoof level,

The essential blacksmith's tools. The protractor on top of the vise enables the farrier to measure the angulation of the foot. (*This photo and the others in this chapter are by James Deutschmann*)

which ensures the same length of feet and the same angle of wall on corresponding feet and is extremely useful for precise shoeing even though it is disdained by many blacksmiths.

When all the feet have been well prepared, the shoes are forged to fit them—and not the reverse. A well-fit shoe should lie level on the whole wall of the hoof and the flat outer rim of the sole. It should be flush with the sides of the hoof all the way around, and each heel should be beveled so that the horn and the end of the shoe are perfectly in line.

Horseshoes are held on by nails and clips. The nails, usually four on the outside and three on the inside, are driven at the proper angle through nail holes in the shoes, into the thin horn of the wall high enough to give a firm hold, but still as low as possible in order to damage the least possible amount of horn. At the point where the nail emerges it is wrung off, except for a tiny portion called the "clench," which is turned back onto the wall and rasped smooth. The clips are built into the shoes—toe clips for the front shoes and side clips for the hind—and they are hammered onto the walls of the feet.

While these are the general principles of normal shoeing, there are many variations. A clever blacksmith can often correct such action defects as winging, toeing in, and toeing out, by fitting corrective shoes.

Removing the old shoe.

Trimming the sole.

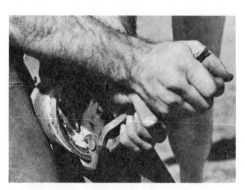

Trimming the wall.

Leveling with the rasp.

Refitting the shoe.

Nailing.

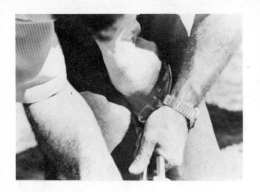
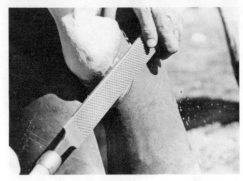

Trimming the clinches.   Rasping the clinches and finishing.

(Conversely, bad shoeing can just as readily cause these and other faults.) He will also sometimes forge special half-shoes to help cure a horse who is suffering from corns or contracted heels. He can even improve foot angulation by adjusting toe and heel length so that the line running from just below the fetlock joint to the toe is absolutely straight and sloping, and not broken into a convex or concave angle. Ideally, it should be parallel to the angle of the shoulder.

There are innumerable types of horseshoes, and literally hundreds of volumes have been written on the art of shoeing horses. But most modern riding hacks are shod in ordinary "keg shoes," so called because these light iron plates are factory-made in various sizes and ordered by the blacksmith by bulk in kegs.

In winter when the going is icy, you should have your horse "sharp-shod," with sharp heels or removable calks fitted into his regular shoes in order to prevent slipping. Horses with tender feet, or those who are ridden or driven a lot over hard roads, will benefit from wearing rubber or leather pads, underneath their shoes, after the foot cavity has been packed with oakum. But "leathers" should never be used in desert regions or during hot spells because of their heatening effect on the feet.

Finally, don't forget to let your horse go barefoot for at least several weeks out of the year, or with only his forefeet protected by metal tips. An annual vacation from horseshoes is one of the best ways to keep the frog and horn in good condition and to give ailing feet a chance to return to normal. You should remember, though, that an unshod hoof grows out at the usual rate and that the natural wearing down is neither uniform nor sufficient; so you must still call on the blacksmith every month or so for trimming services.

As you can see, there is no deep mystery involved in ordinary shoeing. The technique becomes much more complicated, however, when dealing with Standardbred, Saddle Bred, and Walking Horses, and with Hackney and Shetland Harness Ponies, whose gaits and action are very much dependent upon the way their feet are trimmed and the kind of shoes they wear.

Generally speaking, toe weight and length affect the length of stride and increase forward motion, while heel weight encourages higher knee action. Furthermore, the angle of slope of the horse's toe (which is normally the same as the slope of the pastern) is sometimes altered slightly, either to correct a conformation fault or to influence the horse's stride. In Gaited classes you will see many horses with fantastically elongated feet, but as long as the normal angle of slope is respected, the extra length and extra weight should do no harm—except, of course, that the horn becomes very fragile and frog pressure is lost. If you look carefully, you will see quite a few Saddle Bred horses and Harness Show Ponies whose hoofs are reinforced with metal bands where the horn has cracked. Sometimes the horn has been so damaged that the shoes must be held on by cement instead of the usual clips and nails.

Trainers of these breeds work in close collaboration with the blacksmith, since artificial gaits such as the rack and the stepping pace can only be performed really well with the aid of appropriate shoeing. The expert blacksmith studies a Gaited horse's action with special care before a show, for he can do much to perfect its performance by providing the most effective length and weight for each pair of feet. Walking Horses, whose overstride is exaggerated by adding weight to the shoes, may carry into the show ring as much as thirty-six ounces on each foot—which is a far cry from the race horse, whose extra-light aluminum racing plates are so thin that they are good for only one race.

Whatever kind of shoes he wears, you should trot your horse out immediately after shoeing and observe him closely for signs of lameness. Sometimes a badly placed nail will become painful only four or five days later. If an animal goes lame within a few days after being shod, the first thing you should do is to check the shoes; the lameness may disappear if you have the plates removed and reset correctly.

A blacksmith specialist may charge as much as $50 or more to prepare a Saddle Horse for showing. For a show horse with gaiting problems requiring carefully balanced iron shoes, leather pads, and vinyl inserts, the process may take an entire day and cost $150 or more. But an ordinary shoeing job would cost about $20 or $25, resetting the same shoes a few dollars less, and merely trimming the feet no more than $15. Race track blacksmith Tex Cauthen, who is the father of the phenomenal young jockey Steve Cauthen, charges $27 for shoeing a race horse. Even Saddle Bred horses that are used for pleasure hacking are most often shod normally in ordinary flat shoes, just like the other breeds. It is nevertheless understandable that quite a few horsemen are learning to be their own farrier. There are over 100 farrier schools in the country (although the experts say that only a few of them live up to their promises). At the same time, horse-shoeing has become a competitive art, with forging contests, including various classes such as shoeing a horse with contracted heels, corrective shoeing from a foot X-ray, even speed classes for a routine shoeing job.

While you will probably grumble about the monthly blacksmith's bill (most horsemen do), the fee you pay him for a job well done is also a kind of insurance premium that protects the good health, sound action, and pleasant disposition of your horse.

9.   Your Horse's Health

Like the expectant parent who conscientiously bones up on baby care before the happy event, an expectant horse-owner will find less cause for alarm during his first experiences with a horse of his own if he has already acquired some basic notions about equine health problems and how to deal with them.

Fortunately, most horses are robust creatures. Given proper feed and water, suitable shelter, regular grooming care, and enough exercise to keep them physically and mentally occupied, the great majority of them (if they are sound to start with) never become really seriously ill. It is true that horses, like children, are subject to occasional stomachaches and colds, as well as the various minor cuts and bruises that parents and horsemen soon learn to treat efficiently. But infectious disease is comparatively rare in modern riding stables, due to effective control programs and the development of vaccines, antitoxins, and antibiotics. Some maladies that used to be fatal have disappeared completely, and such ordinary troubles as colic and thrush have never been frequent in a well-run barn. Most equine ailments develop slowly and can be avoided entirely if caught in time. So the main role of the horse-owner is a preventive one, and his principal defensive weapons are simply good horse management and plain common sense.

Although insurance cannot prevent an accident or illness from occurring, it may alleviate the consequences. The two principal types of horse insurance are (1) livestock mortality insurance, a form of term life insurance limited to the actual cash value of the horse and covering death due to disease, accident, fire, etc.; and (2) a livestock floater policy, covering death from accidental causes only. The latter is more limited but also considerably less expensive. It is practically impossible to insure a horse against disability or unsoundness, and comparatively few pleasure-horse owners insure their horses' lives. But all of them would be well advised to protect themselves with full liability coverage for injury and damages that may be caused by their horse. It is also useful to know that many hunt and riding clubs can arrange for policies covering personal injury to members during organized sport or competition at special rates.

While he should do everything he can to prevent disease from occurring, even the most experienced horseman should never attempt to be his own veterinarian. Veterinary science is highly specialized, and home remedies or amateur analyses are dangerous substitutes for qualified professional care. Diagnosis of disease in horses is particularly difficult. Lameness, for instance, may be traced to almost numberless causes, each requiring a different treatment. Administering medicine to horses demands skill and experience and may call for intravenous injection. So it is indispensable for every horse-owner to have a veterinarian. In fact, you should get a veterinarian even before you get your horse.

Most specialized veterinarians belong to the American Association of Equine Practitioners, whose members devote practically all of their time to horses. In many areas you may be able to find one of these experts with whom you can establish a permanent and friendly relationship, or who can recommend a colleague qualified to deal with horses in your immediate neighborhood. At first you will probably be tempted to call him at the slightest suspicion of irregular behavior in your horse, like the frantic young mother who summons the doctor every time Baby forgets to burp. But as you become more familiar with your horse, you will soon be able to recognize when he is "not himself," and to tell the difference between the signs of a minor indigestion, for example, and the true symptoms of illness requiring immediate veterinary attention.

What are the warning signals of illness in a horse? Perhaps the best way to identify them is to compare a healthy horse with a sick one.

A HEALTHY HORSE . . .

stands squarely on his four feet, seldom resting a foreleg unless there is something the matter with it.

His coat is shiny and soft and lies down flat and smooth.

His eyes are wide open and the eye lining (as well as the inside of the mouth and nostrils) is a salmon-pink color.

His appetite is normal.

His skin is slightly moist. Not a perceptible sweat, but just enough to keep the coat soft and the skin supple.

His pulse (felt by the tips of the fingers over the large artery where it rounds the lower jaw immediately in front of the heavy muscle of the cheek) is steady and even, when the horse is at rest, with about thirty-three to forty beats per minute in mares and geldings, and twenty-eight to thirty-two in stallions. The younger the horse, the faster the pulse, while well-bred horses usually show a higher pulse rate than cold-blooded ones.

His temperature (taken with an ordinary greased rectal thermometer or a special equine type that is equipped with a ring and string to prevent it from getting lost in the rectum) normally registers between 99.5 and 101 degrees, being lowest in the morning and highest in the afternoon.

His breathing is even and quiet when at rest, with eight to sixteen respirations per minute.

His bowel movements take place four to eight times during each twenty-four-hour period, and the droppings are free from mucus and odor. A healthy horse's digestive system is almost constantly at work; you can usually hear the rumbling of peristaltic sounds when you place your ear against the horse's flank.

His urine is light yellow in color and slightly cloudy; it is eliminated five or more times a day, in a total quantity of four to seven quarts.

His limbs and joints are free from excessive heat and swelling, which are most easily detected by running your hands down the legs and comparing each limb to its matching one.

A SICK HORSE . . .

is apt to assume abnormal attitudes, such as lying down at unusual times or in unusual positions. A horse suffering from advanced laminitis may even sit on his haunches like a dog, or one with colic may lie on his back with his feet in the air in an attempt to relieve the abdominal pain. A lame horse often points the ailing foot.

His coat may be dull and "staring" (with the hairs standing up rather than lying flat and smooth).

The mucous membranes of the eyes, nose, and mouth may be off-color, which sometimes gives a clue to the cause of illness: pale membranes usually denote an anemic condition; a yellow tinge is the sign of liver trouble; dark red may indicate fever; and a blue-red shade can mean that something is wrong with the horse's heart or circulation.

His appetite is abnormal; he may be either off his feed or simply ravenous.

His skin may feel tight and dry (a condition known as "hidebound") or he may, on the other hand, sweat profusely.

His pulse is either irregular or abnormal, more often too fast than too slow.

His temperature is often high (a subnormal temperature is very rare in horses). A reading of 102.5 degrees is considered to be a low fever, 104 a definite one, while 106 is very high and indicates a serious infection.

His breathing may be either too slow or too fast, and perhaps noisy and labored.

His droppings are abnormal in color and consistency. In case of serious constipation, there is an absence of peristaltic sounds.

His urine may be either insufficient or excessive, unusual in color or consistency, and may perhaps be produced with pain.

There may be heat, swelling, or pain in some part of his body—most often in the feet or limbs, in which case his movements will also show unmistakable signs of lameness.

Generally speaking, the most vulnerable points of a horse are his feet and legs, especially the forelegs, which carry the most weight and are most subject to strain. Nature didn't design the horse with the idea that he would one day carry the weight of a rider on his back, jump over fences, and gallop over hard roads. His natural activity is to move about

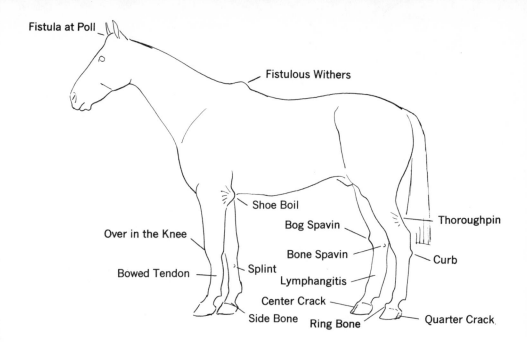

Fistula at Poll

Fistulous Withers

Shoe Boil

Bog Spavin

Over in the Knee

Bone Spavin

Thoroughpin

Bowed Tendon

Splint

Curb

Lymphangitis

Center Crack

Side Bone

Ring Bone

Quarter Crack

in a leisurely fashion most of the time, and instead we ask him to furnish short periods of violent effort, interrupted by long hours of confinement. No wonder lameness is the most frequent ailment of riding horses! The next common source of indisposition is the horse's susceptibility to chills and drafts, followed by his somewhat delicate digestive system. In addition, each animal has his individual points of resistance and weakness, which you will soon learn to recognize in your own horse.

With a new horse you should, of course, inquire into his past history before deciding to buy him, while the veterinary examination will bring to light any serious past, present, or potential unsoundness. A study of the horse's conformation will also give you a preview of future health problems, since certain flaws of structure make him especially vulnerable to certain ailments. You should be sure to learn what inoculations he has had and keep them up-to-date with regular booster shots. An anti-encephalitis vaccination and a Coggins test are practically obligatory if a horse is to be shipped from one state to another, and well-cared-for riding horses are periodically protected against tetanus infection as a matter of course by the administration of tetanus toxoid (and not antitoxin, which gives immunity for only a few weeks). Incidentally, it is a good idea to have your doctor give you the necessary shots and boosters so that you will be protected from tetanus infection too.

In addition, you should ask your veterinarian if there are any inoculations he considers advisable for your particular region.

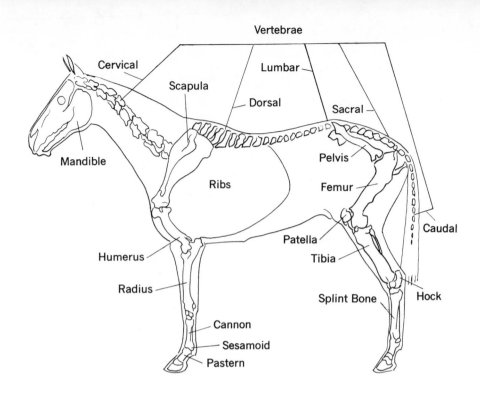

Every horse should receive the following regular medical attention:

1. An annual antitetanus booster shot of tetanus toxoid.
2. An annual Encephalomyelitis vaccination.
3. Once or twice a year an inspection of the teeth and gums, followed by a rasping ("floating") of any sharp places and treatment of any abnormal dental condition.
4. Every six months (at least) an analysis of the droppings for parasites, and administration of whatever worming treatment may be necessary (nowadays most often by tubing).
5. Optional: An Influenza vaccination, to protect against the most common respiratory disease in horses; and an Anthrax preventive vaccine in states where this epidemic disease is still a threat, such as Mississippi, Louisiana, Texas, Arkansas, Nebraska, South Dakota, and California.

Furthermore, every horse-owner should possess one or more of the excellent reference books on equine health care now available, written by a veterinarian, such as:

Horses in Health and Disease by James L. Naviaux, DVM (The Booking Institute, Box 9698, Washington, D.C. 20016)

YOUR HORSE'S HEALTH173

Veterinary Treatments and Medications for Horsemen, Equine Research
Publications (15048 Beltway Drive, Dallas, Texas 75240)
Equine Medicine and Surgery
Illustrated Veterinary Encyclopedia, Equine Research Publications

The magazine *Equus* is an authoritative, thoroughly up-to-date
source of information on equine health care and problems.

While this reading, instructive as it is, cannot replace professional
consultation and care, it is valuable for giving the horse-owner a general
idea of problems he may have to face, and for providing first-aid information in an emergency.

Now let's review the principal menaces to your horse's good health,
always remembering that the role of the horse-owner is to prevent disease when possible, to give first aid in emergencies, and to CALL THE VET-
ERINARIAN WHEN MEDICAL TREATMENT IS NECESSARY!

LAMENESS

Lameness is the most troublesome of all horse ailments because it
makes an animal unfit for work; it is also one of the most frequent, due
to the nature of the work he does. The horse's foot strikes the ground
with a force of approximately 700 pounds per square inch at the walk,
1,600 pounds per square inch at the trot, 2,100 pounds at an easy canter,
and possibly twice as much on landing over a jump, so you can see how
a false step can sometimes result in serious injury. While it is easy to see
when a horse is lame (or to feel, if you are riding him, especially at the
trotting gait), locating the seat of the trouble is another matter.

If your horse suddenly becomes lame while you are out riding him,
you should dismount at once and first of all pick up and examine his feet,
since the most likely cause is a stone stuck in the frog, and prompt re-
moval will also remove the lameness. If the lameness is severe and you
cannot immediately determine the cause, you should walk him back to
the stable unmounted, for riding a lame horse may result in serious damage.

With running and jumping horses, lameness occurs 90 per cent of
the time in the front legs, while trotters and pacers, who move with a diagonal or one-sided two-leg beat, show about the same incidence front
and back.

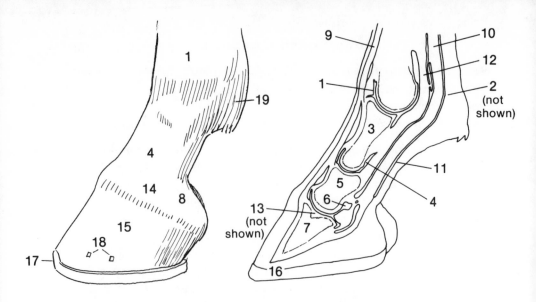

1. Fetlock joint   2. Sesamoid bone   3. Large pastern bone   4. Pastern joint   5. Small pastern bone 6. Coffin joint   7. Coffin bone   8. Lateral cartilage 9. Extensor tendon   10. Deep flexor tendon   11. Terminal branch of the flexor tendon   12. Annular ligament of the fetlock   13. Lateral ligament of the coffin joint   14. Coronet   15. Wall of the hoof   16. Sole of the hoof   17. Clip of the shoe   18. Clinches of the horseshoe nails   19. Fetlock (tuft)

Often a horse will obviously favor a lame foreleg when he is at rest. In action he may nod his head each time the *sound* foreleg strikes the ground. But lameness in the hind legs is more difficult to detect. One way is to have the horse walked away from you and to observe his hocks; the sound hock will be raised higher and dropped lower than the lame one. Listen, too. Sound legs strike louder than sore ones. Sometimes a horse will switch his tail toward the side on which he is lame.

You should examine your horse's legs by hand as well as by eye and ear. Run your hand down the leg that seems to be affected to feel for any abnormal heat, tenderness, or swelling. When in doubt, compare each leg to the matching one. You might feel the pulse in the artery on both sides. Inflammation makes it stronger. Horses usually wince when you touch a tender spot, and you will often feel a lump or puffiness where they have suffered strain. You can also pressure-test the limbs by running your hands over them one by one, pressing firmly. Then have the horse trotted out for inspection. The pressure should have aggravated the lameness and made it more visible.

With cases that are difficult to diagnose, modern vets rely increasingly on selective nerve-blocking injections in order to pinpoint the exact seat of the trouble. If bone damage is suspected, they will of course X-ray.

Lameness in the legs may be caused by a number of different ailments, most of which result from strain, overwork, or an inherited weakness. Among the most common are:

SPLINTS. This is not an unusual occurrence among Thoroughbreds who are put into hard racing training when they are very young, since most splints appear before the age of four. Splint bones are the vestiges of two of the disappeared toes of the ancient Eohippus, and the ailment known as splints is a condition caused by the ossification of tissues between the cannon and the splint bones, usually on the inside of the front legs where concussion is great. Splint formations low on the leg rarely interfere with a horse's action once they are set. But if they are placed near the knee or if they interfere with the ligaments and tendons, the consequences are more serious. While the bony deposit is forming, there may be stumbling and temporary lameness as well as local heat, swelling, and pain. Afterward, the lameness usually disappears, but you can always feel the presence of splints and most often see them too. A horse should be given a complete rest while the splints are forming. Most veterinarians recommend blistering or pin-firing if the position of the splint involves the tendon and causes lameness. Sometimes no treatment of any kind is needed. However, it is wise to notify your veterinarian as soon as you suspect this condition in your horse, so that he can intervene if necessary.

RINGBONE requires very careful attention, because the lameness provoked by this formation of bony enlargements on one or both of the pastern bones is often severe, and there is also a risk of its becoming permanent. Ringbone is caused by overstrain, too much work for too young a horse, or even by faulty nutrition. Heredity is responsible for certain cases to the extent that horses with weak, short, straight, or exaggeratedly sloping pasterns are especially vulnerable. Like splints, ringbone develops gradually and may be hardened by blistering or pin-firing. Your veterinarian should follow its development, for he may be able to suggest special shoeing that will ease the pain and reduce the strain on the ligaments. In any case, you can expect your horse to be out of work for some months before the ossification has been completed.

BONE SPAVIN or "JACK" is a similar bony enlargement, on the inside of the hock joint. It is regarded as a serious defect, although the lameness that occurs during its formation may completely vanish afterward. However, the hock joint will be permanently enlarged when compared to a sound one, and even the enlargement is sufficient to disqualify a horse from Conformation Hunter classes. Rest, special shoeing, counter-irritation (blistering and firing), and surgery are the usual forms of treatment.

CURB is the rupture and thickening of the ligament at the back of the hock about three or four inches below the point, causing an obvious bulge in the hock when seen from the side. It may be more or less hereditary, since weak, narrow, or overbent hocks are more prone to curbs than are other types of conformation. But its immediate cause is violent strain and concussion, as occurs in jumping, racing, and the sliding stops of Quarter Horse performances. There is temporary swelling, heat, and lameness, and the horse must be rested while the hock is probably fired or blistered by the veterinarian in order to strengthen the ligaments and tendons. "Curby hocks" are usually considered to be a blemish rather than an unsoundness, as they rarely cause permanent lameness. But they are definitely an indication of weakness in a horse's legs and constitute a serious conformation defect.

BOWED TENDONS, on the other hand, are an unsoundness, even though race horses may recover and run again after suffering this condition which results from a thickening of the flexor tendons or ligaments in the cannon region and is caused by strain. While the lameness may not be permanent, bowed tendons should be considered a serious defect when buying a horse, for they will never prove as strong as normal tendons.

BOG SPAVIN is a swelling of the joint capsule of the hock, usually caused by bad feeding and insufficient exercise and appearing most frequently in horses with straight hocks. While the joint is inflamed there is heat, pain, and lameness. But afterward the lameness disappears and there remains only a soft, rather unsightly swelling which is often very difficult to remove.

If a lame horse's legs seem to be all right, you should inspect his feet. Some horses' feet are imperfect in conformation, which predisposes them to certain injuries.

Horses with flat feet, for example, are apt to suffer from BRUISED SOLE, usually caused by an injury from a sharp stone or excessive trimming by the blacksmith. Aside from lameness, there will be heat and pain in the sole and sometimes you will see a dark stain on the surface.

Corrective shoeing can do much to relieve pain and prevent a recurrence of this kind of bruised wound.

Foot lameness may also be caused by CORNS, which are usually formed in the heels of the forefeet. Like corns in humans, they are caused by excessive shoe pressure or too tight shoes (often the result of overdue shoeing). Your blacksmith will pare away the corn and fit the foot with a special half-shoe. After a few days of rest, the pain and lameness will usually disappear.

CONTRACTED HEELS is a painful condition in which the frog begins to lose contact with the ground and becomes dried and shriveled, either because of improper foot care, shoes that are too narrow, or too infrequent shoeing. Some horses are believed to inherit a tendency to develop this condition and they should be given more than the usual foot grooming, with regular rehydrating treatments (mud or clay packs, tub soaking) in addition to a daily application of hoof dressing. The offending shoes should, of course, be removed and therapeutic ones fitted.

CRACKED HEELS are similar to severely chapped hands in humans, the skin above the heels becoming cracked when a horse has been allowed to stand around too much with wet feet, or when the skin has been irritated by mud, snow, or medicine dripping down from the upper leg. Sometimes there is a greasy discharge or bleeding in addition to heat and pain. Since it is the result of neglect rather than injury, proper care will prevent it.

CRACKED HOOF or SAND CRACK is a narrow vertical crack running down the wall of the foot, which may be either superficial or deep and painful. It is most often the result of dehydrated hoofs (in other words, careless hoof grooming), and the best prevention is to maintain the suppleness of the horn by the daily application of hoof dressing and proper shoeing. While waiting for the cracked hoof to grow out (which may take a long time, as its rate of growth is only about half an inch per month), you can soften the horn and reduce the pain by soaking the foot in a tub of warm water. The blacksmith should bind the edges of the crack together with a metal band in order to prevent further damage.

SEEDY TOE is an inflammation of the coronet that affects the horn, eventually leading to a separation between the wall of the foot and the horny laminae of its inner surface. You can see the cavity quite clearly when the horse's shoe is removed. Caused by shoes that place undue pressure on the wall of the foot or a piece of gravel that gets under the shoe and works up, and often a result of founder, the only prescription for seedy toe is plenty of patience while healthy horny tissue is growing out again.

FOUNDER or LAMINITIS, an intense inflammation of the sensitive laminae of the feet, can be extremely painful. It usually occurs in one or both of the forefeet and may result from overwork, concussion, abrupt changes of temperature, insufficient work for a heatening diet, or letting a horse stand in a draft or drink too much cold water when he has come in hot from work. Formerly, long sea voyages tended to produce founder in horses. But nowadays the up-to-date horse travels by trailer, van, or plane and if he "founders," it is most often due to careless stable management or to strenuous work, as in the case of the Standardbred racer Adios whose persistent case of laminitis during the last six years of his life fortunately did not interfere with his invaluable activity as a sire.

The symptoms are numerous: heat and dryness in the feet, rapid breathing, thirst, fever, groaning, sweating—accompanied by intense pain and, of course, lameness. The horse wants to lie down most of the time, and when he does walk, it is on his heels. You should remove the shoes from the affected foot or feet, and stand the horse in a tub of cold water, or pack clay or mud around the hoofs to reduce the temperature of the feet and to increase the circulation. You must also put him on a strict diet. But first of all, send for the veterinarian. Treated rapidly, the ailment can often be cured in a week or so; but if it is left unattended, the tissues will be permanently damaged.

THRUSH is an infection of the frog, immediately recognizable by the offensive odor and discharge from the cleft. It is a sign that a horse has been allowed to stand around with wet or dirty feet, which is why it does not normally occur in a well-run stable. Insufficient exercise and inadequate foot care may also cause thrush, because the frog cannot clean itself naturally without hoof movement. The treatment is to clean out the frog, paring away the diseased portion, and then to pack the cavity with a thrush medicine that your veterinarian will prescribe. The dressing must be renewed every day until the frog is healthy. If the first signs of thrush are ignored and no care is given, the entire frog may be destroyed.

NAVICULAR DISEASE is far more serious. It is an inflammation of the navicular bone in the foot, induced by repeated concussion and frequently accompanied by such complications as sidebone, ringbone, and contracted heels. The lameness may appear suddenly or in spells, the horse may stumble a lot and his gaits may become stilted. In advanced stages he refuses to move ahead at all. Thoroughbreds and horses with straight shoulders and straight pasterns who indulge in strenuous sports are most liable to develop navicular disease, which is often difficult to diagnose correctly. There is no real cure either, although some relief may be given to certain cases by shortening the toe of the affected foot, by employing injections of hydrocortisone, or even by severing the nerves that lead to the affected area. In any case, it is your veterinarian who must advise the proper treatment.

SIDEBONE is an inflammation of the cartilages under the coronary band and the wall of the hoof—usually in the forefeet—that brings about an eventual ossification of the affected tissues. The lameness is at first severe, but disappears after the sidebone has become set, although the foot will never regain its original resiliency. Some horses seem to inherit a tendency to form sidebones. It is often the result of repeated strain and too much work at too early an age, which is why it is quite frequent among race horses, trotters, and cow ponies. A horse must be allowed complete rest while the ossification is taking place. Many vets like to hasten the process and harden the tissues by blistering or firing.

THOROUGHPIN AND WINDGALL

Thoroughpin and windgall are two somewhat similar ailments which do not, however, cause lameness. Thoroughpin is a puffy swelling on the sides and just in front of the point of the hock, caused by a distention of the sheath of the deep flexor tendon. It may be reduced by blistering or firing, or it may be allowed to develop untreated.

Windgall is an enlargement of the joint-oil spaces around the fetlock joint, causing a soft, painless swelling that is similar to bog spavin in appearance, but less serious. In both cases the horse should be rested until the swelling has diminished, while the use of elastic work bandages and astringent lotions will help to prevent these ailments from recurring. Trotters with excessive knee action, Hunters, and stock horses are more or less predisposed to windgall, which may be unattractive, but is hardly a major affliction.

DIGESTIVE AILMENTS

The most common digestive ailment in horses is COLIC, perhaps because this term is applied to any disorder that causes abdominal pain.

Actually there are several different kinds of colic, any one of which may develop into a serious condition, so veterinary consultation is advisable. Too often owners "wait and see," which is probably why colic is the number one horse killer in the country. It is also the subject of an intensive research program of the Morris Animal Foundation.

A horse suffering from colic is a pathetic sight. He shows definite signs of abdominal distress and is uneasy, frequently looking around at his flanks; he may try to roll or to kick at his belly, and he continually lies down and gets up again, groaning all the while; he may sweat in patches, his pulse and breathing may be fast, and his abdomen may be distended, but there is usually no fever.

Some of the common causes of colic are:

Faulty teeth, preventing proper mastication and digestion
A sudden change of diet
Giving a large quantity of grain or cold water to a tired horse
Insufficient exercise
Crib-biting or wind-sucking
Bad-quality or moldy feed, or eating bedding
Sand impaction from grazing in sandy pastures (fairly common in the south of Florida) .

When a horse shows signs of colic, you should send for the veterinarian at once. At intestinal torsion ("twisted gut") can easily be mistaken for colic, and need not quite so often prove fatal if it is diagnosed early enough (although some cases are indeed hopeless). You should keep your horse walking about slowly until the veterinarian arrives, in order to prevent him from rolling and possibly getting cast or twisting his intestines. You mustn't give him anything to eat. The veterinarian will probably prescribe a colic remedy. There are many of them, often combined with a laxative, since constipation frequently accompanies colic. Relief will come rapidly, in a few minutes or in a few hours at the most, and during this time you should keep an eye on your horse to see that he doesn't hurt himself. It is simpler to prevent colic than it is to treat it, and good horse management will reduce it to a minimum.

CONSTIPATION is more serious for the horse than for most other animals because of his particular digestive system. You should ask your veterinarian to recommend a laxative that you always keep on hand. At the first suspicion of bowel stoppage, put your horse on a laxative diet of bran and linseed mashes, make sure that he gets enough exercise every day and that he has not developed the habit of eating his bedding.

AZOTURIA is not, strictly speaking, a digestive disorder, even though some of its symptoms are similar to those of a severe colic and although it appears most often in horses who have been stabled on full rations without work or exercise for one or more days. Horsemen familiarly refer to the disease as "Monday-morning sickness," as draft horses who ordinarily do not work on Sundays are much more prone to it than riding horses. The symptoms are rather impressive: stiffness and cramps in the muscles, trembling, sweating, thick and darkly colored urine. Sometimes the animal is unable to walk at all or even to rise to his feet. Severe cases require severe treatment, including intravenous injections. But mild ones clear up with a restricted laxative diet and a graduated amount of exercise after three or four days. Fortunately, the horseman who always takes care to adjust the horse's rations to the amount of work he is doing and avoids leaving him idle in his stall for long periods of time, will rarely come in contact with this pitiful ailment.

INTERNAL PARASITES

Many kinds of parasites are irresistibly attracted to horses. White worms (ascarids), pinworms, tapeworms, blood worms (strongyles), bots, and other varieties have devised ingenious means of entering the horse's system, for in order to survive and propagate, horse parasites are required to pass certain portions of their life cycle within the horse's body. A parasite-infected horse will have a staring coat, an excessive appetite combined with loss of weight, and may become quite irritable. The traditional treatment is periodic fecal analysis followed by worming by the veterinarian, who administers the worm remedy by "tubing" it directly into the horse's stomach through a nostril. The most common worming program for stabled horses is twice a year. On Kentucky breeding farms, the horses are wormed every two months, since they are in pasture most of the time. Besides, foals are more susceptible to worm damage than horses and require more frequent worming.

It is becoming increasingly usual to give riding horses and brood mares year-round protection against strongyles by administering low-level Phenothiazine in tiny doses with the horse's daily feed during the first 21 days of every month. But any worming program should be carried out under the supervision of a veterinarian, because the drugs employed, if not meticulously controlled, can be deadly poisons.

You should also try to limit parasite infection as far as possible by regularly cleaning and disinfecting your stable, by keeping the paddock cleared of droppings, and by situating the manure pit at some distance from the barn. Careful daily grooming, especially around the forelegs where the botfly likes to plant its eggs, will help to eliminate these nasty creatures.

SKIN AILMENTS

The horse's skin is hypersensitive, rather thin, and alive with nerve endings and tiny muscles which permit him to move almost any part of it at will. The skin is also of importance in eliminating waste matter from the body, which is why the horse's daily grooming is more truly health care than a beauty treatment.

Skin eruptions may be caused by infection, nervousness, dietary upsets, chills, or allergies, and they are rarely serious or long to cure. Usually they will clear up very quickly with a light, laxative diet, good hygiene, and grooming. Irritated spots may be soothed by applications of witch hazel or a bland powder such as zinc oxide. Many skin eruptions disappear upon administration of a gentle laxative.

You can avoid chafing a sensitive skin by seeing that your tack is always clean, soft, and supple. You should keep your horse's bed as clean as possible too, because his skin may become inflamed upon contact with irritating liquids such as urine. And incidentally, the horse is particularly susceptible to skin irritations of all kinds during the shedding season.

Insect, fly, and mosquito bites can be avoided by proper control measures, including screens, sprays, and the use of fly sheets. The newest fly-repellents can be safely sprayed right on the horse's coat. But you should still see that your stable is always clean and disinfected regularly and that the manure pile does not become a breeding place for flies.

HIVES or ''FEED BUMPS'' are small swellings under the skin, just like human hives. They appear suddenly and spread rapidly, often after a change of diet (especially to sweet feed), and for some mysterious reason, most often during warm and humid weather. Some horses develop hives as an allergic reaction to certain foods—quite often, corn. With prompt and proper care the hives will disappear almost as suddenly as they have appeared. Mild cases clear up in a few hours, and the stubborn ones in a week or two. The treatment is very simple. First of all, cut down the horse's rations to small portions of bran mash and hay. (In bad cases you should withhold all food for twenty-four hours.) Clear the bowels with a laxative and administer an antihistamine medication as recommended by your veterinarian. If the horse suffers a great deal from skin irritation, applications of witch hazel will have a soothing effect. In any case, you can usually avoid recurrence by introducing all dietary changes very gradually and by making sure that you never feed your horse too rich a diet for the amount of work he is doing.

COUGHS AND COLDS

Some horses will cough if their feed is too dry, and merely dampening the hay slightly will make the cough disappear. However, if the coughing is at all frequent, if it is accompanied by the slightest fever, or any discharge from the nostrils, or even a lackluster expression, your horse has probably caught cold and you must watch him carefully. Horses are particularly sensitive to drafts, and there is danger of bronchitis, influenza, or pneumonia developing if the first symptoms of a cold are not treated promptly.

You should always keep a cough remedy in your first-aid cabinet. Most of them have a honey base and are rubbed on the horse's tongue with a flat wooden spoon. You should also isolate your horse at the first sign of a cold, keep him warm and out of drafts, and put him on a soft diet. If the cough doesn't disappear within a day or two, you would be wise to call the veterinarian, because an untended cold may lead to a more serious ailment that can permanently damage a horse's wind.

If your own horse is unusually sensitive to cold, you should be especially careful to dry him off thoroughly after exercise, to give him adequate indoor and outdoor clothing, and to feed him a slightly heating diet (corn and grains) during the cold winter months.

RESPIRATORY AILMENTS

It is always risky to buy a horse who shows symptoms of any of the respiratory ailments, for they will limit his usefulness and are considered a serious form of unsoundness.

A "windy" horse or a "roarer"—that is, one suffering from BROKEN WIND as a result of overwork or an infection like pneumonia—is automatically disqualified from Hunter classes, although you may occasionally run into one in the hunting field or in a jumping competition. The condition is most frequent in big horses and is characterized by a definite gasping sound as air is drawn into the lungs. Some types of broken wind may be operated on, with varying success. Most often, the horse's soundness is permanently impaired.

PNEUMONIA often results in permanently broken wind if it is not treated immediately, so you should send for the veterinarian as soon as you suspect the presence of this infection, which is particularly dangerous for horses. The onset is sudden, with a high fever (105 to 106 degrees), accompanied by weakness, a short, dry cough, a rapid pulse, and fast breathing. With expert care, good luck, and modern antibiotics, pneumonia may be cured in two or three weeks. But it can also drag on for months and cause permanent damage to the patient's wind and heart.

HEAVES is similar to asthma in human beings. Just as some allergies are hereditary, horses may inherit a predisposition to this chronic ailment, which usually appears as an aftereffect of pneumonia or some other respiratory infection. The symptoms are a dry, distressing cough and heaving flank movements, with a peculiar double expiration following each inspiration of air. A horse with well-developed heaves is usually incapable of leading a normal, active life. But early cases are frequently alleviated and even cured entirely by the regime of a hay-free diet (or a diet based on a special non-allergic feed for heavey horses called New Hope), antihistamines, and only light work.

SHIPPING FEVER

The signs of fever in a horse are a rapid pulse, fast breathing, and shivering, quite often accompanied by constipation. Sometimes it indicates the presence of infection, or it may be merely the result of nervous excitement, or perhaps a case of shipping fever that horses quite often contract during and after a long trip, probably due to the change of environment, feed, and water, retention of urine, or exposure to common microbes different from those to which the horse has already built up an immunity at home. You must keep the feverish patient warm with blankets and standing bandages, give him plenty of water and rest, and feed him a reduced diet consisting mainly of bran mashes and boiled or green food. If his temperature has not returned to normal within twenty-four hours, call the veterinarian. Many low-grade infections can develop into something more serious if not attended to promptly.

YOUR HORSE'S EYES . . .

should be kept free from foreign matter and regularly checked for inflammation due to stable dust, feed dust, or pollen. If they are red and watery, you can wash them out with a warm solution of boric acid, or you can apply an ophthalmic salve.

PERIODIC OPHTHALMIA ("MOON BLINDNESS") is the principal disease affecting the horse's eyes. It is an inflammation of the inner structures of the eye (iridocyclitis to your ophthalmologist), characterized by profuse tearfulness, a swelling of the eyelids, and the accumulation of pus in the watery fluid inside the eyeball. The condition is actually a symptom of a systemic infection in the horse called leptospirosis, which modern veterinarians treat with antibiotics, corticosteroids, and the alternate use of ointments to dilate and constrict the pupil of the horse's eye. While the disease still holds some mystery for veterinary research, it seems very possible that these symptoms of leptospirosis manifest themselves only when the animal's body is deficient in riboflavin, an element of Vitamin B.

TEETH

All horses have twelve molars and ten incisors in each jaw, and the males have two additional teeth called "tushes," which appear only very rarely in mares. Their teeth grow throughout their lives and require regular attention in order to ensure proper mastication and consequently good digestion. Every six months, or at least once a year, you should have your horse's teeth checked and filed down to an even level ("floating" is the technical term for this operation), so that the grinding process is perfectly efficient.

"Wolf Teeth" are small, extra teeth that sometimes emerge in front of the molars. They do not affect the eyesight, as many people believe, but they may very likely impede the bitting of a young horse. Modern veterinarians remove them only when they cause trouble.

CONTAGIOUS DISEASES . . .

are fortunately more unusual in horses than in other livestock. Some of them must be immediately reported to the local authorities. Radical measures have been taken to stamp out infections that formerly caused disastrous epidemics, such as the dread glanders, which raged through the U. S. Cavalry stables during the Mexican-American War. Today it is practically unknown.

The most dangerous contagious disease at large today is probably ENCEPHALOMYELITIS ("SLEEPING SICKNESS"), a virus disease of birds that is transmitted to the horse by the bite of sucking insects, primarily the mosquito. Of the various types, three have been identified in the United States and are known as Eastern, Western, and Venezuelan (VEE). This last, which moved north from South America via Mexico a few years ago, caused the death of many horses in Texas and created a national alert, which was fortunately successful in avoiding a nation-wide epidemic. The symptoms become apparent only after an incubation period of three weeks and start with a fever, then depression and invasion of the nervous system. The final stage is complete paralysis. While there is no sure cure, prevention is almost totally ensured by an annual vaccination, preferably administered in the spring before the mosquito season.

EQUINE INFECTIOUS ANEMIA (EIA) is a mysterious viral disease affecting the blood and lymph systems. It is highly contagious and there is much controversy over its proper treatment. There is no cure. On the other hand, the Coggins test detects it, and a negative Coggins report is required for interstate travel in many parts of America.

CONTAGIOUS EQUINE METRITIS (CEM), a bacterial disease that is propagated during breeding and prevents conception, made the headlines recently when imported brood mares introduced it into some of the leading Kentucky stud farms. Although the disease is not fatal nor even very difficult to cure, it can mean millions of dollars of losses if an infected stallion is obliged to miss a breeding season, and infected mares are unable to conceive. As a direct result of this latest epidemic, a special health certificate is now required for crossing certain state borders, and it is more than ever advisable to request negative CEM cultures from mares and stallions before using them for breeding.

STRANGLES, an equine version of distemper, is a streptococcus infection, causing inflammation of the upper respiratory tract and swollen lymph nodes that often develop abscesses. It is spread by direct contact with afflicted animals and with contaminated food and water, especially at horse shows, race tracks, and boarding stables, although it is much less prevalent than it used to be. Antibiotic treatment usually cures it if administered early enough. Penicillin is sometimes used at the very beginning. Young horses under five years of age are more susceptible than older ones, especially during damp, cold weather. There exists a preventive vaccine, but many vets consider it unsafe.

CUTS AND BRUISES

Wounds are classified as incised, punctured, lacerated, or bruised, and the greatest danger from all of them is tetanus infection. Since tetanus germs cannot grow in the presence of oxygen, the most critical kinds from this point of view are deep wounds and nail punctures. Your horse should be permanently protected against tetanus, but even so, if a wound is particularly deep or dirty he may need an extra booster shot.

Steady bleeding means that the blood comes from a vein, and it can be stopped by applying direct pressure. But if the blood spurts, it comes from an artery. Most often a sterile pressure bandage applied to the wound will stop this bleeding too. But should it be necessary to apply a tourniquet between the wound and the heart, it should be handled by an experienced person and care taken to release the pressure every fifteen minutes until the veterinarian arrives.

If the cut is near a joint, there is also the danger of rupturing a joint-oil capsule. Joint oil, or "synovial fluid," is a thick, sticky liquid which oozes out of a wound if a joint has been damaged. Its loss can be very serious indeed, so by all means call the veterinarian.

Nowadays infection is fought with antibiotics such as penicillin and streptomycin in addition to the traditional antiseptics (iodine, blue ointment, etc.); but antiseptics and antibiotics are never used at the same time. Antibiotics are called upon when the wound is very important or too deep to be reached by an ordinary germicide.

Body wounds on horses usually mend quickly, while leg wounds take longer to heal. You should try to keep the wound dry and avoid the use of grease or ointments that will retain infection. Beware also of over-treating wounds with excessively strong antiseptics, for this may only result in a worse scar. And finally, during the fly season, you should protect wounds with a fly-repellent dressing.

Wounds are healed by *granulation,* when new cells are formed from the capillaries at the base of the wound to fill up the gap. Sometimes this granulation is excessive and rises above the edges of the wound to form *proud flesh,* an unsightly, raw exposed mound which makes further healing impossible without medication or surgery. The best way to avoid it is to have the vet suture deep wounds as soon as possible, to clean all wounds thoroughly, keep them closed and covered with a nonirritating bandage, and remove scabs if necessary. Getting rid of existing proud flesh also requires veterinary skill in order to remove the excess tissue down to skin level either by surgery or by the systematic application of caustic substances under veterinary supervision.

INCISED WOUNDS . . .

whether superficial or profound, are characterized by their clean-cut edges. First aid consists of washing the wound and the surrounding area and applying an antiseptic such as blue ointment (which some veterinarians prefer to iodine); then the edges of the cut should be brought together and a bandage applied to keep it clean. Sulfanilamide powder sprinkled on the wound before bandaging will often hasten healing.

If the wound is a large one, you should call the veterinarian at once, because it may need stitching and this must be done as soon as possible. In this case you should apply no antiseptics or other medicine but simply keep the wound moist with cool boiled water to which you have added one teaspoonful of salt per pint, until the veterinarian arrives.

PUNCTURED WOUNDS . . .

are probably the most common, and they can also be the most serious if antitetanus measures are not taken immediately. One of the most frequent types of puncture wounds is the nail in the foot, picked up during work. (And the best prevention, needless to say, is to make sure that sharp objects never clutter up your barn or paddock.) The appropriate first aid is to remove the nail, open the wound, and poultice. Then keep it clean by bandaging, with the bandage wound loosely enough around the pastern to allow for possible swelling.

In the case of a prick from a horseshoe nail, the horse will probably fall lame within four or five days after being shod. The nail must be removed and the wound treated. Afterward, the foot should be left unshod or else fitted with a shoe that is cut away to avoid the injured spot.

LACERATED WOUNDS . . .

are torn and ragged, increasing the danger of infection and the difficulty of removing foreign matter. Lacerations are also more apt to leave a scar than other types of cuts; one quite often sees the coats of Western-bred horses marred by little skin lumps that are the consequence of improperly treated barbed-wire cuts. (With show horses such blemishes are frequently removed by plastic surgery.) Your wisest course of action is to send for the veterinarian, keeping the wound moistened in the meantime just as if it were an incised wound.

BRUISED WOUNDS . . .

usually take much longer to heal. They may be caused by blows, kicks from another horse, or violent contact with a blunt object such as the pole of a jumping obstacle or a stable partition. If the skin is broken, the injury should be treated as both a wound and a bruise.

The moment you suspect a bad bruise without a break in the skin, you should try to limit the swelling as much as possible by applying cold water to the injured spot by means of a hose, a soaking tub, bandages soaked in cooling lotion, or ice packs. Having limited the swelling, the next step is to attempt to reduce it, by applying hot poultices about twenty-four hours later.

SADDLE and GIRTH GALLS may occur in sensitive-skinned horses as a result of repeated abrasion by an ill-fitting saddle, a stiff, irritating, or too tight girth, or a dirty saddle, girth, or saddle pad. Fortunately, galls are very long to develop. Preventive measures can be taken as soon as you notice any sign of abrasion, by changing to a different type of girth or saddle, by using a saddle pad if you don't already do so, and by proper tack care and saddling procedures. Naturally, no horse should ever be girthed or saddled if his skin is sore, since continued irritation may cause an abscess or ulcer which is certain to require veterinary treatment and may keep your horse out of action for many days.

Permanent blemishes are sometimes caused by repeated bruising, the kind most frequently seen being CAPPED ELBOW ("SHOE BOIL"), an unsightly swelling at the point of the horse's elbow, which is frequently the result of insufficient bedding—in other words, bad stable management. Even more frequently the injury comes from a shoe bruising an elbow when the horse is lying down, in which case it may be prevented by putting your horse in special "shoe-boil boots" when you bed him down for the night.

"BIG" KNEES are usually the result of a blow, such as hitting a fence when jumping or striking the knee against a hard wall, as is very apt to occur during shipping. CAPPED HOCKS are similar, but the point of injury is the hock and the cause is usually rubbing or striking the hock against the stall partitions or kicking at the stable walls. At the first sign of either of these injuries, you should wash the spot, treat it with antiseptic, and prevent all contact with it until it has healed. Cold applications may attenuate the blemish. But the best thing to do is to take immediate preventive measures. As soon as you notice any puffiness around your horse's hocks or elbows, observe his stable habits. If you discover that he likes to kick or rub against the stall partitions, line them with padding. Shipping injuries to the hocks can be avoided by always protecting the hocks with hock boots before you load your horse in a van or trailer.

FISTULA OF THE WITHERS is another condition caused by bruising or an ill-fitting saddle, and sometimes by an infection in the horse's system. It is accompanied by swelling and soreness that comes to a head in an abscess, with a copious discharge. Modern veterinarians treat the affliction by lancing, injections, and surgery.

POLL EVIL (FISTULA OF THE POLL) may result from a sharp blow on the top of the head against the low roof of a shipping van, for example, or a low doorway. (No horseman worthy of the name would ever strike a horse a direct blow on this most sensitive part of the head.) A protective shipping helmet and special care when leading your horse through low doorways should be sufficient to eliminate the ordinary causes of this rather unusual ailment.

Faulty action or bad shoeing may cause bruises on the horse's legs. When one foot brushes against another (usually the insides of the front legs), it is called BRUSHING or INTERFERING, and some horses' conformation reveals a predisposition to this type of injury. Such animals should always wear brushing boots. A good blacksmith can also correct or improve the defective action by fitting special shoes.

OVERREACH occurs when the shoe tip of a hind foot strikes and bruises the heel or back of the leg of the forefoot, which is most likely to happen during fast gallops and with breeds such as the Walking Horse that are encouraged to produce an exceptionally long overstride. Such horses, as well as race horses and racing trotters and pacers, should always wear protective overreach boots. With a fresh injury you should clean and dress the spot and call the veterinarian.

One of the most sensational careers in racing history was cut short because of incurable overreaching. The horse was the legendary Tetrarch, a big, rather clumsy-looking gray, who was probably the fastest Thoroughbred ever foaled. Once at Sandown, for example, he was left at the starting gate and began to run only when the field had a fifty-yard lead. But he still came in first, beating the best racing filly in England by a nose. It was a great loss to racing when repeated injuries caused by overreaching forced this fabulous runner into retirement, undefeated, at the end of his two-year-old season.

ACCIDENTS AND FALLS

Accidents can happen during jumping, hunting, riding cross-country, and at the most unlikely times and places. Fortunately, even the most disastrous-looking spills usually have no serious consequences, and the horse will immediately scramble to his feet again unaided. (Don't forget to catch hold of the reins as he rises!) You should always walk him around a bit to make sure that he is uninjured before remounting. He will probably be rather nervous and frightened at first, and your immediate preoccupation is to help him to regain confidence in himself and in his rider.

If he seems unable to get up alone, perhaps he has fallen in an awk-

"Fortunately even disastrous-looking spills . . ."

ward position, or is caught up in the reins. If so, you must disentangle him, pull the reins over his head, and encourage him to rise. The principal danger of simple falls is a horse's getting cast, because he may break a blood vessel in his frantic efforts to get up again. You must try to keep him calm and prevent him from struggling while you help him to his feet. Sometimes you will need the assistance of another person. Once the horse is up again, examine him for lameness, wounds, and bruises. Lead him back to the stable and give first aid if necessary. If there is any evidence of serious injury, you must of course call the veterinarian.

Should your horse have the misfortune to break a bone, it does not necessarily follow that he must be destroyed. Horses have suffered fractured hips without their owners ever noticing, and the bones have mended all by themselves, leaving only a trace of stiffness. Some small fractures can be treated quite successfully (the sesamoid bones, splint bones, and chipped knee bones often are). Broken limbs are, of course, more serious, mainly because the horse's entire body might have to be suspended in a sling in order to take his weight off the broken leg. This can involve very heavy expense and there is besides a great risk of sling-

". . . usually have no serious consequences." (*Photos by Sue Maynard*)

supported horses contracting pneumonia. As a matter of fact, such cases are usually treated exclusively at veterinary colleges, which are the only institutions well equipped to handle them properly. One of the most modern is the new Bolton Center of the University of Pennsylvania School of Veterinary Medicine, where the late Dr. Jacques Jenny, world famous for sophisticated horse surgery, devised spectacular orthopedic facilities, including devices for safely manipulating injured animals and a horse-sized swimming pool in which four-legged patients can move their limbs while supported in a sling. Seattle Slew was treated here.

Perhaps you have heard of the race horse Your Host, whose owners were paid a full indemnity of a quarter of a million dollars when his right foreleg was shattered at Santa Anita in 1951. Instead of writing off the loss, the insurers (Lloyds of London) had the broken bones reset and when the horse had recovered his strength he was sold to a breeding syndicate. For ten years, Your Host continued to play a prominent role in racing, at stud, siring among many other fine racers the fabulous Kelso, who five times was voted Horse of the Year of Thoroughbred racing. (But it is only fair to add that his veterinary bill came to over $40,000!)

MEDICATION, TREATMENTS, AND DRUGS

Some horses are very understanding when being treated for an ailment, while others are as unruly as spoiled children about accepting medicine, and it often takes two people to handle a sick horse.

Giving a horse medicine is not always as simple as it sounds. Pills are usually given with a "balling gun" (the giant, oval horse pills are called "balls"), which project the pill far back in the horse's throat, giving him no choice but to gulp it down. Liquid medicine is introduced into the mouth by means of a syringe. However, nowadays many remedies (as well as vitamin and mineral supplements) are prepared in powder form to be dissolved in water and sprinkled on a horse's feed or added to his water bucket. While pills and syrups are still occasionally prescribed, most modern veterinarians administer many of their remedies by injection (and worm remedies by tubing them directly into the horse's stomach). If your own horse requires frequent "shots," your vet may show you how to give an intramuscular injection. But laymen should never attempt an intravenous one. Even enemas should be administered only by a veterinarian. An impressive quantity of liquid is employed.

One of the newest forms of equine therapy in America is the ancient science of acupuncture, which has been used successfully to treat chronic sore backs and founder (laminitis), as well as to relieve pain.

Among the common methods of restraining a suffering or nervous animal in order to administer treatment or medication are holding up one leg, employing hobbles or a *twitch*. The latter device twists the horse's upper lip, causing sufficient discomfort to distract his attention from the real project you have in mind. There are three kinds: a hinge twitch, a screw twitch, and a loop twitch (the most common). None of them should be applied too tightly or for a long time, and none should be used too often. The horse may find the twitch more fearsome than the procedure from which you wish to withdraw his attention. A twitch is a traditional item of equipment of the blacksmith, and most stables own one. However, unless there is some counterindication, it is increasingly usual to give restive horses a mild tranquilizer before undertaking any treatment or procedure that causes them anxiety.

Dressings are often difficult to keep in place when the affected spot is near a joint. The proper technique for bandaging a horse's leg

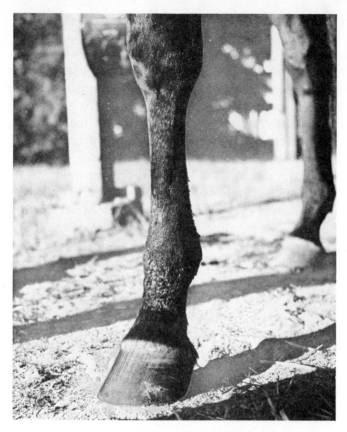

A blistered leg. (*Photo by Ray Woolfe, Jr.*)

is more easily learned by observation than by reading a description in a book. The important thing is to use sufficient cotton inside the bandages and to wind them tightly enough so that they will stay in place, but not so tightly as to impair the circulation. In certain cases you must make allowance for possible swelling.

Blistering and pin-firing are delicate operations designed to increase the blood supply to an affected area in order to repair or fortify damaged tissues and to stimulate the growth of additional new scar tissue. Blistering is produced by a strong caustic ointment, and firing is done with a heated firing iron, the special advantage of the latter being that it can increase the amount of supporting new scar tissue at the exact spot of weakness. Some veterinarians consistently blister or fire ringbone, curbs, and splints. Others feel that rest alone is often just as effective. Perhaps the truth of the matter is that an untreated horse may appear to be sound sooner than he really is and he may be put back to work prematurely, whereas the horse who has been blistered or fired is sure to be given the lengthy convalescence that he needs. It also seems to be true that these treatments are less generally applied today than in former years, or at least not before the pros and cons have been most carefully weighed. In fact, Lloyds of London has ruled that the horses they insure must not be fired or blistered without the express permission of the insurance company.

Naturally, the use of these techniques is reserved for the professional veterinarian. But all horsemen can learn how to hose a horse's legs by playing a stream of cold water on them, to clean out wounds or to reduce pain and swelling. You should start the hose on the foot and work upward. A great labor-saver is a perforated rubber hose which can be circled around the leg, passed over the horse's back, and taped to his blanket. Twenty minutes is long enough for an average hosing treatment, which may be repeated two or three times a day. Always protect the heels and the back of the pastern before hosing, and thoroughly dry the legs and heels afterward, in order to prevent cracked heels.

Finally, no discussion of equine medication and treatment would be

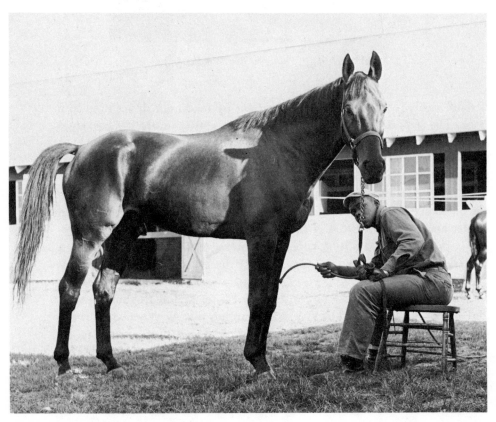

Hosing a horse's leg.

A whirlpool tubbing treatment. (*Photos by Ray Woolfe, Jr.*)

complete if it ignored the question of drugs, which has divided the horse world more violently than anything since the Forward Seat.

Just as the "drug scene" has emerged as part of society as a whole in recent years, so have drugs begun to play different and larger roles in the horse world. While the use of drugs in veterinary medicine is substantially the same as always, nonprofessional administration of drugs has greatly increased. In some equestrian circles, it almost seems that if you don't know how to give an injection to a horse, you aren't really up-to-date.

It's not a bad idea for the experienced professional horseman or seasoned amateur to know how to administer an intramuscular injection, and most veterinarians will provide them with instruction for use in an emergency. People who keep horses in remote areas necessarily have to be more self-reliant about such things. However, the dangers of indiscriminate or incompetent drug administration cannot be minimized.

The problems that have arisen in recent years have mostly involved drugs that influence feeling (thus soundness) and drugs that influence temperament. Local anesthetics such as procaine and its derivatives obviously have many virtues in competent hands, and are invaluable in diagnosing lameness and, as in human medicine, the treatment of injuries. However, when such products are used to conceal unsoundness from a prospective purchaser or a horse show judge, their use is not only illegal and immoral but also extremely dangerous.

The same is true of central-nervous system depressants such as the phenobarbitals, barbiturates, and tranquilizers such as Acepromazine. Tranquilizers in particular have many invaluable and legitimate applications, such as in clipping, showing, or transporting a restive horse, or even in certain training situations such as backing a young horse for the first time. However, there is no question that there has been widespread abuse of these drugs, especially in the show ring and in the trial of horses by prospective customers. (Some dealers have indirectly acknowledged this by furnishing their own "prescriptions" for success along with the horse: "Two cc's of so-and-so forty minutes before the class.")

Fortunately, the vigor with which the AHSA has prosecuted its drug-testing program at horse shows has significantly inhibited what was once a rapid spread of indiscriminate drug administration. Any exhibitor at any member show is liable to testing, and severe penalties are imposed in cases in which "positive" samples are verified. Every horse show exhibitor should possess a copy of the current AHSA "Drugs and Medication" pamphlet, which clearly explains what is and what is not permitted, and he should also provide his vet with a copy to ensure that he too is aware of any liability to which he might unwittingly subject his client. Many colic remedies, worming preparations, and antibiotics contain ingredients that are on the AHSA's list of banned substances, which means that no horse treated with them should be shown for a period ranging from four to five days, depending on the drug involved. The same thing is true of many patent medicines. Even an "ordinary tonic" may produce a positive drug test. The best course of action is to administer *nothing* to a show horse during or shortly prior to competition, unless the formula is known, and known to be exempt.

Among the products specifically exempted by the AHSA are ordi-nary penicillin (*not* the version compounded with procaine), aspirin, and (somewhat controversially) phenylbutazone (Butazolidin, or "Bute"). The latter has been subject to increasing restrictions abroad, and the FEI is considering extending its present prohibition (which affects only Dressage horses) to all of its disciplines. In the United States, however, this drug is permitted by most state racing jurisdictions (with the notable exception of New York State), as well as by the AHSA.

Many horsemen feel that this drug constitutes the course of last resort for older horses showing normal wear and tear as well as for slightly arthritic or navicular horses, and there is little doubt that it has extended the useful life of many star performers in many competitive areas. Basically an anti-inflammatory agent with some analgesic proper-ties too, "Bute" has few side effects and so is regarded by many horsemen as far safer and more conservative than the alternative treatments for the same conditions, which are Steroids and Neurectomy (denerving). For the horseman who must cope with "feely" older horses, it has the advan-tage of being administered in powder form along with the feed, as well as by injection.

Now you should have a general idea of the principal menaces to a horse's health and how to avoid and treat them. But you mustn't be over-impressed by this lengthy list. The fact is that most horses are born sound and stay that way. They rarely require such luxurious therapy as the French race horse who accompanies his owner every spring to the health resort of Vittel, where they both drink the celebrated waters to stimulate their equally sluggish kidneys! If you do no more than provide your own horse with a sensible diet, reasonable care, and sufficient exer-cise, the chances are that he will always remain in good health and work-ing condition.

The First-Aid Cabinet

A Thermometer (of a special equine type or the regular human rectal kind)
Scissors (preferably curved)
A Disinfectant (such as Creolin or soluble pine oil)
A Colic Remedy (that your veterinarian recommends)
A Laxative (the kind your veterinarian prefers)
Cough Medicine
White Lotion (used with soaking bandages for cooling)

Antiphlogistine (used in a poultice for heating) or Poultice Powder

Leg Brace (used under standing bandages for fatigue)

A Liniment (for sore, strained muscles)

Healing Powder (for dusting over wounds, such as B.F.I. or Iodoform)

Healing Spray (such as Furacin or Pelizone)

Ophthalmic Ointment (for the eyes)

Vaseline

A Diuretic (prescribed by your veterinarian, to stimulate kidney action)

Several rolls of Bandages 3 inches wide

A supply of Cotton Wool (a 1-pound roll)

Masking Tape and Adhesive Gauze

Rubber Gloves, clean Towels

A Tub (for soaking feet)

A Measuring Cup

A Dose Syringe

Rubbing Alcohol

10. Tack

"Give me my boots and saddle!" croons the cowboy in the old song, repeating insistently his haunting plea. Such a strong sentimental attachment to leather goods may surprise at first, but it is not as unreasonable as it may seem, for modern riding is dependent upon a number of essential items of special equipment if it is to be practiced effectively and in comfort.

Ever since the beginning of "man's noblest conquest," horsemen have been devising and revising articles of tack (a term which, by the way, is merely an abbreviation of "tackle," used in the sense of "equipment," as in "fishing tackle"). Some of them are veritable works of art which have found their way into museums; others are curious devices that attempt to achieve by mechanical means the same results as long hours of laborious training. Despite the artistic appeal of the first and the miraculous promises of the second, experienced horsemen believe that the simplest equipment is usually the most effective, although they seek a high standard of quality and workmanship. The average rider, too, will find that the conventional kind of riding tack is most apt to help him improve his own and his horse's skill, and that buying the best quality he can afford and taking care of it will prove to be an economy in the end.

Before you venture into the saddler's shop, with its delicious odor of new leather and its irresistible array of bridles and saddles, you must have a pretty definite idea of what you are shopping for. Certain kinds of equipment have proved to be most effective for certain uses, and what you choose will depend upon the breed and conformation of the horse you ride and the type of activity you practice together.

The first piece of tack you take from its rack when preparing for your daily ride is your horse's bridle, and so let's first consider the question of

BITS AND BRIDLES

Bits and bridles are primarily a means of communicating with your horse and encouraging him to adopt the correct head carriage, which permits him to perform his work with maximum efficiency. Never, never should the bit be regarded as a means of coercion, or the bridle and reins as an aid to the rider's balance, like the handle bars of a bicycle!

Before going into the subject of the different kinds of bits, let's look again inside your horse's mouth.

On each side of the lower jaw, between the tushes or canine teeth and the grinders, there are two smooth intervals called the "bars," which occur just about at the corner of the mouth. This is where the bit is placed, over the tongue. The nerve endings of the mouth and lips are very sensitive in an unspoiled horse, allowing an expert horseman to communicate with his mount in a very precise and delicate way, and the horse to respond instantly to the slightest pressure. But they can easily be injured by rough riding, and may eventually become so completely deadened that the horse doesn't register any message at all. It is in these cases that some riders are inclined to resort to more and more severe bits; but the experienced horseman, whenever possible, prefers to repair and re-educate the spoiled animal's mouth by reverting to the lightest possible bit, or even to a hackamore, which has no mouthpiece at all, until the nerves have regained their original sensitivity.

"Signals" are sent to the horse via the bit and bridle by means of pressure brought to bear mainly on the lips, tongue, and nose. In addition, certain bits include a leather strap or metal chain that fits into the "chin groove" underneath the horse's lower jaw; many of the Western bits act on the roof of his mouth. The various kinds have been designed to serve definite purposes with different types of horses at different stages of schooling and for different riding activities. While the familiar claim that "the key to every horse is in his mouth" may be open to argument, it is generally true that at any given stage there is a certain type of bit in which a horse is apt to do his best. Therefore, choosing the most suitable bit for your own horse is not a matter of caprice or fashion, resolved by a casual, "I think I'll try *that* one." Your own degree of riding skill should be considered along with your horse's temperament and training; young riders and novices should follow the advice of their riding instructor, or of an experienced horseman friend.

One of the crucial steps in the early training of a riding horse is his introduction to the bit. The very first bitting usually takes place right in the young horse's stall, where he is fitted to a "bitting rig," consisting of a simple harness and a "mouthing bit" (a straight bar bit to which are attached a number of small dangling metal "keys") that encourages him to play with the bit in his mouth and to keep his lower jaw relaxed and mobile. The bitting rig of Saddle Horses and Walking Horses includes a head-setting device to help them acquire the high head carriage that is essential for Gaited horses.

Bits are made of various metals. The best are of stainless steel. They may also be covered with hard or soft rubber or with leather to make them softer in a tender mouth.

Modern bridles are fitted with hook-in studs for attaching the bit and reins, instead of the old-fashioned buckles, which nowadays are found only on bridles of inferior quality. It is even more attractive to have the bit and reins permanently stitched to the bridle. Sewn-in bits are required when showing Hunters in Appointments classes and are often seen in the hunting field. However, it is useful to keep an extra hook-in stud bridle for the occasions when you may wish to experiment with a different kind of bit.

The basic bitting principles to bear in mind are that:

—thick mouthpieces are less severe than thin ones, because they distribute pressure over a wider area;

—a jointed mouthpiece is more severe than a solid one, because it pinches the sides of the tongue;

—twisted mouthpieces are more severe than straight ones, and wire mouthpieces are the most severe of all.

—wide flat links and wide flat straps are more gentle for curb chains and straps than narrow, thin ones, which can cut;

—on curbs and Pelhams, short shanks are gentler than longer ones;

—finally, and most important of all: Always use the gentlest, lightest bit that permits you to control your horse.

While there are many fancy patented bits on the market, most of the leading horsemen seem to do very well indeed with the conventional types. Bill Steinkraus always works in an ordinary jointed snaffle, although he often used a Pelham for jumping competitions. Probably half

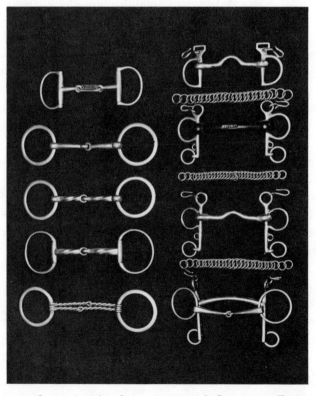

Bits. (From top to bottom) Left column: Dr. Bristol; flat ring snaffle; twisted snaffle; twisted egg-butt snaffle; wire-mouth snaffle. Right column: Kimberwicke; rubber-mouth Pelham; Tom Thumb Pelham with port; double or full bridle (bit and bridoon), with different forms of curb chains in between. (*Photo by James Deutschmann*)

A snaffle bridle. (*Photo by James Deutschmann*)

of the international riders today use a plain snaffle, and the others a variety which experience has proven to be most effective with their particular horses.

You too will most likely find the best bit for your own horse among the standard ones: the snaffle, the curb, the double bridle, and the Pelham.

THE SNAFFLE BIT

In its simplest form the snaffle is merely a straight bar with large rings at each end to which the reins and cheek-straps of the bridle are attached. When the mouthpiece is extended at each end to avoid cutting the corners of the horse's lips or tongue, it is known as an *egg-butt snaffle*. The standard type, which many consider to be the ideal training and general riding bit, is the *jointed snaffle*. Slightly more severe and very common are the *wire snaffle* and the *twisted snaffle;* and much more severe than these is the *chain snaffle*, consisting, as its name suggests, of a series of metal links. All of them act on the corners of the horse's lips, the jointed snaffle acting on the tongue as well, with a sort of nutcracker effect.

While the snaffle may seem ineffective with hard-mouthed or high-headed horses, and while it is never used with Saddle Horses, some kind of a snaffle is often the best choice for the training and normal riding of Hunters, Jumpers, and all-round pleasure horses, and it is definitely preferred for green horses and novice riders. Furthermore, the snaffle is the only bit with which to start "making" the mouth of a young horse and to remake the mouth of a spoiled one.

THE CURB BIT

The curb is a single-bar mouthpiece that may be straight, half-moon shaped, or—the most common—with a central "port," which is an arch in the middle to discourage the horse from slipping his tongue over the bit and thus completely nullify its effect. At each end are two upright bars of varying lengths called "cheekpieces," the upper ones (the part above the mouthpiece) for attaching the cheek straps of the bridle, and the lower ones for attaching the curb reins. In addition, there are two hooks on the upper rings for attaching a *curb chain,* which fits against the chin groove in the lower jaw. With very sensitive horses it may be covered with rubber or leather, replaced by a leather strap, or entirely omitted. Farther down there are two little rings for a *lip strap* that helps to keep the curb chain in place.

The effect of the curb is one of leverage as well as direct pressure on the horse's bars. As the reins are pulled, the bit pivots in the horse's mouth, bringing his head down and in toward his chest and inducing him to flex at the poll and to yield the lower jaw, which is compressed between the mouthpiece and the curb chain. The severity of a curb bit depends upon the height of the port (the higher the port, the more severe the action on the tongue and the roof of the mouth), and also upon the difference in length between the upper and lower cheekpieces (the greater the difference, the more severe the bit). Four inches is considered a maximum length for a Hunter or any other horse in whom overflexing of the neck is undesirable.

Many Polo Ponies and Western horses are ridden in a curb bit, while the Tennessee Walking Horse bit is merely a variation of the curb, with very long shanks (seven to nine inches), curved cheekpieces, a high port in the mouthpiece, and a soft leather strap in place of the curb chain. It is not customary to use a curb alone with Hunters or Thoroughbred-type horses, who are nevertheless quite often ridden in one when it is combined with a snaffle to form:

THE DOUBLE BRIDLE

The bit (curb) and bridoon (which is the name for a snaffle when combined with a curb) make up the bitting part of the double or full bridle—no longer referred to very often as a "Weymouth" or "hunting bridle"—that is the ultimate goal in training Saddle Horses and is required in Saddle Seat Equitation classes because of the high degree of control it permits.

While the snaffle bit (acting on the corners of the mouth) raises the

A double bridle. (*All illustrations of tack are from the catalog of Miller's, New York City, and are reproduced with their permission.*)

horse's head, the curb (acting on the lips, tongue, and chin groove) obliges the horse to flex at the poll and to yield with his lower jaw. The two bits are placed simultaneously in his mouth, with the snaffle sitting slightly higher than the curb, since it must fit snugly in the corners of the mouth while the curb rests on the bars. The two pairs of reins should be of different widths (the snaffle reins being the wider), or else the curb reins may be plain and the snaffle reins laced or braided.

A double bridle is preferred for showing Hunters, and a long-shanked one is always used with Saddle Horses, as it is very effective in increasing the flexion from the poll. It may be employed in the advanced training of many kinds of horses—even stock horses—when the double reins, especially the curb reins, are held in expert hands.

THE PELHAM BIT

Horses who fuss with an extra bit in their mouth but who still require the influence of a curb chain, often go best in a Pelham, which combines some of the effects of both the snaffle and the curb in a single bit. Shaped like the curb bit, it is used with two pairs of reins and a curb chain. Like the ordinary curb, its severity depends upon the

A Pelham bridle. (*Photo by James Deutschmann*)

difference in length of the upper and lower cheekpieces as well as on the tension of the curb chain.

Pelham bits are made in various shapes, but the most common kind has a port in the center to prevent the horse from getting his tongue over the mouthpiece and at the same time to increase the pressure on the bars of the mouth. Hard-rubber mouthpieces are almost as popular as those of stainless steel.

When the cheekpieces are short and the mouthpiece plain, the Pelham is the most common polo bit and is often used for hacking as well as for hunting and jumping. But the long-shanked kind is more often employed with Saddle Horses than with Hunters. Its principal disadvantage is that while it brings a horse's chin in and his head down, it may encourage him to carry his head *too* low.

GAGS

Jumper and Event riders sometimes increase the effect of the snaffle bridle by employing a "gag bit," which consists of round leather cheekpieces that pass from the crown down through special holes at the top

A full-cheek snaffle bit with keepers, worn with a rounded bridle. (*Photo by Sue Maynard*)

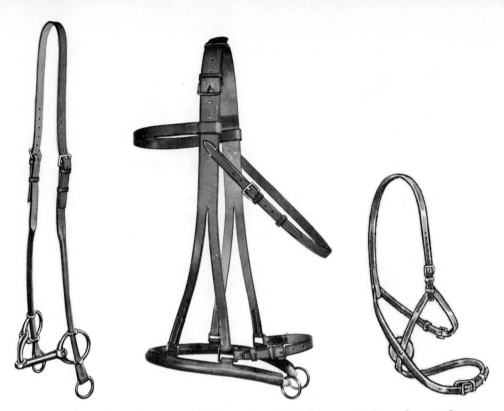

Left, a Shrewsbury gag. Middle, a jumping hackamore. Right, a figure-eight nose-band. (*From the catalog of Miller's*)

and bottom of the snaffle bit rings and then to the reins. When the rider pulls on the reins, the gag acts like a pulley wheel, multiplying the effect, causing the bit to rise in the horse's mouth, thus encouraging him to raise his head. Gags are therefore useful for horses with hard mouths and low head carriage and for strong pullers. But because of their severity, they require sensitive hands and should be reserved for really expert horse-men.

WESTERN BITS

Because Western horses are so often trained to perform special work such as cutting and roping, and are normally taught to neck-rein, the theory and practice of bitting Western horses differs from Eastern traditions.

The most typical Western bit is probably the *spade*, whose long shanks and high central port cause it to act principally on the roof of the horse's mouth. Since it is Spanish in origin, its use is largely concentrated in areas where Spanish customs still prevail, as in California and Texas. It is a very severe bit and can be harmful to green horses unless it is used with great tact and discretion. Another Western type is the *half-breed*, a straight bar bit with a copper roller in the high port to keep the horse's mouth moist, which is worn with a soft leather chin strap. A great many Western pleasure horses are ridden in a *Western curb* with long, curved cheekpieces and a leather strap replacing the curb chain in the chin groove.

In recent years a new element has entered into Western bitting. As the breeding of Western horses becomes more refined by Arab and Thoroughbred crosses, and as other breeds are trained in Western-style riding, more and more Western riders are finding that the use of very severe bits is no longer necessary or desirable. And so today many well-bred Western horses are trained and ridden in an ordinary snaffle.

Quite often with Western horses, the bit is replaced entirely by a

HACKAMORE (OR JAQUIMA)

which is not a bit at all, but a sort of halter-like device (*jáquima* being the Spanish word for "halter") with a leather noseband fitting high across the nose about two inches below the cheekbones and two reins attached under the horse's chin. The narrow, rounded, wire-nosed version is called a *bozal*. Usually made of horsehair rope, it passes around the nose, is knotted beneath the chin, and suspended from the browband by a leather strap. The effect is to exert pressure on the soft part of the nose and on the sensitive nerves on the underside of the jaw. When a hackamore "bit" is added, the reins are fastened to two long metal shanks which permit greater leverage, but there is still no actual mouthpiece.

During their early training almost all Western horses wear a hackamore, since there is absolutely no danger of injuring the young horse's mouth by the rider's hand actions, which may be more vigorous than in Eastern riding methods when teaching such movements as the sliding stop and sharp turns. Nevertheless, while it spares the mouth, the hackamore is hardly a gentle means of control and may result in very irregular performances if the rider's hands are not light and sensitive. Furthermore, many hackamore-ridden horses tend to reach out with their noses, which is not a great fault in a Western horse whose head carriage is low, but is less desirable in an animal whose neck should be flexed.

In the show ring, hackamores are permitted only in the Western Di-

vision, in Jaquima classes of certain Breed Divisions, and in Open
Jumper classes. Kathy Kusner, for example, rode Aberali in a hackamore
and achieved results with that high-spirited Jumper that far surpassed
what his previous riders had attained with conventional bitting. Eddie
Macken, the expert Irish professional, rides his tough, hot-tempered little
super-Jumper Boomerang in a hackamore too. These cases are exceptional, but they show that a hackamore can sometimes provide the answer to a seemingly insoluble bitting problem.

PONY BITS

The majority of the standard bits are made in pony sizes and the
choice of a suitable one should be based on the same considerations that
determine the bitting of a horse, that is, on the degree of training of the
pony and the rider, on the type of work the pony does, and on the sensitivity of his mouth.

The most usual pony bit is some form of snaffle or a short-shanked
curb, with a leather strap instead of a curb chain, as on the Western
curb. The latter is especially indicated for older ponies whose mouths
have become so hardened from being pulled about by young beginners
over the years that they no longer respond to a snaffle.

THE BRIDLE

The purpose of the bridle is to support the bit in the horse's mouth
and to transmit the signals from the rider's hands by means of the reins.
The basic form of bridle consists of a strap going over the horse's head
behind the ears (the crownpiece), with the two ends that hang down on
either side (the cheek straps) attached to the rings of the bit. To hold it
in place, a second strap is attached to the top and runs across the head in
front of the ears (the browband). It is made of plain leather for Hunters,
but is colored for Saddle Horses and ponies. Another narrow strap (the
throat latch) splits off from the crownpiece and runs between the neck
and the jaw. The various elements hold together because the straps all
run through a loop at each end of the browband. Western bridles are
somewhat simpler. Often the throat latch and browband are discarded
and the bridle is held in place by a loop in the crownpiece through
which the horse's left ear is passed.

When purchasing a bridle, you should consider not only the price and size but also the quality, which depends on the quality of the leather rather than on its decoration. Prices range from $15 to $200. Superior bridles have beveled edges on both sides, far more stitches to the inch (giving greater strength), a smooth underside, and nickel or alloy buckles rather than plated ones. Sizes vary from one maker to another, so you should play safe by trying it on your horse before you oil it for the first time. Special bridles are made for certain breeds such as Arabians and Shetland Ponies. Don't be pressured into paying an exorbitant price needlessly. But do be prepared to pay the price required for first-class materials and workmanship if you want your bridle to last.

CAVESSONS

The modern custom is to fit all Eastern bridles with a cavesson, which is an entirely separate noseband going over the horse's nose about two inches below the cheekbones, with a crownpiece that runs behind the horse's ears and through both ends of the browband underneath the bridle crownpiece, and with a strap buckling under the jaw for correct adjustment. A cavesson isn't really necessary with a snaffle bit unless a standing martingale is used; but cavessons are required for Hunters in the show ring and most modern Eastern riding bridles include them.

The *longeing cavesson* is an extremely useful piece of tack, consisting of a crownpiece and a noseband with a D ring on top and two side rings for attaching a *longeing rein* about thirty feet long, with a loop at one end and a swivel snap at the other. An essential accessory is a special *longeing whip,* twelve to sixteen feet long, with a long cord lash. While a good set of longeing equipment may seem an expensive luxury, it is invaluable for training young horses and ideal for exercising and schooling older ones. It cannot permanently replace cross-country riding, but it is a most convenient occasional substitute.

NOSEBANDS

To return to the bridle, some riders find it worthwhile to add still another accessory, a *dropped noseband,* which is buckled below the bit and is more effective than a cavesson with horses who try to evade the bit by opening their mouths wide and slipping their tongues over the mouthpiece. A variation that fulfills the same function and is widely used south of the border is the *figure-eight noseband*. Mexico's Olympic Champion General Mariles was one of the early advocates of the figure eight for Jumpers, and all of the Mexican Equestrian Team horses still wear them. The USET coach Jack Le Goff also always uses them on the Three-Day horses in his charge.

Needless to say, the correct adjustment of a dropped or figure-eight noseband is vital to its effect, for if it is placed too low or strapped too tightly, it can do more harm than good.

REINS . . .

may be made of sturdy cotton webbing (which is perfectly satisfactory for everyday use), of plain leather, or of leather with laced, braided, or rubber hand parts. Many jumping riders prefer the racing reins with narrow handpieces that are covered with rubber, providing a nonslip grip even when they are wet with rain or the horse's sweat, but for some strange reason these are not permitted in Hunter show classes.

Reins may be of various widths, the choice being a personal matter depending largely on the size of the rider's hands. The principal rule to remember is that when two pairs of reins are used in a Pelham or a double bridle, they should be of different widths, with the snaffle reins the wider, or else one pair should be plain and the other laced or braided (the tradition being to use braided reins only with the snaffle bit). The snaffle reins are fastened by a buckle, while the curb reins are stitched together.

Western reins may be open or closed. A portion of the reins may be of chain, in order to increase their weight and thus facilitate ground-tying. When closed reins are used in Stock Seat Horsemanship classes, hobbles must be carried. But if split reins are used and the horse will ground tie, no hobbles are necessary. A popular custom in California is to attach to the center of closed reins a length of braided leather called a "romal," which is allowed to hang down on the horse's right side and is used as a quirt.

All reins should be frequently checked for signs of wear and any weak spots repaired before they reach an actual breaking point. One horseman who learned to his sorrow the unfortunate consequences of broken reins was Lord Mildmay, an accomplished English gentleman jockey. Riding a horse named Davy Jones in the Aintree Grand Na-

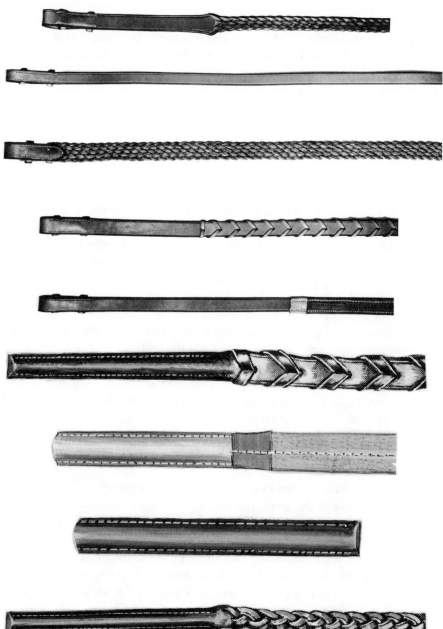

A wide variety of reins. From the top: Braided; Plain; Cord; Laced; Rubber Covered; Raised Plain; Raised Rubber; Raised Laced; and Raised Braided Reins (*All reins from the catalog of Miller's*)

tional Steeplechase of 1936, Mildmay was leading the field as he jumped the next to last obstacle of the grueling course. It seemed that victory could not possibly escape him, when to his horror, as he landed on the far side of the final jump, one of his reins tore apart at the buckle and Davy Jones ran off the course with Mildmay helpless to intervene. It was certainly one of the worst breaks in racing history!

MARTINGALES

One sees a great many martingales these days, especially in Jumping and Hunter Seat Equitation competitions. These devices are designed to keep a horse's head down and to bring in his chin in order to permit the bit to act effectively. While they may be useful with animals who hold their heads too high or those who have the habit of suddenly throwing their heads back, they should not be considered a permanent substitute for correct head carriage, which comes from training, nor obviously are they a substitute for good hands. In classes run under FEI Rules (see Chapter 13), only running martingales are permitted.

As an indispensable safety precaution, all martingales should be fitted with a small red rubber "stop" to fasten the neck strap to the rest of the martingale, thereby ensuring that the slack is held forward of the neck strap and cannot form a loop in which the horse might get his legs caught.

There are three types:

The RUNNING MARTINGALE is a leather strap with a loop at one end attached to the girth; the other end is split and finished off with two rings through which run the reins; an additional strap forms a supporting breastplate. When the reins are pulled, pressure is exerted on the bars of the mouth, encouraging the horse to lower his head, bring in his chin, and to remain "on the bit." While it is often useful with a snaffle bridle, running martingales that are adjusted too short can injure the bars and lead to dead-mouthed horses.

When two pairs of reins are used, there is a difference of opinion as to which ones should be attached to the running martingale, but most horsemen choose the snaffle reins. If the bridle reins are not sewn to the bit, an essential accessory is a REIN STOP on each rein, to prevent the martingale rings from sliding up and getting caught on the hook-in studs

of the bridle, in which event the sudden severe restraint could easily
cause a horse to panic and even to fall.

The STANDING MARTINGALE is a leather strap that joins the
girth directly to the underside of the horse's noseband. It is held in place
by a breastplate that encircles his neck in front of the shoulders. Although imposing a definite limit as to how far back the horse can throw
his head, it does not interfere with a horse's jumping any more than a
running martingale, if it is correctly adjusted—that is, somewhat loose
rather than taut when the horse's head is held in a normal position. Polo
Ponies invariably wear a standing martingale, and so do many Open
Jumpers. The Saddle Horse and Western version, which is called a "tie-
down," is much used in training but forbidden in the show ring and the
contest arena.

A running Martingale. Note the rein stops to keep the Martingale rings from hanging
up on the rein studs.

A standing Martingale. (*Photos by James Deutschmann*)

The IRISH MARTINGALE is quite unlike the other two, being nothing more than a leather strap with a ring at each end to link together the two reins in front of the horse's neck in order to prevent both of the reins from being flipped over onto the same side by an unexpected movement of the horse's head or a sudden stumble. It has no effect on the horse's head carriage or on the bit, but is simply a kind of safety measure that is, incidentally, a tradition among riders of British and Continental race horses.

HALTERS AND LEAD SHANKS

For leading and tying, your horse should have two halters composed of a crownpiece, a noseband with connecting cheek straps, and a throatlatch (or "lash"). The first can be of soft cotton rope, nylon webbing, or heavy oiled leather for ordinary wear in the stable and paddock, or for grooming; the second might be made of bridle leather for show. You must be sure to order the correct size (measuring the length of your horse's head from behind the ears to the tip of his nose), and to adjust it correctly, with the noseband falling no lower than two inches below the cheekbones.

You will also need at least two lead shanks about eight feet long. Cotton rope is much nicer than hemp for everyday use and for tying up, while the second one might be a chain shank with a leather strap six feet long, to be used for leading and grazing.

BRIDLING YOUR HORSE

Only practice will make you really expert at putting on your horse's bridle and bit; however, from the very first time you should make a special effort to be as deft and as gentle as possible. If your horse regards bridling as an unpleasant experience, he may become head-shy, which will seriously complicate the process. One simple way to make bridling more agreeable to him is to warm the bit in the palm of your hand for a few minutes before slipping it into his mouth, because the cold metal can give him a nasty shock. But let's start the entire procedure from the beginning.

You enter the stall holding the reins in your right hand and the crownpiece in your left, approaching the horse diagonally at his left shoulder. First, slip the reins over his head and rest them on his neck. Then unbuckle and slip off his stable halter.

Now you must shift the crownpiece to your right hand, take the bit in your left, and hold the crownpiece near the horse's head, slightly in front of and below its correct position. Insert your left thumb in the near side of the horse's mouth (or two fingers on the far side) to force him to open it. Some horses will open their mouths as soon as they feel the bit against their teeth. Then, as your left hand slips the bit into its proper place over the tongue and on the bars of the mouth, your right hand should slide the crownpiece over the ears, working gently, as the horse's ears are very sensitive. This is what takes practice! Pull the forelock under the browband and out of the horse's eyes; adjust the cheek straps; buckle the noseband and throatlatch; finally, if you are using a Pelham, Kimberwicke, or a full bridle, hook on the curb chain, making sure that the links lie flat in the chin groove and that it is properly adjusted. Strangely enough, the links will lie flatter if you make half a twist backward with the chain when attaching the second (near) hook.

With the bit and bridle in place, you must now check to see that

Bridling your horse. (*Photos by James Deutschmann*)

each piece is correctly adjusted. You may have to experiment before you find the exact fit for your horse, but these are the general rules:

The bit should, of course, be placed over the tongue, the snaffle or Pelham fitting snugly into the corners of the lips, making just one and a half to two wrinkles to ensure that the bit is high enough in the horse's mouth. Novices tend to place the bit too low, which invites the horse to put his tongue over the bit and leads to one of the most common and most troublesome of equestrian problems.

If you use a double bridle, the curb bit should be about a quarter of an inch below the snaffle. (Place them together in your hand and slip them into the horse's mouth as if they were a single bit.)

The bit should be wide enough for your horse's mouth, but not so wide that it can move from side to side and bruise his lips. If there seems to be any danger of injury to the corners of his mouth, you should use leather or rubber bit guards that fit over the ends of the mouthpiece.

Between the throatlatch and the throat there should be room for you to easily slip the four fingers of your hand.

Between the cavesson and the nose there should be *just* room to slip two fingers, and the noseband should lie about two inches below the cheekbones.

If you use a curb chain, the links should lie flat in the chin groove, leaving room for two fingers between the chain and the chin. The tension on the curb chain is correct when, with the reins in a normal riding position, the shank of the curb bit forms a forty-five-degree angle with the horse's lower jaw.

Finally, when you are certain that every part of the bit and bridle is correctly and comfortably adjusted, check on both sides to make sure that none of the bridle straps is twisted and that all the ends are in their keepers.

Now you can slip the stable halter over the bridle, lead your horse out of his stall, and place him in crossties while you go to fetch a saddle.

SADDLES

The purpose of a saddle is not only to protect the horse's back, but also to help the rider maintain a balanced seat without pulling on his horse's mouth, and to permit him to shift his weight smoothly as the horse's own balance is changed whenever he stops, starts, or jumps a fence.

When standing absolutely still, the center of gravity of most horses is located about fourteen inches behind and above the point of the elbow, moving forward during fast action and backward during high collection. The basic principle of modern riding is that the rider's weight should coincide as closely as possible with the horse's center of gravity (except at the walk and standing still, when it is necessarily farther back), and this is the main reason for the different designs of modern saddles. A rider naturally needs a less forward position for slow, high-action gaits (with Saddle Horses and Park Hacks, and for dressage) than he does for fast work such as racing, jumping, and hunting. While Western saddles were originally designed to permit working cattle rather than to promote good riding, the present trend is to construct them in a way that accommodates a modified Forward Seat, more aligned to the horse's own weight center.

The foundation of every saddle is the *tree,* which consists of two arches usually made of beechwood (for lightness), reinforced with metal (for strength), and shaped so as to prevent the saddle from touching the horse's spine. The front arch rises over the withers and is called the *head* or *pommel,* while the back arch, behind the rider, is flatter and wider and is called the *cantle.* To keep the arches in place, to distribute the rider's weight evenly and keep it well off the horse's spine, the two arches are joined by two shaped panels of wood reinforced with metal, which rest on the muscle pads on either side of the back. This framework is stuffed and then covered with leather. On each side there is a *skirt,* covering the *stirrup-leather bars,* which are attached to the tree and pulled through the panel and the outer *sweat flaps* against which the rider's legs rest. Today most stirrup bars are provided with safety gates that are supposed to open automatically should the rider fall. Still, it is a wise precaution to keep all kinds of stirrup-bar catches, even the safety ones, permanently open at one end.

The large saddlery houses provide a wide assortment of saddles for every type of equine conformation and activity, varying in the depth of seat (it being generally agreed that in all saddles the lowest point of the seat should be directly in the center), the angle and form of the flaps, the shape of the head and cantle, the degree of slope from front to rear, and the placement of the stirrups, as well as in the type and quality of materials and workmanship.

For *Eastern-style riding,* there are three general types:

1. The SHOW SADDLE, which is quite a flat saddle with a cut-back pommel and straight flaps designed to show off the horse's forehand and to throw the rider back toward the cantle. It is always used in Saddle classes and for Saddle Bred and Gaited horses who are ridden with long stirrups.

2. The ENGLISH or HACKING SADDLE, for riding Hunter Seat, is sometimes simply called a FLAT SADDLE, even though its seat, which is inclined slightly forward, is somewhat deeper than the show saddle. The best-known model is probably the Whippy pattern, which was the most widely used Eastern saddle before World War II and is still quite appropriate for all-round riding on Thoroughbred-type horses. But for hunting, jumping, and outdoor riding, most horsemen have changed over in recent years to a Forward Seat saddle.

3. The FORWARD SEAT or JUMPING SADDLE was originally created by the Italians. The flaps are cut well forward and incorporate padded knee rolls. The front is often cut back, the cantle is rather high, and the seat may be quite deep. Piero Santini, who did much to promote the Forward Seat developed by his teacher, Federico Caprilli, has lent his name to a popular all-round Forward Seat pattern, and most of the leading saddle-makers here and abroad have produced an adaptation of their own. The so-called "Steinkraus model," for example, originally made by Hermès, the deluxe French saddlers, according to the Olympic Champion's personal design and for his personal use, is one of the best light jumping saddles available—but very expensive.

In addition to these three basic Eastern types, special saddles are designed for certain activities such as cutting cattle, roping, dressage, polo, and racing (the latter are incredibly light, weighing between one and a half and two and a half pounds), as well as for a few specific breeds such as the Tennessee Walking Horse.

The SIDESADDLE, which was the only ladies' saddle a century ago, has never become entirely obsolete and, in fact, is enjoying a lively revival, perhaps because it is so elegant and romantic. In order to permit the rider to wear a long split skirt and to remain in balance and secure with both legs on the same side of the horse, the sidesaddle has a flat seat, only one stirrup (usually the left one), and two padded pommels or horns on the same side, one of them shaped like an upward-curved half moon for the right leg to hang over, and the lower one curved downward

Prix des Nations saddle.

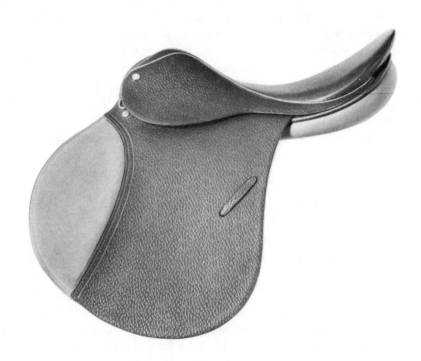

A German all-purpose saddle.

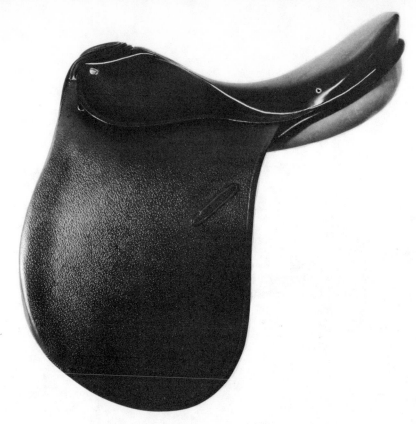

A typical Dressage saddle. (*From the catalog of Miller's*)

to prevent the left leg from flying up. The Washington International and New York National horse shows have classes for Ladies Hunters under Sidesaddle, and there has been an all-Sidesaddle show in New Jersey for a good many years. In Mexico, many horsewomen ride a stock sidesaddle, and there are Arabian classes for sidesaddle too. You are apt to find ladies riding sidesaddle in English and Irish Hunting meets, where it is believed that a lady rider can often control a large, heavy Hunter better in a sidesaddle than astride.

For *Western-style riding,* whether your horse is an Arabian, Appaloosa, Morgan, Quarter Horse, or even a Thoroughbred—or a mixture of any of these breeds—you will need quite a different kind of saddle.

The WESTERN SADDLE is much heavier than the Eastern. An ordinary stock saddle weighs from thirty to fifty pounds, and some of the ornate silver-embossed Parade versions even more. They sit high off

A Hunter ridden in a Sidesaddle. (*Photo by Budd*)

the horse's back, which is protected by one or several thick blankets, rather than by the Eastern-style saddle pad, and they are held in place by one or two leather or mohair *cinches* with a ring at each end through which the *latigo* or *cinch straps* are run. Western saddles are almost always sold completely equipped, including stirrups. The extra-wide sweat flaps are called *sudaderos,* the ornate leather coverings over the stirrups are *tapaderos,* and the stirrup fenders are *rosaderos.* The entire saddle is sometimes hand-tooled and decorated with engraved silver ornaments, so that a fancy model represents a lot of rodeo prize money!

With its very deep sloping seat, high cantle (for fixing a slicker or a blanket roll), and high pommel with a horn for attaching a lariat (to hold roped cattle), the Western saddle was originally conceived for practical ranch work. However, because of the ever-growing popularity of Western pleasure riding, the more refined breeding of Western horses,

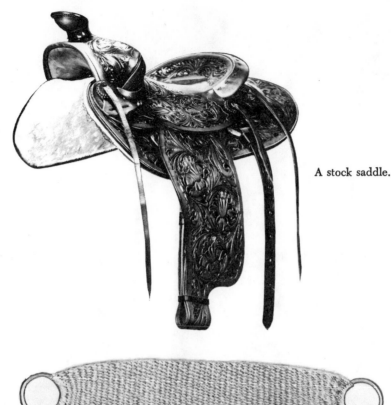

A stock saddle.

A woven cinch.
(*Pictures from the catalog of Miller's*)

and the realization that Western riding can be an art instead of just a rough-and-ready means of transportation, Western saddles are at the present time undergoing some major modifications. The horn, although essential for roping, is of no use at all in ordinary pleasure riding, and it is frequently reduced in height. The built-up seat, sloping sharply down toward the rear and consequently throwing the rider back against the cantle, is incompatible with a balanced seat and so many Western riders request only a moderate slope to permit better balance and easier weight-shifting. The modern tendency is also to hang the stirrups more nearly in line with the center of the saddle, so that the rider's weight is, as it should be, directly over the stirrups. In other words, while Western

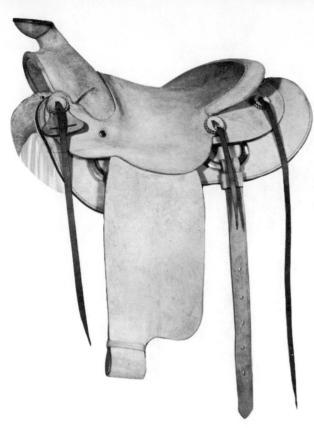

A roping saddle.
(*From the catalog
of Miller's*)

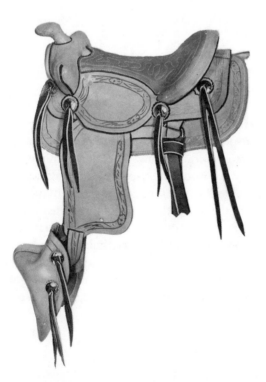

A child's Western saddle.
(*From the catalog
of Miller's*)

riding is invading the East, the principles of the Forward Seat school are influencing Western riding and therefore Western saddles.

The MCCLELLAN or MILITARY SADDLE merits a paragraph of its own. Not because it is especially recommended, but because it has recently been revived (especially for long-distance riding) and is, strictly speaking, neither Eastern nor Western in type.

Designed for the War Department for use during the Civil War, and named after one of Lincoln's generals, it was the standard saddle of the U. S. Cavalry for over eighty years, during which time it underwent little change—or improvement. The McClellan saddle came into widespread use when they were sold as surplus from Cavalry stocks, and today copies are again being made. It is very deep-seated and only lightly stuffed, requiring a thick saddle pad and weighing about 18 pounds. It is, in fact, much too awkward and uncomfortable a saddle for a well-bred horse. Its principal advantage is sturdiness at a low price, but the disadvantages are numerous, especially for a rider who owns a nice horse and is ambitious to perfect and refine his equestrian skill.

Buying and Fitting a Saddle

A good saddle will last for many years if given proper care. Because of its importance to the comfort of both rider and horse (not to mention the considerable investment it represents), you should buy the very best quality you can afford. The maker's reputation is one guarantee of quality, and there is also an advantage in dealing with a large and well-established saddlery house that is prepared to undertake adjustments, repairs, and reconditioning, and thus prolong the life of your expensive tack.

The very best saddles are made by hand and are most often imported from abroad. Among the world-famous names in saddle-making are Hermès of France; Kieffer and Passier of Germany; Pariani in Italy; the English firms of Crosby and Barnsby; and in the United States, Smith-Worthington, M. J. Knoud, Blue Ribbon (specializing in show saddles for Saddle Horses), and Simco (Western). Bargain saddles are imported from Argentina, India, and Spain, but the quality of the leather and workmanship cannot compare to that of the aforementioned saddlers.

While a first-class saddle will gradually shape itself to the horse's back during the breaking-in period, you should "try it on" before buying, and there will always be a saddle stand available in the shop for just this purpose. The saddle's suitability to your horse can be judged by measuring the desired length and by taking into account your horse's conformation. In general, Thoroughbreds tend to have narrower backs than common horses and therefore require a narrower tree arch; Walking Horses, Arabians, and Morgans, on the other hand, are most often round-backed and need a saddle with a wide front arch. If you have miscalculated, it is possible to adjust the fit to a certain extent by altering the padding.

In a well-fitting saddle the pommel clears the rise of the withers (or else the front is cut back completely) so that there is no danger of injury to the withers or interference with the horse's shoulder movements. The front arch should never pinch the withers or press on the shoulder muscles. The side panels rest on the muscular pads on either side of the horse's spine so that no part of the saddle touches the spine itself, and toward the rear, the panels should never press down on the loins. In fact, when you are sitting in the saddle, it should be possible to see daylight right down the horse's spine. If his spine is unusually protruding, the panels may be raised by additional padding.

It is a nice idea for each horse to have his own saddle, but this is not always possible. Unless there is a very great difference of conformation, several horses can share the same saddle, especially if you choose one with a cut-back pommel (to eliminate wither problems) and with a tree wide enough for the widest-backed horse (the others can wear a thicker saddle pad).

A first-grade Eastern saddle costs from $400 to $500, not counting the stirrrups and girth. Western saddles start lower, and fancy ones run even higher, but they are usually fully equipped. The best children's and pony saddles, with a smaller tree and shorter skirts, are less expensive— about $250—and there is a treeless felt saddle made especially for small children and ponies that costs no more than $50.

Your reaction to the prices quoted above may very likely be (after catching your breath), "What about buying a secondhand saddle? Wouldn't that be a good idea?" Yes, indeed, it is an excellent idea—*if* you can find a good one. The trouble is that a broken-in saddle of top quality is a rarity and almost as expensive as a new one. Most saddlery houses have a stock of used, reconditioned saddles they have received as trade-ins, and with luck you might find an interesting buy. In any case, it is always better to buy a top-quality used saddle than a cheap new one.

Breaking In Your Saddle

New leather equipment is stiff and free from oil and requires conditioning before you use it for the first time. A few saddle-makers will condition your saddle for you for a fee, but most horsemen are fussy about their tack and they prefer to do the job themselves. Some of them have their own secrets, like the U. S. Equestrian Team coach Bertalan de Nemethy, whose saddle-conditioning formula is a sponge bath of homogenized milk. But far more usual is the following procedure:

With a sponge and a good supply of saddledressing or dubbing (which many horsemen prefer to neat's-foot oil because of its waterproofing effect), oil the entire saddle, being particularly generous on the underside and wherever there is a bend or stitching. If you warm your new saddle first, either in the sunshine or under a sun lamp, the leather will soak up a great amount of dubbing in a very short time. Otherwise, you must leave the saddle alone for twenty-four to forty-eight hours to allow the leather to absorb as much as possible. Afterward, with a glycerine saddle soap and another sponge, you should work up a good wet lather and remove the oil that remains on the surface. Next, make a heavy *dry* lather and rub it well into the leather, removing the excess with an almost dry sponge and finally polishing off with a chamois.

At the end of a few weeks of normal use and ordinary care, you may want to repeat the oiling process; but this time you should treat only the underside of the saddle, leaving alone the seat and the outer surface of the flaps and skirts.

After its original conditioning, your saddle will need only normal care with saddle soap or cleaner each time you use it. If it is ever drenched with rain, or if you notice at the end of a year or so that the leather seems to be drying out, you may repeat the oiling treatment. But remember that too much oil can be just as harmful to fine leather as too little. While you want all of your leather tack to be soft and supple to prevent cracking and to ensure your horse's comfort and your own, you mustn't rob it of all of its stiffness, or it will become positively limp.

Just as important as the preservation of the leather in a saddle is the soundness of its tree. The best models are constructed for strength as well as lightness, but careful handling can avoid costly repair bills:

Always carry a saddle draped over your arm, or else with the front toward the ground and a finger through the pommel.

Put it away on a saddle stand or rack, with the girth detached and laid across the seat and the stirrups pulled up; then cover it all with a dust cloth.

Lay it down (when there isn't a saddle rack nearby) preferably in a corner, the seat facing the angle of the wall, with the pommel to the ground and the cantle high.

Eastern saddles are held in place on the horse's back by means of a GIRTH buckled onto leather tongues called *saddle billets,* which are stitched to each side of the saddle underneath the flaps. Needless to say, the billet straps undergo very hard wear (you will probably have to replace them several times during the lifetime of your saddle), and so they should be made of the strongest possible kind of leather.

The material of the girth may be a sturdy washable cotton webbing (the most usual kind for Saddle Horses) or folded leather (perhaps the best all-round type and very durable). Since your riding safety depends upon the soundness of the girth, you should treat a leather girth just as you do your saddle: unfold it and condition it on both sides with dubbing or neat's-foot oil before you use it for the first time, keep it clean and supple with saddle soap after each use, and repeat the oiling treatment periodically.

Many top horsemen prefer girths with an elastic inset on the near side. These are practical and fashionable but, oddly enough, not permitted in Corinthian classes, where appointments are controlled and scored. For sensitive-skinned horses, there are specially shaped girths tapered under the elbows to prevent chafing; "balding girths" of braided leather for horses prone to girth sores; and girths of closely woven cord that give a tight grip without chafing. But the most usual antichafing accessory is a tubular sheep's-wool *girth cover* which slips right over any kind of girth. *Girth guards,* covering the buckles, are mandatory in Corinthian Hunter classes but seldom employed under ordinary circumstances.

With some horses a girth is not sufficient to keep the saddle in place, and so BREASTPLATES and CRUPPER STRAPS are made to prevent the saddle from slipping either backward or forward on the horse's back. The breastplate is attached to the front arch of the saddle and to the girth, and may be useful for slender or "herring-gutted" horses, whose underbelly is tucked up between the ribs and the hips. Cruppers, attached to the back of the saddle and looping around the horse's tail in order to prevent the saddle from slipping forward over very low withers, are always worn with driving harness and never by fine riding horses, although plump-bellied ponies sometimes need them.

Non-slip mohair girth. (*From the catalog of Miller's*)

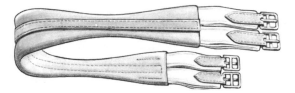

Chafeless girth. (*From the catalog of Miller's*)

SADDLE PADS are frowned upon in the show ring, but many horse-men use them as a matter of course for ordinary riding, for they per-form the double function of absorbing sweat and protecting the horse's back. Attached to the saddle by two straps through which the saddle billets are run, they are usually made of sponge rubber, real or synthetic sheepskin (the woolly side placed next to the back), or felt. In England saddle pads are often called "numnahs," which is derived from the Hindustani word for "felt." You may have one made to order to fit your saddle, or you can buy a standard size and cut it out to the exact shape yourself, following the outline of your saddle. It should extend about an inch or two all around the saddle—after laundering, for it is sure to shrink. The use of a saddle pad not only protects your horse's back, but also protects the saddle from wear and perspiration stains and, inciden-tally, enables you more easily to use the same saddle on different horses. So you see, saddle pads may not be considered smart, but they are very sensible.

Among Western riders there is not the same prejudice. In fact, the SADDLE BLANKET is one of the most characteristic items of Western tack. It may be a folded blanket of Mexican or Navaho Indian design, or simply from Army-surplus stock. Many cowboys prefer a felt or sheep-skin pad. Whatever you use, there should be at least two inches of blanket between a heavy Western saddle and your horse's back. A time-saving tip is to mark the center, so that the blanket will hang down evenly on both sides. The most attractive kind of all is the corona blanket, shaped to fit the saddle, with a striped rolled border all the way around.

POMMEL PADS of knitted wool are used to prevent the saddle from rubbing on a horse's withers. It used to be a fashionable teatime oc-cupation of the wives of race-horse owners to make their own pommel pads in their racing colors. It would be difficult to find a modern horse-owner who does his own knitting and purling, but many of them find a pommel pad necessary for improving the fit of a saddle on horses with prominent withers.

STIRRUP LEATHERS and stirrups are usually sold integrally with Western saddles, but they are separate items of Eastern tack. A rather expensive English import called Gibson Red Chrome Leather is deservedly the first choice of particular horsemen for stirrup leathers, while rawhide or rawhide-lined leathers are very common. All leather stretches (rawhide stirrup leathers may lengthen as much as twelve inches during the first year of use), and so you should remember to change the stirrup leathers regularly from one side to the other, since the mounting side naturally tends to stretch more than the off side. The punched holes should, of course, coincide perfectly, enabling you to adjust the stirrups to exactly the same length.

The best STIRRUP IRONS are made of stainless steel and the proper size is one inch wider than the rider's foot. Lightweight stirrups are more difficult to recover than those with a certain amount of weight. Ordinary straight stirrups are the most widely used and the best, although the Cavalry favored the offset kind, with a backward-sloping tread and the outside vertical bar shorter than the inside one to force the ankles in and the heels down. However, correct distribution of weight achieves the same result with straight stirrups. Novice riders may feel more secure with so-called "safety stirrups," which are designed to open automatically in case of a spill. However, most experienced riders,

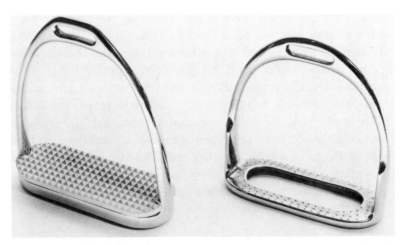

Some riders like a rubber tread in their stirrups, as at left, while others prefer the conventional irons shown on the right. (*From the catalog of Miller's*)

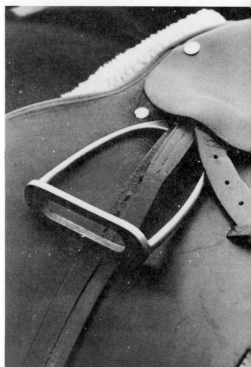

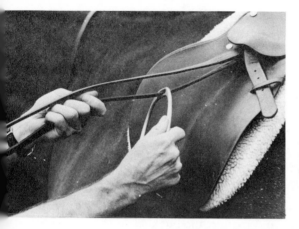

Running up the stirrup irons. (*Photos by James Deutschmann*)

who are even more interested in safety measures than are beginners, have another sure way of avoiding getting "hung up" in a stirrup during a fall. First of all, they use the correct size of stirrup iron; and then they always leave the safety catch on the stirrup bars open.

There is one more customary precaution that will prevent your horse from becoming annoyed or frightened by dangling stirrup irons. Whenever you saddle him, you should push the irons up as high as possible to the saddle on the underneath stirrup leathers; then bring the ends of the stirrup leathers through the irons and leave them that way until you are ready to ride. You should "run up" the irons again as soon as you dismount, and fasten them in the same way whenever you lead a saddled horse.

Saddling Your Horse

While we have been looking over the different kinds of saddles and tack, your horse has been standing patiently in crossties with his bridle on, feeling sadly neglected! At last we will get around to saddling him—

but first, you must brush his back lightly to remove any dust or straw, and smooth his coat down flat in order to eliminate any possible source of irritation under the saddle.

When you bring your saddle, approach your horse from the near (his left) side and lay the saddle as gently as possible a few inches in front of the withers, sliding it backward into its proper place. (If it is an Eastern type, the stirrup irons should be pulled up and the girth should be detached and lying across the seat; with a Western saddle, the far stirrup should be hung over the horn and the cinches and saddle strings should be folded back over the seat so that your horse won't be struck by the cinch rings when you swing the saddle onto his back.) If you use a saddle pad or blanket, you should place it on the horse's back in the same way, sliding it backward into its proper position, and then lay the saddle on top.

A light shake will settle the saddle well in place, and now you should attach the girth, first to the billet straps on the off side, and then on the near side. If you use a shaped saddle pad, you must slip the billet straps through the pad straps before attaching the girth. The English saddle should have three billets, and the girth is buckled to the two outside ones only, leaving the center strap as an emergency replacement. If you use the folded leather type of girth, you must make sure that the open side of the fold is facing the rear, in order to avoid pinching the horse's sensitive skin.

A correctly fitted girth lies about four inches behind the horse's elbow and leaves enough room for you to slip two fingers in between the girth and the horse. But almost all horses have the defensive habit of swelling up their bellies during girthing, so you should fasten the girth snugly at first and then tighten it again a few moments later, making a final check when you are in the saddle. After fastening the girth you should make sure that it doesn't pinch the horse's loose skin behind his elbow and that there are no wrinkles underneath. One way to smooth the skin is to run your fingers underneath the girth from front to back. Another trick is to lift each foreleg and stretch it a bit forward.

With a Western saddle the process is similar, except that you have one or two cinches to fasten instead of a girth. If there are two of them (a "double-rigged" saddle), the front cinch should always be fastened first and unfastened last. The cinches are attached to the long latigo straps by various methods, including a tongued cinch ring that functions like a belt buckle, a cinch hitch, a cinch hook, or a Tackaberry buckle. The last two are perhaps the quickest to manipulate.

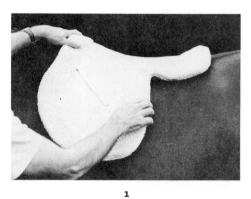

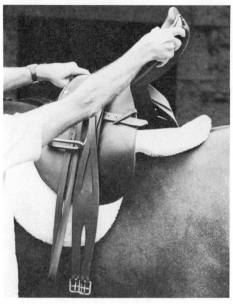

1

2

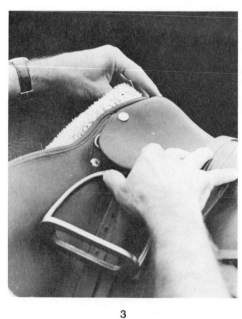

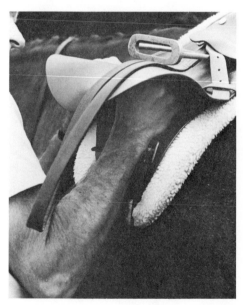

3

4

Saddling your horse. (*Photos by James Deutschmann*)
Position the saddle pad (1). Place the saddle on top, taking care to pull the pad well up into the arch of the saddle (2 and 3). Buckle the girth, starting with the rear billet (4).

CARE OF TACK

Tack-Care Equipment

A supply of Dubbing or Neat's-foot Oil
A supply of Glycerine Saddle Soap and of one-step Harness
Cleaner
Sponges
A supply of cheap Turkish Towels or Rags
2 soft Brushes (one for brushing, one for scrubbing)
Metal Polish (the impregnated pads are convenient)
A Chamois (for polishing)
A Stitcher and Leather Punch (handy for emergency repairs)
A Cleaning Hook (for hanging bridles)
A Saddle Rack (for cleaning saddles)
Rubber Gloves (for horsewomen with well-manicured hands)
A Bucket (for water—if possible, warm)

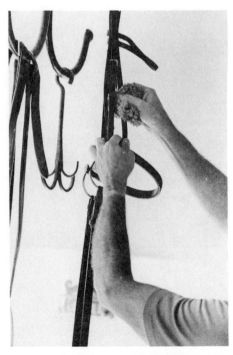
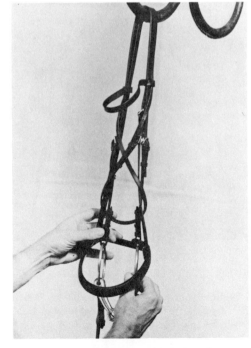

Cleaning a bridle. Bridles are most conveniently hung on a tack hook for cleaning. They will look neater on their racks if the cavesson and throatlatch are closed, but only run through the keepers rather than being buckled. (*Photos by James Deutschmann*)

As soon as possible after riding, every piece of equipment should be cleaned before being put away. While it may seem fastidious at first, you will soon get into the habit and probably even take pleasure in caring for your tack.

The bridle must be completely taken apart each time it is muddy or very soiled, and after each use the bits and curb chain should be washed in water and wiped dry. The traditional way to clean the leather parts is to hang the bridle on a cleaning hook, wash with a sponge soaked in warm water, then treat with a dry saddle-soap lather well rubbed in until no trace remains on the surface, and finally polish with a chamois. Busy modern horsemen often use a lanolin-fortified "One-Step" harness conditioner and cleaner that cleans and preserves the leather at the same time.

Before you use a new bridle for the first time, it should be taken apart and oiled all over, especially around and underneath the buckles, on the undersides of all the straps, and wherever there is stitching. Condition it just as you did your new saddle and leather girth, and repeat the treatment whenever the bridle leather shows signs of drying out or if it has been drenched with rain or sweat. After riding in the rain, you should clean your tack with a glycerine saddle soap while the leather is still moist in order to prevent cracking.

The metal parts of the bridle, as well as the stirrup irons, can be shined up from time to time with metal polish, with the exception of the mouthpiece of the bit.

Now let's tackle the saddle. You should thoroughly brush the saddle pad as soon as it is dry, place the saddle on its cleaning rack, detach the leathers and irons, remove the girth and brush that too. Web girths need to be laundered as they become soiled (Saddle Horse grooms often treat them with shoe whitener or whiten them with pipe-clay for extra dazzle during horse shows). All the leather tack, including leather girths, receives the same everyday care: wash with a sponge soaked in warm water, rub with a saddle-soap lather or harness cleaner, leave to dry for ten or fifteen minutes, and finally polish with a chamois.

As you are rubbing and polishing, keep an eye open for any traces of broken stitching or cracks in the leather, inspecting with special care the billet straps and reins. You may avoid a nasty accident by always attending to repairs at once.

When all of your tack is clean and shining (it will not take as long as it may seem), you should reassemble the bridle and hang it up by the crownpiece on its circular bracket, reassemble the saddle and place it on

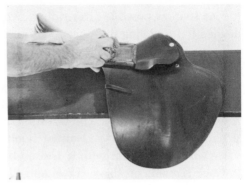

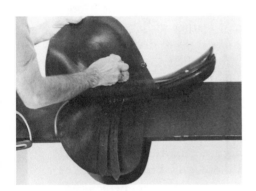

Cleaning a saddle. Start by wiping with a damp sponge all over. Then work up a fine lather on your saddle-soap bar. (It is handy to place the soap bar in a wooden holder.) First clean the panels, then the underside of the skirts, finishing with the top of the skirts and the seat. When you have finished, run up the stirrup irons and place the girth through them as illustrated. (*Photos by James Deutschmann*)

its rack with the stirrup irons pulled up, the girth detached and laid across the seat, and cover it with a dust cloth.

At last, a sigh of relief. Or rather, a sigh of satisfaction for a job well done!

11. Clothing—His and Yours

One of the refinements that civilization brings to primitive creatures is clothing—and the horse is no exception. However, in his case it is not because of modesty that we drape his body in sheets and blankets and wrap his legs in flannel, but a matter of common sense.

In his natural state the horse is amply protected from the elements by a coat that sheds in warm weather, grows heavier in winter, and is practically waterproof. Wild ponies instinctively stand with their backs to the wind and rain, causing their long, shaggy tails to blow between their legs and provide protection for the undersides of their bellies, where they are sensitive to cold. But the civilized horse is usually clipped and his mane and tail are often pulled. He can become overheated by the fast work we ask him to do, and he can catch a chill from standing around idly in a stable stall for hours on end. Furthermore, he must be protected from the contrast of temperature between his comfortable stable and the cold outdoor air. You should always remember, though, that a riding horse's clothing is merely a replacement for his natural coat, and that too much of it is just as unhealthy as none at all.

Naturally, all of his wardrobe should be kept well repaired and clean, and every garment fitted to stay securely in place without causing discomfort. Surcingles and body rollers must never be strapped really tight. There is only one way of putting on blankets and sheets that avoids roughing the horse's coat and causing him irritation. You should always throw them up on his neck and pull them backward, to smooth down the hair; when removing a blanket or sheet, slide it off in the direction of the horse's tail.

STABLE SHEETS . . .

are made of cotton duck or some other light but sturdy washable material. They are held on by two surcingles and a buckle in front to prevent them from blowing over the horse's back. Sheets are worn for protection from dust, flies, and drafts when the horse is in the stable. The USET prefers a lightweight "Haversham" model of quilted nylon with a brushed nylon lining. They are also worn underneath his woolen blankets. It is a good idea to have two stable sheets for your horse, so that one of them will always be clean, and to buy them about four inches too long, (measuring from the withers to the tail), to allow for shrinkage during laundering.

STABLE BLANKETS . . .

are made of plain wool, or of canvas or heavy cotton lined with fleece. The front is fitted to go around the chest, and the blanket hangs down to the elbows all the way around to protect the horse's legs. Top-quality blankets are usually held on by a BODY ROLLER, which is a girth-like band with two pads fitting on either side of the spine and two buckled straps for fastening; many models incorporate one or two sewn-in surcin-

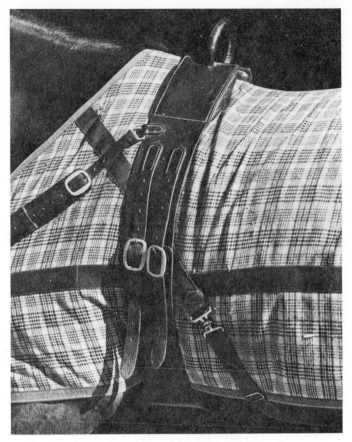

An anti-cast body roller. (*Photo by James Deutschmann*)

gles. The British have invented an ANTI-CAST BODY ROLLER, which is a special leather surcingle with a metal arch that prevents a horse from rolling over on his back far enough to get cast. Very widely used in England, it is expensive but effective and is worth the investment if you own a horse that has a tendency to get cast.

Your horse should always be given a nice warm blanket when you bed him down on chilly nights. Clipped horses should wear a blanket whenever they are turned out in cold weather, for the warm covering will not only prevent chills but also discourage the growth of a heavy coat.

When you blanket your horse with a plain wool blanket, always put a cotton sheet underneath. First of all, it will avoid irritation from the wool underside of the blanket and will help to keep the hair of his coat lying flat. But the principal reason is that a horse's body gives off a lot of heat which condenses when it meets the cooler outside air; if a sheet is

Horses should be blanketed when turned out in cold weather. (*Photo by Sue Maynard*)

worn underneath the blanket, there will be two layers of clothing between his body and the outer air and the condensation will take place on the outside blanket instead of right next to his skin, where dampness is apt to give him a chill.

COOLERS . . .

are light, unfitted coverings that are thrown over the horse after exercise, while he is being walked around to cool out. They are held in place by ties in front of the chest, a soft browband in front of the ears, and a soft rope under the tail. Sometimes you will need the added security of a light surcingle or, on gusty days, a stable-blanket pin holding together the long sides of the sheet under your horse's belly.

There are three main types:

1. The normal Cooler, of lightweight wool;
2. The Breezer, of *very* lightweight wool or woven acrylic;

3. The Fly Sheet, made of fine mesh and used as a protection from flies or for the first few minutes of cooling out a horse in extremely hot weather. (Even when the air is warm, a light breeze blowing on his damp coat is still enough to cause a chill.)

BANDAGES . . .

are the most versatile articles in the horse's entire wardrobe, since they may be used for support, protection, warmth, and faster drying, as well as for the treatment of weary or ailing limbs when used with a heating or cooling lotion. They are always "set" (wound) over four to six layers of cotton wool, to increase the warmth, protection, or drying process, or to effect a treatment if the cotton is first soaked in a leg brace (an astringent solution that stimulates the circulation in the limbs). Now you can buy bandages of synthetic pile, quilted cotton, or with a laminated foam center that greatly simplify this common stable procedure. But it is most economical and most common nowadays to make or purchase leg wraps in which the cotton is covered with cheesecloth and which can be reused many times. Bandages can also be torn from large bolts of flannel or other suitable material.

The setting of LEG BANDAGES is an important and frequent stable operation and all horsemen should learn how to do it correctly. You must start at the top with a three-yard length of bandage and wind toward the bottom and then up to the top again, where you fasten the ends. Always wind from front to back so that when you pull on the bandages to tighten them, the pressure will be on the shinbone and not on the tendon, which can actually cause a bowed tendon if you're not careful.

The traditional way to fasten leg bandages was to tie the end-tapes in a bow and tuck in the ends. But many horsemen removed the tapes and fastened the bandages with special bandage pins or wide adhesive tape in order to cause less of a pressure point and further minimize the danger of a bowed tendon. Nowadays perfectly smooth self-adhesive Velcro closings have replaced pins and tapes in many cases. In fact, bandages themselves have been replaced for many protective purposes by ready-made shaped boots of every imaginable kind.

Whatever the fastening method you favor, you should always take care not to wrap the bandages too tightly and thus impair the circulation of the legs, which may swell or "fill up" after a hard workout. Never

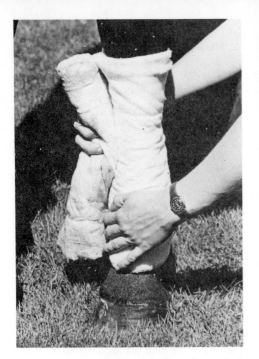

Left, "standing bandages," worn after work. (Cottons last longer if they are covered with cheesecloth.) Right, these homemade bandages have been torn from a large bolt of flannel. Notice the double safety pin fastening. (*Photos by James Deutschmann*)

leave bandages in place for more than twelve hours at a time, and always give your horse a vigorous leg massage after removing them.

There are two principal kinds of leg bandages:

1. Stable (or Standing) Bandages. Of wool or flannel, for warmth and protection. They run from below the knee or hock down over the fetlock.

2. Exercise (or Work) Bandages. Of elastic or elasticized crepe, or (newest and best of all) of laminated foam-centered synthetic material, for support and protection during work.

Saddlery houses also sell a patented Elastic Hose, permanently shaped to fit over the tendon, fetlock, and hock joints without slipping.

TAIL BANDAGES are narrower than leg bandages and are wrapped around the top part of the tail for protection during shipping as well as to beautify and improve the shape of the tail when the bandage (or the tail) is moistened before winding. Like leg bandages, these are often wisely replaced by ready-made Velcro-closed TAIL WRAPS. But care must still be taken not to fasten them too tightly. (See Chapter 7, "Grooming Your Horse.")

Saddle Bred horses, Walking Horses, and Fine Harness Horses, whose tails are set, wear special tail tie-down nets shaped to fit the set of the tail.

BOOTS AND HOODS

Aside from these basic articles of clothing, there are any number of boots, socks, and head, neck, and leg coverings devised to serve a special purpose, such as protection during training or shipping, for teaching or improving gaits, and protection from brushing, overreach, or just plain mud! Among the many different kinds of boots alone you will find hock boots (for shipping), heel boots (for cutting and roping horses), and shin, ankle, coronet, knee, and tendon boots, as well as various combinations, aside from the familiar rubber bell boots and quarter boots that are standard equipment for Hunters, the hinged quarter boots that all Five-Gaited Saddle Horses wear for riding and driving, the polo boots that are indispensable for Polo Ponies, special boots to provide traction for Parade Horses on slippery pavements and protection for Trail Horses on rocky mountain paths.

If a horse does a lot of traveling, he will certainly need a tail guard, a shipping helmet, and perhaps a rain sheet. Saddle Horses and Harness Ponies are usually covered from head to heels to protect their impeccably groomed coats between show classes, and in their tack trunks will often be packed either plain or "sweating" hoods, the latter especially conceived to reduce the jowls of Saddle Bred horses.

When planning your own horse's wardrobe, you needn't be dismayed by the profusion of elegant monogrammed trappings you see illustrated in saddlers' catalogues or hanging in the smartly decorated tack rooms of leading show stables. Some owners find it worthwhile for reasons of prestige or business to spend considerable sums of money on their horses' appearance. But it is very likely that your own mount will be just as attractive and correct in more modest garb. The sensible horse-owner provides his horse with clothing that is suitable to the kind of life he leads and to the social circles in which he travels.

The Wardrobe of a Well-Dressed Horse
A Saddle and Fittings (about $600 for superior quality)
A Saddle Pad ($20 minimum for sheep's wool; $25 or so for a Western blanket, and at least twice as much for the elegant corona blanket cut to fit the shape of a Western saddle)

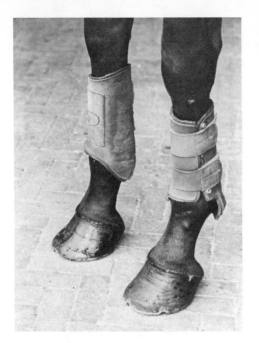 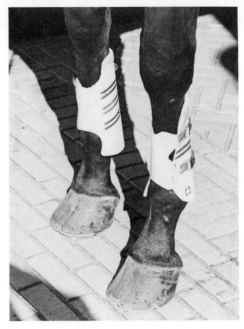

Left, protective shin boots with Velcro fastening. Right, plastic shin boots. (*Photos by James Deutschmann*)

A Bit and Bridle (or 1 for everyday use and 1 for show; about
$75 complete with cavesson and reins; Western bridles range
from $50 to $80 for a Parade model, and hackamores from
$20 to $60)
A Longeing Cavesson and Rein ($45 to $80 and well worth it)
2 Cotton Stable Sheets ($20)
2 Blankets ($20 to $35 each; 1 very warm, 1 medium)
1 or 2 Coolers (about $35 each; plus a Fly Sheet at $20 or so if
flies are a problem in your region)
1 Body Roller ($30)
Boots (as required for protection and work)
Leg Bandages (absorbent Stable Bandages and elastic Exercise
Bandages)
Tail Bandages (slightly narrower than leg bandages—or a
ready-made Tail Wrap)
A supply of Sheet Cotton (to wear underneath leg bandages)
2 Halters and Lead Straps (1 of nylon—$15 complete with tie-
rope—or an ordinary leather grooming halter—$10; 1 of bri-
dle leather, complete with lead strap and chain shank—$30)
For traveling: Shipping Boots ($30 for a complete set of foam
or fleece-lined vinyl; $100 for fleece-lined leather), Helmet
($11), and a Tail Guard ($8)

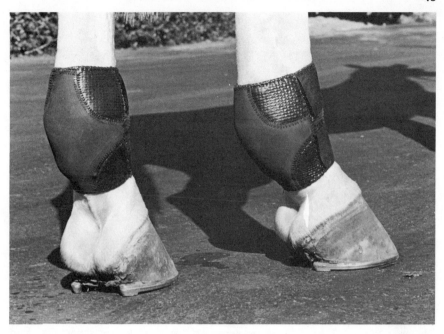

Above, Sesamoid boots. Right, open front boots. (*From the catalog of Miller's*)

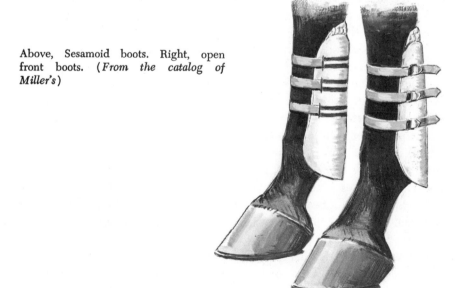

THE WELL-DRESSED HORSEMAN

Clothes may not make the man, but they can certainly help the rider —at least to the extent that well-cut garments and well-fitting boots give maximum protection, comfort, and freedom of action and enable him to devote all of his attention to his work, undistracted by the pain of a blistering heel or the restriction of tight-fitting shoulders. Riding clothes can also be informative when you know, for example, that a professional hunt servant wears the bow on his cap turned down, while an amateur turns it up (and just the opposite is true in England); or that in Driving, a gentleman whip or owner wears a gray hat and suit, and a professional coachman a black hat.

Fashions in riding clothes don't change very fast, and so there is little to lose and much to gain by buying the best quality you can afford. The smooth, skin-tight new look resulting from the use of stretch fabrics and Velcro fastenings that replaced the traditional Cavalry line is probably here to stay. Experienced horsemen go to extravagant lengths to find the perfect pair of boots or the best-cut coat, and their investments usually pay off not only in comfort but in actual years of wear. With growing children the problem is, of course, quite different. But you can still select a good, workmanlike quality, if not the very top. In any case, avoid the shoddy kind of riding clothes that is more suitable for wearing to a costume party than for serious work in a schooling ring.

When shopping either for yourself or for a child, it is wise to deal with a well-established, specialized firm, where the personnel is qualified to give expert advice and the fitters are experienced in the correct adjustment of riding jackets and breeches. Most of the large saddlery houses offer a complete selection of riding attire as well, and you can often order quite successfully by mail.

Before you slip into your handsome riding clothes, you will need a sturdy outfit for working around the stable. Most horse-owners find that nothing surpasses blue jeans and a work shirt when attending to their daily chores, with a heavy sweater or jacket to wear during cold weather —in fact, during much of the year, because the early-morning hours can be very cool. Quilted down-filled nylon windbreakers or vests are very useful and so are leather jackets, since neither of them retain stable odors. You will need a pair of work gloves, which can be worn over thin woolen gloves during freezing weather (if you cannot find the excellent foam-interlined kind), and also heavy woolen socks (or two thin pairs worn together), because your shoes are bound to get wet when you hose down the stable floor, and there is always the danger of being stepped on by a horse. It is a pity to spoil expensive riding boots or leather jodhpur shoes by wearing them around the barn. A sturdy old pair of leather shoes or hard rubber boots are much more sensible. Both attractive and practical, if you can find them, are Newmarket boots with rubber feet and waterproof nylon or canvas tops, which can be used for wet-weather riding as well as for stable work. But the current status symbol in this field (especially in the East) is a pair of low, rubber-soled boots made by L. L. Bean of Freeport, Maine.

Western horsemen usually choose much the same outfit for riding: Levis or Frontier Pants, a cotton or woolen shirt, with or without a plain or windbreaker-type jacket or a vest and, needless to add, a wide-brimmed hat and Western boots. Cattle-working cowboys wear high-heeled boots that permit them to get a good grip on the ground by digging in their heels. But Western boots are also made with ordinary heels, and these are often preferred for pleasure riding. Carved boot leather is more pliable than plain, and also more decorative. The trouser legs are usually worn outside short boots, in order to prevent pebbles and sand from entering, but inside high ones, after smoothing the trousers and pulling over them a pair of high socks. Leather chaps are hot and heavy, but they are indispensable in really rough country and are required in certain show classes and contests. Deer and elkskin are soft and luxurious, but most Western riders prefer to go to the trouble of breaking in leather chaps that will last a lifetime and will not ride up on the legs. Chinks are short apron-like chaps which only reach the middle of the calf and are open at the back. Cooler and lighter than long chaps, they are especially favored by women riders. Eastern riders have also adopted tight schooling chaps, worn over blue jeans. In fact, this has become one of the most common schooling outfits East or West.

For hacking Eastern style, riders who practice the Hunter Seat wear either breeches and boots or jodhpurs and jodhpur shoes, with a riding shirt or sweater, a tweed or woolen split-tail riding jacket, and an ordinary soft hat or cap, or a hard hunting cap or derby. T-shirts, practical for everyday wear (just about everywhere), are being replaced by the current "in" fashion: a collarless "Equestrian" shirt worn with a matching or contrasting choker and a stock pin. The universal hacking attire for Saddle Horse riders is jodhpurs.

There are no formal rules for pleasure-riding dress, but your own good taste and common sense will impose certain limitations. It is obvious, for instance, that breeches with reinforcements inside the knees are necessary in view of the wear and tear the garment is subjected to at this spot and because nothing gives a better grip than leather on leather. Some horsemen with sensitive skin who spend a good deal of time in the saddle find it necessary to increase the protection by taping a pad of sponge rubber to the inside of their legs. Flat-soled shoes or sneakers are unsuitable for riding because they would permit the entire foot to slip through the stirrup during a fall and could cause a rider to get "hung up" and be seriously injured. In fact, you will soon discover that there is a sound practical reason for almost every item of traditional riding attire. Beginners should start out by conforming to the customs that have been established by more experienced horsemen.

Even though fussy riders no longer have to spend endless hours in the fitting room, thanks to the invention of four-way stretch fabrics and Velcro closings that eliminate trouser leg buttons, it is still advisable to have your ready-made coats and breeches checked by the fitter (if there is one). Breeches should fit well in the seat and be somewhat snug in the knees. A coat should be large enough to fit comfortably in the shoulders. As far as fabric is concerned, your principal consideration should be the climate in which you live. In areas where there is a great divergence of temperature between the summer and the winter seasons, you will be far more comfortable if you own a lightweight coat and breeches for warm-weather wear, and a second heavy woolen outfit for the winter months. Colorwise, you may exercise your own judgment, taking into account the local scene which is at the moment still relatively conservative in the East, more colorful in the Middle West, and quite flamboyant on the West Coast as well as in some Southern and Southwestern states.

Whether you wear boots or jodhpurs is a matter of personal taste and convenience. Some horsemen find gaiters the most comfortable for everyday hacking. Generally speaking, novice riders look best in jodhpurs, because boots seem to emphasize every weakness in a rider's seat and legs. But it is a fact that most of the leading Hunter horsemen and those who do a great deal of riding prefer boots. Jodhpurs are probably more sensible for young children, principally because of the extravagance of buying a costly pair of boots that may be outgrown in a short period of time. But outside of the show ring, they, like many of their elders, ride in blue jeans rather than in breeches or jodhpurs.

In order to make sure of getting the correct size, you should try on your jodhpur shoes or boots over the socks you intend to wear with them (or over two thin pairs of socks, which many riders find more comfortable and warm than one heavy pair). They should be snug in the heels, looser in the toes and ankles, and not too tight in the calves. If you decide to buy boots, don't forget to order at the same time a pair of boot hooks for pulling them on and a boot jack to help in taking them off. New boots need to be broken in gradually, and it is wise to resist the temptation of inaugurating a new pair the day of an important horse show or hunting meet.

Both boots and jodhpur shoes should be kept on trees and given regular care to preserve the suppleness and appearance of the leather. They are cleaned with saddle soap and shined with boot polish. Fox-hunting people who hunt in rough country often order boots in reverse calf, from which scratches can be removed by applying boot polish with a "boot bone," a smooth shank bone of a stag sold by most saddlery shops. Wet boots and shoes must be dried on trees away from any direct source of heat. An extra saddle-soaping with a dry lather well rubbed in will help

A well-appointed Hunter rider. (*Photo by Sue Maynard*)

to restore the softness of the leather after they have been soaked with rain.

Show-ring appointments are prescribed by the American Horse Shows Association and outlined in detail in the AHSA *Rule Book*. In classes where appointments are scored as well as conformation and performance, it is vain to enter the ring unless you are dressed in perfect accordance with the rules. Riders in the Open Jumper division may dress as they please. But even so, most horse-show committees request (and some require) that the competitors wear suitable hacking attire, including a coat, a tie, and a hat—preferably a hard one. Western riders must always appear in the show arena wearing a Western hat and leather chaps, or chinks, and carrying a rope or a riata. The elegant Saddle Horse suit for show wear consists of Kentucky jodhpur trousers (somewhat bell-bottomed and very slender) and a long-skirted, tight-waisted jacket.

If you intend to do any showing, you will find it worthwhile to do your daily riding in the same type of clothing you will have to wear in the show ring, and to carry the same accessories. Some riders who habitually school without a hat are quite disconcerted when they have to wear one in the ring, for a derby is required in most Saddle classes, and either a bowler or a derby in the Hunter division, or a hunting cap for children. Many riding and Hunt clubs have ruled the wearing of a hard hat obligatory at all times, for safety reasons. Even if you only ride in your own back-yard ring, it is a good idea to always wear one, especially when schooling over jumps. The safest is the Caliente protective helmet, which includes a chin harness. It was borrowed from the race track and is worn by all Three-Day-Eventers during the Cross-Country as well as by Harness racing drivers.

Gloves pose a similar problem. There is no doubt that gloves protect a rider's hands not only from the cold, but also from rein burns and irritation. While some horsemen argue that they destroy sensitivity, such expert "hand-riders" as Italy's world-renowned d'Inzeo brothers, Piero and Raimondo, and all of the Olympic dressage competitors, never enter a ring barehanded. But you must start the glove habit during schooling, or you may indeed feel off your riding form when you are suddenly obliged to wear them during competition. Young Saddle Seat horsemen should bear this in mind, since gloves are a required accessory in Saddle Seat Equitation classes. As a matter of fact, it is correct to wear gloves and a hat in all Saddle Horse events.

Many competitive riding events have special dress requirements, for that matter. In Parade and Costume Horse Show classes they are an important element in the scoring, as they are in many Harness Driving events. Even Three-Day riders have to invest in an extensive wardrobe, because they need different attire for each of the three days: one for Dressage, another for the Cross-Country, and a third for Stadium Jumping. These are all described in detail in the AHSA *Rule Book*.

Of all the different forms of riding dress, the most becoming to the rider and the most appealing to the artist is undoubtedly hunting attire. Strictly governed by traditions that are enforced by alert Hunt-club Secretaries, hunting appointments permit very little expression of individual taste. Some Masters prepare a list of their particular vestimentary requirements, as these may vary from one Hunt to another. So it is advisable for a new member or a guest to consult a regular member or the Hunt Secretary before venturing forth to his first Meet with a strange pack. It is also wise to order your hunting kit from an experienced hunting outfitter who is familiar with the conventional details of this somewhat specialized branch of tailoring. Undoubtedly the simplest course is to patronize, when possible, the shop or tailor that already supplies members of the Hunt with which you intend to ride.

The basis of your first formal hunting appointments might well be a black riding coat with plain black bone buttons. Your breeches should be colored (buff or tan), with which you should wear plain black boots and a black hunting bowler. (Juniors, however, should not wear formal hunting attire before the age of sixteen, and in 1963 the American Horse Shows Association abolished all Junior classes requiring hunting attire.) A more formal costume for gentlemen consists of a black hunting frock coat worn with a black reinforced top hat and white breeches, in which case top boots (black boots with brown-colored tops) and white garter straps are obligatory. Top boots are worn only—but always—with white breeches.

With either costume you will need a special plain white hunting shirt to which a plain white stock is buttoned before being tied. Many hunters appreciate the convenience of ready-tied stocks that fasten behind the neck, although they are prohibited in Appointments show classes since they cannot, like standard stocks, be unfolded and used as an emergency sling or tourniquet in the event of an accident. Actually, a stock is quite simple to tie once someone has shown you how. The important point is for it to stay securely in place during several hours of galloping and jumping without flapping up in your face. In addition to the regulation plain gold stock pin (always worn horizontally, in order to

A rider in a Corinthian (Appointments) Class, equipped with hunting crop and sandwich case. (*Photo by Budd*)

avoid pricking one's chin should it happen to break open), experienced hunters fix the loose ends of the stock to their shirt with small safety pins. Strategically placed, the pins will be completely concealed by your hunting waistcoat, which should be canary-colored and of conventional cut, adorned with plain brass buttons. Your gloves should be of white string, brown leather, or yellow chamois.

To the layman, the most characteristic article of fox-hunting clothing is the brass-buttoned scarlet coat, which used to be fashionably referred to as "hunting pinks"—not because hunters are color-blind, but in honor of a famous nineteenth-century London tailor whose name was Pink. What the uninitiated do not always realize is that a scarlet coat is a sign of experience in the hunting field and is reserved for gentlemen riders with at least four or five active seasons to their credit. For a beginner to appear in a scarlet coat would be ridiculously pretentious. And scarlet is never worn by a lady except when she is an MFH or when it is the uniform of an Equestrian Team, in which case a feminine member of that Team will wear it during competitive performances. Its correct accompaniments are the same white breeches, top boots, canary waistcoat, and black silk top hat that are worn with a black coat, with gloves of white string or tan leather.

Another common misconception among nonhunters concerns the hunting cap. A hard cap, it is true, is one of the most practical and popular forms of headgear for everyday riding. But during actual fox-hunting, black hunting caps are the distinguishing mark of the Master and the Hunt officials and servants. Traditionally, they were never worn by any member of the field except for very young ones, but now some Hunts permit women to ,wear them as well. (Play safe by checking first with the Hunt Secretary.) The alternative, of course, is a bowler or a top hat. For safety reasons, some Masters now encourage young riders and novices to wear a Caliente helmet with a black velvet cover and a chinstrap.

Hunt colors, which are worn on the collars of ladies' black coats and of gentlemen's black or pink ones, like the Hunt insignia engraved on the buttons, must be earned. Granted by the Master, usually only after several years of active membership in a Hunt, they are not lightly awarded —very rarely, in fact, to Junior members—and to "receive the button" is a distinct honor.

No such stringent rules govern the riders' clothing during cub-hunting, which precedes the regular hunting season. Fox-hunters call their attire on these occasions "Ratcatcher," in contrast to their formal appointments. The term seems to have been handed down from early hunting days when there actually existed professional ratcatchers who hunted the vermin on foot with terrier packs. Even during the regular season, some Hunts hold meets on "Bye Days" (unscheduled hunting), when it may be announced that Ratcatcher clothing is acceptable. Nevertheless, it is a courtesy to the Hunt officials and fellow members to maintain a certain standard of dress. For example, to appear in a turtle-neck sweater, jodhpurs, and a cloth cap would be considered too casual even for a Ratcatcher day. While your breeches should be colored (tan, beige, brown) rather than white, and your coat a classically cut tweed or linen split-tail model, you should take the trouble of putting on a shirt with a collar and tie. Even better would be a soft hunting shirt and stock, either white or colored. The waistcoat may be of any shade, or even dispensed with entirely.

Your boots may be either plain black or brown, with matching garter straps. Black is perhaps the better choice, since these can also be worn with a formal black hunting coat, while brown boots are suitable only for cub-hunting. Likewise, your hunting bowler may be gray or brown as well as black. It is a matter of personal taste. But again, the budget-conscious horseman would point out that a black bowler is correct on more occasions than is a brown one.

A well-appointed Western rider. (*Photo by Judy Frederick*)

Gloves are an optional accessory to Ratcatcher clothing. Most experienced subscribers appear with white string, brown leather, or yellow chamois ones. Elasticized vinyl gloves are a practical recent invention. In any case, gloves are the only tried and true means of holding on to wet reins without slipping during rainy weather.

Speaking of rain, an unfortunately frequent occurrence during the hunting season in many parts of the country, you may wish to invest in a specially designed split-tail riding raincoat. While cleverly conceived to afford a horseman maximum protection from the elements with a minimum of encumbrance, raincoats are considered hot and bulky by many hunters, who claim that a good-quality wool hunting coat is sufficiently waterproof to offer protection from scattered showers, if not from a genuine downpour.

A well-appointed Saddle Seat rider. (*Photo by Jamie Donaldson*)

You may be wondering how much this magnificent finery is going to cost. There is virtually no maximum limit for de luxe custom-made riding clothes and boots, and minimum prices are of little interest to the serious horseman who seeks a reasonably good, serviceable quality. If you plan on well-made, better-than-average wear, an outfit consisting of riding breeches and jacket will cost $125 to $150 (almost as much for children's sizes). Jodhpur breeches and a coat will amount to about the same. A regulation Saddle Horse suit represents an outlay of from $125 to $150, and an evening show tuxedo somewhat more. Boots run between $80 and $150 ($60 to $75 for children) and jodhpur shoes around $45. Everyday Western wear is comparatively reasonable, except for Western boots, which start at about $35 and go very much higher for a fancy handmade pair.

A well-appointed Dressage rider. (*Photo by Julia Radigan*)

An elegant sidesaddle rider. (*Photo by Sue Maynard*)

The most expensive of all are hunting appointments. A gentleman Hunt member may spend—for clothes alone, not counting boots—as much as $500 or more if he wishes to cut a fine figure in "hunting pinks" at a fashionable Meet.

SPURS AND STICKS

To spur or not to spur? That is a question which never fails to rekindle an ancient argument among horse-lovers.

Spurs have been extolled as indispensable, and condemned for being as dangerous as "a razor in a monkey's paw." To follow through the latter metaphor, it would indeed be imprudent to give a razor to an irresponsible monkey, but millions of men wield this hazardous tool every morning and, aside from an occasional nick on the chin, no great harm is done. The same distinction might apply to spurs. No novice rider should ever wear them, but many expert horsemen rarely put a foot in the stirrup without them.

Spurs demand perfect control of the rider's leg, and when this condition is met, they permit a very precise communication. As a matter of fact, what the advanced rider seeks from spurs is not so much greater se-

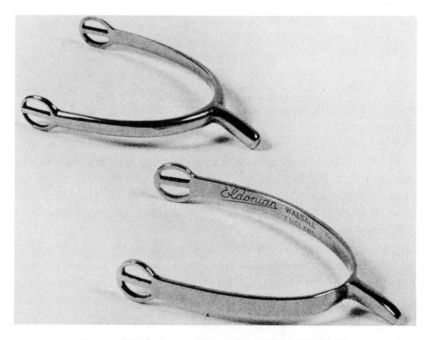

Prince of Wales spur. (*From the catalog of Miller's*)

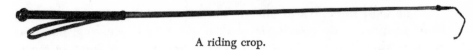

A riding crop.

A feathered jumping bat.

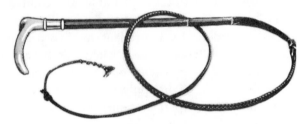

A hunting crop.

A Western bat.

(*From the catalog of Miller's*)

verity of leg signals as greater delicacy. Since precision and not pain is their principal object, there is little justification for sharp spurs under normal circumstances, and so all spurs, even roweled ones, should be dull. Properly fitted, they are worn at right angles to the boot at about the height of the horizontal seam. Spurs are of no use at all when worn too low, but the exact adjustment is an individual matter. Many riders have small leather "spur rests" placed at the back of their boots to prevent the spurs from slipping.

It is very easy for a rider who hasn't perfect leg control to jab his horse with the spurs unintentionally, which can cause the animal confusion as well as pain if it results in conflicting signals. Consequently, young riders should buy their first set only when their instructor feels they have acquired sufficient leg control so that the use of spurs will be a means of increasing their riding skill rather than an agony for their horse.

On the other hand, every horseman should become accustomed to carrying a stick. There are many different kinds, including the slender "cutting" whip for Gaited horses, the hickory Walk-Trot stick, the feathered jumping bat, the traditional hunting whip with a crook handle for opening gates and a long lash which is allowed to hang down toward the ground in order to keep the hounds away from the horses' heels, and also various longeing and driving whips. You should select one that is appropriate to your particular riding activity.

The stick is not so often a means of punishment as of reinforcing the actions of the legs and alerting the horse's attention. Like spurs, its principal purpose is communication, not necessarily by inflicting pain. If you think of your stick as an extra leg, you will not be inclined to abuse it. (And since you have a leg on each side of your horse, you should learn to use the stick ambidextrously.)

The effectiveness of sticks depends upon promptness of application rather than intensity, so it is a good practice to carry one every time you ride. You never can tell when you may need it, and when you do need a stick you need it *immediately*. Nobody has yet invented an adequate substitute. Can you think of one?

12.   Training Your Horse

Every time you ride your horse you are training him—for better or for worse. Whether you have given him an hour's serious work in the schooling ring, a brief limbering-up at the end of a longe line, or merely a pleasant walk along familiar bridle paths, the animal you bring back to the barn will not be *quite* the same one you originally led from his stall.

Some riders never do become fully aware of the fact that they are inevitably trainers as well, whether they like it or not; others seem to have been born with an extraordinary gift for making a horse understand what they wish him to do and for dealing with difficult horses. But every rider can increase his horse's ability and his own pleasure by learning something about the basic theories and techniques of training.

When dealing with elephants, college students, or horses, sound educational methods take into account not only the kind of knowledge one wishes to impart, but also the intellectual capacity and the particular psychology of the pupil involved. And so in order to appreciate the principles of horse-training, it is essential to understand how the horse's mind works and how his psychological reflexes function.

Horses vary in mentality just as human beings do. They have their individual characters, individual moods, individual reactions, and (like us) they are continually developing and changing, although they generally settle down to a more or less constant behavior pattern around the age of six. Individual animals, different breeds, and sometimes certain families within the same breed possess distinctive traits. The manner and environment in which a colt is reared will also influence his character. Nevertheless, there are certain valid generalizations that apply to all horses.

Considering his size, the horse has a tiny brain (only half as heavy as ours), and his intelligence, while it can be developed by training, is limited. He has been compared to an amiable, not very bright three-year-old child, and the image is apt if not very flattering. Like a child, he has a brief attention span and is easily bored. Like a child, he enjoys attention and will try to attract it by using any means at his disposal. His reasoning ability is rather slight; equine logic, if it exists at all, is much more elementary than the human kind. Fortunately, his mental weakness is compensated by an excellent instinctive memory and a remarkable ability to form new habits—good or bad.

How can a horseman profit from his awareness of the horse's intellectual shortcomings? First of all, by exercising unlimited patience when dealing with horses; second, by presenting instruction in the simplest possible form, and by progressing very gradually from each lesson to the succeeding one. You mustn't try to push your horse ahead too fast, and you should never correct him for disobedience unless you are sure that he really understands what you have asked him to do; otherwise, he may associate the punishment with quite another cause. Punishment and praise must be immediate if he is to form the correct connection between cause and effect.

Because of his slight intellect, the horse's power of concentration is limited. That is why your schooling ring should be situated in a spot that is free from distracting lights and sounds, particularly from the sight of other horses at play. When introducing new or difficult work, you should try to school your horse alone (not forgetting, of course, that he needs to become accustomed to being with other horses too). Several short schooling periods are more effective than one long one, and you must resist the temptation of continuing for "only ten minutes more" at the end of an encouraging schooling, for you run the risk of undoing all the good work you have just accomplished. You should always try to end each lesson with something your horse does well, and to break up every workout with frequent periods of relaxation. Merely a short stroll on loose reins will do wonders to refresh his interest. You will also retain his attention better if you vary his work as much as possible; above all, avoid following the identical sequence of exercises and always turning and stopping at the very same spot. Professional trainers believe that five one-hour lessons a week are quite enough for most horses and that all of them should be given at least one day of rest each week. Even the world-famous Lippizaner stallions of the Spanish Riding School in Vienna, who are probably the most highly trained horses in the world, are schooled for only forty-five minutes a day. The early-morning hours are favored for schooling by most trainers, since the horse is refreshed after a long night's rest and the sun is not yet hot. The traditional race-track training hours are between 6 and 10 A.M., although many horses are taken out even earlier in especially sultry climates.

Like most living creatures, the horse has five senses through which he receives impressions from the outside world. Each of them is utilized in one way or another in modern training methods.

His *sense of smell* is not outstanding, but it definitely exists. Desert horses are even believed to scent water from very far away. Stallions used at stud are stabled well apart from the other animals and exercised in their own personal paddock, for the scent left by strangers in their yard can infuriate them, and of course they will immediately distinguish the exciting scent of a mare in the neighborhood.

The horse's nose plays a part in his recognition of inanimate objects in addition to animal and human beings, so you should give a green horse ample opportunity to overcome his natural timidity by allowing him to sniff unfamiliar things such as new clothing, jumping obstacles, or the saddle you are introducing to him for the first time. Incidentally, the gypsies believe the best way to make friends with a horse is to blow gently on his nostrils, an act that is widely practiced in the animal world as a friendly greeting.

His *sense of taste* is well developed. Many horses have very definite likes and dislikes in feeding. An extension of this perception is the *gourmandise* that is characteristic of most horses, which can inspire them to unsuspected degrees of cleverness, such as figuring out how to operate light switches and to open feed-room doors, and even to recognize the need for stealth in escaping the attention of a sleeping groom when attempting a midnight raid on the feed bin!

In training, the horse's sense of taste can be exploited very little. While it is true that tidbits he particularly relishes (such as carrots, apples, sugar, a handful of oats or grass) make very acceptable rewards, especially with young colts, it is never wise to overdo hand-feeding with older horses, who soon acquire the habit of nipping. Besides, the best reward of all for good behavior is a release from restraint, such as dismounting or riding with loose reins. The horse's mentality being what it is, you cannot bribe him with food; he will not work in anticipation of a reward, as will dogs, for example.

The horse's *eyesight* is generally excellent, especially his night vision, although some experts believe that all horses are more or less myopic. Others claim that they have a blind spot that extends as far as six feet in front of the nose, which explains the value of the sheep's-wool noseband or "shadow roll" used on many race horses, trotters, and Hunters, to prevent them from literally being frightened by their own shadow. In any case, because of the placement of the horse's eyes on the side of his head, his peripheral vision is outstanding. Race horses are sometimes put in blinkers to prevent them from being distracted or discouraged by the sight of horses running alongside them.

A horse can see distant objects best when his head is held high, close objects when it is held low. When horses are grazing and can look back between their legs as well as to the side and forward, they have almost a 360° scope of vision. While some authorities claim that the horse, like many mammals, is color-blind, he can apparently distinguish between bright colors and gray shades.

Some horses have such acute powers of observation that you will almost be persuaded that they can see behind them. Of course, they can't, so you should never approach a horse from the rear but from the front, or better still, diagonally. When you cannot avoid approaching from the rear, be sure to speak to him as you do so. Your horse will probably notice at once that you are carrying a stick. Often the mere awareness of its presence will keep him on his good behavior and you will not have to use it.

A few Hunters and Jumpers possess a remarkable natural ability to judge distances, but they are exceptional individuals. Normally, the horse's eye travels from the ground up, and therefore elementary training obstacles should always include a well-marked ground-line. Even expert Jumpers are apt to have more trouble with a single rail that has no ground-line than with a much larger, well-marked oxer.

Far more than his sense of smell, the horse's vision can be used to help him overcome his natural timidity. Horses generally overreact to unfamiliar objects. It is an instinctive safety measure rather than genuine fear, and the best way to deal with it is to offer reassurance. Always calmly walk your horse up close to anything that seems to frighten him needlessly and let him have a good look at it. Often, the nature of the object will surprise you. It may be a mud puddle, a baby carriage, an open umbrella, or merely a piece of paper fluttering to the ground.

The horse's *hearing* is very keen. He is sensitive to all kinds of sounds, recognizing different voices, animal and human, and even able to distinguish between the footsteps of his friends and strangers. He loves gentle sounds and quiet music. The ancient Greeks played soothing melodies during foaling, and today many racing grooms believe that soft music on the barn radio keeps the horses calm and happy. Others prefer louder, livelier works as a means of preparing them for the crowd noises they will have to face at the race track.

Sudden loud noises can be most alarming to a horse and set his nerves on edge. Some of the Olympic Team horses who are marvels of obedience during exacting competitions behave more like skittish colts when they are obliged to stand at attention in front of the band during the ear-splitting concert of national anthems that precedes the Nations' Cup.

A horseman can utilize his pupil's sense of hearing in many ways. Young trainees are taught to respond to voice commands before any other kind of signals, and the voice is used as an aid even in advanced work (except for dressage and cutting competitions, where it is forbidden). You should always talk to your horse a lot and frequently use his name. The horse's vocabulary will never be as extensive as that of a clever dog, but it is true that he can learn the meaning of many words and phrases, and he will always be most responsive to the expression of your voice. You can calm him, stimulate him, praise him, or correct him vocally merely by adopting the appropriate tone, without necessarily pronouncing any intelligible words at all. Trainers usually raise their voices slightly when signaling faster work, and drop down to a soothing note for commands to slow down and to halt. (And here's a tip to trilingual horse-trainers, for what it may be worth: a French dressage rider once maintained that horses respond best to training when commands are given in the guttural German tongue and praise in melodious Italian!)

The horse's *sense of feeling* is extremely acute. He is highly responsive to different forms of contact all over his body, especially if he belongs to one of the thin-skinned, hot-blooded breeds. We capitalize on his unusual sensitivity by developing a veritable tactile language whose vocabulary is vast, thanks to the rider's "aids" (the hands, legs, and seat), in addition to the voice. All equestrian techniques are based upon the horse's sense of feeling. If he were an insensitive creature, we would long ago have had to find some other animal to be our riding partner.

Does the horse possess a *sixth sense?* Some experts believe that he does, and in evidence they bring accounts of amazing exploits where horses indeed seem to have manifested some uncanny kind of ultrasensory perception. Farmers claim that field-kept horses are infallible weather prophets once you learn how to interpret their behavior, and their premonition of impending danger has often been illustrated by fact and fiction.

One widely reported incident took place during World War II, when the Russian mounted cavalry was advancing over territory that had been mined by the retreating Germans. The Russian commanding officer ordered his men to ride with free reins over the snow-covered mine fields, and those who did so, letting their horses find their own way, came through unscathed, while the soldiers who insisted on guiding their horses' footsteps perished on the spot.

There is no doubt that a horse is quick to sense a rider's anxiety or fear, although many riders believe that this is due to his powers of observation or to his sense of smell rather than to intuition. In any case, a trainer must always be in complete command of his own nerves and emotions if he hopes to control those of his horse. The most successful trainers have been noted for unwavering self-control as well as inexhaustible patience.

Whether you choose to believe that the horse has six senses or only five, all horsemen should be aware of the dominant instincts that inspire and influence his behavior.

Because he is a vegetarian and has never had to attack other animals for food, the horse is not by nature an aggressor. Horses don't have territories to defend either, like many other animals. In natural wild life they traveled about in herds, leading a very independent kind of life. Their original sense of independence has been attenuated by centuries of domestication (the equine runaway most often returns to the stable of his own free will) and most modern breeds are surprisingly willing to accept discipline. Perhaps this is due to the tradition of hierarchies formed in the herd, where leadership seems to be based more on some innate quality other than age, sex, or size. It is not unusual to see a stable of horses practically tyrannized by a small, assertive pony. On the other hand, some horses may be very domineering with their stablemates and quite submissive with human beings.

Horses have remained gregarious and they love company, human and animal—with the exception of pigs, which most horses loathe. Consequently, a horse will undertake an activity for the first time much more readily if he is asked to follow the lead of a more experienced comrade—for example, when entering a van or trailer. Due to their herd instincts, horses generally work better in a ring with other horses than alone. For the same reason, there are fewer jumping refusals in the hunting field than in the show ring, where the horses jump individually. You have certainly noticed that horses always move more spontaneously in the direction of other horses or toward the barn.

Friendship seems to mean a lot to these sociable creatures. You will often see two "best friends" huddled close together in a pasture, sniffing and nuzzling each other, swishing flies off each other, or simply standing side by side.

The horse's herd instinct can be usefully exploited during training in various ways, for example, in teaching a foal to halter-lead, and inducing him to enter a van for the first time; it also partly explains the utility of lead ponies at the race track. But in advanced training it is a tendency that must be controlled. A well-trained horse should have learned to obey his rider's commands, not his impulse to follow the leader. In fact, whenever you take your horse out with a group of riders, you should occasionally turn him away from the others and then rejoin them, in order to avoid your horse's becoming "herd-bound."

Another powerful equine instinct is for movement. It is natural for a horse to move about most of the time, and his immediate reaction to fear or danger is to flee. The most terrible experience of all, from the horse's point of view, is to be thrown off his feet and thus deprived of his only defense—a fact that is fully appreciated by Western-style horse-breakers, as we shall see. It also explains his reluctance to step on unfamiliar surfaces, like a bridge or a loading ramp. Excitement, nervousness, anger, and confusion, as well as fright, may be expressed by running faster or running away. Thoroughbreds are particularly susceptible to speed, sometimes becoming so intoxicated by it that they lose their heads completely; it may take some time to sober them up again. It is evident that the training of hot-blooded horses should be firmly founded in work at the slower paces.

A normal horse is a generous soul, good-natured, honest, anxious to please, endowed with a special brand of courage and a simple sense of justice. Trainers try to preserve these worthy qualities by being meticulously fair in asking their pupil to do no more than he is physically and temperamentally capable of doing, and by meting out correction only when absolutely necessary, with a promptness that leaves no confusion in the horse's mind as to why he is being punished.

We have already mentioned the horse's remarkable memory, and it is worth returning to, because this is probably his outstanding mental attribute, as well as the most valuable of the trainer's tools. The easiest way to teach a horse something is by repetition. He learns by association of ideas and by forming habits rather than by reasoning or logic. While everything he sees or does leaves an impression on him, the more violent the experience, the longer it sticks in his mind. Unpleasant impressions can take a long time to disappear and should be avoided, except when it may be desirable to deliberately provoke an incident in order to uproot a bad habit.

Past lessons should always be reviewed before attempting new ones, repeating each exercise until it has become firmly fixed before going on to the next. Needless to say, you must be scrupulously consistent in the way you communicate commands to your horse. If you praise him for responding in a certain way to your aids, and then suddenly correct him because *this* time you mean something different, your horse's poor brain will become utterly confused and many hours of schooling will have been in vain. This is why only a very experienced rider should attempt to train a green horse. A trainer must possess complete control of all the riding aids, and it goes without saying that he must be perfectly schooled himself in the technique of correctly producing the different gaits and movements before he can hope to teach them to his horse.

Memory and habit lead to other typical equine traits, such as an attachment to routine and a dislike of change. More often than not it is memory rather than instinct that explains the horse's uncanny ability to find his way home.

When all is said and done, the horse's memory and habit-forming aptitude provide the cornerstone for all traditional training methods. In fact, to put it very simply, one of the ultimate aims in training a horse is to reach the point where, like a good dancing partner, he always responds to your actions immediately and in a consistent way.

There are as many methods of training horses as there are trainers—or rather, as there are horses, because each animal requires a slightly different, individualized approach. Methods also vary according to the type of activity a horse is being taught to perform, and each trainer also has his personal schooling secrets. It is not often possible to lay down definite rules, because the trainer must exercise his judgment at every step of the way. As a result, every thoughtful training program is really made to measure for each individual horse. A horse can be broken in only a few weeks, or he may be brought along gradually at a much slower pace. Often the trainer's choice is governed by practical considerations—he simply cannot afford to devote the time required for training by the most careful traditional methods.

The trainer's skill comes partly from science, but mostly from years of experience in working with all kinds of horses and facing all kinds of training problems. An astonishing number of trainers have enjoyed their most successful periods when they were well in their sixties and seventies, like the dean of American Thoroughbred trainers, the late "Sunny Jim" Fitzsimmons, who was still going strong at eighty-eight. The late Aly Khan's will specifically provided that his valuable racing operations be managed by Madame Vuillier, widow of the noted breeding theorist, since the astute Moslem leader considered that her years of experience and mature judgment more than compensated for the handicap of being a woman—and seventy-four years old.

The horse's education can be divided into five separate stages of learning:

1. *Early training of the colt* from birth until he is strong enough to carry the weight of a rider (usually between two and three years).
2. *Introducing the rider.* Often referred to as "backing" or "breaking." Teaching the young horse to accept a rider and to respond to the basic aids.
3. *Schooling in the saddle.* Teaching the horse collection and correct head carriage, and completing his bitting education. Furthering his physical development and his response to the aids; more advanced schooling in his natural gaits.
4. *Specialized Training.* Developing the horse's ability to perform special tasks and teaching him specific techniques, for example, training a Gaited horse, developing cutting, roping, or other Western specialties, schooling for hunting, jumping or dressage.
5. *Re-education,* which may be either to correct the training of a badly broken or badly schooled horse, or to perfect the work of a well-trained one.

Now let us examine in more detail the curriculum of these different "schools" and the training methods that are most frequently employed.

EARLY TRAINING

On modern breeding farms, foals are handled from the day they are born, especially around the head (to prevent head shyness from developing) and around the feet (so that they will accept having their feet picked up for monthly trimming and for shoeing when the moment arrives). Simple grooming and hoof care from the very beginning will make it seem quite natural to them to be touched on different parts of the body, while good stable manners acquired early can avoid a lot of trouble later on.

The first real lesson the foal must learn is to be halter-broken, that is, to move along willingly while being led by a rope from the halter. A tiny halter can be slipped over his head for a few minutes when he is only a few days old, but the first halter must be soft, with sheepskin covers on the head and noseband, or it will bruise his tender skin. At one month of age he can be taught to lead. A foal naturally follows his dam until he is weaned and he need only be led alongside of her at first and then gradually coaxed away, being amply rewarded by petting or a few oats when he obeys. With a foal who refuses to move ahead, a long lead rope is looped around his croup so that a pull on the lead automatically forces the hindquarters forward. The best position for the foal is beside and slightly in front of the person who is leading him, the leader remaining level with the youngster's shoulder.

While walking on a lead, the foal learns to obey the discipline of the lead rope and already begins to associate different pressures and pulls with different movements, such as turns and stops. He is also exposed as soon as possible to all sorts of usual sights and sounds: the traffic on a road adjoining the pasture, the presence in the stable yard of children, other animals, and various vehicles. He can even be persuaded to follow his dam into a horse trailer and to back out again, a useful lesson he will never forget.

After he has been weaned, at about six months of age, the charming young colt learns to stand quietly when tied by the halter, inside and outside of his stall, as well as in crossties. When he has become accustomed to standing still without nervousness, he can be taught to stand correctly, squarely balanced on his four feet.

The Thoroughbred stands with the near foreleg a few inches in front of the off foreleg, and the near hind leg slightly behind the off-hind, a position that shows him off to best advantage by accentuating the slope of the shoulder and giving the impression that he "covers a lot of ground."

The tradition with Saddle Horses, Tennessee Walkers, and Shetland and Hackney ponies is to train them to park or stretch, that is, to stand with their forelegs planted in front of their bodies, the hind legs stretched behind the croup. It is easily learned at a tender age, when the trainer can move the colt's slender limbs into position, making a fuss over him as soon as he assumes the desired pose.

When the colt has become used to following the trainer quietly on a loose lead with free forward movement, he is ready to learn a few elementary signals and voice commands.

To take a simple example, the trainer restrains the colt from moving by firmly holding onto the rope attached to the halter. Then he says "Walk," and at the same time he steps forward himself, gently leading the rope forward and perhaps lightly touching the colt's flank with the other hand, preparing him for the rider's leg signals which will come much later. Soon the colt associates the command "Walk" and the hand signals with the act of moving ahead, and he will obey immediately— especially if he is rewarded with a few oats. This elementary process of forming associations is the foundation of all his training, even though later on, of course, the signals will be given by the rider's hands, seat, and legs and will be much more precise, and the horse will have acquired a wide repertory of associations. But the basic principle forever remains the same.

In succeeding lessons the colt is trained to move forward at a walk or slow trot, to stop straight without altering his head position, to move backward a few steps, and to come to the trainer. The customary spoken commands are simple: "Get up," "Back," "Walk," "Trot," "Whoa," "Come here." Leading him alongside a fence encourages him to move in a straight line and keep his body straight, while leading him from both sides and making turns to the right as well as to the left will help prevent him from becoming one-sided. These early lessons should be brief. Until he is a year old, the playful infant is given only small doses of work with plenty of time for romping in the pasture.

When the colt has celebrated his first birthday, the next step is to drive him on foot in long reins in order to acquaint him with the idea of responding to rein signals from behind. Long-rein driving (called "ground driving" in the West) also teaches him to keep his body straight

Longeing. (*Photo by Ray Woolfe, Jr.*)

and is a means of developing correct head carriage, which makes it a vital step in the education of Saddle Bred horses.

At first the reins are attached to a halter, hackamore, or cavesson, with the trainer walking six or eight feet behind holding the reins slack, and the exercises are the same as when the colt was led by the halter: spoken commands to stop, start, change direction, and back up straight, only now the rein signals are given simultaneously with the voice commands. During the first few lessons an assistant walks at the colt's head and guides him until he understands the meaning of these new sensations. When the colt responds correctly on his own, he may be driven cross-country, uphill and down, and even urged to step over simple obstacles such as logs which he may meet along the way. These outside excursions enlarge his horizon at the same time that they further his physiial development.

As he approaches his second year, the colt may be exercised on the longe rein in the schooling ring. Longeing (pronounced and sometimes spelled "lungeing") is one of the most useful of all training techniques. Having a young horse move freely in a circle around the trainer with even, relaxed strides is invaluable in preparing him for the rider. Later on, it is an excellent means of perfecting the balance and action of a trained horse, and it always enables an expert trainer to improve a horse's physical development by supervised exercise.

A standard or improvised longeing cavesson may be used, along with a twenty-five- to thirty-foot longeing rein, snapped onto the D ring on top of the noseband, and a long longeing whip. (Older horses are more often longed in their regular bridle and saddle.)

During the first few lessons the trainer has an assistant lead the colt by the halter while he himself stands a few feet away, gradually moving to the center of the ring as he plays out the longeing rein. The colt is moved around in circles of varying size and in both directions, while the trainer moves in a much smaller circle in the center of the ring. Spoken commands are reinforced by a flick of the longeing whip below the hocks and an appropriate movement of the longeing rein. Since most horses move more readily to the left than to the right, the introductory lessons start in the left direction; but later on, the right direction is stressed, to prevent the horse from becoming one-sided. The initial longeing lessons are devoted to walking and slow trotting with no fast work, since the purpose is to induce the colt to overcome nervousness and to acquire confidence at the same time he is building up his muscles, developing flexibility and balance, and—most important of all—learning to produce free forward impulsion, which is the foundation of all his more advanced training. Eventually he will be longed in all three natural gaits: the walk, trot, and canter.

Longeing is not a simple technique to master, since it requires much sensitivity and judgment on the part of the trainer and expert coordination of the rein, whip, and voice. He must avoid monotony by constantly changing the gaits, pace, and direction of movement (which means changing the rein from one hand to another), as well as by varying the size of the circles, always taking care not to overtire his young pupil and to provide frequent moments of relaxation at a slow walk and occasional rewards, including edible ones.

The driving lessons continue too, perhaps three or four times a week, with longeing on the other days. When the colt performs his elementary lessons well, he may proceed to more advanced exercises, driving in figure eights and nines and serpentines, with the reins held gradually higher.

At about two years of age the colt is ready to be bitted. His first bit is a mouthing bit, a straight bar bit with a hard-rubber or leather-covered mouthpiece and dangling keys, fitted to a light bridle. To start with, he wears it only in his stall for an hour or so a day. After several days he wears it underneath the cavesson during his driving lessons, although the reins are still attached to the cavesson and not to the bit rings.

Only an experienced trainer can recognize the opportune moment for attaching the longe reins to the bit rings. The colt must be psychologically ready to accept the bit and his mouth must be physically

Driving a yearling in long reins. (*Photo by Ray Woolfe, Jr.*)

prepared as well. At the chosen time the cavesson is removed and the longe reins are hooked directly onto a light riding bridle with a snaffle bit. Spoken signals are gradually abandoned as the colt learns to respond correctly to direct rein signals on the bit. Instead of establishing contact with the colt's mouth by pulling the bit back, the trainer urges him forward against it, thus encouraging him from the very beginning to "reach for the bit."

Now the colt is introduced to the saddle. Again, the first lessons take place right in his stall. In order to distract and quiet him, he may be given a few handfuls of oats while a lightweight saddle is laid gently on his back, just long enough for him get the feel of its unaccustomed weight. Each day it is left in place a little longer. Then the girth is loosely attached, and finally the saddle may be worn during his driving lessons, with the stirrups pulled up and tied securely to the girth and the longe reins run through them.

When a colt has reached this stage in his education, he is ready to be ridden. But is he ready for it physically? He has probably been growing in size and strength at a phenomenal rate, but he won't attain his full growth for several more years and in the meantime his bone structure and muscles are unable to withstand great strain. It is true that race horses make their debut at the age of two, but even with the minimum

Longeing the yearling under tack. (*Photo by Ray Woolfe, Jr.*)

weight they carry, many a promising racing career has been interrupted by leg or foot unsoundness resulting from excessive early exertion. There is no point in jeopardizing the riding future of a precocious colt by mounting him prematurely.

INTRODUCING THE RIDER

The most conservative trainers like to "back a horse" (have him mounted) for the first time when he is about three years old. Since the decision depends upon the condition of the individual animal, it may be a bit sooner—as early as two years—with those who are physically advanced for their age and destined for an early hunting, jumping, or showing career, or as late as four years with those whose development is slower and whose trainers are in less of a rush. Sometimes a horse is broken at two and then turned out to pasture until his education is resumed in the saddle a year later.

If a horse has already been given adequate early training, the act of carrying a rider will be a natural continuation of his previous lessons and should present no special difficulty. Often the horse is further prepared for the rider by having the stirrups dangle freely from the saddle while he is being longed and by carrying a sandbag tied to the saddle during several preceding lessons. But even so, a careful trainer may take an entire week to progress from the point where he puts a foot in the stirrup while the horse is standing saddled in his stall, to where he actually sits on the horse's back for more than a minute or two.

The initial lessons require the aid of an assistant or even two, to lead the horse by the bridle. Five minutes is quite long enough for the very first ride, which often takes place at the end of a schooling session, when the horse is a little bit tired and least likely to act up.

Only an excellent rider should be the first to mount a young horse. There is always danger of injury to the horse's mouth or to the horse himself, and it is absolutely vital that the rider should not be unseated. Furthermore, the riding aids must be applied correctly from the very beginning if the horse is to establish a correct foundation. At this stage the colt should have no bad habits, but he will acquire them very rapidly if he is confused by the rough, inconsistent, or conflicting aids of an inexperienced rider.

During the first two months all mounted work is done only at a walk or trot—often on the longe—during the last fifteen or twenty minutes of the longeing and driving sessions, and the schooling periods are gradually prolonged. When the horse accepts the rider without nervousness or apprehension, the entire program is resumed from the very beginning, only under saddle. The colt may be shod now in light plates, with leather pads if the going is rough. Voice commands, leg signals, and weight shifts are used to start with, the bit and rein effects being introduced very slowly. At every step of the way the trainer must exercise good judgment and self-control, especially when dealing with a talented horse, where the temptation is great to push him ahead too fast.

Western horses who are let loose on the range as foals, except for a brief period of branding and veterinary care at the age of six to twelve months, often start their training abruptly at this stage with no previous schooling. Needless to say, their sudden loss of freedom and the intro-

Backing a young horse to introduce him to carrying a weight on his back. (*Photo by Ray Woolfe, Jr.*)

duction of a bridle (or, more often, a hackamore), saddle, and rider all at once can come as quite a shock, and somewhat violent methods are required to get them to accept this disagreeable new state of affairs. The actual process is called breaking.

While it is much less widespread than it used to be, horse-breaking is still practiced on the large Western ranches. The basic principle is to invite resistance and to overcome it once and for all, the horse acknowledging defeat and remaining submissive thereafter.

Sitting on his back for the first time. (*Photo by Ray Woolfe, Jr.*)

There are many different breaking methods. Since the most terrifying sensation a horse can experience is to be deprived of his freedom of movement, most of them employ various hobbling devices of rope and leather that pull one or more of the horse's legs up in order to restrict his movements or to throw him to the ground. Certain pulley-like contrivances put the animal in the helpless position of having either one or two legs pulled out from under him; the "Scotch hobble" links one hind foot to his neck, while the so-called "W" rope may be used to force a horse to his knees. Sometimes particularly wild or recalcitrant horses were deprived of feed and water as a "gentling" preliminary, or tied up in solitary confinement to the limb of a tree for twenty-four to forty-eight hours before they were saddled and ridden for the first time.

It is obvious that all of these methods are unsuitable for a well-bred horse. Some of them involve real risk to his physical and mental well-being. Not only is the horse broken, but sometimes also his spirit and per-

Reassuring the horse.

Leading the horse by the halter at a walk. (*Photos by Ray Woolfe, Jr.*)

haps a few bones. And so their use is restricted to cold-blooded, range-bred animals who are to be used as working stock horses. Nowadays, when so many Western horses are far from worthless animals, bearing a strong strain of Thoroughbred blood and being raised to become Hunters, Jumpers, and pleasure hacks, they are broken to the saddle whenever possible in the slower, nonviolent, conventional way.

SCHOOLING IN THE SADDLE

A great many riders who buy a horse of their own acquire him at this stage of his education, the early training and elementary riding techniques already having been taught by the breeder, the dealer's training staff, or the previous owner. At this point a horse is said to be "broken," but he is far from "finished."

If the preceding lessons have been thoroughly learned, he will have a sound foundation for becoming a good riding horse. As a matter of fact, as soon as a horse "steers well" by responding correctly to the basic riding aids, you can start jumping, hunting, or learning Western specialties on the novice level. But if you wish him to develop into a really fine riding horse, you will want to teach him such advanced refinements as *collection* and *flexion.*

Every rider is probably familiar with the terms. But in order to fully understand their meaning, it should be remembered that all movement is nothing more than a loss and recovery of balance. Collection is a refined state of balance which is achieved by closely coordinating the forehand and the hindquarters of a horse. The forehand is lightened by increasing the load on the hind legs, which are brought under the croup with an increased bending of the hindquarter joints, and the shift of weight is accompanied by a proportionate raising of the horse's head and flexion of the neck.

A collected horse is like a wound-up spring. His paces are animated and brilliant, since relieving the forehand allows the forelegs to reach out higher and more freely; his strides are shorter and his action higher; the hindquarters, which generate his motive power, produce increased impulsion. There are many different degrees of collection, from the high collection required to perform certain advanced dressage movements to the almost imperceptible collection of the Hunter and Park Hack. Saddle Horse collection is achieved mostly by the rider's hands; dressage and Jumper collection by the legs.

Correct collection is not a tense, imposed position, but a relaxed, elastic one. The horse's muscles must be prepared by flexing and bending exercises, such as figure eights, serpentines, and lateral movements, which help to remove stiffness from various parts of his body. His confidence must be built up to eliminate tension due to anxiety or fear.

In order to obtain a state of collection, the stimulating action of the rider's seat and legs which drives the horse's hocks forward underneath his body is combined with the restraining action of the hands, causing the horse to yield with his lower jaw and to flex his head from the poll (that is, to bend his neck not from the shoulders, but from behind the ears), which brings his chin in and his head into a vertical position. Flexing at the poll is the basis of all good head carriage and also permits a horse to balance himself.

As an initial exercise, the trainer simply asks the horse to yield his lower jaw while standing still by urging the horse's hindquarters forward with his legs, at the same time preventing any forward movement with his hands. This procedure encourages the horse to flex from the poll, and as soon as he does so, he should immediately be rewarded by relaxation and praise. When the horse fully understands what is desired of him, the trainer may ask him to produce gradually increasing degrees of collection lasting a few minutes while performing his regular schooling exercises. But it should not be overdone with Hunters and Jumpers, and no horse should be asked to remain collected for a long period of time.

Meanwhile, work is continuing in all three basic gaits: walk, trot, and canter.

The *walk* should be an even, flat-footed four-beat gait. Oddly enough, it is the most difficult of all to perfect.

The *trot* is a two-beat gait, with the diagonal pairs of legs moving simultaneously (the left front and the right hind are in the air while the right front and left hind strike the ground, and vice versa). The rider should take care to alternate the diagonal set of legs with which he rises to the trot (posts), in order to avoid uneven strain on the horse's legs. Show-ring rules require that when circling clockwise around the ring, the rider should be on the left diagonal and be sitting in the saddle when the left front leg is on the ground; when circling counterclockwise, he should be on the right diagonal, sitting in the saddle when the right front leg is on the ground. In theory, the rider's weight will fall into the saddle at the moment when the horse's legs are in the best position to receive the burden—although some equestrian experts maintain that the opposite is actually true. A slow trot is called a "jog" or "dogtrot."

The ordinary trot. (*Photo by James Deutschmann*)

The *canter* is a three-beat gait. The horse leads out with one foreleg —let us say that it is the left foreleg. The left hind leg and the right foreleg next follow in unison, and finally the right hind leg strikes off. There is one brief moment when all four feet are off the ground. The canter is actually a schooled version of the horse's natural *gallop*, a fast gait that is no more than a series of leaps. Other variations are the *hand gallop*, produced with a definite degree of collection, and the Western *lope*, which is as slow as the hand gallop but freer, with little collection or none at all. The horse is on the correct lead at a canter when the leading foreleg is the one on the inside of a turn or a circle. When they are at pasture, most horses naturally canter on the correct lead and make the proper changes of lead when necessary, just as they usually jump on the correct lead. But later on, the presence of a rider on his back seems to disrupt a horse's natural movement, which is why the rider must help his horse to

The extended trot. (*Photo by James Deutschmann*)

select the proper leading leg. If the forelegs are on one lead and the hind legs on another, it is called a "disunited canter" and is a serious fault.

Many expert trainers maintain that the best gymnastic exercise of all is the extended trot, since it develops flexibility, balance, strength, and control and also tends to settle down overspirited horses. Trotting over cavalletti (see page 297), set slightly wider apart than the horse's natural stride, automatically obliges him to extend. The trainer intersperses frequent halts, backing, and turns in both directions. Later on in horse shows, Hunters will turn only toward the inside of the ring, but Saddle Horses are allowed to turn either way. The horse is also trained to stand perfectly still while being mounted and dismounted from either side.

The trainer constantly seeks to develop immediate obedience, good balance, smooth transitions from one gait to another, regularity of pace and stride, and dexterity in changing directions. As weak spots show up during riding, he attempts to correct them by concentrated work on the longe line. The aids become lighter and voice commands are abandoned

Cantering on a loose rein. (*Photo by James Deutschmann*)

Training over cavalletti. (*Photo courtesy of the USET*)

as they become unnecessary. Schooling takes place over varied terrain, since every change of footing requires a readjustment of the horse's balance and develops him physically. To vary his program from time to time, he is taken on cross-country rides in company with other horses as well as alone. He may be permitted to run from time to time, but no really fast work is done until the horse is well schooled in his basic riding techniques. There is another strictly physical reason for avoiding too much galloping with a young horse. During the gallop stride there is a moment when all of the weight of the horse and rider (which may amount to over a thousand pounds) is placed on one single leg, and you must remember that the young horse's bones are not fully set before the age of five or six. It is not surprising that horses who have been galloped excessively as colts often break down when they should be in the prime of life.

When the horse is ready for it (again in the wise judgment of the trainer), he may be introduced to the double bridle, which helps to further the flexion of the jaw and poll and permits an expert rider great delicacy of communication. Arabian and Saddle Bred horses, who are naturally high-headed, will take to it easily, but other breeds may have more difficulty, especially if their neck muscles have not been adequately prepared by flexing and suppling exercises. At first the curb part of the double bridle is worn with the curb chain very loosely attached, the curb reins hanging quite slack, and only the snaffle part actively used. Little by little, the curb is put into action too.

Long before reaching this relatively advanced stage of training, some horses will have revealed an aptitude for hunting, jumping, gaited work, driving, cutting, or roping, and so forth, in which case the trainer will probably have given them instruction in one of these specialized techniques. However, the early training should be frequently reviewed, as the basic lessons that have been so laboriously assimilated form the foundation for all the rest. A resistance or flaw in advanced work can often be traced back to an elementary exercise incompletely mastered or improperly executed.

The everyday schooling exercises are much the same for all kinds of horses. It is not so much *which* movements a horse performs as *how* he performs them that makes the difference. A conscientious rider will school his horse regularly in the following exercises—not in order, of course, but all mixed together:

Walk, Trot, and Canter in a small circle in both directions

Halts and Half-Halts (a corrective check to improve balance, without breaking the gait or losing forward impulsion)

Walk, Trot, and Canter on straight lines, serpentines, figure eights (with changes of lead) and figure nines in both directions (the latter is a half turn, obliging the horse to turn on his haunches, which is the foundation movement for the pivot)

Backing Up in a straight line (always followed by a forward movement)

Turns on the Forehand to both sides (this is the most natural way for a horse to make a turn)

Turns on the Haunches to both sides (a pivot on the hind legs)

The training program should also include a good deal of cross-country hacking.

TRAINING THE PLEASURE HORSE

If you are interested in all-round pleasure riding or park hacking, you will probably have selected your horse more because of his pleasant disposition and attractive appearance than for outstanding athletic ability. As a matter of fact, all he really needs to know in order to give you many years of riding pleasure is how to walk, trot, canter, stop and back, have good manners, and be obedient. You can both keep very busy simply perfecting these basic skills.

Entertaining tricks are easy to teach, but most horsemen consider them suitable only for pet horses or ponies and out of place in the education of a fine riding horse. Some of the cute ones that may seem charming for a young colt become actually dangerous in a full-grown horse and may interfere with his usefulness as a riding mount. For example, if you teach him to shake hands—and he will learn it quickly—your blacksmith is one person who will definitely not be amused!

However, there is no reason why a pleasure horse cannot learn some other things as well, such as a few simple dressage movements, or a little elementary jumping. Many trainers believe that the rudiments of jumping should be integrated into the basic schooling of all horses. In any case, bringing your horse back to school from time to time will not only keep him from getting bored and sluggish, but will improve your own riding, and enhance your horse's resale value too.

TRAINING THE HUNTER

While it is almost always a Thoroughbred that wins the Conformation Hunter Show Championship, what distinguishes a Hunter from other kinds of horses is not so much his breeding as his way of going. A good Hunter's movements are free and easy, with long, low strides and free shoulder action. His paces are smooth and even, his obedience is exemplary, and, ideally, he should jump out of stride.

Because soundness is vital, prospective Hunters are never pushed ahead too fast during early training or mounted prematurely. If restraint is exercised during his early years, a sound and well-trained Hunter can be shown at three years, hunt a full season at five, and provide delightful sporting companionship until the age of fifteen or twenty.

Hunters are trained to walk, trot, and canter with natural, free movements and just enough collection to keep their bodies in perfect balance. Hunter Hacks are schooled for showing in a hand gallop, which is a smooth, collected gallop. But generally speaking, there is far more emphasis on extension than collection in training Hunters. They must also learn to execute all kinds of turns, to reduce and extend their stride at all gaits, to develop sure-footedness by working over uneven terrain, and to strengthen their shoulders as well as fortify their wind by riding uphill and down. Hunters must be able to jump all kinds of natural obstacles up to a height of four feet six inches, including ditches, spread fences, and combinations, in good form and out of stride at an even hunting pace. Their characters are developed for obedience, confidence, steadiness, and perfect manners alone and in company.

Early work on the longe is the best means of establishing the desired gaits: a square, even walk; a well-extended, low trot; a smooth, ground-covering canter. Expert longeing also helps to develop smooth increases and decreases of speed and regularity of pace. During his early mounted training, the Hunter wears a snaffle bit. When he is ready to be ridden outside the schooling ring, a Pelham or double bridle is often used, although many Hunters are ridden all their lives in nothing but a snaffle. Cross-country hacking, alone and in company, is stressed throughout his training to accustom the future Hunter to all kinds of sights, sounds, and ground conditions.

Jumping training usually starts on the longe, first by merely walking the horse over a rail placed on the ground and then by trotting over it without changing the rhythm of his gait. The rail is gradually raised, and eventually the horse is cantered over. Poles must be placed between the top of the jumping standard and the ground, so that the longeing rein will slide up and down over the standards without getting caught in them.

When the horse is able to clear two or three feet correctly, he can be mounted for jumping, and returned to the first exercise of walking over a rail on the ground. The weight of the rider is bound to upset his balance at first, so his legs are protected by bell boots as well as bandages in order to prevent bruises during his early lessons.

The safest and perhaps the best way to proceed is to progress from that single rail, taken at a walk. As soon as the horse walks over a single rail satisfactorily, he learns to trot over a single rail. Then a second rail is added, then a third, and finally a fourth, the rails being spaced to accommodate the horse's normal trotting stride. (About five feet is a good average for most full-size horses.) Once the horse is trotting through the four "cavalletti" with only occasional mistakes, a fifth rail can be introduced, but spaced an extra stride away—say, ten feet from the fourth rail, if five feet spacing has been used. This rail can then be gradually raised, first to a height that is only barely big enough to jump, then to three feet or three and a half feet over a period of days or weeks, depending on the talent of the horse. Eventually, fences can be altered and distances adjusted to develop the horse's jumping form and gymnastic capabilities, and this same kind of work can continue throughout the horse's entire career. Bertalan de Nemethy, the coach of the U. S. Equestrian Team, is an especially strong and expert advocate of cavalletti work, as anyone who has watched the team in training will have seen.

Once the single fence following the cavalletti has been mastered, additional fences can be added in varying distances. This pattern of training is virtually foolproof, since the cavalletti keep putting the horse in the perfect spot from which to jump. But obviously both horse and rider must eventually learn to do without this helpful "crutch" and jump all the same fences from a trot and finally a canter without any rails or cavalletti to help them.

Some professional trainers still start their young Hunter prospects jumping in a jumping chute or "Hitchcock pen," which is an enclosed jumping lane with high walls and solid adjustable obstacles, where the horse is let loose to jump in complete freedom. While this installation may be an extravagance for a small stable, it is a most useful and effective facility where there are a number of young Hunters in training. It is certainly more effective than the contraptions devised by some inventive trainers; for example, the Frenchman who encircled his entire jumping arena with overhead wires on which ran a wheel and a number of cords; whenever he schooled over fences, he would fasten the cords around his body so that if his horse went down or an accident occurred, he would remain safely suspended in the air!

It is unnecessary to school a Hunter over very high jumps. Consistency of performance and good jumping form are far more important than height. Obstacles of three feet or three feet six inches are quite enough for everyday schooling, although a few fences may be set at four feet or four feet six inches once or twice a week during the month before a horse show or the reopening of the hunting season. The important accomplishments are for the horse to approach the obstacle smoothly, to be perfectly obedient at the take-off (which is usually at a point a foot or two farther away from the jump than its height), to leave the ground

Schooling over jumps. A good way to develop jumping ability is to place a low fence 9 or 10 feet from a series of rails on the ground and then gradually raise and/or spread the fence, as described in the text. Eventually the rails on the ground can be removed, and bigger fences like the larger oxer can be jumped from a canter. (*Photos by James Deutschmann*)

with sufficient impulsion, extending his neck and rounding his back as he clears the fence with his body straight, and finally to collect himself immediately upon landing and to continue cantering on in an unbroken stride.

A Working Hunter shouldn't jump like an Open Jumper, who clears his fences high and clean. The Hunter may meet a great many obstacles during a long day's hunt, and if he consistently jumps too big over his fences he will only tire himself needlessly.

When he is jumping well under saddle in the schooling ring where the take-off and landing are level, the apprentice Hunter may be asked to jump over the natural obstacles on uneven terrain that he encounters during his cross-country rides, first at a trot and eventually at a canter.

At the end of twelve months or so of jumping training, he can be introduced to the hounds and the Hunt. The cubbing season, when the young hounds are trained before the official season starts, takes place in

Learning to jump in a Hitchcock pen. (*Photo by Ray Woolfe, Jr.*)

August or September in most parts of the country and is the ideal occasion to show a young horse what the Hunt is like. Remember that the purpose of cubbing is to perfect the training of the hounds, not to train green horses, and your presence is tolerated as a courtesy on the part of the MFH on condition that you do not interfere with the work of the pack. At first your horse will be very excited and must be kept at a distance. In fact, the first few times out he should not be asked to jump every fence, but merely to follow a part of the chase in order to become accustomed to the stimulating spectacle of the hounds, the sound of the horns, and the presence of so many other horses and riders.

If he has behaved well during several cubbing meets, he may follow part of the regular Hunt, turning for home as soon as he shows signs of fatigue. Any weakness that is exposed in the hunting field should be corrected later on at home in the schooling ring.

During the next year the young Hunter's ring training becomes more advanced, with a variety of new jumps added and the obstacles placed in varying series and combinations. But the work should never be beyond his means or so difficult that his confidence is shaken. Once that is lost it is not easily recovered, and the horse's confidence in himself and in his rider is absolutely essential to all successful jumping activities.

TRAINING THE JUMPER

The horse is not very well designed for jumping when you compare him to other animals such as cats, gazelles, and deer. Nor is jumping one of his favorite pastimes, although Pat Smythe's famous mare Tosca is said to have jumped fences just for the fun of it. Nevertheless, if a horse possesses suitable conformation and temperament, an experienced trainer and an expert rider can develop his natural ability to the point where he is capable of astounding athletic achievements. Just consider the present official Federation Equestre Internationale (FEI) world jumping records:

High Jump: 8'1¼" (2.47 meters) by Huaso, ridden by Captain Larraguibel at Santiago, Chile, in 1949

Long Jump: 27'6¾" (8.40 meters), set by Andre Ferreira of South Africa on Something at Johannesburg, in 1975 (over an obtacle of that width)

The present North American Indoor Puissance (high jump) record is 7'5", set at Toronto in 1978 by Barney Ward riding Lucky Hit. But such "records" during competition cannot be taken too seriously, since they are not produced under identical, controlled conditions . . . and especially since sophisticated show managements have recognized the publicity value of setting a new high jump record whenever possible.

While certain physical qualities help to make a good Jumper (strong quarters, sound feet and legs, good shoulders and heart depth, a rather short back and a closely coupled body), as well as certain natural aptitudes (good natural balance and impulsion, freedom of movement, instinctive bending of the knees and rounding of the back when clearing an obstacle, and a natural instinct to jump clean), one of the most important requisites of all is undoubtedly courage. Some horses who look quite unimpressive outside of the jumping arena simply fly over the fences once they have passed through the In Gate, their generous hearts making up for their obvious deficiencies of conformation.

Because of its strenuous physical demands, concentrated jumping training rarely starts before the age of four. Until then, all of the preliminary schooling, especially the Hunter program, provides the best possible foundation. Cross-country work is perhaps less important for the Open Jumper than for the Hunter, although a certain amount of it, especially over uneven terrain, helps to develop sure-footedness and accustoms the horse to making last-minute adjustments of balance.

The difference between the obstacles jumped by Hunters and by Open Jumpers lies not only in their size (there is no limit in Open Jumping, international Puissance jump-offs frequently reaching a height of seven feet, and six-foot spread fences being commonplace), but also in their difficulty. Jumping courses are designed to present knotty problems to the horse and rider as a test of obedience and judgment as well as gymnastic ability. Combinations of fences are placed at awkward distances, requiring a meticulous adjustment of the horse's stride; a vertical obstacle may be placed right after a very spread one, necessitating a split-second change from an extended jumping position to a collected one. Basically, obstacles are difficult to the degree that their form conflicts with the natural arc of the horse's jump and their separating distances with the horse's normal length of stride. Thus, experienced riders know that innocuous looking parallel rails are a very difficult obstacle, while the more imposing triple bars and hog backs are much easier to jump clean.

Consequently, the Open Jumper must be trained as a veritable athlete, with advanced schooling to enable him to adjust his strides in order to arrive at the precise take-off point and to produce the degree of collection necessary to furnish the impulsion for clearing very broad or very high obstacles—all the while remaining perfectly relaxed and supple.

His initial jumping lessons are just like those of the Hunter, starting either on the longe or loose in a jumping chute, with a rail on the ground and then simple fences, eventually progressing to wider obstacles such as parallel poles and oxers, and finally combinations of fences placed at easy one- or two-stride distances apart. The length of a Jumper's stride is important to the rider in planning the way he will ride a course (the average horse's jumping stride measures about four yards), and so the longe work that develops even, uniform strides is very useful. Flexing and suppling exercises are also effective: figure eights, serpentines, turns, halts, and backing. Special attention is given to changing leads, including flying changes of lead (at every stride).

But the most valuable tool of all in training Jumpers is a set of cavalletti, which is a series of poles 10 to 12 feet long, placed on low trestles that raise them 6 inches or so from the ground, and over which the horse is walked and trotted, on the longe as well as under saddle, at first over a single pole and then over an entire series. The initial object is merely to measure the horse's strides, and then to regulate his approach to a fence. At the beginning, the cavalletti are adjusted to the horse's normal stride, which means that they are placed 5 or 6 feet apart, with an 11- to 12-foot distance preceding the obstacle. Afterward, the distances may be lengthened or shortened, thereby obliging the horse to lengthen or shorten his strides. Finally, any number of variations can be devised, arranging the cavalletti in combination with one or several fences. Hunters, as we have seen, are increasingly trained over cavalletti too.

At the same time, the Jumper is schooled over jumps without cavalletti, in order to help him acquire an eye for distances—and to train the rider's eye as well.

The key to successful jumping is in the approach to the obstacle, rather than what happens once the horse and rider have left the ground. That is why experienced Jumper trainers devote more training time to the approach than to the actual clearing of obstacles. Besides, the best way to train a horse to jump in response to the rider's actions, instead of merely because there is a fence in front of him, is to turn the horse away from an obstacle at the very last minute, so that he does not develop the habit of anticipating the rider or of rushing into his fences uncontrolled. During a typical schooling session the horse may be circled or halted in front of a fence three or four times or even more, for every fence he is actually asked to jump.

Gradually the obstacles are raised and their appearance varied. In the show ring a Jumper may encounter such odd-looking barriers as a row of oil drums, a railroad-crossing gate, or a garishly painted poster on a fence, in addition to the simple rustic fences and gates. During the cross-country phase of recent Three-Day Olympic Events, contestants have been required to jump over a hayrick, a water trough, and a garden table set for tea.

As the horse's physical ability increases, he may be faced with more difficult gymnastic problems, such as jumping a fence at an angle, and jumping when coming out of a turn.

In Jumping classes conducted under Table I of the American Horse Shows Association rules, contestants are penalized for touching the obstacles as well as for knocking them down, and so American Jumpers must be taught to jump not only well, but clean. Occasionally one meets a horse who is a naturally clean Jumper, but even he may become careless from time to time, especially when he has learned that ordinary jumping poles roll to the ground without causing him any great personal inconvenience. Trainers have many methods for teaching a horse to "respect" an obstacle. One of the most common is "poling" with a taped bamboo pole which an assistant holds at the top of a fence and raps sharply against the horse's legs as he clears it. Another is to place a light iron pipe directly on top of the fence, so that the horse's carelessness will cause him pain. The use of solid fences during early training instills respect at the very beginning, but after the obstacles have become bigger, solid ones are dangerous.

Patience is essential when training all kinds of horses, but especially Jumpers. There is no short-cut. While it can happen that an exceptionally talented horse, even insufficiently schooled, may win a few classes or have a brilliant season, it is most likely that his career will be brief and that sooner or later he will have to be retrained correctly from the very beginning. There is no substitute for a carefully planned, step-by-step schooling program adjusted to the aptitudes and learning ability of each individual horse. Excellent general guidelines can be found in such books as:

Training Hunters, Jumpers and Hacks, by Harry D. Chamberlin (Van Nostrand, 1973)
Effective Horsemanship, by Noel Jackson (Arco, 1967)
Riding and Jumping, by William Steinkraus (Doubleday, 1969)
The Complete Book of Show Jumping, by Michael Clayton and William Steinkraus (Crown Publishers, 1975)
Hunter Seat Equitation, by George Morris (Doubleday, 1971)

The average age of the top Jumpers is about twelve or thirteen years, and some of the most successful ones have been much older, so there is no need for precipitation. The extra months devoted to laying a sound foundation at the very beginning are sure to reap generous dividends in the end, by prolonging a Jumper's active career by many years. In other words, in Jumping (as in many other activities), it pays to "make haste slowly."

TRAINING THE SADDLE HORSE

Three- and Five-Gaited Saddle Horses, as well as Morgans and Arabians destined for Three-Gaited show events, are trained to produce high action and a high degree of collection with a proud head carriage. To a certain extent, this is quite natural to them, much more natural than to Thoroughbred-type horses, for instance, since their basic conformation lends itself particularly well to high collection and head position.

A bitting harness or "dumb jockey." (*From the catalog of Miller's*)

While the early training of Saddle Horses is the same as for all young foals and colts, the introduction of the bit is slightly different. At the age of eighteen months or so, a special bitting harness is fitted. This is a bridle, harness pad or backband, and a crupper with a tie-down strap and two side straps, a large snaffle bit and an overhead check rein, and its purpose is to obtain the correct head set and to induce flexion from the poll while the young colt's neck muscles are still developing. The bitting harness is fitted quite loosely at first and tightened gradually by shortening the check rein and side straps. Introduced first in the stall, it is worn for only five or ten minutes at the beginning, and later as long as thirty minutes or an hour a day. Finally, the pupil wears it during his driving and longeing lessons.

Saddle Horses aren't longed as much as they are driven in long reins, since this prepares them for driving to a cart later on if they are to be trained as Combination or Fine Harness Horses. Even if they are only to be shown under saddle, harness driving is an excellent means of developing the shoulder muscles that are important to their particular kind of action.

When the Saddle Horse drives well in long reins with the trainer on foot, he is shod in light plates and hitched to a two-wheel breaking cart. At first he is merely led by the halter while pulling an empty cart behind; next he is led and then longed while an assistant is seated in the cart; finally he is driven by the trainer directly from the cart. Only three or four introductory lessons are usually necessary before he has become accustomed to the strange sensation of hauling a vehicle. But the first few times the trainer must be alert to any signs of alarm and he will need the assistance of one or even two helpers. Very often a horse's immediate reaction to dragging a weight behind him is to bolt, and this might lead to injury if precautions have not been taken. Only the walk and trot are practiced in harness, but the horse must also learn to stand, and it is useful if he is taught to back up a few steps.

At about two and a half or three years of age the young Saddle Horse is introduced to the rider in the traditional way, and work under saddle is begun just as with other types of horses. Prospective Five-Gaited horses are often started younger and worked harder than the Walk-Trot or Fine Harness types.

The first two gaits to be schooled are the walk and the trot. Beyond this stage there is no well-defined teaching technique. Saddle Horse trainers are obliged to vary their methods with each individual horse, the only accepted rule being to concentrate on perfecting just one gait at a time. Even then, there is always the danger when a new gait is being learned that the horse will lose or mix up the ones he has previously mastered.

Generally speaking, the stronger a horse's natural gaits, the more difficult it will be for him to acquire the artificial ones. Most trainers try almost anything that their ingenuity and experience suggests in order to induce the horse to produce the desired movements, and then to impress upon him that this is what they wish him to do. Only when the form of a gait is well set are speed, collection, and brilliance sought. Of course, the trainer must be an excellent rider and know exactly what the different gaits should feel like in the saddle when they are properly performed. Special shoeing is an indispensable aid in acquiring and perfecting the artificial gaits. The horse's legs are always protected during exercise by bandages, and hinged quarter boots worn on the forefeet.

Unless a horse shows a special inclination to rack, the trainer first attempts to teach his pupil the stepping pace, which is a slightly syncopated, four-beat gait, during which the horse crouches on his hindquarters and more or less trots with the forelegs while walking with the hind. Many horses learn it best from the trot, since it is sort of a midway gait between the trot and the pace. Others learn it better from the walk. The movement should be rather slow, collected, and rhythmical, with a maximum of action.

The rack is difficult and tiring to perform and no less challenging to teach. It is, like the stepping pace, an artificial gait, and not all horses learn to do it well, although an aptitude is inborn in certain American Saddle Bred families. Usually, a horse is put into the stepping pace and then urged on to greater speed in order to induce him to break into a rack, which is produced from the same crouching position, only with an even four-beat rhythm and gliding speed. Of all the gaits the rack is the hardest on the horse. If it is practiced too long at a time, he is very apt to slip into a pace or a mixed-up gait in order to relieve his weary limbs.

The canter is taught in the usual way, always by urging the horse into it from a walk, putting him on the correct lead, and working equally on both leads. It should be a rather slow, collected canter instead of a gallop, and the horse must be restrained from going too fast or from moving too high or extending too far. Cantering in small circles tends to reduce the stride and limit the speed.

As a colt, the Saddle Horse will probably have learned to stretch or park, which is the stance he must assume when he is judged in the show ring. The early lessons are repeated from time to time so that they remain fresh in his mind, and he is taught to park in harness too, which is a bit more difficult to learn.

While being schooled in each of his gaits, the Saddle Horse is trained to respond immediately to the rider's signals for going into a certain gait, and then to maintain it without a break until receiving a signal to change. The rider's leg aids are less important than with Hunters or Jumpers, and the action of the bit more so. Moreover, Saddle Horses are often taught to associate the direction in which they turn or move with a certain gait.

As training progresses, the lessons may take place in a round or oval ring instead of on a straight-of-way, because the horse needs practice in maintaining his gait without a break while bending around a curve.

Backing is also schooled, under saddle as well as in harness, for it is a required movement in showing.

The Saddle Horse is ridden and shown in a double bridle. He is introduced to it gently, just like the other types, with particular care being taken to avoid spoiling his mouth or throwing him off the gaits he has learned. The curb part is more important for him than for other horses, as it tends to increase his flexion at the poll. But he must never be permitted to overflex, with the forehead falling forward of the vertical line, which is a very bad fault.

Many considerations enter into the decision as to whether a Saddle Horse is best suited for a Three-Gaited or a Five-Gaited career. One of the most important is the horse's natural conformation and temperament, since the desirable features of a Three-Gaited Saddle Horse are a fine head, a long tapering neck, an excellent vertical head position, and perfect manners. His most important gait is a flashy trot. The Five-Gaited horse should be bolder, fiery and handsome, somewhat heavier in build, and perhaps less refined, but he should possess greater skill and brilliance, excelling in the slow gait and the rack, especially the latter. If a horse performs only three gaits well but is also good at driving, he may make a Combination show horse. Perhaps he will be best not as a riding horse at all, but in Fine Harness, in which case he should be of the Five-Gaited type with flowing mane and tail and needs to learn just two gaits, aside from the walk and trot: an animated walk and a park trot. But he should acquire exceptionally good manners.

When his future has been decided, the horse is groomed accordingly by setting his tail (Five-Gaited and Fine Harness), or by roaching his mane and setting and clipping the upper part of the tail (Three-Gaited).

From now on, his lessons follow a program designed to polish and perfect the skills he will eventually demonstrate so proudly in the show ring. It is only fair to add, however, that training Saddle Horses is a very difficult specialty. Few amateurs learn to do it well enough to excel in competition when matched against such great professional experts as Red Crabtree, Ed Teater, Jim B. Robertson, Tom Moore, and Don Harris, to mention only a few of the best.

TRAINING THE WALKING HORSE

The Walking Horse requires less lengthy training than either Saddle Horses or Hunters, because he only needs to perform three gaits—the

A Saddle Horse in a tail set. (*Photo by James Deutschmann*)

flat-footed walk, the running walk, and the canter—all of which are natural to him. His conformation is well adapted to produce them with the required style, and a strong strain of Saddle Horse blood endows him with an unusual aptitude for mastering them. In addition, his steady, adaptable, easygoing temperament makes him a model student.

The early training of the Walking Horse may follow the traditional program for all young horses. But frequently he is handled as a foal and colt just enough to make him gentle, to learn to lead well and to park, while being permitted to develop his natural way of going by running loose at pasture until he is about two years old.

It is most often at this age that his serious schooling begins. He may be bitted in the usual way, starting with a soft snaffle; or, as is frequently the case, the leading lessons may proceed in a hackamore, and a curb bit is introduced later when he is ready to be ridden. This usually occurs sooner than with other breeds, for the Walking Horse may be broken to the saddle as early as the age of two by a very lightweight rider, the preliminary steps of head-setting, longeing, long-rein driving, and hitching being entirely eliminated.

The first gait to be taught is the flat-footed walk. Shod in light rac-

ing plates with thick leather pads, the young Walking Horse carries a little added toe weight to help him keep his walk straight and square. The
trainer encourages his natural tendency to nod his head in rhythm, and
tries to develop a good forward reach with the legs as well as speed,
evenness, and boldness. Schooling exercises consist of straight lines, circles, turns, stops, and backing, with periodic refresher lessons in parking.

When the flat-footed walk is well established, the time has come to
work on the running walk. The basic teaching method is not very complicated. The trainer urges more and more speed at the walk, while preventing the horse from breaking into a trot or pace by a restraining action of the hands. In order to develop a fast and flashy gliding running
walk, special shoeing is employed, as well as Walking Horse heel boots
that prevent injury to the front legs by the overstepping hind feet. In addition, light chains or wooden trotting balls may be placed around the
forefeet to make the horse lift them higher. The longer the overstride, the
greater his chances of winning a ribbon at a horse show! Extreme speed
is also one of the earmarks of a show-quality running walk, but it should
never be demanded until the young horse's physical development is far
enough along, and then only after the pupil has been well warmed up by
schooling in the flat-footed walk. Another requirement of the running
walk is that the horse's head should swing up and down from the shoulders in an exaggerated fashion, nodding with the lift of each front foot,
as the horse at the same time flicks his ears and clicks on the bit. Light
chains dangling from the bit rings are sometimes used to encourage this
distinctive head movement. The principal difficulty in schooling the running walk is to develop maximum speed without allowing the horse to
slip into another gait such as the stepping pace or a mixed-up trot. However, the feeling in the saddle of the running walk is so unique that an
experienced trainer is able to detect any irregularity at once.

Finally, the Walking Horse is schooled in the canter, which should
be an easy, high, rolling gait that comes quite naturally to him. For show
horses, the "rocking-chair" effect is nowadays highly exaggerated. But
the trainer's only real problem is to encourage the desired movement
while restraining the horse's tendency to gallop.

In his general way of going the Walking Horse may be more relaxed
and less collected than the other Gaited horses. In fact, a certain
looseness of stride is desirable. His head carriage is obtained by bitting
rather than by wearing a head-set or bitting harness. If he has started
training in a hackamore, his first bit is usually a low-port curb with a single bridle, and eventually the regulation Walking Horse bit, which is a

curb type with a higher port, a soft leather curb strap, and very long, curved cheekpieces. If he has been introduced to bitting with a simple snaffle, the snaffle must be replaced by a low-port curb before beginning the gaiting lessons. His head should be held high and flexed at the poll, with his muzzle slightly tucked.

When he performs his three gaits well, the Walking Horse is ready to graduate from school. If he shows particular style, with great speed and overstride at the running walk, he may have a brilliant future in the show ring, and so his tail will be set and his subsequent schooling carefully supervised, probably by a professional trainer.

TRAINING THE WESTERN HORSE

Western-style riding has become so popular in recent years that nowadays all kinds of horses are trained the Western way: Thoroughbreds, Arabians, Morgans, and mixed breeds as well as the horses of more definite Western origin, such as Quarter Horses, Palominos, and Appaloosas. Actually, any horse can be trained for pleasure riding in Western rig, but advanced activities such as cutting and roping do require special aptitudes and often a certain kind of conformation, both of which must be inborn. That is why the most successful cutting and rodeo horses at the present time are Quarter Horses, while Thoroughbred types seem to win the judges' favor in Working Stock Horse and Reining show classes.

The best Western methods of training well-bred foals and colts vary little from traditional systems, with the same early handling, grooming and hoof care, breaking to the halter, leading and tying, and teaching of simple voice commands. One of the differences is that Western colts are often taught to be led from another horse ("snubbing"), as well as on foot. Another is that they are accustomed from an early age to the feeling of having ropes slid all over their bodies and swung about their heads in the air. In addition to being trained to stand square and still when tied by the halter, they are taught to stand calmly when placed in hobbles (which link the two fore feet or the two hind feet together), in side lines (which link one fore foot to the matching hind foot), or in cross-sidelines (linking one fore foot to the opposite hind foot).

Western horses are often trained to stand *ground tied*, which can be a great convenience on the range when it may be desirable to dismount and tie the horse in a spot where no natural hitching post is available. In learning the ground tie the horse must gradually come to associate the idea of the split reins lying on the ground in front of him with immobility. In order to establish this association of ideas, the trainer either drops the reins and snaps them to a weighted ring imbedded in the ground, or he places the horse in hobbles as he drops the reins in front of him. After sufficient repetition, the horse will associate the rein position on the ground with standing still until his master returns and picks up the reins again.

The first year in the life of a Western foal is devoted mostly to play. But at twelve months or so he can attempt a little serious work in the corral. Often his first real lesson is in *whip-breaking,* which is a process of teaching the colt to come to his trainer on command and sometimes to follow him as well. Maneuvering the colt into a corner of a small corral, the trainer holds a long whip which he flicks lightly across the colt's cannons at the same time he pulls on the halter rope and commands, "Come here." The colt is rewarded when he obeys, and flicked with the whip across his legs when he turns away from the trainer or tries to evade him. After a little practice the exercise is repeated without a halter, and usually in a very short time the young trainee will obediently trot over to his master and face him standing still as soon as he hears the words "Come here." This is very common obedience-training for Western horses who are often kept loose in pastures. For working stock horses, the lesson is slightly different, since they are whip-trained to turn around and face the trainer and to stand still without approaching him.

There is no reason why a Western yearling cannot be longed, just like his Eastern cousins, and many of them are (but Western trainers usually refer to the longe line as a "gyp rope"). However, it is even more common to ground-drive Western colts in long reins when they are fifteen or sixteen months of age, and later to hitch them to a cart. For this purpose they wear a hackamore more often than a cavesson noseband, but the exercises and the technique are the same. A tie-down strap or a simple bitting rig may be worn during the driving lessons to encourage correct head carriage. After a couple of months of ground-driving in a hackamore, the colt may be bitted with a mild snaffle in the traditional way and driven in the bit and bridle. But many Western trainers prefer to continue with the hackamore until the pupil is more advanced, since it cannot possibly damage his mouth. There is a special risk of bit injury with Western colts because they are broken later and are trained to do sharp turns and short stops much sooner than other horses.

In any case, the first ride almost always takes place in a hackamore as soon as the colt's physical development permits him to be mounted safely. It is not uncommon for Western colts to be ridden during very brief periods by a light rider as early as the age of two, although actual schooling in the saddle should only start when they are physically prepared to withstand the strain, usually between two and a half and three years. The early riding lessons are frequent—perhaps several times a day—but very brief.

The initial sessions are devoted to walking, turning, stopping, and mounting and dismounting from both sides, with the rider emphasizing his spoken commands by leg actions and particularly by shifting his weight in the saddle. Then the jog trot is practiced, to which the Western rider never posts. It is easier to sit comfortably to a slow jog, but this takes the most training. (Green horses almost always jog too fast.) Next, the trainer works on the lope. Again, a slow lope is harder to learn than a faster pace. Finally, he works on the gallop.

During this faster work it is wise to intersperse exercises in stopping and backing a few steps to prevent the young pupil from becoming overexcited.

Work on figure eights accustoms the young horse to weight signals and changes of lead; the loops may be longer and leaner than Eastern figure eights, in order to make him practice sharper turns at the ends. Galloping into corners obliges him to turn correctly on his hind legs in order to get out again. Going around in circles of decreasing size, aside from teaching him to take the correct lead, helps him to learn to maintain his balance and develops the suppleness necessary for executing the sharp turns and pivots he will be taught later on. It is customary to practice backing alongside a straight fence, in order to oblige the horse to keep his body straight. In Stock Horse show classes, he may be asked to back up as much as fifteen feet or more in a perfectly straight line.

Often the work of Western horses requires them to stop short from a fast gallop. While the foundation for this characteristic Western movement can be laid during the early training period, concentrated work is not attempted until the animal is fairly mature physically, for the exercises are very hard on the feet and legs and premature work can lead to unsoundness. First, the young horse is frequently asked to make short stops from all gaits on the hind legs, until he responds promptly and with precision. Then the trainer runs the horse alongside a fence and at the same time that he stops him, he turns his head in toward the fence. In order to avoid hitting himself, the horse must slide and squat back on his hocks as he turns, which is the basis of the rollback and the *sliding stop*.

Some trainers gallop their horses straight up to the side of a barn or some other solid wall, stopping and turning them at the last minute. The exercise is repeated with gradually increasing speed, but never for more than a few minutes at each lesson, because it is tiring and very hard on a horse's feet. Sometimes his front feet are left unshod to make them tender, so that the horse will more readily shift his weight to his haunches when sliding to a stop. The hind legs should be protected by heel boots. In a good sliding stop the stop should be smooth and gliding with the hocks well under the horse and the forelegs braced.

Cross-country rides are very important for a Western horse. Steadiness is one of his most desirable attributes, and the best way to develop it is to acquaint him with all kinds of experiences at an early age so that nothing will take him by surprise later on. He is ridden around cattle as well as other horses and various farm vehicles. As a matter of fact, by observing his reactions to livestock, an experienced trainer can already tell whether his pupil has inherited that curious cow sense that is an essential trait of stock and cutting horses.

After a year of schooling in his basic skills, the colt is ready to be bitted. A gradual transition is made from the hackamore to a standard Western curb bit by first using a bozal, which has a rounded, wired nosepiece narrower than the hackamore. At first the bozal and curb bit are worn at the same time, with just the bozal actively employed; little by little, more pressure is placed on the bit and less on the bozal, until the latter may be removed entirely. Professional trainers sometimes start out right away with a spade bit, but this is very severe and can easily damage a young horse's mouth if the rider does not possess light hands and perfect control.

When his gaits are well set and the horse is used to the bridle, he may be schooled in *neck-reining*, which will permit riding with the reins held is only one hand. As all well-trained riders know, there are two principal types of rein effects: the direct rein (which turns the horse's head in the direction in which he is to move), and the indirect rein (which places a slight pressure on the horse's neck on the side *opposite* to that in which he is to move). In many kinds of riding both effects are used simultaneously. But with Polo Ponies, stock horses and most Western pleasure hacks, only the indirect rein effect is used, and this is what is referred to as "neck-reining."

One of the most usual training methods is to cross the two reins under the horse's neck. When the trainer wishes the horse to turn to the right, for example, he pulls lightly on the left-hand rein, at the same time laying it across the horse's neck. The horse will obey the bit signal he has already learned by turning to the right, but gradually he will also associate turning to the right with the feeling of the rein on the left side of his neck. Weight shifts reinforce the rein signals. Eventually the trainer puts no pressure on the mouth at all, but signals turns entirely by laying the rein on the horse's neck and by shifting, ever more slightly, his own body weight.

Another method is to use two hands, the signal for the turn being given by an outward pull on one (direct) rein, while the opposite (indirect) rein is laid across the horse's neck, the direct-rein effect being gradually lightened and finally discarded entirely. All early work in neck-reining is done only at a walk until the horse has learned to obey accurately and promptly the slightest touch of the rein against his neck.

Aside from constantly trying to develop his horse's physical ability and obedience, just like his Eastern counterpart, the Western trainer stresses the exercises that prepare his horse for the specialties he may be asked to master later on: sharp turns, immediate stops, backing, galloping in small circles, half and full turns on the haunches (pivots or "rollbacks"), and the sliding stop.

From now on, the Western horse's advanced schooling varies according to the particular role he may be asked to play on the ranch or in the contest arena.

The *roping horse* may be trained either as a working stock horse or as a show performer. Although calves aren't branded as much today as they used to be, they still are roped in order to be earmarked and vaccinated. (When branding is still practiced, it is apt to be "freeze branding," which is relatively painless, produces no open wound, but destroys pigment cells so that the hair in the area treated grows in again completely white, leaving a visible pattern.) As an arena sport, roping now occupies a place not only in rodeos and Quarter Horse shows, but in the Western division of regular horse shows all over the country.

Schooling in roping may start as early as the age of three if a horse has already completed his basic training. He must learn to follow a running calf, and when the rider ropes the animal from the saddle and dismounts to throw it to the ground, the horse must slide to a stop as soon as the slack of the rope is thrown in front of his head, back up and drag the calf a few steps to tighten the noose, and then stand quietly unmounted, always facing the calf and holding the rope taut until the cowboy has tied the calf's three legs together, released the rope, and remounted.

The first step in training is to let the horse run after calves without roping. Then he must practice taking the necessary steps backward to tighten a rope which is merely held in the trainer's hands while the trainer is on foot. A long training whip may be used, or the trainer may flick the slack of the rope in his horse's face in order to get him to back. Sometimes a pulley-like system of ropes is attached to the horse's hackamore, so that a pull on the lead rope forces him to move backward by exerting pressure on his nose. Next, a sandbag or a heavy log is used to represent the calf while the trainer, now mounted in the saddle, goes through all the motions of the actual calf-roping procedure. This is called "dry work," during which the horse learns to brace himself for the jerk on the saddle horn when the calf is roped.

"Wet work" begins when a live animal is substituted for the sand-bag. The first one may very well be a goat rather than a calf, and the scene is rehearsed at a walk at first and finally at a gallop. The choice of an animal suitable to the stage of the horse's training is very important, for too clever and experienced a calf can elude the horse, and confuse and discourage him. Roping is rather strenuous work for an apprentice cow pony, and overwork must be avoided.

To be a good enough roping horse to compete in the contest arena, a horse must possess perfect soundness, high strong withers, plenty of early speed that can last up to two hundred yards if necessary, very short, clean stops, and innate cow sense. For rodeo contests he must also learn to stand quietly in a chute until asked to move out at top speed, and this requires more special schooling. In rodeos, only time counts in the scoring, but in Quarter Horse performances it is the horse's ability that is rated. Needless to add, in any kind of a roping performance as well as in successful training, the horse's rider must also be an excellent roper.

Training the *cutting horse* is one of the most difficult, and also exciting, projects that any horseman can undertake. But even the most expert professional trainer won't get very far with an unsuitable horse. A promising cutting horse is calm by nature and has outstanding cow sense. His neck-reining should be impeccable, for he must be ridden with very slack reins, and his pivots and short stops on the haunches must be superb. Nowadays, practical cutting of individual calves from a herd is often done with pens and chutes, and so cutting is becoming more and more an arena sport, while the training that used to take place on the range is now accomplished in a corral by a professional trainer. The word *cutting*, by the way, does not originate from the action of the horse, although he does indeed "cut out" certain calves from a herd. The "cut" is the name of the pen into which the calves are driven.

Training a Cutting Horse. (*Photo courtesy of Mrs. W. Sheldon Winans*)

Cutting lessons are strenuous and rarely start before the age of three. Some trainers begin to work a horse with only a rope around his neck, signaling by leg squeezes and weight shifts. But it is more common for the horse to wear a snaffle bit or a hackamore.

The cutting horse's job is to separate a selected calf from the herd and to prevent him from rejoining it by blocking any attempt to run or dodge past the horse. Needless to say, he must be able to make fast sprints to keep up with the elusive calf, short stops and sharp turns to prevent the calf from slipping by the inside of the arena fence, and he must be smarter and just as agile as the calf if he is to stay with it. When training a cutting horse for competition, the ultimate goal is for the horse to do the work unaided by the rider, whose principal preoccupation is to ease rather than to hinder the horse by remaining in perfect control of his own balance and actions. In actual practice, though, the top cutting riders may help their horses more than the spectator realizes, for they are very clever about concealing their aids.

Nevertheless, no horse is selected for cutting training unless he has shown definite evidence of cow sense. This may well be an inherited trait, or a combination of inherited traits. At least, a number of Quarter Horse stallions, such as Doc Bar, have consistently passed on outstanding cutting ability to their offspring. His inherent instinct is encouraged and developed by taking him around to observe all kinds of cattle. During his elementary training, the emphasis is placed on schooling short sprints, sharp turns (half as well as full turns), and changes of lead during figure eights, all of which develop the muscles and agility the horse will need for actual cutting.

When he is well-schooled in the fundamental techniques, he starts to work in a corral with calves or goats, aided by one or two assistants on horseback who act as turn-back men. As the horse begins to understand what is expected of him, the trainer allows him to work with less and less prompting. Some horses will grasp the idea very quickly, but others may require a good deal of patient coaching.

Because of its physical demands and the intense concentration necessary, the lessons are divided into several brief sessions. Some horses appear to enjoy the work so much that they would keep it up indefinitely if the trainer did not intervene!

It has been estimated that it takes at least six months to prepare a talented cutting novice for competition, and at least one or two years of experience to make a finished performer.

TRAINING PONIES

Because their limited size generally permits them to be ridden only by children, the schooling of riding ponies is less complete than that of horses. Their training program is less extensive, the lessons shorter, the jumping obstacles smaller, and trainers don't attempt to put as much finish on their education as they do with riding horses. Fortunately, the average pony is very clever and quick to learn. His natural self-reliance and resourcefulness amply compensate for his relatively limited training.

His early education as a foal and colt is just the same as if he were a horse. As a matter of fact, it is often a temptation to treat an appealing little pony like a foal throughout his entire adult life. But even though he may never grow big, he should never be prevented from growing *up*. Nothing is more disagreeable and more likely to develop bad riding habits in a child than an overpetted pony.

The basic mounted training takes place, whenever possible, with an experienced child rider in the saddle. It is most unwise to let an inexperienced child attempt to train an unschooled pony. Not only is there a risk of injury to the child, but also a strong probability of developing a spoiled and stubborn pony who never will give riding satisfaction. Some of the larger breeds such as the Welsh and Connemara may have their advanced training perfected by a lightweight adult. Those who are to be used for hunting and jumping pursue a simplified Hunter or Jumper program. Gaited ponies, like the Shetland, are given training similar to that of the Saddle Horse.

The most highly schooled of all are the Harness Ponies, especially the Shetlands and the Hackneys, for their small size is no longer a handicap to a trainer and may even be an advantage. From their earliest lessons, long-rein driving and hitching are stressed. They learn to stand in a stretched position and are schooled in a park trot, which is a slow trotting gait with high, showy action that is facilitated by the use of specially weighted "rocker" shoes.

Since Harness Ponies are usually bred and trained exclusively for showing, their education is most often supervised by a professional trainer and driver or "whip." Riding ponies, on the other hand, have often been successfully trained by expert amateurs. One of the trainer's principal preoccupations is to develop the physical aptitudes of these winning creatures without spoiling their dispositions. Young ponies need a lot of exercise, with plenty of time in the pasture or paddock in addition to their daily riding lessons.

DRESSAGE TRAINING

To speak of dressage training is really redundant, because *dressage* (pronounced to rhyme with "garage") is a French word literally translated as "training," and also as "straightening," in the military sense of "dressing the ranks."

This systematic method of schooling horses, based on the classical principles of horsemanship, is not trick riding, as some people still seem to believe. Although a highly trained dressage horse can indeed perform a number of school figures, rather like an equine ballet dancer, the basic purpose of the art is to perfect his natural movements and to develop his suppleness, balance, and responsiveness, thus improving his performance whatever it may be. Dressage training can also preserve a horse's soundness and even prolong his life, because it makes him better balanced, with his weight more rationally distributed between the vulnerable forehand and the sturdier hindquarters, and therefore less apt to suffer from wear and tear. Many dressage horses have remained sound enough for competition in their twenties.

There is a distinction between elementary dressage, in which the object is to produce a superior riding horse that is keen but submissive, supple, obedient, forward-moving, and free from resistance, and advanced or Grand Dressage, in which the horses and riders are so highly trained that they are finally also able to perform movements demanding a high degree of collection and instant response to imperceptible commands, at the same time maintaining an appearance of lightness and elegance. Then there is a distinction between Olympic Grand Prix Dressage and Haute Ecole or Exhibition Dressage, as practiced by the famous Spanish Riding School of Vienna, with its specially bred and trained Lippizaners, in France by the Cadre Noir of the Cavalry School at Saumur, and in Spain by the Andalusian Riding School of Jerez de la Frontera. Circus dressage is something else again. Nevertheless, the same basic principles and training underlie them all.

Dressage is concerned with perfecting the walk (with working, collected, medium, extended, and free strides), the trot and canter (with working, collected, medium, and extended strides), as well as halts and half-halts, rein-backs (backing), and Figure Eights and serpentines with simple and flying changes of lead. More advanced are turns on the haunches, half and full pirouettes, the counter-canter (leading with the outside legs), the passage (a slow, shortened, very collected, elevated, and cadenced trot), and the piaffe (a collected trot in place). Turning figures include the volte, where the horse turns in a circle about six meters in diameter, and the change through the circle, which is half of a Figure Eight. There is also a series of lateral movements, in which the horse is bent uniformly from the poll to the tail and moves with his forehand and quarters on two distinct tracks. These are known as the shoulder-in, the travers, and the renvers, and the foundation exercise for them all is called "leg-yielding," in which the horse is slightly bent in his entire length toward the side of the rider's active leg, with the fore and hind legs on that side crossing in front of the others. While these advanced movements are most impressive, experienced Dressage riders say that the extended walk is the hardest of all to perfect. The competitive tests formulated by the AHSA indicate the best sequence of schooling these dressage exercises, from the simplest level to the highest.

Dressage training. (*Photo courtesy of Mrs. William Steinkraus*)

Needless to say, the horse who is gifted with the physical and temperamental aptitudes to make a finished dressage performer is a rare creature indeed, and the rider who is willing and able to undertake the arduous schooling is almost as exceptional. But a little basic dressage training can be of immense benefit to any average horse and conscientious rider, as many Hunter, Jumper, and Pleasure horsemen have learned. Even Stock Horse trainers have discovered that dressage improves their horses' work in the corral or show ring. Elementary dressage is also part of the Pony Club program and is a phase of the popular sport of Eventing.

Dressage training has become increasingly available throughout the country. Young riders can find it by joining a Pony Club. The U. S. Dressage Federation has regional representatives and sponsors clinics, while Combined Training Association clubs feature dressage as part of their Eventing training. The American Horse Shows Association can provide information about these organizations and their activities. In addition, world-renowned dressage trainers and riders give private lessons to advanced students and occasionally hold clinics. Even if none of these possibilities is available, there is no reason why an ambitious horseman cannot attempt to teach his horse the fundamentals of dressage with the aid of one of the detailed works on the subject, such as:

Hilda Gurney riding her home-trained dressage horse, Keen, in the World Dressage Championship at Goodwood, England. (*Photo courtesy of the USET*)

Bengt Ljundquist, *Practical Dressage Manual* (12711 River Road, Potomac, Maryland 20854)

Alois Podhajsky, *The Complete Training of Horse and Rider* (Doubleday, 1967)

Jean Saint-Fort Paillard, *Understanding Equitation* (Doubleday, 1974)

A. L. Endrödy, *Give Your Horse a Chance* (J. A. Allen, London, 1971)

Albert Decarpentry, *Academic Equitation* (J. A. Allen, London, 1971)

Keen, an American Thoroughbred, was basically trained by his owner-rider Hilda Gurney, a California schoolteacher, and the pair won the Pan American Games Gold Medal in 1975 and placed Fourth in the Olympic Grand Prix Dressage event in 1976—which proves that it can be done!

RE-EDUCATION

Re-education is the process of discovering the defects of an already trained horse and then attempting to correct them. Since horses are living creatures and none of them is perfect, you will never reach the point where you can say "He's finished," put an end to his schooling, and live happily ever after with a perfectly well-trained mount!

It is more than likely that your own horse already has learned to respond to the basic aids more or less correctly. He probably produces all of his gaits reasonably well, and this is all that many young riders expect of a horse. They are content to jog along, year after year, without ever attempting to improve their horse's ability or their own. They adjust themselves to their horse's faults and the horse adjusts to theirs, and often it never occurs to the riders that they are getting only a fraction of the pleasure that they might from their riding partnership.

Even the apparently flawless performer is bound to have a resistance somewhere. Most horses favor something, usually one of the hind legs. Crooked movements can often be traced back to some part of the body that the horse is favoring because of a training or conformation weakness. Some trainers claim that because of the unborn foal's asymmetrical position in its mother's womb, its physical development is bound to be one-sided. In any case, the first defect an experienced horseman looks for is any sign of unevenness, and once it is detected he sets about to correct it.

Almost all horses need help in finding their own natural balance. With older animals it may mean going back to the very beginning of elementary training, but the efforts spent in balancing your horse really well are most worthwhile. Not only will it permit him to do more things better, but also it will keep him sounder by removing the cause of uneven wear and strain on his body mechanism.

Many registered Thoroughbreds have been trained for racing rather than as riding horses, and it is often advisable to retrain them almost from scratch as well, for they have probably learned little of the rudiments of hacking. One of the most frequent causes of unevenness in Thoroughbreds may be traced back to the fact that American races are run counterclockwise, and consequently race horses learn to use only one lead. Also, because their work requires them only to walk or gallop, few race horses have occasion to develop a good natural trot. Furthermore, the riding technique of race-track jockeys, as excellent as some of them may be, is quite different from normal hunting or hacking. For example, most jockeys ride with the left stirrup longer than the right (called "acey-deucey"), because all of our race track turns are taken to the left. William Hartack was one of the very few American turf stars to ride with stirrups at an almost even length, although all European jockeys do so—for example, Jean Cruguet, the French jockey who rode Seattle Slew to his Triple Crown.

Even with the best-trained horses, problems will crop up from time to time. Different forms of resistance, evasion, and stiffness may develop quite unexpectedly. An older horse may become cunning as a result of bad riding. Any horse can pick up a few bad habits during his riding career.

The experienced horseman is always alert to this danger, since he knows that it is much more difficult to correct bad habits than to teach good ones. For example, with a *hard-mouthed* horse, the only solution is to rest his mouth and then start his entire bitting education all over again. Some horses become careless because they are simply *"sour"* from overwork, and they too need a long rest before resuming training.

In the event of *pulling*, the rider should first of all check his own actions to make sure that he himself is not the unwitting cause. Otherwise, his horse may have to be retrained completely so that he will accept the bit as he should.

Ponies, as they grow older, tend to become guilty of *napping* (refusing to advance), for which there are two traditional cures: first, to simply outstay the pony by making him stand still much longer than he likes; or second, to force him into motion by turning him around sharply in small circles.

You may have a horse who suddenly decides to try to *evade the bit* by throwing his head up or by getting his tongue over the mouthpiece. A change of bitting system is one immediate solution, although diagnosis often reveals that the source of trouble is not in the horse's mouth at all, but in the rider's hands.

Rearing is usually caused by heavy-handed riding. But it is also possible that a horse rears in order to evade the bit because his mouth is sore. In this case it may be that you are using a bit that is unsuitable in size or type. If the horse's mouth is badly damaged, you may have to rest his mouth completely or ride him only in a hackamore until the mouth is sound again.

The rider's first reaction when his horse rears should be to throw his weight forward and above all to remain in control. If he pulls the horse's head around sharply to one side and forces him to spin around, the horse should abandon all ideas of acting up, at least for the moment. At any rate, try to keep a rearer moving, because he cannot do it when he is in motion.

Horses who become excited and attempt to *run away* may be simply trying to burn off excess energy that is the result of too much feed and too little exercise. A romp in the paddock before riding, or working in deep sand, which demands greater muscular effort and attention to balance, are two temporary expedients. But the basic problem is one of insufficient control by the rider and insufficient obedience on the part of the horse.

A most unusual runaway incident occurred during the running of the Maryland Hunt Cup cross-country steeplechase in 1896, when the horse Kingsbury, leading the field after two miles of fast galloping, lost his head completely, threw his rider (T. D. Whistler), and ran off the course, racing in the direction of the stable. There the rider found him, comfortably settled in his own stall, happily munching oats. Furiously remounting, Whistler rode back to the course, picking up where the horse had run away. He caught up with the leaders and, to his great astonishment, won in the last few yards of the four-mile race.

Some equine runaway stories may have a happy ending, as you see, but the consequences of *kicking* are always most unpleasant. Sometimes a horse will kick because he is not getting enough exercise while being fed too rich a diet, and kicking is his way of blowing off steam. But if he is merely being disagreeable, you must apply immediate correction with a stick. You might even provoke an incident, if necessary, because the punishment must be practically simultaneous with the offense in order to be effective. If your horse seems to be preparing to kick while you are riding him around other horses, the best thing to do is to hold his head up and keep him facing the object or animal he wishes to kick while you pull him out of striking range. In the hunting field you should also hold your arm horizontally behind your back as a warning to the rider behind you.

Like human beings, a horse can be adversely influenced by bad company and can pick up bad habits from his stable or riding companions. If spotted in time, you can usually prevent them from taking root.

Perhaps it is not bad habits but bad manners that your horse has learned, such as *nipping* and *biting*. More often, you will find during your horse-owning career that animals have been too severely or improperly chastised in the past, so that a nipper, for example, will no longer nip by the time you acquire him, but he may very possibly have become head-shy. In any case, there is no reason why a rider should feel that he has to live with such unpleasantness, when it is usually possible to eliminate it after accurate diagnosis and patient corrective schooling.

Where your horse's actual performing specialty is concerned—jumping, hunting, gaits, cutting, roping, and so forth—horse shows serve as an invaluable guide to his retraining needs. Competition in the show ring will reveal weaknesses that you never suspected in the home schooling arena, and the period following a show is an excellent time for some serious re-education, brushing up your own technique as well as your horse's, in view of what you have observed during the show.

But in the long run, it is your horse himself who will be your best guide to a sound schooling program. His reaction to your actions and the degree to which he develops his natural ability are infallible evaluations of your success as a rider and as a trainer.

13.   Horse Shows

Few sporting events attract a more varied group of spectators than a horse show. From the weather-beaten ranch hand leaning over the ringside to watch a Western roping class to the bejeweled society leaders who fill the front boxes at Madison Square Garden during the National Horse Show week . . . from the conscientious beginner hoping to improve his own equestrian form by studying the experts to the city-bred child whose only chance to see real-life riding is to buy a ticket to a show, all of them have one thing in common—a love of horses.

Television broadcasts have introduced what used to be considered a rather exclusive event to a larger audience than ever before, while the list of exhibitors and the number of shows are growing steadily. The American Horse Shows Association recognizes more than 1,600 shows a year, and many more are organized under the rules of other associations.

As in any other competitive event where rivalry is keen, it requires thorough training and preparation in addition to ability in order to compete successfully in the "major league." But showing can be a lot of fun for every horse-owner, no matter how limited his skill, if he is sensible in his choice of shows and classes and sporting in his attitude.

There is a good deal of camaraderie among the horse-show regulars, and a show is an excellent place to make friends and to establish contacts with other horsemen. If you are a newcomer to the ring, you should be friendly without being forward, and scrupulously respect the unwritten rules of show-ring etiquette: Never disparage a rival's horse; never ridicule his riding; and never dispute the decision of the judges, no matter what your personal opinion may be. Only by exhibiting good sportsmanship as well as good horsemanship will you profit fully from your show experiences.

Speaking of profit, you shouldn't expect to find the material kind. Competing on a large scale, or following the horse-show circuit every weekend, can be quite a costly hobby, since the prize money offered rarely covers the showing expenses of even the most successful stables. A weekend at an "A" show now represents an investment of several hundred dollars. On the other hand, showing on a smaller scale need not be expensive, and it is impossible to measure in dollars the wealth of pleasure and knowledge you will acquire. (If your horse should happen to do well in the ring, it will probably increase his monetary value, too.)

The national governing body of horse shows in the United States is the American Horse Shows Association (598 Madison Avenue, New York, N.Y. 10022), with which most of the major shows and many of the smaller ones are affiliated. A membership application is enclosed in the Prize List of all recognized shows, and the dues are not excessive: $25 for Senior members (over eighteen) and $15 for Juniors. In order to compete in an AHSA show, you must be a member of this or of an affiliated organization, or pay a $4 registration fee at each show. While Juniors are exempt from this rule, only as AHSA members are they entitled to have the points won in shows throughout the year officially recorded for Horse of the Year awards and to compete in the AHSA Medal Classes for Juniors and in international competitions. The Association publication, *Horse Show*, will keep you up-to-date on announcements of shows and amendments to the current rules, while the AHSA *Rule Book* ought to be considered as indispensable a piece of horse-show equipment as your stable grooming kit.

There are three classes of official shows: A, B, and C, depending upon the amount of money awarded and the number and variety of classes. Placements in A shows are worth the most points toward the annual high-score totals in each of the twenty different divisions, so their standards are high and the ribbons hotly contested. Many shows are of mixed classification. For example, a show may be A for the Hunter and Jumper divisions, B for Saddle Horses, and C for some other division.

In addition, the annual calendar is filled with numerous nonrecognized horse shows organized by Pony Clubs, riding clubs, and various local groups. Some are run in a decidedly informal fashion, but all of them use as a model the Association rules, which are checked and revised each year by committees that include the nation's outstanding horsemen. The American Quarter Horse Division has rules of its own, being governed by the American Quarter Horse Association, while cutting contests are conducted under the regulations of the National Cutting Horse Association.

Sometimes a show will be devoted to a single breed, such as Arabian, Morgan, or Appaloosa. Other shows may make a specialty of Hunters, Saddle Horses, Fine Harness Horses, or Westerns, with a lesser number of classes for some of the remaining divisions. Often there are Halter and Breeding classes for mares, stallions, colts, and fillies, shown in hand (without being ridden) and judged on conformation only. Not all shows, even the major ones, schedule events for every type and breed. But almost always there will be classes in Equitation. Sometimes an entire show is restricted to riders under eighteen years of age, and great amusement is provided for the younger set by Gymkhana events and shows, composed of competitive mounted games for Junior exhibitors.

In short, if you enjoy competition and if your horse is well trained in the specialties of his type or breed, you should have no difficulty in finding horse shows in which to demonstrate your skill before the public.

On the other hand, if your own horse is a lovable but homely creature of only average ability, not at all a show type nor of a registered or even clearly defined breed, there are still many opportunities for you to enter him in Gymkhana events and smaller shows. Perhaps you'll even win a ribbon in a jumping, reining, trail, or hack class restricted to local exhibitors, or place in a Maiden Horsemanship event. Many a nimble pony who wasn't much to look at has introduced his young owner to the heady atmosphere of the winner's circle by carrying him to victory in an egg-and-spoon race, or a game of musical chairs.

While they may differ in detail, all American horse shows respect the same traditional colors of winners' ribbons.

Grand Champion	Blue, Red, Yellow, White
Reserve to Grand Champion	Red, Yellow, White, Pink
Champion	Blue, Red, Yellow
Reserve Champion	Red, Yellow, White
First Prize	Blue
Second Prize	Red
Third Prize	Yellow
Fourth Prize	White
Fifth Prize	Pink
Sixth Prize	Green
Seventh Prize	Purple
Eighth Prize	Brown
Ninth Prize	Gray
Tenth Prize	Light Blue

The show Championship in most divisions is decided in a Championship Performance class, which is often a Stakes event. But the Championship of the Hunter and Jumper divisions is presented to the horse who has won the most points throughout the show, according to the following scale:

Blue Ribbon	5 points
Red Ribbon	3 points
Yellow Ribbon	2 points
White Ribbon	1 point

Only the first four ribbons in each class count toward the Championship, while bonus classes in the Jumper division are awarded bonus points, with a scale of 7–5–4–3–2–1.

Each year in every division the points are recorded by zones as well as nationally, the horse with the largest totals being declared Horse of the Year. A similar award is presented at the end of each year to the Small and Large Pony who have won the most points in International Pony Classes. Other horse-show associations also offer High Score classes and annual awards. In fact, the AHSA recently voted to adopt an "Honor Roll" program similar to that of the Quarter Horse and International Arabian Associations, awarding titles for four different levels of achievement: AHSA Honor Roll, AHSA Champion, AHSA Grand Champion, and AHSA Supreme Champion.

The first step in successful showing is to pick the right shows. The major ones attract the leading horses and riders from all over the country and an amateur must possess a well-bred, well-trained horse and considerable equestrian skill if he is to hold his own in such accomplished company. There is as much difference between a Class A show horse and a family horse as there is between a pedigreed show dog and a pet. Show stables start their green horses out in C shows, which are used for schooling until the horses are ready to confront the Bs and finally the As. Like them, you should plan on acquiring experience in several small local shows to prepare yourself and your horse for more advanced competition.

Horse shows are advertised in the horse publications, listed in *Horse Show* and the calendar of the annual *Rule Book,* or merely announced by a bright poster in a village shop window. The present trend is to coordinate a number of shows to form a "circuit" in a particular region, such as the winter circuit in Florida and the New England circuit in the summer.

When you hear of one that interests you, you should contact the show Secretary and ask for a prize list describing the classes, rules, time schedule, and conditions of the show. You will also find in the prize list information concerning feed and stable arrangements. In the large shows lasting two days or more, these facilities are most complete and include the available services of a blacksmith, feed man, and veterinarian. But at smaller ones, you must take care of your horse's accommodations yourself. Sometimes you will simply have to tie him to a shady tree or, if it's not too hot, show him from the van.

You will also receive an entry blank with the inevitable waiver to be signed, relieving the show management of responsibility for damage or injury caused by your horse, as well as a statement affirming that riders showing in Amateur classes possess a current Amateur Card. This document is issued by the AHSA, free to members and for a fee of $20 to nonmembers. Riders under eighteen years of age are automatically considered to be amateurs. In classes restricted to ponies the entries must also possess a current Measurement Card to prove that they are under 14.2 hands high. Ponies are measured at recognized shows and must be remeasured every year until the age of six, when they are given an official card that is valid for the rest of their lives. Riders wishing to compete as amateurs in international competitions under FEI rules must possess an International Amateur Card, obtainable from the AHSA.

There is nothing complicated about entering your horse in a show. You simply fill in your entry blank and return it with payment covering the total amount of your entry fees and stabling charges.

You shouldn't try to enter every event in the show. Four classes a day are ample. Usually the program is arranged to make it possible for a horse to compete in every class for which he qualifies. In smaller shows, where the events are less numerous, it is sometimes permitted to make cross-entries, that is, to enter a horse in two different divisions, such as Open Jumper as well as Working Hunter, or Working Hunter as well as Conformation Hunter.

When filling in your entry blank, you should be sure that your horse is eligible for the classes in which you wish to show him. Generally speaking, eligibility is based upon the horse's age, height, sex, and weight, as well as upon his past showing experience. A "Maiden" is a horse (or rider) who has not yet won a blue ribbon at a Regular AHSA Member Show in the division in which he is showing. A "Novice" has not yet won three first ribbons; and a "Limit," six. There are no limitations in Open classes. A Green Hunter is a horse of any age who is in his first or second year of showing over jumps, while a Preliminary Jumper is a horse that has won less than $1,000 in Jumper classes at any show since March 1, 1969. However, once a horse has won $1,000 in any given show year, he may continue to show as a Preliminary Jumper for the remainder of the year. After that stage, he advances to the Intermediate Jumper section, where he remains until he has won $3,000. (These figures may be increased, so play safe by consulting the current *Rule Book.*) Many classes are restricted to certain categories of riders: Lady, Amateur, Amateur-Owner, Junior, Local (residing within a specified area), and so forth. Stallions are usually barred if a lady or child is to ride or drive, although eligible for Open classes. You must note the conditions of each particular event, and there are also a few general regulations of which every horse-show exhibitor should be aware:

Any horse showing evidence of lameness, broken wind, or impairment of vision will be refused an award (except in Equitation or Jumping classes, or stallions and mares in Breeding classes, if the infirmities do not seem to be of a nature that can be passed on to their offspring).

An animal over 14.2 hands is considered to be a horse and is ineligible for Pony classes; animals 14.2 and under are considered to be ponies (with the exception of Arabian, Palomino, Half Arabs, Appaloosas, Paints, Pintos, Paso Finos, Western, and Morgan horses, who may measure 14.1 or even slightly less).

All horses should be free from any contagious or infectious disease. If an entry is found to be suffering from such a malady, his owner must pay an indemnity to the show and withdraw his horse.

No horse is eligible for competition in a recognized show if it has been given any drug which might affect its performance or any substance which would affect its circulatory, respiratory, or central nervous systems. Exhibitors are particularly cautioned against the use of patent tonics and medicines, many of which contain a forbidden substance, since the penalty for "doping" a horse, even unwittingly, is disqualification of all the exhibitor's entries throughout the entire show. With drug testing now frequent and the penalties for infraction of the rules most severe, all horse show exhibitors should procure a copy of the AHSA Drugs and Medication pamphlet and read it carefully.

In some shows, last-minute "Post Entries" are accepted, with a slight additional charge—but not nearly as frequently as they used to be. As a rule, you must decide which classes you wish to enter at the time you fill in your entry blank and return it promptly. A popular show may limit the number of entries on a "first come, first served" basis.

All over the country, horse shows are held indoors and outdoors throughout the year, the busiest showing months being from May to October. At least four to eight weeks before the show with which you have chosen to inaugurate your personal season, you should start your preparations.

The first thing to do is to gradually take your horse off pasture, increasing his grain ration and daily schooling, with emphasis on the work he will be asked to demonstrate in the show ring. The Association *Rule Book* is a useful guide to your training goals, since it describes in detail the performance requirements of all the show divisions, as well as the standards that govern the judging of each breed and every class.

Whatever the division in which your horse may be competing, you should make yourself familiar with the ring procedure of each of his classes and rehearse them thoroughly at home. If you are entering Equitation classes, you will practice the riding patterns outlined in the prize list; you can set up eight jumps on a figure-eight course at the same heights used in the Hunting Seat Medal Class, and build in your own ring a jumping course similar to the ones you will encounter in Junior Jumping events.

For Hunters, you can build a replica of the course described in the program, but it would be a mistake to overdo schooling over jumps. Long daily walks with some brisk trotting and slow work up and down hill is the best exercise for building up the muscles of a Hunter.

If you are going to show an Open Jumper, school him over fences of every imaginable appearance: broad jumps such as hog backs, oxers, triple bars, and Liverpools, in addition to single rails, railroad gates, a pile of oil drums or barrels, and all sorts of odd-looking obstacles and combinations. You might occasionally school him over a few fences a bit higher than those announced for his classes in order to be prepared for a raised jump-off. You might also build a water jump, which is a feature of all Grand Prix classes and increasingly of others, and which requires practice. Nevertheless, just as with a Hunter, it is much more important to build up his jumping muscles and general condition by plenty of work on the flat than it is to do a great deal of actual jumping over obstacles. The German Olympic Team horses rarely jump higher than 4 feet during training, while the U. S. Equestrian Team perfects its horses' jumping form over schooling fences set at 4 feet or under, with only occasional larger courses to "raise their sights."

When preparing for a Handy Hunter Class, you should practice jumping fences at an angle and making sharp turns, because the courses will be twisty and your time limited. Sometimes you will be asked to lead your horse over a fence after dropping the top rail to the ground. Try it. You may find that *you* need schooling too.

The special performance requirements of Western classes will be outlined in the prize list, and you should practice each exercise separately, but only occasionally the entire pattern, since overtraining will be marked against you. (But any deviation from the set pattern will cause elimination.) Be sure to work on opening and closing gates without dismounting if you are showing a Trail Horse, for a gate will invariably figure among the selected trail obstacles. Frequently there will a span of water that must be forded, not jumped.

Saddle Horse workouts should never become tedious, the idea being to produce brilliance, for which the horse must be somewhat fresh, and to stop before he begins to tire or to lose enthusiasm. A show horse cannot be hacked in the ordinary way before or during the horse-show season, for he is sure to become careless and slip below the high standards of precision required of him in the ring. During the schooling lessons your own riding should be just as careful as if you were already in front of the judge, and it goes without saying that it is a risky business to allow a show horse to be ridden by anyone but an expert horseman.

No matter what his breed or type, you ought to devote a little time each day to placing your horse in his show position until he learns to stand without fidgeting. And don't neglect to train your horse to remain perfectly still while you mount and dismount him. He should also become accustomed to all sorts of sights and sounds, if he isn't already, including motor traffic, music, and applause. A radio turned up high is a favorite trick of show as well as racing stables.

You must take care to avoid injury and strain and even scratches or cuts that might mar the beauty of your horse's coat during the last three or four weeks before a show. Groom him thoroughly every day, employing conditioning feeds and supplements to make his body fit, his muscles hard, and his coat glossy. Clip him if necessary seven to ten days before the show, but avoid soap baths, which tend to dull a horse's coat. You should, however, wash his mane and tail a day or two beforehand, trim any long stray hairs around his head and feet, and run the clippers over a hogged mane to make it neat and smooth.

Since a horse may move with soreness during the first few days on brand-new shoes, it is better to have him shod about a week before the show, which will give you time to adjust a shoe that pinches or to treat the ill effects of a nail prick. This is not the moment to try out a new blacksmith! If he is a Saddle Horse or Fine Harness Horse, he will need special shoeing, but his weighted shoes should be fitted at the last possible moment before the show or the horse will become accustomed to them and they will be less effective. For the same reason, they should be removed as soon as the show is over. If you are going to an outdoor show, it is advisable to have your horse shod with shoes in which studs can be screwed in case of muddy or slippery going.

Your horse's mane-, tail-, and foot-grooming must comply with show regulations, which are particularly explicit in certain divisions. For example, shoes no heavier than twelve ounces are permitted in the Arabian Horse division, and a maximum toe length of 4½ inches. Morgans must wear a full mane and tail without braids, false hair, or evidence of tail-setting; in order to avoid disqualification, they must, like Welsh Ponies, respect certain maximum toe lengths and shoe weights according to the classes in which they are entered. Shetland Ponies are forbidden any kind of artificial appliance. Saddle Horses, on the other hand, are allowed to wear mane and tail wigs, a tail brace and mouth controls, although other artifices such as dyed coats and wired ears are specifically prohibited. Tailsetting has been declared illegal in some states, due to a vigorous campaign waged by the Humane Society and the ASPCA, but the courts have since ruled that a horse may be shown in a state where tailsetting is banned as long as the operation was performed in another state. Grooming and equipment restrictions for Tennessee Walking Horses are perhaps the most detailed and the most strictly enforced of all. Like the others, they may be amended from year to year in order to combat new abuses invented by overzealous exhibitors. So, before preparing your horse for a show, it is advisable to check his grooming and equipment requirements in the current AHSA *Rule Book*.

Well in advance of the date of the show, you should make arrangements for your horse's transportation. Unless you own a horse trailer or can rent or borrow one, your best plan is to send him by van. Often your local riding club, Pony Club, Hunt club, or breed organization will hire a commercial horse van accommodating four, six, or nine horses. Sometimes all of the van space will not be filled and you may discover upon inquiry that even a group of which you're not a member will welcome your horse in exchange for your participation in the expense.

Some horses are balky about being loaded into a van until they are used to it. Professional horse shippers know all the tricks for loading reluctant horses. But if you are going to handle your horse's transportation yourself, it is a good idea to practice the loading procedure and even go for a short drive as a part of your horse's general education, in order to avoid a last-minute struggle that may make you late for a show. Just letting your horse sniff the van or trailer may be enough to convince him that there is nothing to fear. Many horses travel better in the company of another horse or a person. The first experience is the most important, so try to make it as pleasant as possible by being patient and reassuring.

Every precaution must be taken to avoid injury or chafing during shipping. The van should be padded of course, with a nonskid floor mat, and the horses should be outfitted with shipping boots or bandages and a tail guard (not too tightly wrapped), a leather head guard or "bumper," and a padded or sheepskin-covered shipping halter. A useful new product, consisting of Velcro-closed sheepskin bands, transforms an ordinary halter into a shipping halter in a few seconds.

In cool weather, you might give your horse a light sheet to keep his coat clean, or a warm blanket if it is really cold. Remember, though, that the horse's body gives off a lot of heat in a confined space and horses in a van need less clothing than in the stable.

Loading a horse into a trailer. (*Photo by James Deutschmann*)

While some owners leave their horses untied in a single horse trailer, it is generally safer for them to travel in crossties. A rubber-covered butt chain, to prevent them from leaning against the tailgate, is always essential. It should be fastened *before* the head strap when loading, and removed *after* the head strap when unloading. Some experienced horsemen say that horses travel better facing backward, if facilities permit. In any case, your horse will greatly appreciate a hay net, if only to alleviate boredom. It is impractical to supply water during a short trip of three or four hours. During a longer one, it is customary to schedule periodic stops and overnight layovers, when the horses can be unloaded, watered, given a chance to urinate and to stretch their legs.

If you have to cross a state line, make sure that your horse's travel documents are in order. Regulations vary from state to state according to the current epidemic situation, but practically everywhere you will need a valid negative Coggins test certificate and a Health Certificate from your veterinarian.

Although horses are often given tranquilizers when they are shipped by plane, be careful about using them on the way to a show, since they are among the "forbidden substances" that incur severe penalties as well as cancellation of any show winnings. If you own a really bad shipper

Shipping a horse by plane. (*Photo courtesy of Mrs. William Steinkraus*)

who absolutely requires tranquilizers in order to be vanned safely, you will have to schedule his shipping far enough ahead of time for all traces of tranquilizer to have disappeared before the show, and this may mean (depending on the drug administered) as much as four or five days. However, if you have taken the proper precautions in introducing your horse to van or trailer travel, and if you do everything possible to make the trip as safe and comfortable as possible for him, he should not really need them anyway.

If it is a local show, you may be able to hack your horse to it, a very common practice in Great Britain, where horses are often ridden to shows from considerable distances. Once, in order to give a gray gelding named Desire a chance to prove himself as a show Jumper, the British Olympic Team Rider Wilf White rose at the crack of dawn and hacked over twenty miles, because the owner considered his horse's ability too meager to warrant the investment of a trailer. As it turned out, the expedition was highly successful. Desire won all of his classes and, in fact, was seldom defeated during fifteen years of show jumping. Although the owner finally did buy a trailer, White often preferred to hack to shows even at the peak of Desire's career, believing that the road work used up the spirited horse's superfluous energy and improved his jumping.

Undoubtedly the longest hack to a show in history was undertaken by another dauntless Britisher, Mrs. Brenda Williams, nine-time Senior

Dressage champion of Great Britain, and her remarkable Connemara pony gelding Little Model, whom she rode in the Grand Dressage event of the Rome Olympic Games. Because her horse hates traveling in a trailer, Mrs. Williams covered the twelve hundred miles between London and Rome entirely on foot, with Little Model alternately undersaddle and on the lead shank, her trailer cruising along behind only to provide shelter during the night and when passing through congested city streets.

If you are going to a one-day show, you should plan to be there early in the morning, shipping your horse the day before if the trip is a long one. For a two-day show or longer, try to get there a day ahead of time so that your horse will have a chance to become acclimated before the show starts and to school over the courses whenever possible. If the distance requires a van ride of over twelve hours, it is best to ship your horse *two* days ahead, because he may run a fever ("shipping fever") and you should give him a day in which to recuperate. When there is a considerable difference in climate or altitude, as at the Olympic Games held in Tokyo and Mexico City, the competing horses may be shipped weeks or even months ahead of the event in order to give them time to adapt themselves to the new conditions.

It's lucky that there is no baggage limitation for horse-show exhibitors! There are quite a number of things that you should bring along if you are to be well prepared for any eventuality. In your tack trunk (an essential acquisition if you plan to do much showing) you will stow your saddle and the tack you need for the events in which you intend to compete. Even though you'll check the sound condition of every item as you pack it, it's a good idea to include a few replacements, such as an extra bridle, bell boots (if your horse wears them), a stirrup leather, and a stirrup iron. For some mysterious reason it always seems to be during a show that something breaks. You'll also need bandaging material, your grooming equipment (including heavy thread and a needle for braiding), a first-aid kit, a cooler, a stable sheet, a blanket (or a fly sheet, depending upon the weather), one or two stable halters, two shanks for leading and tying, and a flashlight.

Feed as well as bedding will probably be available at the show grounds, but it is preferable to keep your horse on the diet he likes and to which he is accustomed, so for a short show, less than three days, you should bring along all the grain and hay he will consume during the show. You will probably feed him a little less hay than usual and a bit more grain, diminishing his daytime feed and increasing his evening rations. You may have to modify his normal feeding schedule so that he will always have ample time (at least an hour) to digest his meal before competing in a class. Some horses are very fussy about their water, and will turn up their noses at a bucket that does not taste quite the same as the water at home. While it is not unheard of for international race horses to travel with a supply of home-drawn water in their luggage, show horse owners can solve the problem by adding a few drops of peppermint or wintergreen or cider vinegar to the water buckets a few days before shipping to a show, and then flavoring the water at the strange stable in the same way.

It is a good idea—and attractive, too—to paint your initials and stable colors on your feed and water buckets (one for each horse), as well as on your tack trunk and on all your stable tools. If it is an outdoor show, you should prepare for the worst by packing wet-weather clothing for yourself and your horse.

As for your personal equipment, make sure that you lack none of the appointments required in your different classes. You will probably run through two shirts a day and you'll find it convenient to have an extra coat and pair of breeches on hand in case of rain or a muddy tumble, plus ordinary clothes to wear when schooling and doing stable chores. Before you lock your trunk, wait a minute! Have you remembered your boot hooks and jack?

Large stables send along a groom for every two or three horses, but it is quite possible for you to look after your own mount all by yourself. However, if you are showing in Conformation classes where the horses are stripped (unsaddled) in the ring, it is customary to have a groom enter the ring to take off the tack, rub down the horse, and carry the saddle while you hold your horse by the bridle in his conformation position. Most Championship classes require the horses to be stripped and then resaddled before the ribbons are awarded. It is also handy to have a groom at the Out Gate to take over your horse after a round. It's indispensable, in fact, if you are showing two horses in the same class.

If you haven't a groom of your own, you may be interested in the services of one of the "floating" grooms who are sometimes still found at the larger shows, many of them specialists in show-grooming techniques such as braiding manes and tails. Well-done neck braids, by the way, will stay in place with just occasional touch-ups throughout a two- or three-day show, but it is better to take them down and rebraid them daily if you wish them to be perfect. Besides, leaving braids done up for too long a time will cause the hairs to break off, and your horse's mane and tail will become thinner and thinner. Tail braids, in any case, need

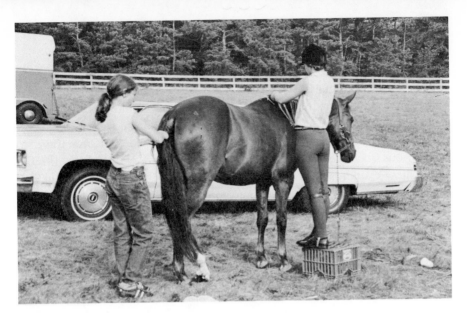

Last-minute grooming. (*Photo by Sue Maynard*)

to be taken down after the last class every day and redone before the first class the next morning, so you might as well rebraid the mane at the same time.

Every time you enter the ring your horse should be as well turned out as possible, which means that you—or somebody—will have to brush his coat, arrange his mane and tail, and clean his feet several times a day. In order to keep them sound throughout a show, many horses have their legs done up in standing bandages or in cold-water swabs every night, especially if the going is hard and their legs are delicate. A Jumper may benefit from wearing bandages between classes if he has a strenuous program.

If you bring along your own groom, you will of course be responsible for his (more likely her) transportation, meals, and sleeping accommodation. If it is an overnight show, you may reserve an entire tack stall where the groom can sleep on a folding cot. However, at such large shows you will probably van with a group, and only one of the accompanying grooms needs to sleep with the horses, while the others usually stay in a nearby motel.

Unless you ride along in the van or drive your own car and trailer, you should schedule your personal transportation so that you arrive at the show grounds before your horse and will be there to welcome him when he walks, a little wobbly, down the unloading ramp. You'll have plenty to do while waiting for him. The first thing is to check in at the show Secretary's office to see about the stabling that has been assigned to you, to make the necessary arrangements for bedding, feed, and water, and to pick up your exhibitor's pass, if you haven't already received it by mail. Usually your groom will need a pass too. At large shows the Secretary may hand you a thick envelope filled with tickets and invitations to the various social events that have been planned to brighten up the horse-show evenings—and to make it very difficult for you to get up and exercise your horse early the next morning!

Either at the Secretary's office or at the In Gate, you will be given the numbers assigned to each horse you are to ride as well as the numbers for Equitation classes, which are usually different from those used in Performance classes. Be careful not to lose them or to get them mixed up, because you are required to wear the appropriate one every time you enter the ring. It is a good idea (and the only way to keep them straight if you are riding more than one horse) to write each horse's name on the back of his number. And don't be surprised if you are asked to make a deposit. Many managements have learned from experience that this is the only way to ensure all of the numbers being returned at the end of the show.

If your van still hasn't appeared on the horizon, you will have time to get two programs and mark the classes in which you are entered on the timetable. Post one in your horse's stall, making a note of any special tack or clothing that may be required, as a reminder to yourself and instructions to your groom, and slip the other in your pocket.

As soon as your horse arrives, remove his traveling gear, give him some water, and walk him around a bit to stretch his legs before settling him down in his stall with a pail of fresh water and a hay net, which will keep him busy and content without allowing him so much hay that his belly swells.

After he has rested a bit, you can ride him around the grounds to get acquainted with his new environment and the sight and sound of the other horses and riders. If permitted, you should take advantage of schooling in the ring or over the outside hunting course. Should this be forbidden, you can at least walk the course on foot. There are always schooling facilities set up near the stable area or In Gate at a recognized show, sometimes with special hours reserved for each division, in which case a schooling schedule will probably be printed in the prize list or program.

You should plan your time so that your horse is tacked up, warmed up, and ready to go through the In Gate when his class or number is announced. How much of a limbering up you'll give him depends upon the individual. The average schooling time before each class is about ten or fifteen minutes of work in the schooling area. However, a "hot" horse can often be taken into the ring with very little preliminary exercise if any, while a sluggish one may need a long workout before reaching his top form. A Jumper may be trotted over a few low fences, or he may be asked to jump several big ones; it depends entirely upon the horse. Hunters who are scored on "Manners" may need quite a lot of work to tone high spirits down to the calm, steady way of going that Hunter judges prefer.

The classes are announced over a loudspeaker in the stable and schooling area, and you should appear promptly at the In Gate when your class is called. It can start without you if you are more than three minutes late. In the Jumper Division, failure to enter the ring within one minute after being called will incur elimination. No matter how great your haste, wipe off your horse and your boots with a stable towel just before you enter the ring.

In classes that are judged in a group, all of the entrants pass through the In Gate when the class is called in the order in which they arrive. There is little advantage in being among the first or the last, so your principal preoccupation should be to avoid being caught in a crush at the gate, to make your entrance at the required gait, and to "start showing" as soon as you are visible to the judge. Sometimes there is a delay in collecting a class, particularly when you have to wait for entries still being judged in a previous class in another ring. This is one instance in which you might be well advised to wait a bit at the In Gate before making your entrance. A few warm-up rounds of the ring are fine, but too many might take the freshness off of your horse.

Once inside the show ring, you should put on your performance for the judges and not the public; in fact, try not to think about the audience at all. Above all, don't wave or speak to friends at the ringside, but concentrate on riding your horse and on responding promptly to the judge's instructions. Until you are a very experienced show rider, you shouldn't even be overly preoccupied with the judge, but think only of your horse. The same advice is valid for Equitation classes. Young riders whose only thought is of a pretty hand position and a riding-manual seat seldom make as favorable an impression on the judge as those who simply concentrate on giving their horse a good ride.

In the large shows where there are many professional horsemen and the competition is very keen, you may notice that some riders have sub-

Getting a leg up. (*Photo by Sue Maynard*)

tle methods of attracting the judges' attention and even of trying to make their competitors appear inferior. Hardened pros can spot at a glance the entries that will be most threatening to them, and in Saddle Horse classes, for example, they have been known to force a rival horse to break his gaits. But these and other dubious methods are exceptions to the general rule of show-ring manners, and many amateurs could take a lesson in good sportsmanship from the pros. Besides, such maneuvers do not fool experienced judges. Your personal aim should be to ride your best rather than to beat the others. This doesn't mean that you shouldn't look out for your own interests. On the contrary, if you refuse to allow your horse to be concealed behind a group of other horses (unless you wish to correct a fault such as a wrong lead at the canter as discreetly as possible), and if you try to attract the judge's attention when your horse is performing a movement in which he excels, you will be displaying showmanship, not a lack of sportsmanship.

You never can tell when a judge will cast his glance in your direction, so you should start competing the moment you enter the ring and not let down until you have passed through the Out Gate. Some Hunter judges consider important, for example, the way a horse comes around the corners at the ends of the ring, and they may mark down an entry even though he clears his fences well if he is careless on the turns. Many a clean jumping round has been spoiled by a knockdown at the very last obstacle, and many an Equitation competitor has been moved down a place, because after a good performance the judge spotted him pulling up in a sloppy manner.

Speaking of judges, their role is often misunderstood. The prize list of every horse show announces in advance the names of the judges for each division, and by entering the show every exhibitor implicitly engages himself to accept the opinion of these particular experts. How much bitterness would be avoided if all horse-show competitors were fully aware of this simple fact! To become an official AHSA judge, an Association member of recognized competence and authority must be recommended by at least three judges and approved by a special committee. Only after a trial period and approval by the Judges Committee may he be promoted from the status of Recorded Judge to that of Registered Judge and thus be permitted to officiate alone in one or more specified divisions. His judge's card must be renewed each year and can be revoked by the Committee if ever an investigation and hearing proves that he has violated the judging rules.

Despite these controls, it is inevitable that every judge should have his individual preferences. Since the perfect horse has not yet been born, a horse-show class is often decided by choosing the lesser of two imperfections, an exercise that is more often than not a question of personal taste. The judge's preferences are no secret. You merely have to notice the type of horse he "pins" and the sort he "puts down." A good judge is consistent in his standards, and this is a practical consideration in selecting the most promising shows to enter. For example, some judges appreciate brilliance, while others prefer a horse that is "agreeable to hands" and of more docile nature. Some Hunter judges like a faster pace than others. Many Equitation judges prefer a relaxed and natural riding style to a stiff but perfect "textbook seat."

If you watch the other classes in your division or if you have already observed the judge in question, you will know what he likes and to a certain extent you may be able to adjust your horse's performance and your own to fit his standards. On the other hand, if your horse's type or your own riding style (in Equitation classes) differs considerably from those the judge has favored in the past, you should be neither surprised nor disappointed if you finish out of the top ribbons. Remember, you enter each particular show to accept the opinion of a particular judge. It is only one opinion, of course. Another judge might have placed you higher or lower, but that is beside the point. The only time you have a right to criticize a judge is when he does not run a class according to the rules.

After completing your round you should leave the ring promptly. Now is the moment to show your appreciation to your horse for doing well, so give him a pat, a kind word, or a more tangible token such as a piece of carrot or a lump of sugar. But now is *not* the moment to scold him if he has done badly; he will never understand what he is being punished for. Instead, if you are disappointed in your performance, go over the course in your mind, find out what spots caused you trouble, and plan to work on them later in the schooling ring, if it is a minor matter, or at home after the show, if the weakness is a basic one.

As your show experience increases, you will take the excitement in your stride, but at first it is only natural for you to feel your heart in your mouth and butterflies in your stomach. If you are nervous, remember that a certain amount of tension is not necessarily undesirable when extraordinary effort is required. But always remain in control of your actions. Ride as you did during schooling in your own ring. Don't suddenly change your style radically because of the presence of an audience and a judge; you will surely upset and confuse your horse and make it impossible for him to do his best. Most of these kindly creatures are anxious to please, so give your horse a chance!

The ring procedure varies somewhat in the different show divisions, so let's examine the principal ones individually.

HUNTER DIVISION

If you own a Hunter, there are three general types of classes in which he can be entered: Breeding (shown in hand, with conformation only to count); Conformation classes Green and Regular (shown under saddle, with conformation *and* performance scored); and Working Hunter classes Green and Regular (where soundness and performance over a jumping course determine the winners).

Green Hunter fences are 3'6" high; second-year Green Hunters must be able to jump 3'9", and Regular Hunters 3'9" to 4'6", all of them over courses consisting of typical hunting obstacles such as a post-and-rails fence, brush, a stone wall, a white board fence or gate, a chicken coop, an Aiken, a hedge, and sometimes an in-and-out pen. A show Hunter should not be asked to jump over a pole over brush, hog backs or triple bars, but in many Western shows the Hunter courses are, in fact, very similar to Open Jumping ones. All courses, except for Handy Hunter events, must be posted ahead of time or printed in the prize list or catalogue.

In regions where fox-hunting is widespread, there will be a great variety of classes for every imaginable category of Hunter horse and rider, such as:

Small Hunters (under 15.2½ hands)
Lightweight Hunters (able to carry up to 165 pounds)
Middleweight Hunters (able to carry 185 pounds)
Heavyweight Hunters (able to carry up to 205 pounds)
Thoroughbred Hunters
Non-Thoroughbred Hunters
Qualified Hunters (with one or more seasons of hunting with a
 recognized Hunt)
Hunter Hacks, Bridle Path Hacks, Handy Hunters, Appoint-
 ment, Formal Hunting Attire Under Saddle (judged 60 to 75
 per cent performance, 25 to 40 per cent conformation, with 15
 per cent appointments in Appointment classes)
Hunter Pair, Hunter Team, Amateur Owner
Open, Stakes, Hunter Classic

For children under 18 years old with ponies 14.2 hands or under, there is a highly popular Hunter and Jumper Pony Division, with fewer classes, lower jumps (from 2'3" to 3', depending on the pony's size), and

A conformation Hunter class being judged at the National Horse Show. (*Photo by Budd*)

in general more indulgent jumping standards, but very keen competition.

Not all show classes award points toward the Championship to the top four winners. Some are Half-Point classes and others Full-Point. Champion and Reserve titles are awarded to two of the four horses that have acquired the most points throughout a show, performing over a regulation Hunter course with fences at the full height required in the section in which shown. It all sounds even more complicated than it is. However, a careful study of the AHSA *Rule Book* is essential in order to select your classes wisely—and this is good advice for all Divisions.

Competitors in the Hunter division enter the ring or the outside course when their number is called and ride the jumping course individually. Afterward, if conformation as well as performance is considered, all of the riders, or a list selected by the judges, lead their horses back into the ring unsaddled, and line up in the center to be checked for soundness.

When lining up, you should try to avoid the heels of the horse next to you by staying ten to twelve feet away from your neighbors; if your own horse is unreliable, try to place him at the end of the line. You should stand about two feet in front of him, jiggling the reins from time to time to get him to stretch out his neck and head. Waving a handkerchief or throwing a bit of grass or sand will alert him and make him prick up his ears.

Hunters are supposed to be presented in a fit hunting condition, neither too fat nor too thin. The current show-ring practice is to have them a little plumper than is normal for actual field hunting. "Honorable" scars and blemishes won't count against a horse, but those that indicate any past or potential unsoundness are heavily penalized.

Entries will be asked to jog their horses one at a time in front of the judges. A horse showing signs of lameness, impaired vision, or broken wind must be examined by the show veterinarian; if the horse proves to be unsound, he will be disqualified. It often happens near the end of a long show that a horse will be a bit sore, but not really lame. In this case, the best thing to do is to keep him moving all the time he is in the ring and he will probably pass inspection. But if you allow him to stand absolutely still, the soreness will appear to be worse than it is when you move him out again.

Aside from soundness, conformation, and good manners, the Hunter judge gives great consideration to jumping style and an even hunting pace. A horse that moves with long, low strides and jumps in cadence without clearing his fences overly high is the one that wins his favor—and perhaps the class. Consequently, in order to show a Hunter to best advantage, riders try above all to maintain a smooth pace. Occasionally it may be necessary to fake it. For instance, they will use imperceptible half-halts to slow down a horse who is gathering momentum, or stimulate a sluggish horse by invisible seat actions in preference to using the stick, because hitting a Hunter with a riding crop while on the course is certain to rule him out of the ribbons.

The pace you set should be suitable to the course you are jumping: rather brisk over a long course with high fences; slow and easy over a short, low one. In most Hunter events, good manners and way of going are the qualities the judges seek. Since these are seldom compatible with the handsome Thoroughbred type which the judges also prefer and which, as you know, is a hot-blooded animal bred to race, the use of tranquilizing drugs became so widespread in the Hunter as well as in the Jumper Division that the AHSA has taken severe measures to detect and penalize this illegal practice. While the anti-doping campaign is in full swing, exhibitors should avoid giving their horses any medication without knowing its exact formula. Even an innocent-seeming cough remedy may contain a prohibited ingredient.

Most judges prefer a double bridle to be worn in Hack classes, but a

A jumping course at a small outdoor show. (*Photo by Sue Maynard*)

snaffle, Pelham, or a double bridle may be used in Hunter classes ridden over the outside course. A cavesson is obligatory, a breastplate and martingale optional. Judges are instructed to consider the quality, condition, durability, and cleanliness of a Hunter's tack, so the exhibitor should do the same.

Jumping courses for Hunters are very straightforward in comparison with those designed for Open Jumpers. But you should be quite sure of your course before entering the ring, because you will be disqualified for clearing an obstacle out of order or for jumping a fence that is not included in the course. If your horse refuses at a fence, you have already lost any chance of being placed. So hit him with your stick if you are carrying one (or with your hand, if you are not). In any case, do not fail to express your displeasure with his behavior in terms he understands. Then calmly circle him around and try again—only not from too far back, which would make it easier for him to refuse a second time. One refusal will lose you any chance of consideration for the ribbons, but three refusals mean elimination, even though they take place at different fences. You still have the right, however, to two more jumps before leaving the ring and it is usually sensible to take them. If you don't, your horse may conclude with typical equine logic that all he has to do is refuse often enough and he will be led back to his comfortable stall.

Jumping faults are scored with much greater leniency for Hunters than for Open Jumpers. A Hunter is penalized for "ticks" or "rubs" that result from faulty jumping, but theoretically his score will not be affected by occasional light touches, except in classes where there are a great many good rounds and the competitors are difficult to separate. On the other hand, it is virtually impossible to wind up in the ribbons of an average Hunter class if your horse has had a rail down. When the entry is large, you practically always have to go clean in order to win.

OPEN JUMPER DIVISION

Horses of all breeds, any conformation, and almost any degree of soundness are eligible for Open Jumping classes, although the most successful are Thoroughbreds or possess a high percentage of Thoroughbred blood. Any kind of tack or bitting may be used (except that standing martingales are prohibited in FEI classes). Any style of riding is permitted. Sometimes it is fairly unorthodox! There is only one thing that counts: to jump the courses clean.

When starting out in show jumping, your choice of classes is more important than in the other divisions. As a matter of fact, it is better for a novice rider and a green horse to make their debut not in the Jumper division at all, but in Green Working Hunter classes. After a first year of showing over fences with a minimum height of 3′6″, and perhaps a second year over a minimum height of 3′9″, you will be ready for the more difficult courses of Preliminary Jumpers with obstacles up to 4′3″. Once your horse has won $1,000 with these conditions, he is probably ready to advance to the more challenging problems of the Intermediate and Open Jumper courses. Even though he may have fantastic natural ability, it is unwise and may be dangerous to enter him in classes over his head. You may cause him to lose confidence, which can be disastrous to his future jumping and undo months of careful schooling.

The Jumper is the only show horse whose number of classes should be deliberately restricted. His work is the most strenuous, and besides, the Association rules require that all ties must be broken. As a result, many classes are decided in one or more jump-offs over a raised course. Four events a day is a lot for a Jumper and five excessive in most cases. Experienced riders try to pace their horses' efforts throughout a show in order to spend their energy to best advantage. They like to start them out perfectly fit, even a bit fresh, so that they will finish still in top condition, ready to confront the raised jump-offs at the end of the class and the more difficult classes at the end of the show.

Since performance is all-important, careful preshow schooling and conditioning are essential for the show Jumper. Unlike the race horse who is trained for one or two specific races, a Jumper must be in condition to compete every week during several months, in spite of the added strain of traveling from one show to another and the frequent changes of hay and water. Most experts agree that a Jumper should have a day of light work before leaving for a show and a complete holiday the day he travels, plus a day or two of rest after the show. A horse that is being shown in jumping classes every weekend or two during the summer season doesn't really need any exercise between shows other than daily light work, with an occasional schooling to work on the weak points that have shown up in competition.

While your preliminary training must be very thorough in order to remain reliable under the stress of competition, you shouldn't try to cram a lot of last-minute drilling into your horse just before a show, for he will only become bored and stale, and consequently careless. One of the most trying problems with top Jumpers toward the end of a busy season is to

Kathy Kusner riding Night Hawk over a water jump in an international event in Germany. (*Photo by Conrad Horster*)

keep up their interest, so don't let your own horse become jaded before he has even started.

Upon arriving at the show grounds, walk your horse around so that he feels at home. Unless he's traveling the same day, you might feed him a little more than his usual ration of grain the morning of the show, but give him a bit less hay. Race horses are taken off hay completely the day of a race, and the U. S. Olympic Team horses are given just enough hay in a net to keep them occupied.

Courses for the different jumping classes and the rules under which they are to be scored must be described in the prize list and catalogue (except for the FEI courses, which we will come to in a minute, and which are posted only half an hour ahead of time). Be sure to study the diagrams carefully and, wherever permitted, to walk the course and see for yourself the dimensions of the jumps and the distances between the elements of combinations. Notice any poles that can be rolled off by a light touch, and any loose rail where a slight rub might cause a knock-down. You should also consider the condition of the ground at every fence, and observe the flag positions—the course passes between them. If you are not among the first few riders to go in a class, be sure to watch several rounds of the other contestants, for you may discover difficulties that escaped your notice, such as an awkward turn or an unnatural distance. Furthermore, in certain classes it can be a great advantage to know that you will need a very fast clean round in order to beat the others, or, on the other hand, that a more cautious faultless round still stands a chance of winning. You should decide on your strategy before you go through the In Gate.

It pays to study your course with care, for an error can be very costly. Just ask the great racing jockey Willie Shoemaker who, during the excitement of the Kentucky Derby when he was well in front on Gallant Man, stood up in the stirrups at what he mistook for the finish pole and thereby lost the race! Even the far from absent-minded Eddie Arcaro once lost track of the distance at Pimlico and pulled up after the second lap of a three-lap race, only discovering his error when he helplessly watched the rest of the horses gallop past him.

You should be mounted and near the In Gate at about the time the second rider ahead of you is jumping the course. If the class is a Fault and Out, it is safer to get ready while the third or fourth rider ahead of you is in the ring, because you never can tell when a horse will be eliminated at the very first fence, and you must be there when your turn comes. Pass through the In Gate promptly when your number is called and cross the starting line within one minute of entering the ring. Before crossing the line you may make a circle or do whatever you wish, but any turning away from an obstacle during the course is considered to be a refusal, as is any loss of forward movement at a trot, canter, or gallop (which means that you cannot stop or walk).

If you have had a good round and seem to have a chance at the ribbons or to qualify for a jump-off, don't stray too far away from the In Gate. And don't neglect to let your horse know how pleased you are with him. You should dismount, pull up the stirrups, loosen the girth, cover your horse with a fly sheet or cooler, and walk him around to cool him out or to keep him warm, depending upon the weather, until his breathing is back to normal. Fussy show grooms bring a halter and chain shank to the In Gate to avoid leading a horse by the bridle when they handwalk him between jumping rounds. On very hot days they will have a sweat scraper handy too. Some riders prefer to walk their horses mounted, while waiting for a jump-off to be called.

If you are definitely out of the ribbons or eliminated from the class, remove your horse's saddle and walk him under a cooler for fifteen to twenty minutes before returning him to his stall, until it is time to prepare him for the next class or for the night.

At the end of each event the lucky winners ride back into the ring for the presentation of ribbons. If you are fortunate enough to be among

Katie Monahan on The Jones Boy during a jumping event of the Lake Placid Horse Show. (*Photo by Sue Maynard*)

them, you should accept your rosette from the ring steward, canter once around the ring, and leave. In addition to ribbons, some classes (including all Stake events) offer prize money. You may be asked to collect it at the end of the show in one lump sum at the Secretary's office; it may be mailed to you; or it may be presented to you right in the ring in the form of a check or a bag of silver dollars. In any case, you won't risk losing your amateur status, because it is the horse who wins the money and not the rider. Only when a rider is paid for actual riding is he no longer considered to be an amateur.

SCORING RULES

Show jumping in most of the world (and in the Pan American and Olympic Games) is conducted under the rules of the Federation Equestre Internationale (FEI), the world-wide horse-show governing body with headquarters in Europe, whose President is usually elected from the equestrian-minded nobility, like Prince Bernhard of Holland

and Prince Philip of Great Britain, both of whom have been President of the FEI. The AHSA is the officially recognized affiliate in the United States, but it is also an older organization whose rules existed prior to the formation of the FEI in 1921. In consequence, there has been a parallel evolution of two sets of scoring rules, those of the FEI and those of the AHSA (which were originally based on the British rules).

The scoring of knockdowns and disobediences has long since been standardized at four faults for a knockdown, and three faults for the first disobedience (such as a refusal or run-out), six for the second and elimination for the third. However, the Americans and the British did not choose to follow the FEI in abandoning the scoring of penalties for "ticks" or touches—those slight "rubs" which can be seen or heard, but which do not result in a knockdown, and for many years these "touch" classes have been a part of the horse-show scene in the English-speaking world, but nowhere else.

The principal problems involved in scoring touches concern the judges (who are hard pressed to stay close enough to each separate fence, even with two judges in the ring, to insure accuracy of scoring) and the public (which, being outside the ring, has little chance of following the scoring itself).

Nonetheless, when touches are scored (1 fault for the front touch, ½ fault for the hind touch) it is usually possible to break ties through successive jump-offs without having the fences raised very high; and there has always been a segment of the show-jumping public in the United States which preferred this system to the FEI's, in which the contestant's elapsed time over the course is often used as the means of breaking ties, either in the first round or in one of the jump-offs. Thus touch classes have survived in this country, even though they have disappeared entirely in Canada (where all jumper classes are now run under FEI Rules) and are found only in the smaller shows in England.

Since 1950 the AHSA has swung more and more toward the use of FEI Rules, partly due, no doubt, to the substitution of the civilian U. S. Equestrian Team for our now-defunct Cavalry in the Games and other International competitions. Increasing familiarity has underlined the advantages of FEI rules for both spectators and competitors, and it seems likely that "touch" scoring will eventually disappear in the United States as well.

Currently, however, the AHSA permits its member shows to offer classes under Table I (in which touches are scored), Table II (which is similar to the FEI's Table A except that it is not mandatory for the con-

Michele McEvoy and Sundancer clearing a vertical plank and rails during a winning round in the American Invitational jumping competition at Tampa, Florida. (*Photo by Jay Morris, courtesy of the AHSA*)

testant to carry a minimum weight aside from Grand Prix classes in which the minimum required weight is 165 pounds for men and women, 154 pounds for Juniors), Table III, IV, or the FEI rules themselves.

SCORING TABLES

AHSA TABLE I–TOUCH CLASSES

At least two judges or one judge and a competent scorer, other than the Steward, must officiate in Table I classes.

(a) Touch of obstacle with any portion of horse's body behind stifle .... ½ fault

(b) Touch of obstacle with any portion of horse's body in front of stifle or with any part of rider or equipment .... 1 fault

(c) Touch of standard or wing in jumping obstacle with any part of horse, rider or equipment .... 1 fault
(Touches of any obstacles placed before, in or beyond water or ditch, or touches of groundlines are scored as in (a) and (b) above.)

(d) Touch of flag or marker at obstacles or on starting or finishing line with any part of horse, rider or equipment .... 1 fault

(e) Knockdown of obstacle, standard or wing with any portion of horse, rider or equipment .... 4 faults

(f) Knockdown of flag or marker at obstacle or on starting or finishing line with any part of horse, rider or equipment .... 4 faults

(g) Placing any foot in the water or on the marking strip of the water jump .... 4 faults

(h) First disobedience (anywhere on course). 3 faults

(i) Second cumulative disobedience (anywhere on course) .... 6 faults

(j) Third cumulative disobedience (anywhere on course) .... Elimination

(k) Fall of horse and/or rider (except in Fault and Out and Table III Classes) ... Elimination

(l) Jumping obstacle before it is reset or without waiting for signal to proceed .... Elimination

(m) Starting before Judge's audible signal to proceed; jumping obstacle before start or after crossing finish line whether forming part of course or not; jumping obstacle out of order; off course .... Elimination

(n) Failure to enter ring within one minute of being called .... Elimination

(o) Failure to cross the starting line within one minute after Judge's audible signal to proceed .... Elimination

(p) Jumping any obstacle before crossing starting line unless said obstacle is designated as a practice jump .... Elimination

(q) Failure to jump in designated order .... Elimination

(r) Leaving the enclosure of a closed obstacle not in the proper direction .... Elimination

(s) Deliberately addressing an obstacle ..... Elimination

AHSA TABLE II—KNOCKDOWN CLASSES

Faults and eliminations are scored in exactly the same manner as in Table I above except touches are not penalized.

When time penalties are to apply, the Time Allowed must be based on a speed of 360 yards per minute for courses under 700 yards long, and 382 yards per minute for courses 700 yards and over, with ¼ time fault charged for each overtime second or fraction thereof.

Failure to complete the course within the Time Limit (which is double the Time Allowed) causes elimination.

AHSA TABLE III

This scoring system converts faults into seconds according to a scale based on the length of the course and the number of jumps. Falls and the first two refusals are automatically penalized by the extra time taken, but a third refusal causes elimination.

AHSA TABLE IV

a) The first round may be scored exactly as in Table I, with a timed jump-off in case of a tie for first place.
b) The first round is not timed, nor do touches count. The fastest, cleanest round wins the jump-off in case of a tie for first place.

TYPES OF JUMPER CLASSES

In Preliminary, Intermediate, Open, and Amateur-Owner classes conducted under AHSA Table I, touches are scored and ties are broken by successive jump-offs over the original course, whose fences are progressively raised and/or broadened.

There are a number of different knockdown classes (FEI or AHSA Table II), but these can be divided into two general types: (1) classes in which only jumping ability within a time allowance counts; and (2) classes which are conducted against the clock, so that horses are tested not only for jumping ability, but also for handiness and obedience, and speed becomes a deciding element. In the so-called "time the first time" classes, the elapsed time in the original round breaks any ties, and thus is the dominant factor. (In fact, under the FEI's Table B and C, the faults are translated into seconds and added to the elapsed time, so that the rider's complete score is given in seconds.)

More common, however, is the class that has a time allowance for the original round (with "time faults" penalized at a rate of ¼ fault for each second over the allowance), and only the first or second jump-off is scored against the clock. In a one-jump-off class, for example, all horses with equal faults within the time allowance go forward to the jump-off, but in that second round, horses with equal faults are classified according to their elapsed times.

Classes in which time counts only in the second jump-off tend to place the premium somewhat more on accuracy than on speed (since the fences are high, having been raised twice) while Knockdown and Out and Puissance competitions are really tests of strength and accuracy entirely. The Puissance, in fact, is almost like a high-jump class, for the time allowed is generous for the first round and eliminated thereafter, and the course is quickly reduced to two fences, one a spread and one a vertical. It is quite common, both in this country and in Europe, for the Puissance winner to clear a vertical wall over 7' high.

Buddy Brown and Viscount, a successful U. S. Equestrian Team combination. (*Photo by Sue Maynard*)

The Six-Bars is a special test of power and skill in which six identically constructed obstacles are placed in a straight line. They may all be at the same height (such as 4'0") or they may be of progressive heights (such as 3'9" to 5'0", or 3'9" to 4'6"). The winners are decided by elimination.

A show may also offer Bonus Classes which provide higher rewards for more difficult competition. These are most often judged under Table II rules.

As in the other Divisions, the Championship is decided on the basis of points won in classes throughout the Jumper section. Credit toward the Championship is given only to the first four ribbons, except in Bonus Classes, and ties are left unbroken. Tied horses receive equal legs on any trophy. However, an increasing number of shows have eliminated Jumper Championships in an effort to cut down the entries in Jumper classes.

On the other hand, there is a new (since 1978) and prestigious Jumping prize in the FEI World Cup, which consists of a series of Grand Prix events during certain international horse shows from October to April, culminating in a grand final event for the top 16 European and top 8 American qualifying riders at one of the major horse shows either in America or Europe, and consisting of two rounds over a Grand Prix course with a day of rest between, scored on cumulative points.

It is easy to see that speed classes require quite a different riding and training technique than that employed when only accuracy is involved. The careful, slow clean round that serves the rider best in touch classes or Puissance competitions is usually out of the ribbons entirely when speed is a factor. The speed rider must calculate his risks judiciously, especially when fast, clean rounds have already preceded his. He must try to shave seconds by cutting corners and angling fences even more sharply, for every second counts and the winning margin is often only a matter of tenths.

You will soon learn that the horse who *looks* the fastest seldom has the fastest time. Racing from one fence to another at breakneck speed tends to make most horses flatten out, and too much speed is incompatible with sharp turns. In general, the horse who travels the shorter line and never has to be pulled up will beat the horse who actually gallops faster but who has to be checked. The fastest rounds are usually economical, and deceptively smooth, while the flashiest rounds by wildly spurring riders are seconds slower on the clock. The race is to the swift,

Melanie Smith and Val de Loire, a former Spanish Olympic Team horse, won five Grand Prix classes in 1978 to capture by a wide margin the AHSA Open Jumper Horse of the Year award. (*Photo by Sue Maynard*)

but swiftness on a jumping course comes from obedience and agility on the part of the horse and well-controlled, tactically sound riding by his rider.

SADDLE HORSE DIVISION

Most of the horses entered in a show lead quite ordinary normal lives the rest of the time. Not so the American Saddle Bred horse! Here is a creature bred and trained for the show ring, and he seems to love it. While horses of other breeds, such as Arabians and Morgans, can be trained in the Saddle Horse gaits, they are shown in their own divisions, for they would offer little competition to the peacocky Saddle Bred when it comes to performing the flashy rack and brilliant slow gait of Five-Gaited events, or to producing the animated high action required of a Three-Gaited horse.

Training being of vital importance, this is a division in which professional trainers and show riders abound, especially at the major shows where the Stakes classes are always dominated by the pros and a few highly experienced amateurs. But in local shows, owner-riders find ample opportunities to experience the excitement of showing their own Saddle Horse, and perhaps even the thrill of winning a blue.

There is probably a greater difference between a show Saddle Horse and a pleasure Saddle Horse than between the show and working types of any other kind of horse. When a show horse is being prepared for a season of competition in the Saddle Horse division, he is handled with the greatest of care. It is not only the correctness of his gaits that must be schooled. The style with which he performs them is developed too and particular attention is paid to his appearance, since such qualities as brilliance, presence, quality, and neatness may be scored as well as performance and conformation. Nowadays, flash and glamour may influence a Saddle Horse judge, and so most of the show stables invest in all sorts of artificial beautifiers such as mane and tail wigs in order to dramatize their horses' appearance. Wired ears became so common that they had to be specifically prohibited. Saddle Horse grooms often devote an hour or more to hand-rubbing before a class, in order to put a gleam on their horses' coats, and the day of a show the mane and tail are "picked." With the finger tips dipped in olive oil or brilliantine, each hair is separated from the rest to make the tail and mane appear fuller and shimmer in the show ring. Modern silicone sprays are simpler to apply. Even though you may not be able to emulate the professional's technique, you should see that your horse is perfectly groomed for every class; keep his coat clean between events by covering him with a sheet, and give him a last-minute brush and polish each time he enters the arena.

As in other divisions, Saddle Horse classes are broken down according to height, sex, past show winnings, as well as the quality of the rider, with Ladies', Children's, Junior, Amateur-Owners', Local classes, and so forth. Many of them have detailed requirements as to the grooming and tack that you may use, and you should check the rules to make sure that your horse's presentation complies with the official regulations. Martingales and plain snaffle bits are prohibited in almost all Saddle Horse classes; a double bridle is "preferred," which means that in actual practice, it is, like the flat saddle, obligatory.

THREE-GAITED SADDLE HORSE events may include Model classes shown in hand with conformation only judged, as well as various performance classes, such as:

A Champion Three-Gaited Saddle Bred Horse, Flamenco, ridden by Helen Crabtree. (*Photo by Jack Holvoet*)

Three-Gaited Park Saddle Horse Class (judged on style, finish, quality, manners, and all around brilliance)

Open and Limit Classes (judged on performance, quality and manners)

Combination Class (the horse first being shown to an appropriate four-wheel vehicle at a walk and trot, then under saddle at a walk, trot, and canter. Judged 50 per cent on the work in harness, 50 per cent under saddle, with emphasis on the trot.)

American Saddle Bred Pleasure Horse and Country Pleasure Horse (restricted to registered mares and geldings of this breed. The classes may be subdivided in many ways, including separate ones for lady and gentlemen riders. There may be a class under Western saddle, another for Eastern.)

Championship Classes, which may be divided into different height sections (judged on manners, presence, quality, conformation, and performance)

FIVE-GAITED SADDLE HORSES compete in such events as Model, Open, and Combination classes, as well as in Stakes, in classes

A Champion Five-Gaited Saddle Bred Horse, Lad O'Shea, ridden by Mary Lou Gallagher. (*Photo by Jamie Donaldson*)

for Junior Amateurs, Owner, Amateur-Owner, Ladies, and Championships of several kinds. There are also riding and driving classes for Pleasure and Country Pleasure Five-Gaited Horses.

The FINE HARNESS HORSE section is entirely restricted to registered Five-Gaited American Saddle Bred Horses wearing long manes and tails, shown to a small 4-wheel topless buggy, in a light show harness and a snaffle bit and overcheck. The entries are asked to perform an animated park trot and an animated graceful walk. Extreme speed is penalized.

They must stand quietly, but are not required to back. The judging is based on quality, performance, and manners, but the Championship usually goes to a horse that possesses a quality of showmanship as well, like the long-time king of the Fine Harness Division, The Lemon Drop Kid, who retired at twelve after winning four World Championships and countless show ribbons.

Finally, there is a section for Saddle Horses and Ponies with West-

ern Equipment, shown at a walk, trot, and canter and judged 60 per cent on performance and manners, 40 per cent on conformation and soundness.

All of the Saddle Horse entries go into the ring at the same time. Many professional riders like to be the first or last to enter. In any case, you should avoid being swept along in the middle of a bunch, which is sure to get your horse off to a bad start. The Five-Gaited horse makes his entrance at a graceful, brisk trot, with his hocks well under his body and his head well flexed at the poll. The Three-Gaited is expected to be ridden into the ring at a flat-footed walk, his head held high, with a somewhat loose rein.

As they circle around the ring, they are asked to change from one gait to another and also to change direction by the judge or judges (there may be two or three of them in an important show). Transitions from one gait to another should be prompt and accurate, with the horse always moving on the correct lead at the canter and the rider posting on the correct diagonal. While it is vital for the horse to maintain his gaits without breaking until a change is requested, the rider should at the same time appear to handle his horse with ease, since manners constitute an important part of the final score in many classes.

As a matter of fact, you will notice that Saddle Seat show riders have developed a somewhat exaggerated style that is quite different from that required in Saddle Seat Equitation classes. They sit far back in the saddle, their legs outstretched in very long stirrups and with long reins held high, the purpose being to enhance the horse's appearance no matter what the rider's seat resembles.

The trot is the most important gait for Three-Gaited horses, and it should show extreme hock and knee action. For the Five-Gaited, speed and flashy action at the rack and an excellent slow gait most often determine the winners. When the judge requests "Rack on," the riders urge their mounts on to the smoothest, most dazzling pace possible. Although speed never fails to impress the judges in Five-Gaited classes, it is a sound policy to choose the pace at which your horse produces his finest form, and if it is a rapid one, so much the better. Once established, don't alter it until the judge requests a change. It is better to cut across the ring, if necessary, rather than pull your horse out of his stride by trying to slow him down. If your horse is performing well at a brisk pace, you will show him off best by riding on the inside circle of the ring. But when the command to walk is given, preparatory to going into the canter, you might bring your horse over to the rail, as this will facilitate your putting him promptly and cleanly into a slow, collected canter on the correct lead.

You may have to demonstrate your horse's gaits for quite some time before the judges are able to arrive at a decision. Then you will be asked to line up in the center of the ring. Your horse should be posed while the judges walk around the entries to examine them more closely. Usually, the riders remain in the saddle, but in Championship classes you may be asked to dismount and to strip your horse. In both cases, your horse should stand squarely on his four feet in a stretched position, and you should try to keep him alert with his head held high and his ears pricked. If he is to be stripped, you should have a groom at the In Gate prepared to run into the ring as soon as the order to "strip saddles" is given.

Afterward, the judges will have a selected list of qualified competitors ride off again together, while the rest remain in the center or are dismissed from the ring.

When at last the placings have been decided, the riders advance to accept their ribbons from the ring steward as their numbers are called, circle once around the ring, and leave promptly by the Out Gate.

WALKING HORSE DIVISION

The procedure is identical for Tennessee Walking Horse events, except that only three gaits are demonstrated. Entering the ring at a flat-footed walk, they must maintain it until the judge calls for the remaining gaits: running walk and canter. You will be asked to ride in both directions. When the horses are called to line up following the initial workout, the judge individually instructs one boot of each horse to be removed and handed to him for inspection. A horse will be immediately disqualified if the judge detects on his legs or feet any traces of the use of painful gait-producing devices, or if his mouth shows any signs of severe bitting.

Walking Horse classes include Breeding classes, shown in hand, Pleasure classes for Park, Show, and Plantation Walking Horses (shown at a flat walk, plantation gait, and canter or lope), a Light Harness class (shown at a flat walk, running walk, and an extended running walk, hitched to a two-wheel bike), a Costume class called "Southern Belle Walk," as well as Equitation classes (Eastern style).

WESTERN DIVISION

The phenomenon of present-day horse shows is the enormous growth of interest in Western classes, which have won an increasingly prominent place in the show ring. Rules and procedures have been established by the AHSA, and today a wide variety of classes is offered in horse shows all over the country for different types of Western horses.

The STOCK HORSE may be of any breed or combination of breeds as long as he measures at least 14.1 hands, is serviceably sound and of stock-horse type. His single most important accomplishment is skill at reining. The judges are instructed to assign 50 per cent of the total score to reining ability, and only 20 per cent to conformation, 20 per cent to manners, and 10 per cent to appointments.

The entries must be shown in stock saddles without tapaderas, so it will be perfectly evident that the rider is communicating with his horse by using his seat and reins and not his legs. Light hands are essential to successful reining and the leading Stock Horse show riders are noted for them. While the horse is in motion, the rider's hands must be held clear of the saddle above the pommel, with one hand (always the same one) around the reins, the elbow bent, and never with the fingers held between the reins. The most usual position for the other hand is resting on the thigh, although many Western riders prefer to hold it bent at the elbow in front of the chest. The riders must wear a Western hat, a long-sleeved shirt, a necktie, kerchief, or bolo tie, chaps, shogun chaps or chinks, and boots. Spurs are optional. Tack and bitting requirements are described in detail in the AHSA *Rule Book*.

The ring procedure in Stock Horse classes varies from one show to another and from one part of the country to another, with considerable liberty accorded to the individual show committees to respect local traditions concerning tack, bitting, and performance requirements. However, the AHSA specifically prohibits bozal or cavesson-type nosebands, martingales, choke ropes and tie-downs, as well as the use of any wire, chain, or rawhide device as part of the leather chin strap. It also requires that hobbles be carried when closed reins are used. The usual performance procedure is for the horses to enter the ring in a flat-footed walk, going into an easy jog-trot and a slow lope at the judge's command, both ways of the ring, on a reasonably loose rein, without undue restraint. Extended gaits may also be requested. Sometimes the horses are judged for soundness and conformation before entering the arena. After the group workout, the entries either line up or withdraw from the ring while each horse performs individually.

The standard test pattern of a Working Stock Horse begins with a small figure eight at a smooth, even lope, followed by a larger figure eight at a faster pace, changing both front and hind leads correctly. Then the horse is ridden to one end of the arena, turned around a standard in a specified direction, and run the full length of the ring to a straight, sliding stop; turned about another marker and run to the other end of the arena to make another straight, sliding stop; turned back again and run to the center of the arena to a straight, sliding stop. After allowing the horse to gather himself, the rider must back in exactly the opposite direction in a straight line for ten or fifteen feet. Then the horse is brought up to the judge, stopped again and, with his weight on the hindquarters and the legs in one position, he makes a half turn once each way. The riders may also be asked to execute one and a half turns on ends and full turns each way in the center. The horses are judged on a basis of 60 to 80 points on the rein work, 70 points being considered an average performance.

In some shows, Working Stock Horses are tested on live cattle, after the reining test, in which case the judging is slightly different. With 160 points considered to be a perfect score, 60 to 80 points are assigned to the cow work, and 60 to 80 points to reining. A cow is turned into the arena and the contestants must hold the animal at one end long enough to indicate that the horse is watching the cow. The cow is then allowed to run down to the side of the arena and the contestant must attempt to turn it at least twice each way against the fence. Then the cow must be taken to the center of the ring and circled once each way.

Among the Working Stock Horse classes you are most likely to find in a horse show program are events for:

Green (First and Second Year), Open, Stallions, Geldings, Mares, Ladies, Amateur, Amateur-Owners, and Junior Exhibitors, as well as a Stock Horse Championship class and a Jaquima class open to horses under 5 years old.

At the moment there are probably as many Western horses being trained in stock work exclusively for sport and show as there are for practical ranch use. But an even greater number is used merely for pleasure riding, and a separate horse-show section is devoted to the WESTERN PLEASURE HORSE. He too may be of any breed or combination of breeds over 14.1 hands, and is shown at a walk, jog-trot, and lope, moving around the ring in both directions on a reasonably loose rein, without undue restraint. He is judged 60 per cent on performance, 30 per cent on conformation, and 10 per cent on appointments, which of course consist of Western tack and cowboy attire.

Theoretically, equipment such as hobbles, riata, breast collar, and chaps are considered optional, but in actual practice all experienced competitors are equipped with them. Fancy equipment is not supposed to count for more than a good working outfit, but practically all of the winners seem to have shiny silver appointments on their saddles, headstalls, and breast collars. A final tip for entrants in this keenly contested class: Try to look as if your ride really is a pleasure, by giving an impression of relaxation, self-confidence, and comfort in the saddle.

A fairly recent innovation is the section for WESTERN RIDING HORSES, which are required to perform a pattern designed to test the performance and characteristics of a good, sensible, well-mannered, free, and easy-moving ranch horse that can carry his rider around on the usual ranch chores, over the trails, and give a quiet, comfortable, and pleasant ride in open country through and over obstacles. It is judged principally on performance, with emphasis on manners (70 per cent), appointments, equipment, and neatness (10 per cent), and conformation (20 per cent).

WESTERN TRAIL HORSES have classes of their own, since this sturdy, reliable type of horse or pony is required to give evidence in the show ring of his ability to carry his master over rocky trails and through mountain streams, his saddle packs filled with the fishing, shooting, or camping equipment that will be put to good use once he has reached the daily destination. Trail Horse events are also very popular in the New England states and are a regular feature of Morgan horse shows.

Beauty is a relatively negligible quality of the Trail Horse, counting for only 20 per cent of his score, while 70 per cent is accorded to performance and way of going, with emphasis on manners. It is a practical necessity for the horse and rider to be equipped with the proper gear and the horse must be capable of carrying it, so the remaining 10 per cent of the show points is attributed to appointments, equipment, and neatness.

The Trail Horse is shown in a stock saddle, with a fancy silver-studded model being considered in no way superior to a good, plain working outfit. Any standard Western bit may be used, even a bozal or cavesson noseband, provided that it is loosely fitted. The riders must wear Western dress and carry rope or a riata.

The entries are first shown all together at a walk, jog-trot, and lope, over and through obstacles, on a reasonably loose rein without undue restraint.

This is a diverting challenge to an ingenious course committee, for a wide variety of typical trail obstacles may be included to test the surefootedness, self-reliance, and courage of each horse. There may be a water obstacle to be forded, a bridge to be crossed, logs or brush to be stepped over, a mailbox to be opened from the saddle, a ditch that must be crossed by sliding down one side and climbing up the other, without jumping or lunging. The horses may be required to carry objects from one part of the arena to another, without "spooking" when asked to carry game or flinching under a heavy load. They may be asked to stand unattended in one part of the arena either in hobbles or ground-tied, while the rider leaves the ring for a specified length of time. There is sure to be a trail gate through which the horse must pass, side-stepping as the rider opens it from the saddle and again when he closes it on the other side, always permitting him to remain in control of the gate. A Trail Horse

A Champion Parade Horse. (*Photo courtesy of International Arabian Horse Association*)

must allow mounting and dismounting from either side and sometimes he is required to be loaded into a trailer right in the ring.

Since the test diagram is outlined in advance, the competitors may school their horses at home over obstacles similar to the ones they will encounter in the class. It is probably the gate that will require the most practice. However, no amount of work in the schooling ring develops a horse's self-reliance, steadiness, and stamina as surely as does practical experience over miles and miles of natural trails.

Highly popular in some parts of the country, classes for PARADE HORSES were first introduced to horse shows in the Western states just after World War II. Shown to music at a flat-footed animated walk and a prancing parade gait (in which speed exceeding five miles per hour is penalized), the Parade Horse is judged 75 per cent on conformation, performance, and manners, and 25 per cent on appointments. In certain shows, eye appeal may count for as much as 50 per cent or 75 per cent. Because of their appearance and bearing, American Saddle Bred horses,

Palominos, Pintos, Morgans, Arabians, and Walking Horses are most successful in this specialty. Due to the emphasis on appointments, many Parade outfits are extremely lavish, weighing as much as 165 pounds and costing thousands of dollars, with silver, ribbons, flowers, sequin powder sprinkled over the horses' hoofs and quarters, and any other ornamentation the contestants can imagine, so long as it does not (in theory, at least) exceed the limits of good taste. Where this division attracts a large entry, it may be broken down into separate classes for different breeds and colors, such as Palomino, Pinto, and Golden American Saddle Bred. Arabian, Appaloosa, and Morgan divisions, among others, also feature a Parade class. There may also be events for Children's Parade Ponies under 14.2 hands, ridden by Junior exhibitors. Many Parade Horses are home-trained and almost all of them are ridden by amateurs, although it is not unusual for them to be owned and exhibited by commercial concerns as part of a public-relations program.

While large numbers of AMERICAN QUARTER HORSES are shown in the Jumper, Western, or some other division of AHSA horse shows, many owners of registered Quarter Horses prefer to train and enter them in competitions governed by the rules of the American Quarter Horse Association, where their horses will have an opportunity to win qualifying points for the annual Register of Merit (ROM) and toward the title of AQHA Champion.

In order to become a Champion, a horse must not only look like a Quarter Horse, he must also perform like one. He earns the title by winning not less than twelve points in the halter division, not less than twelve in performance competition, and at least thirty points in the two categories, the point value of a class depending upon the number of horses competing.

Most of the performance classes are based on traditional rodeo events, in which the Quarter Horse has always excelled. According to the horses' age (whether they are over or under five years old), there may be Senior and Junior divisions of some of the eleven different events: Cutting (the only contest open to non-registered horses); Reining (which may be subdivided according to the horses' age and to whether they are ridden in a bit or a hackamore); Calf Roping; Steer Roping; Barrel Racing; Working Cowhorse (including reining, sliding stops, backing, and possibly actual work with a cow); Jumping (with touches scored, and obstacles set at a minimum of three feet, to be raised four inches for each jump-off); Western Pleasure Horse (a Hack-type class); Western Riding (over a course including a gate and a small obstacle); Pole Bending Races; and Trail Horse (in which the horse must go through a gate, over an obstacle, across a wooden bridge, and into a trailer, among other tests).

The Quarter Horse Halter Division features a wide variety of classes judged on conformation only and shown in hand, including events for registered stallions, mares, foals, colts, and fillies of almost every age and breeding condition. As with Hunters, the current fashion is to present Quarter Horses in a much plumper condition in the Halter Division than in Working classes.

For Western riders under eighteen years of age, there are "Youth Activity" events, many of them versions of the adult classes, and at the end of the show the highest-scoring young contestant is awarded a trophy as All Around Champion. Two events are obligatory in order to qualify for the trophy: Western Pleasure Riding, and Showmanship at Halter (in which the condition, grooming, and tack of the horse count 40 points, the appearance of the rider 10 points, and his manner of leading, posing, and showing his horse 50 points). The other Youth Activity events are: Cutting, Reining, Barrel Racing, Calf Roping (with the ability of the rider counting as much as the performance of the horse), Breakaway Roping, Western Riding (horsemanship scored as well as performance over a prescribed course), Trail Horse Class, a Stake Race (over a figure 8 course), Pole Bending, and Stock Seat Equitation (walk, jog, lope, changes of lead, figure eights, square stops, backing—and for riders over fourteen years of age, mounting and dismounting). Perhaps it should be mentioned at this point that the AQHA rules are not always exactly the same as the AHSA ones. Western riders should therefore keep both rule books on their bookshelf, and be very sure to study the right set of rules before they go to a show.

The alert and agile CUTTING HORSE has been a star of the horse-show ring only since 1946, when the National Cutting Horse Association was formed to establish rules and procedures for transferring cattle cutting from the corral to the contest arena. The NCHA rules are the official ones of the American Quarter Horse Association and of the American Horse Shows Association. Starting out with only fifty-four members, the NCHA today has flourishing affiliates in every state of the union. Far from being limited to cattle ranchers, the membership includes men and women from every walk of life, who own a cutting horse exclusively for the pleasure of show-ring competition.

A Cutting Contest. (*Photo by Budd*)

The cutting contest resembles closely the practical ranch work from which it is derived. The horse must demonstrate his ability to separate a selected calf from a herd and to prevent the animal from rejoining it. A cutting competition normally consists of two eliminating "go-rounds" of two and a half minutes each, with a third two-and-a-half-minute round for a limited number of finalists. The horse with the highest total combined score is declared the winner.

A herd of cattle is released at one end of the contest arena, where it is supervised by two mounted "herd holders," and prevented from escaping to the opposite end of the ring by two "turn-back men," all of them usually fellow contestants. The judge or judges are also mounted, in order to give them the best possible view of the horses as they work.

Each timed go-round begins as a rider heads his horse into the herd to cut out a selected calf, which he then leads to the center of the arena. One of the rider's most important contributions to the partnership is to select an animal that appears most likely to show off the ability of the horse, and to do so requires an experienced eye for cattle. Whenever possible, the herd consists of yearling or two-year-old whiteface cattle, who most often seem to give the horses enough play to put on a lively show. It goes without saying that a horse, no matter how accomplished he may be, cannot produce a top performance unless the animal he cuts out really makes an effort to get back to the herd.

After cutting out his calf, the horse must demonstrate his skill in working it to keep it separated from the herd without the slightest help from the rider. When the horse holds a definite advantage over the calf, the rider may decide to abandon it and return to the herd for another. On the average, a horse will work three different calves during each go-round. A lesser number would give less opportunity to show off his ability, while a greater number would cause him to lose too much time in riding back to the herd. One of the many subtleties of riding cutting contests is to judge the best moment for dropping one calf and returning to select another spirited adversary.

Each contestant is allotted a score that ranges from sixty to eighty points, with seventy considered to be an average good performance. A horse is given special credit for bringing out a calf from the herd without disturbing the others, and he is penalized for scattering the herd. An entry will be marked down two points for using the back arena wall for turn-back purposes; one point each time the horse is reined or cued in any manner; five points for losing a calf (allowing it to return to the herd); and three points for quitting a calf when the horse is out of position or does not have the advantage over the animal. The score will also suffer if the rider uses a tight rein or falls from the horse, if the horse runs past the calf to the point where he loses his working advantage, or if he indulges in unnecessary roughness, such as biting or pawing. The most severe penalty of all occurs when a horse turns the wrong way, placing himself in a position with his tail toward the calf. In this case he is disqualified and no score is given for the go-round.

Because the cutting horse is supposed to work unaided by his rider, mechanical as well as natural aids are severely restricted. The horses must be ridden with a bridle or a loose hackamore; bozals, choke ropes, tight nosebands, and tie-downs are specifically prohibited, as well as any other device that might give a rider undue control. Spurs may be worn (although there is a penalty for spurring a horse in the shoulder), but quirts or bats are forbidden. In other words, it is really the skill of the horse that is tested, and not the art of the rider. In the long run, a horse's natural ability and patient training will triumph over a rider's clever arena technique. It doesn't hurt, however, to have a bit of luck as well!

Throughout the year, the NCHA maintains a record of the points won by member-owned horses at approved contests. At the end of the season the Top Ten Cutting Horses are announced, the first two being recognized as the World's Champion and Reserve, with special awards for the Champion Stallion, Mare, and Gelding.

OTHER DIVISIONS

In addition to the above, there are AHSA Divisions for certain breeds such as the Appaloosa, Arabian, Hackney, and Harness Ponies, which are presented in Single, Pair, Tandem, and Trandem harnesses and must respond to the commands "Park Pace" and "Show Your Pony" (a smart trot); the Morgan, Paint, Pinto, Palomino, Pony of the Americas, Shetland, Connemara Pony, Welsh Pony (with riding and driving classes), and the Paso Fino (the riders wearing a Western or special Spanish-style "Show Outfit"). An entire show may be devoted to a single breed or to Gymkhana events. All-Pony shows are common, as are those consisting entirely of Hunter and Jumper classes, or of Saddle Bred events. Quarter Horse shows are immensely popular and are run under the rules of the AQHA. Special regulations also govern the running and

A happy winner in the Pony Division. (*Photo by Sue Maynard*)

judging of Dressage shows, Driving shows, and Combined Training Events. Many of these rules are described in the AHSA *Rule Book,* which is, to repeat, a mine of information, and an indispensable item of equipment for all horse show exhibitors.

EQUITATION DIVISION

While the rider's skill influences the outcome of every horse-show class, in most of those that we have seen so far it is the horse that is judged rather than the horseman. In the Equitation division the situation is reversed. It is the rider whose ability the judges score.

Even so, in order to win a horsemanship competition today, a child needs to have a good show horse or pony. In Stock Seat Equitation classes each entry is scored on the suitability of the horse to the rider and even on the fit of the saddle, so you cannot expect a child to do well if he is given a borrowed horse and hand-me-down tack.

It is true that in Hunter and Saddle Seat Equitation classes the judge may ask a good rider on a poor mount to exchange horses with a

The Maclay Cup finalists walking the course with their instructors at Madison Square Garden. (*Photo by Budd*)

better-mounted rider. Frequently several riders change horses. Nevertheless, a young horseman's chances will be far better if he has a good horse of his own to start with.

A child must have an excellent instructor too, one who understands not only riding but showing as well. There is a world of difference between the kind of equitation that wins a Good Hands Class and the simple science of sticking to a horse's back without falling off!

The appointments and grooming of both horse and rider should be correct, neat, and conservative. Fancy dress and trappings designed to attract audience attention are quite out of place. They may delight the parents, but they will certainly be unfavorably noted by the judge as an indication that the rider has a rather distorted idea of the meaning of horsemanship. Because, in this division, it is horsemanship in every sense of the word that is judged, and not just ring performance.

The judge takes into consideration the general appearance of the rider and his horse and the rider's attitude toward his mount, as well as his hands, seat, legs, his alertness and accuracy in responding to the ring instructions, and his good manners. The method of correcting a disobedience can make or break a young rider's score. The fall of either horse or rider also disqualifies an entry, and a young exhibitor may be asked to leave the ring if he does not appear to have his horse under sufficient control.

There are three types of Equitation classes: Hunting Seat, Saddle Horse Seat, and Stock Saddle Seat. All are open to children under eighteen years of age, and for horse-show purposes Junior riders, like Thoroughbreds, are given the same birthday of January 1, maintaining the age they had on the first of January throughout the entire year (with the possibility of competing during December in classes for which he will not be eligible until the following January, if he wishes). Sometimes an entry list is so lengthy that an Equitation Class is subdivided into smaller age groups. It may seem at times that the girls are separated from the boys. But the sad fact is that girl riders are simply far more numerous than boys, except in the Stock Saddle Seat events.

Among the most coveted awards in Equitation are the Alfred B. Maclay Trophy for Jumping, offered by the ASPCA (The American Society for the Prevention of Cruelty to Animals), and the Good Hands Award for Saddle Seat horsemanship, presented at the National Horse Show in Madison Square Garden, both of them open to riders under eighteen who have qualified for the finals by winning a preliminary competition during the year.

Waiting for the class to be called. (*Photo by Sue Maynard*)

The American Horse Shows Association offers to its Junior members Medal classes in each Equitation division, the riders qualifying for the national finals by winning individual classes during the season. In some states you must win three blues in order to be eligible, in others only one. The Hunting Seat and Saddle Seat Medal Class finals are held at a specified Eastern show each year, with the Stock Seat finals taking place on the Pacific Coast. The three happy victors of the finals retire from subsequent competition in the Medal events they have won in order to give other talented young horsemen a chance. But there is nothing to prevent them from entering more than one division, if they wish. Miss Luann Beech was awarded the AHSA Medal for the Stock Saddle Seat in 1954 and then came back to win a second medal in 1956 as the national winner of the Saddle Seat division.

The U. S. Equestrian Team also sponsors a Medal Class for young riders that is a combined test consisting of two phases, one over a slightly more demanding jumping course, and one on the flat. Winners of five USET classes are awarded a bronze medal, winners of ten a silver one, and winners of twenty receive the USET medal in gold.

It is an indication of the quality of the riders and the jumping in these special competitions that the rosters of past winners read like a veritable "Who's Who" of the horse world. For example, the AHSA Hunter Medal Class list includes such names as Buddy Brown, Katie Monahan,

Conrad Homfeld, Crystine Jones, James Kohn, Bernard Traurig, Mary Mairs, Michael Page, George Morris, Victor Hugo-Vidal, and Ronnie Mutch, all of whom went on to greater equestrian triumphs after that early teen-age triumph. To win an Equitation class in first-class competition, a child needs a really first-class horse these days, which probably means an expensive one. But he still needs to ride very well.

In HUNTING SEAT EQUITATION there may be classes of two types: with and without jumping. In the former a course is first jumped by the competitors individually, just as if it were an Open Jumper event. Then, if the judge desires, he may call back into the ring any or all of the young riders to follow the same procedure as the nonjumping Hunting Seat Class, performing at a walk, trot, canter, and hand gallop and executing individual figures. The judge chooses his instructions from an AHSA list, so they may vary from one class to another. Among the suggested exercises are backing, mounting and dismounting, stopping from a gallop, figure eights at a trot (demonstrating the correct change of diagonals in the center) and at a canter, with flying or stationary changes of leads. (If you should happen to start out on the wrong lead

Francine Steinwedell, winner of the Maclay Trophy for Hunter Seat Equitation at the 1977 National Horse Show. (*Photo by Sue Maynard*)

or diagonal, it is better to stop and start off again correctly, than to continue as if you hadn't noticed anything was wrong.) The riders may be asked to jump a low fence at a walk as well as a canter, to pull up on turns between fences, to jump fences on a figure-eight course or in the middle of the ring at right angles to the course.

The way you enter the ring is important. Entering at a sitting trot or a smart posting trot, followed by a halt or half halt and then a smooth transition to a canter, makes a very good impression. Hunter Seat Equitation judges like smooth, free strides, a confident manner, and a natural rather than a "posed" seat. They like bold approaches to the obstacles. If there is an option, for example, between jumping a fence from four forward strides or five cautious short ones, the riders who take the bolder option will score higher.

Often a judge will request the competitors to repeat the course after exchanging horses, and this is the downfall of many a rider whose horse is better trained than he. You must dismount and slip your stirrups off the saddle and then (remembering to keep the sides straight) replace them on the saddle of your borrowed horse. Experienced horsemanship riders watch the previous rounds of jumping and observe their competitors' horses at every opportunity in or out of the ring, because any information they can glean may prove helpful when the moment comes to change mounts.

Occasionally it may happen that the judge will ask a few riders to ride a perfectly strange horse provided by the committee, although this occurrence is rare. However, you will often be asked to ride without stirrups. Finally, the judge may ask every rider three questions, one each on the anatomy of the horse, on tack, and on equitation.

For SADDLE SEAT EQUITATION, the competitors are required to demonstrate each gait (walk, trot, and canter) as they circle around the ring, first in one direction and then the other. When the riders are lined up at one end of the arena, each one is called upon to execute an individual test which will differ slightly from one judge to another. You may be asked to mount and dismount, to demonstrate your horse's gaits around the ring, and to back. (If your horse backs very well, you might ask the judge how many backward steps he wishes, for a perfect performance may result in bonus points in your favor.) Most tests include figure eights at a trot and canter (changing the diagonal exactly in the center of the eight and making two really round, full circles); serpentines at a trot or canter, changing leads down the center of the ring with

Mary Ellen Ronco, Saddle Seat Equitation winner at the 1977 Devon Horse Show. (*Photo by Budd*)

stops at each change; riding as directed without stirrups; changing horses; riding a strange horse, and answering the judge's questions, just as in the Hunting Seat Class. In addition, Saddle Seat riders may be asked to perform a one-minute demonstration ride of their own composition.

STOCK SADDLE SEAT EQUITATION classes are quite different from the other two, since the horse is scored as well as the rider. You might say that they are scored as a team, for there is never any changing of mounts. Basically, it is a modified version of a regular Open Stock Horse Class, with emphasis on good hands.

A light hand is considered by the judges to be the most important single attribute of the young Western horseman, who should hold the reins with only one hand (and not change hands), the hand to be kept clear of the horse and saddle, above and close to the pommel. It is a mistake to imitate the exaggeratedly high rein position of some cutting-horse riders, whose interest is not to ride a correct seat but to show that their horses are working unguided by the reins. In Equitation classes all of the signals for the different movements should be given by reining and shifting the weight in the saddle.

The saddle must fit the rider. Either a half-breed, spade, or curb bit may be used with a leather chin strap. Hackamores, tie-downs, draw-reins, bozals, cavessons, and running martingales are strictly forbidden. The riders must wear Western dress, including chaps or chinks, and carry a rope—and hobbles, too, if closed reins are used. Since the correct position of the feet in the stirrups is with the weight on the ball of the foot, it is better to avoid using very wide stirrups in Western Horsemanship classes, for they may give the impression that your feet are "all the way home," when actually they are perfectly well placed. The stirrups should be worn quite long. When you are standing in them, there should be room for about three fingers between your seat and the saddle.

The ring procedure begins quite conventionally, with all of the competitors riding into the ring at a walk and circling around the rail to be judged at a walk, jog, and lope, working in both directions and always on the correct lead. A subsequent individual performance is optional, except in AHSA Stock Seat Medal classes where it is obligatory. The riding pattern is outlined in the current *Rule Book* and is identical with the test for most Open Stock Horse classes, including figure eights at a smooth, even lope, changing both the front and hind leads; runs the length of the arena and straight sliding stops; backing, quarter turns, and half turns in both directions off the haunches with the horse's feet in one position.

Since the test diagram is published in advance, you will have time to practice each separate element as well as the entire performance. But you shouldn't drill to such a point that your horse anticipates each move instead of waiting for your rein signals. Overtraining is considered a fault and will be penalized, and besides, the horse's performance is given less weight in the judging than are the methods you use in obtaining it. If

Doug Evertz, AHSA Stock Seat Medal Winner. (*Photo by Judy Frederick, courtesy of the AHSA*)

your horse is hard-mouthed, tosses his head about, switches his tail a lot, tugs on the bridle, or shows other signs of indiscipline or nervousness, it will be inferred that your hands are not as light as they should be and that your training methods leave much to be desired. The ideal is for your horse to be in perfect balance at all times, working off his haunches with his body straight, his head held at a normal Western height, that is, low rather than flexed, and with his mouth closed over the bit.

HALTER AND BREEDING CLASSES

Riding, good or bad, doesn't enter at all into Model, Halter, and Breeding classes, where the entries are shown "in hand." But if your horse is registered in a stud book and is an outstanding example of his breed, you may care to enter him in a contest where only conformation and breeding quality are scored.

Breeding classes are offered for stallions, mares and brood mares, foals, yearlings, two-, three-, and four-year-old colts and fillies registered in their respective stud books. Model classes are actually a part of the performance section, but are often held prior to the Breeding Class in order to provide a standard for judging. They may be offered for any breed or type of horse for which there is a division in the particular show, and they may be divided as to age, sex, and height.

The ring procedure is very simple. All of the entries walk into the ring together and are led by the halter in a circle around the judge before being lined up in the center, often with the aid of an assistant handler. The judge inspects each animal and asks for him to be walked away, turned, and walked back; then moved away at a trot, stopped, turned, and trotted back. When every horse has performed alone, the judge sorts them out, sometimes requesting two or more entries to move together, in order to clarify the comparison in his eye and to help him make his placements.

The best preparation for a Halter Class is simply to rehearse the actual ring routine at home some time before the show. Every foal, whether you plan to show him or not, should be taught at an early age to stand squarely on his four feet with his legs straight, his head up, and his whole little body alert. He should know how to move straight with well-balanced strides and perfect manners, to turn in a collected manner both to the right and to the left, and to stop straight without altering his head position or allowing his body to become crooked and his legs askew.

In the Breeding Division, mare and foal are often judged together. (*Photo by Sue Maynard*)

While it is impossible to conceal your horse's inherent conformation faults, you can enhance his natural appearance by conditioning and grooming. He should be neither fat nor thin, but perhaps a bit on the plump side, and as well muscled as you can make him by daily exercise, good grooming, and conditioners. Many breeders swear by linseed mashes; others add a couple of raw eggs to the morning and evening grain during the last few weeks before a colt is shown. His mane and tail should be groomed in the fashion suitable to his breed and conformation, the long hairs clipped off his face and legs. Most often his feet are left natural but well trimmed. However, some breeders like to shoe weanlings and yearlings just for the show with very light plates on the forefeet only, believing that this "dresses up" their feet. The shoes are put on with tiny nails a week or so before the show, so that the colt can become accustomed to them; they are removed immediately afterward.

And that's about all there is to it. But don't wait until the night before a show to train your colt or horse to move quietly and obediently on a lead shank. Manners aren't supposed to count in the judging, but—just like children—well-behaved horses always seem more attractive than unruly ones.

And now your last class of the show is over! Unless you have qualified for a Championship Class, you may leave whenever you like.

You should prepare your horse for the trip home just as carefully as when you sent him to the show. Unbraid his mane and tail, groom him well, and give his legs a good rub before wrapping them in shipping bandages or boots. Protect his head and tail and blanket him if the evening air is cool and the van drafty. Before you close the gate of the van or trailer, look over your stall one last time to make sure you haven't left anything behind. (And don't forget to turn in your exhibitor's number!)

You may wish to say good-by to your friends and watch the final Championship events. But don't linger too long, because you'll want to arrive home before your horse does in order to welcome him with a warm bran mash in his own stall.

You'll surely have a lot to think about on the way back, reviewing the show in your mind. Perhaps you've done less well than you had hoped. If so, the show ring may have brought to light weaknesses that escaped your notice during your regular schooling sessions or riding lessons. Perhaps, on the other hand, you've had greater success than you imagined possible. If so, don't forget that a large share of the credit be-

Awarding the ribbons of a Hunter class at the Devon Horse Show. (*Photo by Budd*)

longs to your horse. In short, whatever your show results, you should leave the grounds neither overconfident nor discouraged.

You should realize that the exhibitor's job during a horse show is to make the most of his particular horse, while the judges' job is to pick the best horse in the ring, not to allow a poorer horse to beat a better one. Often a novice cannot understand why it is possible to produce a perfect ring performance and still be placed below another entry who may have made a glaring mistake. The explanation is simply that the winner was undoubtedly a better horse according to the standards of the class in question, and this was evident despite a less perfect presentation. For example, a Morgan horse may give an impeccable performance in a Hunter class and still be placed below a high-class Thoroughbred, because the latter is incontestably a better Hunter type, even though his actual ring performance may not have been superior. (The Morgan would, of course, have won in the Open Jumper division, where only performance counts.)

The best that you can hope to do is to make the very most of your horse; you can never alter his intrinsic limitations. As one philosophical exhibitor puts it, "A Ford is a Ford and a Rolls is a Rolls!" In other words, you cannot conceal a horse's faults beyond a certain point. Consequently, the real measure of your success at a show is not the color of the ribbons you won, but whether or not you have succeeded in making the

A horse trailer ramp at the end of a show. (*Photo by Sue Maynard*)

The closing ceremony of the Royal Winter Fair Horse Show in Toronto. (*Photo by Budd*)

most of your horse. Once you have learned to consistently show to his advantage a fair horse, you deserve a chance to see what you can do with a better one. But no horseman deserves a really good horse until he knows how to make the most of a fair one.

As a matter of fact, the more you show, the sooner you'll learn that the most important thing you bring into the ring is not your equestrian ability or even your horse, but a spirit of good horsemanship. If you enter a show primarily for the enjoyment of the sport, you cannot possibly lose, no matter where the judges place you in your classes. You will learn a lot about horses and riding, have a lot of fun, and probably make a few new friends. Whether you take home a pocketful of ribbons or merely happy memories, your showing experience will enrich your riding career and both you and your horse will be the better for it.

14. Riding Sports

Equestrian sports are as old as civilization itself. They used to be more or less spontaneous competitive versions of military and working activities, but today they have become ends in themselves.

With more leisure time, better recreational facilities than ever before, and what seems to be a national passion for horses, it is not surprising that riding sports of all kinds are flourishing. Each of them could be the subject of an entire book—an entire library, in fact—and in these few pages it is possible to present only a rapid survey of the most important ones. So let's waste no time and, honoring diplomatic protocol, first pay our respects to the "Sport of Kings," which is, of course:

RACING

Informal racing has probably existed ever since an anonymous pre-historic rider defiantly claimed, "My horse can run faster than your horse!" But Thoroughbred racing as we know it today originated in England, where the first recorded flat race was run in 1377 between King Richard the Second and the Earl of Arundel, each on his favorite and fleetest steed.

In 1730 the first Thoroughbred race horse was brought to the United States. He was *Bulle Rocke, a son of the Darley Arabian, and he holds an uncontested place in American Thoroughbred history despite the fact that he was too old when he set foot on these shores to do any racing or even to engage in more than a limited amount of activity as a stud.

The earliest race track in the United States had been founded in 1665 by New York's first British Governor, Colonel Richard Nicholls, on Long Island's Hempstead plain. But the Puritans frowned on flat racing and the sport first took a real foothold in the Southern and Southeastern states, where the major turf activity was quarter-mile sprints. The Civil War interrupted all racing, and afterward it reappeared principally in the North, its renaissance inaugurated by the Passaic County Fair Derby that was run in Paterson, New Jersey, in 1864. Since that not too distant era, horse racing has become the leading spectator sport in America, as well as a thriving industry. While the Triple Crown races are run on the historic tracks of Lexington, Kentucky (the Kentucky Derby), Pimlico, Maryland (the Preakness), and Belmont Park, New York (the Belmont Stakes), vast new racing complexes have developed in other parts of the nation, especially in Florida and Southern California. A modern racing enthusiast can go to the races somewhere every day of the year.

The purpose of racing is not only to bring thrills to the spectators, joy and riches to the fortunate owners of the winners, and profit to the lucky betters. The sport is of real value in testing the quality of many light breeds. As long as FLAT RACING exists, the value of a Thoroughbred will be determined by his actual functional ability and not merely by his beauty. And in this sense, racing protects the horse from unsoundness and degeneration.

In England, racing is governed with autocratic omnipotence by the historic Jockey Club. But the American Jockey Club, while it established our original racing code and still controls the American Thoroughbred

One of the most famous racing photographs of all time, the finish of the 1944 Carter Handicap in which three fine stakes horses, Bossuet, Wait a Bit, and Brownie, all differently weighted, finished in a triple dead heat.

Stud Book and the registration of names and racing colors, has turned over most of its past prerogatives concerning licensing, rules, and regulations to the various state racing commissions. In addition, the major race-track managements have formed a governing body of their own, the Thoroughbred Racing Association, one of its principal activities being to maintain the integrity of its member tracks by sponsoring the Thoroughbred Racing Protective Bureau.

Today, racing in America is big business, employing mostly specialized professionals. A gentleman jockey would find it very difficult to compete on modern flat tracks. Even if he happened to be born small enough to be able to ride at 115 pounds or so including clothes and saddle (which is the weight he would need to make in order to obtain a reasonably large number of mounts to ride), no weekend rider could ever match the superb racing technique of Eddie Arcaro, who piloted five Kentucky Derby winners to victory; Willie Shoemaker, the most successful jockey of all time as well as one of the few small things to come out of Texas (he measures four feet eleven inches); Johnny Longden, long-time holder of the world record for the number of winning rides (nearly 6,000 of them); or such consistent and outstanding jockeys as

Louisiana's Lafitte Pincay, Jr., and the Latin-American contingent that has dominated the jockey lists in recent years, including Jorge Velasquez, Ismael Valenzuela, Manuel Ycaza, Angel Cordero, and Braulio Baeza (whose weight problems induced him to turn trainer in 1978). Steve Cauthen is a case apart, a genuine phenomenon. Starting his meteoric racing career as an apprentice jockey in 1976, the seventeen-year-old son of a race track blacksmith, he has broken many jockey records, was voted Athlete of the Year in 1977, and won the Triple Crown in 1978 on Affirmed, riding as always with flawless technique and instinctive strategy.

Continental race tracks occasionally schedule flat races for gentlemen riders. The late Aly Khan donned the silks each year at Deauville and Ostende. But in America, flat racing at the big tracks remains for the amateur a spectator sport.

Nor is it generally possible for the average horse-lover to view the spectacle from the owners' stand, because the price of a promising racer and the cost of training and campaigning him have become so high that even millionaires form syndicates to share the bills and the risk. There are still quite a few low-budget owners in Europe, where there are far more small race meetings (especially in England and Ireland) and where the cost of maintaining a race horse is relatively reasonable. But in America, aside from a few exceptional "rags to riches" horses like Alsab and Seattle Slew, the statistics are discouraging:

Of the 40,000 Thoroughbred foals registered each year, less than half are raced, and these favored few average 9 to 10 starts a year for average earnings of $6,000. Since it costs at least $14,000 a year to keep a race horse in the most modest conditions, a horse of average ability would have to start at least 25 times in order merely to earn his keep, and that is far too grueling a schedule. These harsh facts of life explain

Triumphant Steve Cauthen has just won the 1978 Triple Crown with Affirmed over his archrival Alydar in a close finish of the Belmont Stakes. (*Photo Communications*)

why racing (without a profitable breeding operation to support it) is an expensive hobby. They also explain why so many Thoroughbreds sold "off the track" as Hunters and Jumpers suffer from various unsoundnesses due to overwork during their early years.

HARNESS RACING has been aptly compared to a country lad who made good in the big city. And in fact, the sport that used to be widely practiced in a rather informal way at county fairs and on back roads is now one of our major metropolitan sporting attractions.

While there are still hundreds of county and state fairs that feature harness racing, the major events take place on a nationwide circuit of tracks, some of which rival in luxury and capacity the leading Thoroughbred show-places, and the most modern race tracks, like Meadowlands in New Jersey, are equipped for both Thoroughbred and Standardbred racing.

Three contributing elements to this phenomenal success story cannot be overlooked: the attraction of night racing; the appeal of pari-mutuel betting; and the invention of the mobile starting gate which permits all of the horses to get away evenly from the starting-line, in position, on gait, and in a minimum of time.

The major harness-racing tracks are members of and governed by the United States Trotting Association, and the horses are, with few exceptions, registered Standardbreds. Harness races are handicapped according to a horse's speed per mile and are most often run in "dashes" varying between six furlongs (a furlong being the equivalent of one-eighth of a mile) and two miles, although many track events at fairs and a few important races (including the Kentucky Futurity and the richest of them all, the Hambletonian) are still run in heats, usually the best two out of three.

On each day's harness-racing card there will be listed a variety of races for different grades of trotters or pacers. The two are never raced together (the pace is, as a matter of fact, very slightly faster than the trot). The pacers usually wear pacing hobbles to prevent them from breaking into a gallop; with trotters it is the driver's sensitivity and skill that must maintain them in their gait. A horse is not disqualified for breaking, but it may cost him the race. Since he is not permitted to gain ground while galloping, the driver must pull him up and put him back into his proper stride. If a horse who has broken finishes less than a horse's length ahead of the runner-up, the latter is said to be "lapped on," and the breaker is automatically set back behind him in the official race result.

Competing for very considerable purses in the major events, the harness racer pulls a racing sulky (often called a "bike" because it is fitted with bicycle wheels) weighing about thirty pounds and driven by a reinsman wearing racing silks and equipped with a safety helmet and goggles, to protect his eyes from the dirt kicked up by the horses' hoofs. Harness drivers at the major tracks must possess a license that is granted by the USTA only after strict qualifications have been met.

Since there is no weight or age limit for a reinsman, some of them weigh as much as 200 pounds, and many are gentlemen well along in years. Fred Egan, for example, celebrated his seventy-eighth birthday by driving Cassin Hanover to victory in the 1957 Kentucky Futurity. It even used to be thought that youth was a handicap, until Stanley Dancer and

A night Harness race. Most Happy Fella, driven by Stanley Dancer, winning the Messenger Stakes. (*Photo courtesy of the U. S. Trotting Association*)

Herve Filion came along to explode that myth. Still, the average age of harness drivers, including the sixteen- and eighteen-year-old provisional licensees, is well in the thirties. The career of a harness race horse is also unusually long, with many of them competing during ten seasons or more, and with the legal retirement age set at fifteen years.

This does not imply that driving is any less of an art than flat race riding. A trotter or pacer requires the same pampered care and skilled handling as a Thoroughbred race horse, and an expert reinsman—such as Dancer, Filion, Delmer Insko, William Haughton, or Joe O'Brien—enjoys the same advantage over his rivals as does a top jockey. Even though amateur Harrison Hoyt won the Hambletonian back in 1948, and Neal Shapiro used to divide his time between riding international Prize of Nations courses for the USET and driving his own harness racers at Roosevelt Raceway, most amateur drivers appear only on the county fair circuit, because harness racing at the major tracks is dominated by the professionals, just as in Thoroughbred racing.

Racing over obstacles is another matter. While amateurs are permitted to ride in STEEPLECHASE EVENTS at the major tracks, which are concentrated in the states of New York, New Jersey, and Delaware, the

Ray Woolfe, Jr., riding Hampton Roads over the water jump at Saratoga. (*Photo by Bert Morgan*)

professionals are prohibited from many Hunt races. Although the professional steeplechase riders far outnumber the amateurs, and some of them, like Jerry Fishback, set standards that are hard to match, an outstanding amateur with a good horse can still meet the pros on equal terms.

George "Pete" Bostwick has been as successful at training and riding 'chasers as any of the professionals, against whom he competed at the major tracks with great success. (One of the pillars of the horse world in America, he has also excelled as a polo player, a Thoroughbred breeder and trainer, and as a gentleman jockey on the flat.) All-round horseman Thomas Hitchcock, Sr., had no peer as a steeplechase trainer, while none of the pro riders could outmatch such excellent amateurs as Rigan McKinney (who rode many Hitchcock winners), the late Johnny Harrison, William H. Turner, Jr. (later to win fame as Seattle Slew's trainer), and D. M. Smithwick. Outstanding in the younger generation are Janon Fischer, George Strawbridge, Jr., George Sloan, Turney McKnight, and Louis "Paddy" Neilson. U. S. Equestrian Team members Kathy Kusner, Frank Chapot, Michael Plumb, and Bruce Davidson have also competed in jumping races from time to time with considerable suc-

cess. But the unrivaled hero among amateur jumping jockeys is Cromp-
ton "Tommy" Smith, Jr., whose father and grandfather were also prominent amateur riders. Tommy won the Aintree Grand National
Steeplechase in 1965 riding Jay Trump, the third American horse in history to finish the challenging Liverpool course victoriously, and the first
to be ridden by an American. He is now a successful horse breeder, specializing, needless to say, in steeplechasers. The runner-up for steeplechase hero honors would have to be George Sloan, joint MFH of the
Hillsboro Hunt in Tennessee, who was the leading United States steeplechase rider in 1977, and then went overseas to win the British amateur
title in 1978.

Owning, training, and riding steeplechasers tends to be a family tradition, and many of the names on a steeplechase racing card end in Junior, II, III, and even IV, reflecting successive generations of 'chasing enthusiasts. Among the professional dynasties there are the Aitchesons, the
Smithwicks, the Fenwicks, and the Walshes, now in its fourth generation.
Mrs. Ogden Phipps, who owns one of the nation's most successful
steeplechase stables, is Pete Bostwick's sister.

Tommy Smith and Jay Trump at the thirteenth fence of the Maryland Hunt Cup. (*Photo by Marshall Hawkins*)

While steeplechase horses seldom become as famous as flat racing champions (except for Jay Trump), the sport has produced some outstanding stars, such as Winton, who won the Triple Crown in 1946 under his owner-rider Stuart S. Janney, Jr., and Neji, a great-grandson of Man O' War, who won the Belmont Park Grand National Handicap three times under stupendous weights and was a top money-winner for Marion du Pont Scott's Montpelier Stables, one of the few establishments in America devoted exclusively to breeding and racing steeplechasers.

Across the Atlantic Ocean, steeplechasing is very widespread and has long been one of the favorite sports of equestrian-minded gentlemen. Sir Harry Llewellyn, noted for his Olympic show-jumping exploits, finished second in the Aintree Grand National of 1936. Derek Kent, now a leading British steeplechase trainer, used to alternate between riding show jumpers and 'chasers. Laurie Morgan, the Australian Three-Day Olympic Gold Medal winner at Rome, was a frequent competitor in Point-to-Points, and his teammate, Bill Roycroft, could hold his own among the very top steeplechase pros. In 1965 he rode his home-trained Olympic mount, Stoney Crossing, in the prestigious Cheltenham Gold Cup and finished third to the legendary Arkle and his great rival Mill House. As a matter of fact, members of the Three-Day Olympic teams of many nations have been recruited from the ranks of amateur steeplechase riders.

The principal reason for the greater number of opportunities for amateurs in steeplechase than in flat racing is simply a matter of weight. In amateur steeplechase events the usual weight allowance is a comfortable 165 pounds (although the horses running in most professional or mixed events are generally handicapped in such a way that a rider at the major tracks should be able to weigh in at 130 or 135 pounds). Furthermore, ever since the sport was originated by eighteenth-century country gentlemen who would race together cross-country from one point to another, selecting church steeples as the most easily visible reference points, 'chasing has been somewhat more exclusive in character than flat racing. Like other equestrian sports, it is on the upswing, with larger purses (thanks to the trend for commercial sponsorship), more entries, better horses, and greater attendance everywhere.

Governed by the National Steeplechase and Hunt Association, there are three principal types of jumping races:

First of all, there are those taking place on a prescribed oval course, usually around the infield of the major flat-race tracks. These may be *hurdle races,* with obstacles approximately four feet six inches high (which nowadays resemble smaller brush fences rather than the sheep hurdles for which they were originally named); in these events, speed is all-important, making them suitable for three-year-old horses, the minimum legal age for a steeplechaser. Or they may be *brush races,* with obstacles generally between four feet six inches and five feet, including ditch and water jumps, requiring more stamina and greater jumping ability and open to horses four years old and up. Many flat-racing cards include one such steeplechase event a day during the season, the most famous being the Belmont Grand National, the Temple Gwathemy Memorial, and the Saratoga Steeplechase Handicap (in which Hampton Roads was ridden to victory in 1951 by a sixteen-year-old amateur, Ray Woolfe, Jr., who photographed a number of the illustrations for this book).

Then there is the *point-to-point,* a race for Hunters across country over natural obstacles from one specified point to another. Sometimes there is a marked course to be followed and set timber (post-and-rail) fences to be cleared. Sometimes, although less often than formerly (which is why they are often announced as "Old-Fashioned Point-to-Points"), the riders take their own line between several specified checkpoints on the five- to ten-mile course. The day before the event, they are permitted to walk the course and plan their route. Needless to say, the shortest, fastest one is also the most difficult. Nevertheless, almost any

Jerry Fishback on Augustin Stables' Cafe Prince, Steeplechase Horse of the Year in 1977 and 1978. (*Freudy Photos*)

field Hunter, if he is fit and reasonably fast, can have a lot of fun in these events.

Finally, there is the *Hunt race* meeting, an informal all-day program of perhaps six or seven races. A typical Hunt race card might include two hurdle races, a timber or a brush race, and two or three flat races run on turf (grass) rather than dirt. Some meetings schedule races restricted to ladies or children, with perhaps a Hunter Pace or "pink-coat" race, in which amateur gentlemen ride in hunting attire, with a weight allowance as high as 180 pounds.

Very popular in the Eastern and Southeastern states, these occasions often take place on private estates or at Hunt clubs in an atmosphere that is friendly, festive, and fashionable. The Radnor and Rosetree Hunt Clubs sponsor famous Hunt race meetings; the Carolina Cup draws as many as twenty-five thousand spectators each year to Camden, South

Amateur rider Charles C. Fenwick, Jr., riding Ben Nevis II on the way to a second consecutive victory in the Maryland Hunt Cup. (*Photo by Douglas Lees*)

Carolina; the prestigious three-mile races My Lady's Manor and the Grand National Point-to-Point are run over fences averaging 5 feet in height; and the most famous of all is the Maryland Hunt Cup, a four-mile race over twenty-two timber jumps at Glyndon, Maryland, which attracts some of the best riders in America, including World Champion Three-Day Eventer Bruce Davidson and his teammate Michael Plumb, veteran of five Olympic Games, who finished second in this race in 1976. The late great steeplechase rider Noel Laing once said that of all the steeplechase events in the world, the Aintree Grand National was the most difficult to win, but the Maryland Hunt Cup was the most difficult to ride.

A steeplechase horse competing on the major American tracks must be a registered Thoroughbred; even at Hunt races the horses are almost without exception Thoroughbred. A promising 'chaser can make his debut at three in hurdle races and progress to brush races the next year. A horse who jumps slower but clean may succeed best over timber. If he

A Hunt team going over a rail fence. (*Photo by Ray Woolfe, Jr.*)

remains sound, he can expect to race ten or twelve times a year until he reaches the age of ten, which is the average retirement age from steeplechasing. Horses often turn from flat racing to steeplechasing when they are older, but seldom does the opposite occur. It is true that Azucar, a converted steeplechaser, won the Santa Anita Handicap of 1934; Our Jeep, the outstanding three-year-old hurdler of 1960, achieved a fair measure of success on flat grass courses in 1961; Mrs. Ogden Phipps's Top Bid had won several important flat races before turning to jumping and becoming the Steeplechase Horse of the Year in 1970; and Hunter's Rock performed as a three-year-old equally well over hurdles and on grass. Turf racers are more apt to make the switch than dirt racers, but even they are exceptions to the general rule.

Sometimes, however, a talent for steeplechasing reveals itself in the show ring or in the hunting field, as in the case of the handsome horse Sir Trouble, whom Mrs. Clara Adams trained to become a successful steeplechaser after five years as a show horse. One of America's leading lady riders, Miss Betty Bosley (now Mrs. Charles S. Bird, Jr.), used to win show ribbons with her home-trained Thoroughbred Hunter Count Stefan at the same time that he was bringing home silver plate from Hunt races and following hounds in his spare time. In 1946 the versatile gray gelding won the Ladies' Hunter Championship at the Devon Horse Show only two weeks after placing second in the Maryland Hunt Cup.

Although the sport is by no means devoid of danger and, in fact, requires a good deal of courage on the part of both horse and rider, the steeplechase race horse often finishes his life happily as somebody's prized Hunter or hack. In the meantime, many of them really seem to enjoy their work. Take the case of the eight-year-old gelding Firebet, who was entered in the 1949 Belmont Grand National. Losing his rider at the very first jump of the one-and-three-quarter-mile hurdle race, Firebet never for a moment considered running off the course and returning to his stall. Continuing to race, he successfully negotiated one obstacle after another, pacing himself with unerring skill. Among the last horses coming into the backstretch, Firebet decided to make his move. Rounding the final turn he was in third place. He moved up to clear the last jump neck-and-neck with the leader and then sped ahead of him across the finish line. On that memorable occasion, many a horse-lover must have regretted that the regulations do not permit a riderless horse to win a race.

POLO

Far from being a playboy's pastime, first-class polo requires top physical condition, lightning-fast muscular reactions, keen judgment, courage, plus the technical skill that comes only from hours of practice on the playing field. Oh yes, first-class polo also requires money.

Due to its high maintenance cost, this ancient and aristocratic game, which can trace its origins as far back as 600 B.C. in Tibet (where *polo* is a word meaning "ball") and perhaps even earlier in India, might seem doomed to disappearance from the American sporting scene. But while international high-goal polo has indeed decreased, club play is growing stronger. Many young riders learn to play the game at Hunt clubs, Pony Clubs, or at riding academies that sponsor polo clubs and maintain a polo field. Polo training is given and polo teams are formed by many colleges and schools and almost all military academies, since polo was the traditional recreation of the Cavalry. In order to promote the game, the United States Polo Association, which is the official governing and rule-making body in America, has instituted a program offering the services of qualified instructors to polo clubs all over the country, in order to coach the young players, from thirteen to eighteen years of age, who will ensure the future of the sport. When necessary, the Polo Association provides the ponies for these schools, although experience has shown that many well-trained ponies who have never seen a ball or mallet before be-

come reasonably good polo mounts within a very few weeks. An increasing number of teen-age boys (many of them Pony Clubbers) are thus discovering that polo is an even more exciting sport than baseball or football. Furthermore, thanks to this initiative of the U. S. Polo Association, it isn't nearly as expensive as they thought it was either!

Just about any kind of a horse or pony can learn how to play polo for fun. But for international matches, every player must have several carefully trained, well-bred Polo Ponies. Since the height of the pony is no longer restricted, actually small horses are used, generally about 15 or 15.2 hands high and of basically Thoroughbred blood, either full or combined with Quarter Horse or Arabian strains to produce the necessary strength, speed, hardiness, and handiness in a compact body. Even the world-famous Argentine Polo Pony, the most sought after of all, based on the foundation of the sound, tough little Criollo pony, is now predominantly Thoroughbred. Arabians and Quarter Horses are particularly adept at indoor polo, where the playing field is smaller.

For international play, it used to be customary to travel about with a string of up to forty ponies for a four-man team. But today there are seldom more than three or four ponies per player, each one being ridden during two nonconsecutive chukkers a day, three times a week. This is the most that can be asked of a polo pony, who may travel seven miles during a single chukker at top speed, punctuated by sudden stops and turns. Even so, his playing life is seldom more than three years.

The regulation polo field measures 300 yards long by 200 yards wide (120 if there are side-line boards), making it three times as large as a football field. Covering this turf terrain are two umpires, a referee, a flagman behind each goal, and eight players, four to a team, who attempt to drive a four-ounce willowroot ball just three and a quarter inches in diameter into the eight-yard space between the opponents' goal posts, and at the same time to protect their own goal from enemy attack.

Official indoor polo, correctly called Arena Polo, is played over a much smaller surface, 100 by 50 yards, and there are no goal posts, the ball being hit at a recessed or painted portion of the end walls. The game is the same, but there are only three men to a team, and a larger, inflated leather ball is used.

Polo matches are divided into periods called "chukkers" or "chukkas" of seven and a half minutes each. The number varies. In this country it is usually six, with a fifteen-minute half-time recess. In case of a tie, the last period is prolonged until the ball goes out of play; then, after a five-minute interval, the game continues in periods of seven and a half minutes until one side scores a goal and is declared the winner.

The two mounted umpires patrol the play, one of them literally starting the ball rolling by lining the teams opposite each other in the center of the field and bowling in the ball. From this moment the action is wide open and continues at breakneck speed (as high as twenty or thirty miles an hour) until the end of the chukker, being interrupted only if a goal is scored (in which case the teams change sides and the play recommences by bowling in again in the center of the field), if a foul is committed, the ball is driven from the field, or a player injured. Injury, incidentally, is not infrequent, for polo is one of the "high risk" sports. The players continually run the risk of being struck by a mallet or the ball, having a nasty fall, or being kicked by a pony.

Each player wears white breeches, boots, a protective helmet with a chin-strap, and a jersey in his team colors bearing a number that indicates his theoretical playing position. The Number-1 man is supposed to be the star goal scorer; Number 2 the aggressive setup man; Number 3 the long-drive specialist and master strategist; and Number 4 the back or goalkeeper. In actual practice there is much overlapping of roles, and flexible teamwork is vital to winning play. A sense of timing, anticipation, and concentration are more important than sheer strength or even than equestrian ability. However, to be a good polo player, you definitely need a good polo pony. Some players estimate the ponies' contribution to the game as being at least 75 per cent.

Every player carries a mallet made of Malacca, cane, or Duralumin, or a combination of these materials. It must be carried in the right hand, even by a left-handed player. The length of the mallet stick varies according to the player and the size of his pony—a player may own twenty different mallets of varying length, weight, and flexibility—but the heads are all set on at an angle of 77.5 degrees, so that they lie flat on the ground when the ball is hit. It is hit, incidentally, by the side of the head of the stick and not the point.

There are eight basic polo shots and innumerable variations. "Near shots" are struck on the pony's left side, either forward, backward, or diagonally; "off shots" from the right side. Players also attempt to swing at the tiny ball from underneath the pony's neck or across his tail. There are different forms of interception. "Riding off" occurs when one pony pushes another away from the ball in order to place his own rider in hitting position. Another method of preventing a player from hitting the ball is to hook his mallet with your own (but "cross-hooking" by reaching across the opponent's horse in order to hook his mallet is a foul). A player cannot cut off an opponent who is in pursuit of the ball by crossing in front of him; he must approach from the side or behind and scrupulously respect the rules that govern the right of way. Fouls are judged on a scale ranging from one to five, the mildest being bad sportsmanship (5) and the worst (1), creating a dangerous situation in order to block a goal. Five gets a free shot from midfield for the opponents. One scores an automatic goal for them.

Individual players are handicapped annually according to their ability, expressed in the form of goals, the optimum being a ten-goal player (which is so rare that there have been only forty-five in the world since 1891). Among our players in this category were Robert Skene, Dr. William Linfoot, and Cecil Smith, who set a phenomenal record of twenty-five consecutive years as a ten-goaler. But there is still a lot of polo talent in the country, such as Tommy Wayman, Roy Barry, Jr., Harold A. Barry, and Red Armour, who are handicapped at nine goals. There are only four current ten-goal players, all of them Argentinean.

Team handicaps are calculated by totaling the goal ratings of all its members so that, in theory at least, every polo game is evenly matched. Some tournaments are limited, such as "a seven-goal" match, in which an

Two legendary 10-goal polo players, Cecil Smith and Thomas Hitchcock, fight for the ball. (*Photo courtesy of the U. S. Polo Association*)

eight-goal team could not compete. The Cup of the Americas and other international competitions are rated at twenty goals or higher.

Because of the financial burden of maintaining a string of polo ponies, not to mention the sum required to underwrite the training and traveling costs of an entire team, it is hard to see how high-goal polo can ever become as widespread in the United States as it is in Argentina and other South and Latin American countries, or in some parts of Europe and Asia. But intercollegiate polo (arena polo) is expanding, as is low-goal polo, particularly in the Midwest and the West. Thanks to the devotion of a few sporting philanthropists such as Paul Butler (who created the polo center at Oak Brook, Illinois, which is now headquarters of the United States Polo Association) and William T. Ylvisaker (who helped found the Polo Corporation of America in 1976 to promote the game), high-goal polo too has managed to survive inflation.

At the same time, some ingenious enthusiasts have invented variations of the game that require a more modest outlay in facilities and funds. The most successful version was developed by some enterprising Texans. Usually called "Cowboy Polo," there are five men to a team, two

Two high-goal American polo players follow the flight of the ball during an exciting moment of the 1977 Gould World Cup. (*Photo by Jim Higgins*)

forwards, two guards, and a center, each man riding one horse throughout the entire game and playing in a designated area of the field. Western tack is worn, while rubber-headed mallets and a large inflated rubber ball are used. Playing technique is also different from classic polo, since the ball generally spends a lot of time in the air and is sometimes hit before it lands. Because the Quarter Horse is the most popular mount for the game, it is also referred to as "Quarter Horse Polo" and has become increasingly popular all over the country and even abroad. Who knows? The ancient game of polo, originated by the Indians, will perhaps be saved by the Cowboys!

FOX-HUNTING

Far less widespread in this country than in the British Isles, where the suitability of the countryside and centuries of tradition have made it as integral a part of British life as afternoon tea, fox-hunting is nevertheless more widely practiced in the United States than is generally realized.

There are organized Hunts in practically every state. (A complete descriptive listing is published in the annual fox-hunting issue of *The Chronicle of the Horse.*) Some of them are sponsored by clubs, others are organized on a subscription basis, and a few are still privately owned packs. Aside from the exhilarating days of fox-hunting in the open country, most Hunt groups organize a number of related activities during the year, such as drag Hunts especially for Junior members and pony Hunts for very young ones. Many of them sponsor a Pony Club, since one of the original aims of this splendid organization was to interest and prepare young riders to become well-trained, well-mannered fox-hunters. Horse shows, Hunter trials (in which the horses are ridden over an outside course in pairs or teams to show how well they go in company), Hunt race meetings, and point-to-points are planned to occupy Hunt club members outside of the fox-hunting season. As a matter of fact, in order to qualify for many of these events, a horse must actually have been ridden to hounds with a recognized pack.

Except for the privately owned packs, which require introductions, most Hunt clubs welcome guests in the hunting field. Prospective visitors apply in advance to the Master or the Hunt Secretary and contribute a "capping fee" of perhaps $15 to $35. In many cases, arrangements can be made to provide a horse.

American Hunts vary in size, with an average Field of twenty-five or thirty persons. In England and Ireland there may be several times that many, not counting the throngs of spectators who follow the chase by every imaginable means of locomotion—in trucks and cars, on bicycles, on cart-horses, and on foot. In America too, there may be almost as many enthusiasts following a Hunt by car as there are mounted participants.

While it is thus possible to enjoy the spectacle of a fox hunt without a horse, the sport could not exist without a well-trained pack of hounds. It is the hounds who do the hunting, after all; the horses and riders merely follow. In this country we use American or English foxhounds, or a crossbreed between the two. A hunting pack may group as few as six or eight couples (with the odd hounds counting as half a couple), or as many as twenty-five, the average being about twenty couples. Their fox-hunting instinct and ability to "give tongue" or to "speak" is inherited, but they are also given special training under the supervision of the Huntsman, usually a professional, who is responsible for the pack and the strategy of the Hunt. A male hound, by the way, is referred to as a dog or a dog-hound, and a dog that is not a hound is called a cur even

The Huntsman and some of the Field out with the Fairfield County hounds. (*Photo by Ray Woolfe, Jr.*)

though he may be a pedigreed poodle with a case full of show ribbons; a female hound is always called a bitch, even in the most polite circles.

As for the horses, almost any sound, robust horse or pony that can gallop and jump may be used for fox-hunting. But the most desirable are Thoroughbreds of a suitable, steady temperament, because of their incomparable combination of speed, jumping ability, and courage. Irish Thoroughbred Hunters have long been highly appreciated. However, in rugged regions of the United States where the countryside includes rocky hills, marshy, sandy, or muddy stretches, and a comparatively limited amount of open galloping, a half, three-quarter, or seven-eighths Thoroughbred is often preferred to a full-blood, and Quarter Horses are increasingly popular.

Modern Hunters are ridden almost exclusively in a modified Forward Seat, with a jumping or hunting saddle, and a snaffle, Pelham, or double bridle in which the reins and cheekpieces should be stitched to the bit or fastened by invisible studs. By tradition a plain browband (never a colored one) and a leather noseband are worn. Hunting breastplates and martingales are often seen in the hunting field these days—perhaps more often than is really necessary. The horses are shod in shoes with calks if there is slippery or muddy going.

The rider's appointments are rigorously prescribed (see Chapter 11). Some Hunts even furnish members with a printed list of their particular requirements. Visitors and guests might inquire of the Hunt Secretary concerning the customs of the Hunt in question, in order to avoid the embarrassment of arriving in unconventional attire, or in formal hunting appointments on a "Ratcatcher" day.

Fox-hunting takes place over terrain that ranges from a few acres of suburban real estate to hundreds of square miles of Western ranchland. It may be composed of plowlands, rocky mountains, swamps, cornfields, meadows, grasslands, plains, and woods. Occasionally the land is owned or leased by the Hunt. But more often, arrangements are made with a number of individual farmers and landowners to grant the privilege of hunting in return for an indemnity for any possible damage to their land or crops. Sometimes the obstacles are natural ones: stone walls, post-and-rail or log fences, ditches, streams, gates, and snake fences. In these days, unfortunately, more and more fields are enclosed by wire, and so the Hunt must install jumping panels or else cover a portion of wire with a chicken coop to permit the horses to clear the barrier without running the risk of injury. Where there are no natural obstacles at all, the Hunt builds artificial ones.

Since the chase is run principally over land that has been cleared for cultivation, the hunting season starts in the early fall, after the harvest has been gathered, and continues until it is time for spring planting, in March or April. The "cubbing season" takes place shortly before the regular one, in order to complete the training of the young hounds that have been reared by neighboring farms. When permission has been asked and granted by the Master, cub-hunting days also offer an excellent opportunity to school green Hunters.

The object of these elaborate preparations is a small, clever, and fast red or gray fox, who is the bane of the farmer's existence. In certain parts of the West the customary quarry is coyote or hare. The coyote is just as cunning and swift as the fox. But the hare tends to run in circles and rarely provides the Field with the thrill of a long, fast run.

An average Hunt rides to hounds two or three times a week during the season. The "Meet" is the place where the hounds and "Field" (the

Hunt subscribers and their guests) gather. The spot is frequently changed, and a "fixture card" is sent to the members at the beginning of the season, listing the different hunting dates and their respective rendezvous. Where foxes are scarce or nonexistent, a Hunt schedule may consist in part or whole of drag Hunts, in which no live animal is chased, the pack of hounds following a scent that has been "dragged" beforehand over a cross-country course by the Huntsman and his staff.

Bright and early on a hunting day, you will feed and groom your horse and then either ride, lead him from another horse, or drive him in a van or trailer to the Meet. If you decide to hack, you should stick to the roads instead of cutting across country where you may disturb the foxes who are to provide your hunting pleasure; if you go by van or trailer, select a parking place five or ten minutes hacking time away from the Meet. It is courteous, especially if you are a guest or Junior member, to arrive half an hour ahead of time, ride up to the Master, tip your hat, and introduce yourself. This important personage, whose full title is "Master of the Foxhounds" (MFH)—even though she is often a lady nowadays—is in complete command of the Hunt, and you are expected to obey promptly all of his instructions.

While standing around quietly waiting for the Field to assemble, you will become acquainted with the other Hunt officials and servants. It is easy to recognize the Huntsman (he is the one with the horn), as well as his aids, the "Whippers-in." There are usually at least two of them, either professionals or experienced subscribers, appointed by the Master to aid the Huntsman in keeping the pack together and in "whipping in" any stray or lagging hounds. Sometimes there is also a Field Master in charge of the mounted followers, especially if the Master is acting as his own Huntsman, or, as they say, if "the Master carries the horn." This unique instrument, by the way, produces only a single note. But a good Huntsman is able to communicate a wide range of instructions to the pack by varying its tone and rhythm, as well as by the use of his own voice. In addition to directing and encouraging the hounds, he has learned to interpret the "music" of the pack. It takes years of experience to master the art, and each Huntsman has his own style and signals. But the better you can learn to understand the technique of the Huntsman and the work of the hounds, the more appreciation you will bring to fox-hunting, and the more enjoyment you will get from it.

When the Master indicates that the appointed hour has arrived, the Huntsman gathers the hounds and moves on to the first "cover" or patch of forest, where he expects to find a fox. The hounds begin "casting"

The Huntsman gathers the hounds by blowing his horn. (*Photo by Ray Woolfe, Jr.*)

(looking for a fox), their noses to the ground and their "sterns" (tails) animatedly moving from side to side ("feathering"). The quarry, when roused, usually makes off for the open country. A series of distinctive blasts on the horn is the warning that the fox has left the cover or "gone away." And now the chase is on.

An unwritten protocol determines the places in the Field. The hounds go first, of course, directed by the Huntsman and controlled by the Whippers-in, with the Master leading the Field far enough behind to avoid interference with the work of the pack. The most proficient and faithful regular subscribers are accorded the choice positions up near the Master. Novice riders, Junior members, and green horses should keep to the rear and never gallop past the leaders. It would be very ill-mannered for a guest to try to ride "in the Master's pocket" unless he were a distinguished fox-hunter, a visiting MFH from another Hunt, or something of the sort.

And so the hounds pursue the scent of the fox as the Field follows. If the hounds become confused or lose the scent, there is a "check," or forced stop, during which the Huntsman gathers and recasts the pack. Sometimes the hounds are unable to recover the scent, which may have been disturbed by wind, soiled land, or unfavorable weather conditions. If the cast has been unsuccessful, the Huntsman may decide to "lift" the pack, that is, to lead it rapidly to another spot where he believes the fox must have passed. As soon as the line has been picked up again, off you go once more in hot pursuit.

This process of runs and checks continues until the fox is either caught and killed, or has been lost completely. Most often he "goes to earth," that is, in his den or in a hole where the hounds cannot follow. As a matter of fact, it has been estimated that only about one fox in five is actually killed by hounds, even under the very best scenting conditions. But when a kill does occur, there follows a traditional ceremony during which the Master honors certain members of the Field by presenting the fox's tail (its "brush") to the first member present at the kill or to a distinguished guest, and the fox's feet ("pads") to others present at the finish. The fox's head ("mask") is customarily reserved as a trophy for the pack or the Master. The first time a child assists at the kill, the Huntsman marks the occasion by "blooding" him (or her), which is merely smearing his cheeks with a bit of the fox's blood. Frequently the Master also presents the child with a pad.

Now the Huntsman leads the pack to another cover where a new fox is raised, and you're off again. Thus the work of the pack and the pursuit of the Field continues until the Master decides that it is time for the riders, horses, and hounds to return home.

Needless to say, both horse and rider must be very fit in order to put in four or more hours of practically continuous exercise. A horse who is not properly conditioned might have his soundness permanently impaired if pushed beyond his strength. But a Hunter in hard condition is perfectly capable of following hounds two or three times a week, and if he is of the right type, he will simply love it.

It is easy to become carried away by the excitement and spectacle of a successful day's hunting. But never should you permit yourself to forget your hunting etiquette. Good manners are even more important in the hunting field than in the drawing room, because safety as well as courtesy is involved.

The principal rules to remember are:

Always leave two horses' lengths between your own horse and the one in front of you.

Do not chatter during a check when the hounds are working.

Try to keep out of the way of the hounds, but never turn your back on them (especially if your horse has a tendency to kick). Get out of the

Moving along a lane during a fox hunt. (*Photo by Ray Woolfe, Jr.*)

way by backing up rather than by turning around. Never jump a fence when there is any chance of landing among a group of hounds on the other side; never get between a hound and the Huntsman.

Never jump a fence until the hounds have cleared it first. Then allow the Senior members to pass. Wait your turn at a fence without crowding and give the previous rider time to get well over the obstacle and on his way. Remember that a horse approaching a fence in a straight line has the right of way over one coming at it diagonally.

If your horse refuses at a fence, get out of the way as quickly as possible, go to the rear of the Field, and try again after the others have jumped it.

Don't attempt to jump fences beyond your horse's means. There will always be a gate through which you can pass instead. If there is a rider coming through behind you, don't let the gate slam in his horse's face, but hold it open until he can take it over. If you are the last to use the gate, do not fail to close and fasten it.

If you hear the cry "'Ware hound" (meaning to beware or watch out for the hound), "'Ware hole," or "'Ware whip," pass the warning on to the rider behind you. (In present-day suburban Hunts you are just as likely to hear " 'Ware Coca-Cola bottle!") On the other hand, you should leave hunting cries such as "Tally ho" to the Hunt servants and experienced members.

Try to cause the least possible damage to the land over which you ride, especially during damp weather. The Field Master will probably lead you around the edges of plowed land, and you should follow him obediently, keeping close to the hoofmarks 'of the horse in front of you. Never frighten a hospitable farmer's stock by galloping through a herd of cattle or a flock of sheep.

Don't gallop unconcernedly past a fallen horseman. Stop to help him.

If your horse becomes overtired, lame, or unruly, turn for home at once.

Unless your horse is a very quiet and experienced Hunter, keep him well away from the hounds at the kill. Many horses are alarmed by the smell of blood and the experience might cause them to kick or even to try to run away.

At the end of the Hunt, ride up to the Master and thank him for the day's pleasure, for he has been your official host. Visitors should also send the Master a polite thank-you letter within the following few days.

In addition to these basic rules of etiquette, there are rules of hunting horsemanship that you should know. All of them can be summarized in just three words: Spare your horse! It is a hunting adage that the best horsemen finish the day with their horses in the best condition.

To start with, you should remember that the footing may not always be easy on your horse's hoofs. A cornfield where the stubble is left standing, for example, should be negotiated with care, for it might cut your horse's feet. Plowed land is better ridden lengthwise or diagonally rather than crosswise; the presence of water in a deep furrow usually indicates firm earth at the bottom. You should not hesitate to pull your horse up at difficult places where excessive speed may cause him to stumble or even to fall.

It is easier on your horse to approach all the fences in a straight line, and it is prudent to avoid jumping the pointed angles of zigzagging snake fences. When riding down a steep hill, take a straight descent rather than a slanting one, because if your horse should slip he will in the first case merely slide on his hindquarters, while a false step on an oblique line may throw him over on his side.

When you and your horse have returned home from a day of hunt-

Coming home from a drag hunt. (*Photo by Ray Woolfe, Jr.*)

ing, make sure that he is well fed, clean, and comfortable before you start to think of your own hot bath and waiting dinner. Fix him a warm bran mash and groom him carefully, feeling for any heat in the legs and treating any cuts or scratches. It is a good idea to bandage his legs in order to prevent them from filling, before bedding him down.

The next morning, walk and trot him just enough to test him for lameness. But don't attempt to do more than half an hour of easy walking. Your horse has worked hard to provide you with one of the finest sporting pleasures known to man, and he deserves a day of rest.

DRESSAGE

As more and more riders discover the advantages of elementary Dressage training for their horses, it is not surprising that the competitive form of this supreme riding art is also expanding. In each recent year, the number of Dressage events and participants has more than doubled. A Dressage competition was a rare curiosity only a few years ago, but today the United States Dressage Federation (USDF), the AHSA, and local Dressage clubs sponsor competitions and organize classes and clinics throughout the country.

Dressage competition consists of the individual performance of a prescribed test, which is scored by a judge or a panel of judges scoring individually, according to a scale that allots a certain number of points to each exercise, as well as collective marks for the quality of the paces, the horse's impulsion, his submission, and for the rider's position, seat, and use of the aids. After deductions have been made for errors and for exceeding the time limit (generally from 6 to 12 minutes), prizes are awarded to the riders with the highest scores.

The test patterns progress in difficulty, starting with a series of national tests, which vary from one country to another and are open only to riders from that country. These comprise:

Training Level (equivalent to the Pony Club C Level)
First Level (like Pony Club B)
Second Level (like Pony Club A)
Third Level (the beginning of specialization in Dressage, with the introduction of collected gaits and extended paces. The Dressage tests of Three-Day events do not go beyond this level.)
Fourth Level (specialized Dressage of medium difficulty, including flying changes of lead at the canter and pirouettes)

Distinctly more advanced are the international tests under FEI rules:

Prix St. Georges (higher standards for the Fourth Level exercises, with more difficult transitions)
Intermédiaire I (relatively advanced)
Intermédiaire II (even more advanced and more strictly judged, including flying changes of lead at every stride and the piaffe)
Grand Prix de Dressage (the highest standard of artistic equitation. This is the Olympic Dressage test.)

There are also other tests at various levels, such as:

Grand Prix Special (the same as the Grand Prix, only shorter, so that transitions are more important. This is the ride-off test for the Olympic Individual Dressage title.)
Kuer or Kür (a free-style display that may have a musical accompaniment, as in ice skating)
Pas de Deux (a pair class)
Sidesaddle
Dressage Prospect (judged on aptitude as well as on performance)

Elizabeth Lewis, representing the United States in the World Dressage Championship in Copenhagen, performing a half pass on Ludmilla. (*Photo by Udo Schmidt*)

All of these tests are performed individually in an oblong Dressage area (60 by 20 meters for international tests, 40 by 20 meters for national ones), with lettered markers around the edges to indicate where the horse must make various changes of direction, gait, and movement. The judges or jury, stationed opposite the entrance to the arena and sometimes at the sides as well, score each movement by comparing it to a theoretical perfect performance, and evaluate their "general impressions." The scores are pooled to determine the final placings.

A Dressage horse usually starts with the Training Level test (which

Hilda Gurney at the Montreal Olympics. (*Photo by Judy Frederick*)

any well-trained riding horse should be able to perform), then works his way up through the other levels as far as his ability and schooling can carry him. Almost any sound horse can be taught the Training Level exercises. Appaloosas, Quarter Horses, Full and Half-Arabians, Morgans, and many unregistered horses have succeeded in performing them well. But it takes a horse of exceptional aptitude, temperament, and conformation to advance to the International tests, in which Thoroughbreds, Hanoverians, and Trakehners are at the moment the most favored breeds. Unlike jumpers, most Dressage horses are owned by their riders. In order to save training time, international level riders often buy a trained Dressage horse that has already reached the Prix St. Georges level, which generally means an expensive imported horse.

It also takes special aptitudes and temperament to become an accomplished Dressage rider. Aspirants often begin with Pony Club training, then join a Dressage riding class or club. If they advance to the international level, it is practically essential to work with a private coach. The top Dressage riders never stop taking lessons. Although there are still too few Dressage coaches in America to fill the growing demand, some of them, such as Melle van Brugger, Jean Saint-Fort Paillard, Gunnar Østergaard, and Karl Mikolka, give clinics in various parts of the country from time to time. Another essential aid to an advanced rider is the opportunity to ride an experienced, perfectly trained Dressage horse, in order to get the "feel" of the movements that must be taught to his own mount. These four-legged teachers are just as rare as the two-legged ones, and are far more apt to be found in a Dressage trainer's stable than in a riding school barn.

Because the art of Dressage was perfected and preserved by the cavalries of such horse-minded nations as Sweden, Austria, France, Germany, and Switzerland, international competition is still dominated by men. Nevertheless, Liselotte Linsenhoff won the Individual Olympic Gold Medal for Dressage in 1972 and former World Champion Elena Petushkova the Silver, while the 1976 Olympic and 1978 World Champion was Christine Stueckelberger of Switzerland. In the United States, where the boys and men are seldom interested in pursuing Dressage beyond the level of Combined Training Event requirements, almost all of our outstanding riders are women. "Trish" Galvin (now Princess de la Tour d'Auvergne), who won the Dressage Gold Medal in the Pan American Games of 1959 and again in 1963, the Grand Prix of Aachen, placed sixth in the 1960 Rome Olympic Dressage event and eighth at Tokyo in 1964, was a leading figure, and an elegant one, in making the transition between our masculine military Dressage team and the present predominantly feminine civilian one. Among the current outstanding riders are Hilda Gurney (fourth in the 1976 Olympic Dressage Grand Prix at Montreal), Dorothy Morkis, and Edith Master.

If the sport of competitive Dressage continues its impressive growth rate, superior instruction may become more widely available in America. At the present time, Dressage competition on the national level is an absorbing sport for the serious rider; on the international level, it is still a rather exclusive activity, reserved for a privileged few who possess the talent, the horse, and the means to indulge in it.

COMBINED TRAINING EVENTS

Whether it is called Combined Training, Three Day, Eventing, Horse Trials, or "Concours Complet d'Equitation," as in France, this relatively recent riding sport is one of the fastest-growing equestrian activities. In England it often makes the headlines, due to Princess Anne's enthusiastic participation, while the success of our own international Three-Day teams has inspired horse men and women throughout the United States to enter this demanding and rewarding discipline.

There are several kinds of Combined Training events, conceived and governed by the U. S. Combined Training Association and the AHSA. The pinnacle of them all is the FEI international Three-Day Event, first devised for the Olympic Games of 1912 as an all-round test of a cavalry officer's mount. (At that time, Olympic equestrian events were open only to the military.) Its name comes from the fact that three phases take place on three successive days:

The First Day: An FEI Dressage test, generally no higher than the AHSA Third Level.

The Second Day: A grueling test of stamina, speed, nerve, and jumping ability, divided into four phases: First (A), a short warm-up over "Roads and Tracks" at a speed of 240 meters per minute; immediately afterward (B), a 3,105 to 3,450 meter steeplechase over 1 meter timber and 1.40 meter brush obstacles at 690 meters per minute; next (C), more Roads and Tracks over varied terrain at 240 meters per minute which, added to the A phase, totals 10 to 16 kilometers. At the end of this there is a veterinary inspection, with unfit horses being eliminated from further competition; finally, the most spectacular portion of the test (D), a Cross-Country course 5,200 to 7,410 meters long, studded with some thirty formidable and ingenious solid obstacles, including slides, drops, combinations, and water hazards, to be ridden at 570 meters per minute. The maximum height of the jumps is 1.20 meters (3'11"), and they may be as wide as 2 meters (6'7"), with the water jumps 2.50 meters (8'2"). On a rainy day, or for a rider late in the starting order, treacherous footing increases the hazards of the course. Since the obstacles are solid, there is greater risk of injury but none of incurring faults for knockdowns, as only refusals and falls are scored. Three refusals at the same obstacle cause elimination, as does the third fall during the course and the second fall during the steeplechase phase. There are penalties for exceeding the Optimum Time, and elimination for exceeding the Time Limit.

The Third Day: Another veterinary examination eliminates horses that are not in condition to perform the final test of Stadium Jumping, with ten to twelve obstacles not exceeding 1.20 meters (3'11"), including combinations and a water jump, on a winding course 700 to 800 meters long and a required speed of 400 meters per minute, which tests the horse's suppleness and fitness after the rigors of the day before. The penalties for the three days are then totaled, and the lowest-scoring horses are the prize winners.

Princess Anne riding Goodwill during the Three-Day Event of the 1976 Olympics. (*Photo by Sue Maynard*)

An International Level (Advanced) Three-Day Event is so hard on a horse and rider that even the best conditioned pair can compete in no more than two or three a year. But at Training or Pre-training Level, a horse in top condition should be able to do as many as eight or ten. Aside from some notable exceptions, it is a young person's sport. But there are also less demanding versions, one- or two-day programs including modified forms of the same three phases. Some of these are within the abilities of almost any well-trained, well-conditioned horse and rider. In fact, they are probably more enjoyable and certainly less expensive than Horse Shows.

The *Three-Day Event* is offered at Junior, Preliminary, and Intermediate levels as well as in the Advanced FEI form. *Two-Day Events* exist in Preliminary, Intermediate, and Advanced versions and include the same three phases in modified form. *Horse Trials* usually take place on one day and consist of a Dressage test, an abbreviated Cross-Country, and Stadium Jumping, at Training, Preliminary, Intermediate, and Advanced levels. *A Combined Test* consists of only two phases on the same day: a Dressage test and a Jumping event, with Training, Preliminary,

Intermediate, and Advanced levels. You cannot enter these events merely by paying a fee. A horse must qualify for them by accumulating points to earn a grading. A green Event horse would start "unrated" and attempt to move up to Grade 1, 2, and finally 3 (the tops).

There are several red-letter events on the Combined Training calendar: the USET Challenge Trophy Three-Day Event in the fall (for Grade 1 and 2 horses), the USET spring Gladstone Trophy Two- or Three-Day Event, the AHSA Autumn Three-Day Event offering its Combined Training Trophy, and the Autumn Horse Trials of the U. S. Combined Training Association, which awards the DeBroke Trophy. American riders also often compete in the two most famous British Horse Trials: at Badminton in the spring, and at Burghley in late summer.

What does it take to compete successfully in one of these Combined Training Events? Just about everything! Both horse and rider must be brave, fit, and all-round athletes. In international competition, a skilled coach is practically a necessity (Jack Le Goff, the USET Three-Day coach, is considered the best in the world) not only in order to supervise the training program and bring the horses and riders to the peak of condition on the crucial date, but also to advise on strategy during the riding of the Event. In lower level competitions, a superior Dressage performance is most important, since the modified Cross-Country and Stadium Jumping phases are seldom difficult enough to separate the contestants.

Due to their size, speed, and heart, most of the best Three-Day horses are full or part Thoroughbred. Mike Plumb's marvelous Better and Better, for example, is the grandson of Epsom Derby winner Never Say Die and of a sister of Assault, the 1946 Triple Crown winner. When the horse failed to show his illustrious ancestors' aptitude at the track, he was sold as a Hunter and eventually turned to Eventing, with outstanding results. Thoroughbred-Standardbred crosses often do well. Tad Coffin's Karama Kazuri proved that Quarter Horses also possess the necessary qualities. Some horses take longer than others to develop their full potential. Bally Cor of the USET was twelve years old when she produced her best efforts, which were rewarded by an Olympic Gold Medal. Better and Better, the silver medalist, was only seven (but with three years of competition under his girth). There is certainly no substitute for experience—or, as the riders say, for "mileage."

Whatever the breed, conditioning is all-important. Event horses follow a carefully planned, progressive training and conditioning program designed to develop their stamina, wind, hardness of limbs, and muscular

Michael Plumb and Better and Better warming up before the Dressage test of a Three-Day Event. A mainstay of the USET Three-Day Event Team, Plumb is the winner of an Olympic Individual Silver Medal and a team Gold. Within a period of thirteen years, he was the leading Rider of the Year of the U. S. Combined Training Association nine times. (*Photo by Sue Maynard*)

elasticity, in addition to Dressage and Jumping schooling, and plenty of opportunity to become acquainted with the types of cross-country problems and obstacles that they will face in competition later on. Jack Le Goff's method of "interval training" has been widely adopted. It consists of alternating short gallops (3 to 6 minutes) at moderate speed (400 to 550 meters per minute) and 2- to 3-minute rest periods, in order to build up resistance to stress. Uphill trotting is also a valuable training exercise. As in so many other horse sports, the best trainers "make haste slowly." It takes several years to develop a good Event horse. If a horse is injured or loses confidence from being faced with challenges beyond his means, you can lose an entire year, or perhaps ruin him forever. Eventing with an insufficiently prepared horse and rider is not only a hopeless enterprise; it can also be dangerous.

Even with a well-conditioned horse, the rider must do everything possible to minimize the wear and tear of the Event itself, for example, by taking care to:

Michael Plumb and Better and Better clearing the "elephant trap" jump on the cross-country course of the 1977 Ledyard Horse Trials. (*Photo by Sue Maynard*)

—Never trot downhill, but slow down to a walk;

—Change the diagonals at the trot frequently in order to alternate the work load on the horse's legs;

—When going uphill, rise from the saddle in a galloping position in order to relieve the horse's back;

—When galloping, rise out of the saddle in a "galloping crouch" after shortening the stirrups; this also relieves the horse's back;

—Study the cross-country course with the greatest of care. Denny Emerson likes to walk the course three times: first for a general impression, then in an analytical way with an advisor, and finally alone, visualizing his actual ride.

In spite of its comparatively recent popularity in America, the United States is already able to muster one of the best Three-Day teams in the world. Our top riders such as Michael Plumb, Bruce Davidson, Tad Coffin, Jimmy Wofford, and Denny Emerson have won almost everything there is to win in the field, including a fistful of Olympic medals. Bruce Davidson accomplished the unparalleled feat of winning two consecutive World Championships. We have a number of superior women Eventers too. Lana du Pont Wright was the first young woman to be named to an Olympic Three-Day team. Now there are Mary Ann Tauskey, Beth Perkins, and Caroline Treviranus, among others, who compete with the men on equal terms. During the past decade, the European Three-Day Event Championship has been won more often by young women than by men: Mary Gordon-Watson in 1969, H.R.H. Princess Anne in 1971, and Lucinda Prior-Palmer in 1975 and again in 1977.

The best way to enter this exciting sport is to follow the example of many of these stars: Start young by joining a Pony Club, which features elementary Eventing in its program; then graduate to a Combined Training club. Even if you are not interested in competition, it will be excellent training for you and your horse.

TRAIL AND ENDURANCE RIDING

Pleasure trail riding is a rewarding activity for nature-lovers who are also horse-lovers, since it provides complete "communion with nature," animal and vegetable and, on mountain trails, one could add mineral too.

Trail riding is a part of every horseman's life in the sense that any country lane or city bridle path is a kind of trail. But magnificent riding trails are also maintained in National Parks and Forest Preserves all over the United States. The only requirements for enjoying them are a sound horse, a fit rider, and respect for a few basic rules:

—Obey all trail signs.

—Never take unnecessary risks. Always put safety first.

—Carry a halter and lead rope for tying up your horse if necessary. A breastplate is advisable for very hilly terrain.

—Keep to the right on roads and trails, and pass on the left at a walk (never a gallop), after asking the preceding rider for "Trail."

—Maintain a steady, moderate pace. Gallop only when there is a wide open space before you and perfect visibility.

—Although most hikers will step aside for a horse, do not count on it, because hikers have the right of way.

—Horses going uphill have the right of way over those coming down. Downhill riders should stop sidewise to the slope and pull aside in order to give uphill riders room to pass without losing their momentum.

—When negotiating a long uphill trail, a zigzag line is safest and least tiring for the horse. Give him a breather on the way up a steep hill, stopping sidewise to the slope, and remount from the uphill side. (Easy, if you have trained him to be mounted from both sides.)

—Ride with loose reins when the going gets rough, and let your horse find his own footing. Should the trail get even rougher, dismount and lead him.

Many riding clubs organize *group trail rides,* which may be more fun and are certainly safer for the young and inexperienced. In addition to the above rules of the road, you should:

—Always follow the orders of the group leader, and never attempt to ride ahead of him.

—Remember that, as in the hunting field, the fastest horses ride at the head of the column, with the slow and tired ones bringing up the rear.

—Keep a distance of one horse's length between your mount and the horse in front of you.

—Keep kickers at a safe distance from the other horses, and tie a red ribbon in their tail.

—When you have to stop or dismount, if only for a moment, pull over to the side of the trail.

—Signal to the riders behind you any hazards you encounter, such as broken glass, low branches, or barbed wire.

—When you have to cross a highway, obey the leader's orders to the letter. (The safest way to cross is for the horses to stop all at once in single file on one side of the road. When the leader and the drag rider—the last one—give the signal, the entire column crosses at the same time, and then resumes its single file on the opposite side.)

Pack riding is the most adventurous form of trail riding, because it involves overnight camping stops, often in the wilderness, perhaps for several days, a week, or even longer. Each rider is expected to carry the necessary equipment for his horse in securely tied, evenly weighted saddlebags, while the fodder (in pellet form to reduce bulk), provisions, and camping material (including an ax, shovel, pail, and sleeping bags) are loaded onto pack mules or horses. Professional pack stations in many National Parks provide this service, along with the necessary camping gear, experienced guides, and riding horses that are already acclimated to the region and are familiar with the trails. In fact, unless you are very experienced in this kind of an adventure on horseback, you should not attempt it without the aid of a professional guide.

A group of trail riders with their instructor on Squaw Pass above Lake Tahoe. (*Photo by Charles Barieau*)

In addition to these exhilarating leisure activities, Trail Riding has become a fast-growing, increasingly serious competitive sport. National and regional Trail Riding associations as well as local clubs organize events throughout the country, some of which have become world-famous, like the Tevis Cup 100-Mile Ride in California (now officially the "Western States Trail Ride"), the Vermont 100, the Virginia Trail Riders' 100, and the Boston Marathon. Complete schedules are published in *Trail Blazer* magazine, while competitions are supervised and results recorded by two principal governing bodies: the American Endurance Ride Conference and the North American Trail Ride Conference.

There are two general types of long-distance competitive Trail Rides:

Competitive Trail Rides, which are rather like automobile rallies in that the entrants are required to cover a marked trail of 25 to 40 miles per day over one, two, or three days, at an average speed of 4 to 7 miles per hour, arriving at the finish within a maximum and minimum time limit. Stamina rather than speed is tested. There are veterinary inspections along the way, and at the finish a variety of prizes is awarded to the horses in the best condition as well as for horsemanship, grooming, tack care, trail courtesy, and so forth. In some rides the horses' manners and way of going are also scored.

Endurance Rides are more of a race, with a maximum time limit but no minimum. These one-day contests may cover 50 or 100 miles. The speed, depending on the distance, may average 5 to 15 miles per hour, according to the terrain, which usually includes mountainous regions. The horses' condition is checked at various points along the way, since soundness as well as speed count in the final awards, among which is a prize or medal merely for having completed the ride. Frequently, only half of the starters succeed in doing so.

Any horse five years old or older is eligible for these events. Arabians and part or full Thoroughbreds excel by a wide margin, although Appaloosas, Quarter Horses, Morgans, Palominos, and Pintos have also proven their aptitude for the sport. Arabians win the most awards for Best Condition, and there are more geldings than mares among the top winners—but there are also more geldings than mares among the entries. The average age of Endurance winners is 8½ years, and most of them have had at least three years of Endurance riding experience.

This relatively new sport, which first attracted wide attention with Wendell Robie's founding of the Tevis Cup Ride some twenty-five years ago, has already produced a number of equine heroes. One of the most famous is the Arabian gelding Witezarif, who won six Tevis Cup rides and numerous 50- and 100-Milers. Another is the Arabian stallion Kosciusko, who never competed in an Endurance Ride himself, but sired a fantastic number of outstanding competitors, including El Karbaj, two-time winner of the Tevis Cup and of the even more coveted Haggin Cup for Best Condition in this event. Wendell Robie's own "Smokey" (BANDOS in the Arabian registry) set an unsurpassed Tevis Cup record both as a competitor and as a sire. He won the first two years, his daughter won the next two, three offspring were later winners, another was second twice, and his get have completed the Ride 38 times.

Even the most gifted endurance horse will not get far unless he is in superb condition. Experienced competitors start their conditioning and training of a novice horse at least six months ahead of time, and begin to condition an experienced horse at least two months before the first Ride of the season. Five to 15 miles per day, including uphill trotting and downhill walking, is the usual work program, with a "training ride" of

Drucilla Barner, Tevis Cup winner, on Nagiya at Cougar Rock. (*Photo by Charles Barieau*)

some 20 miles once a month when the horse has no competition scheduled. Due to the exceptional rigors of the Ride itself, a horse is generally given up to a week of rest beforehand and again afterward.

In addition to a progressive conditioning program, endurance horses are regularly wormed, as often as every two months, and never fewer than four times a year. Nothing is more debilitating to a horse's stamina than worm infestation. The blacksmith pays them a visit every four or six weeks. They are also accustomed to being handled by strangers, as will occur during the Event by the veterinarians, judges, and P&R teams who check the horses' pulse and respiration recovery rates at regular intervals.

In order to win (or even to complete) an important Endurance Ride nowadays, not a detail can be overlooked. Most successful competitors prefer to use an English saddle with a double saddle pad, a breast collar, a hackamore or a snaffle bit (occasionally a curb), and to wear tennis shoes (which for once are acceptable in these exceptional conditions), leather gloves, and a hat.

During the ride itself, they do everything possible to limit the wear and tear on their horses by:

—regularly changing the diagonals of the trot;

—relieving the horse's back of weight during uphill stretches by rising out of the saddle, or steadying the horse by "tailing" (grasping his tail and being pulled along behind);

—readjusting the saddle pads, saddle, and girth as exertion causes the horse to lose weight;

—avoiding dehydration by frequently sponging the horse off from the saddle during hot weather, by administering electrolytes before, during, and after competition, and by permitting the horse to drink water at every opportunity—a little bit at first, then a stroll, and afterward all he wants;

—verifying their tack at each checkpoint;

—giving their horse and tack meticulous care during overnight stops and periodic rest points, no matter how hungry and tired they themselves may be;

—applying all of their skill, experience, and understanding of their horse to "rate" his efforts throughout the ride, that is, to control his expenditure of effort and energy in the most economical and effective way in order to achieve a specific goal. In this endeavor lies both the challenge and the art of Trail Riding.

RODEO

Back in the days when the West was wild, what could a cowboy do for amusement after the day's work or the season's roundup was over? On the open range far away from town, his sole resources being his rope and his horse, he engaged in informal contests, matching his skill against that of his comrades. What began as a cowboy's pastime gradually grew into a new American sport that was called rodeo, after the Spanish word for "roundup." (It is usually pronounced, by the way, "ROE-dee-oh," although you may hear "Roe-DAY-oh" in areas where Spanish influence still prevails.)

Practically all regular rodeo contestants are members of the Professional Rodeo Cowboys' Association (PRCA), which approves the prize lists and rules of all rodeos in which their members may compete and maintains the records of contest winnings throughout the year, inviting the fifteen leading cowboys in each event to compete in the annual National Finals that determine the World's Rodeo Champions. The PRCA also provides such benefits as hospital insurance, a very useful thing to

have in a sport where injury is so frequent (although hardly ever really serious) that one seldom sees a rodeo cowboy enter the arena toward the end of a busy season without a bandage or a brace on some part of his body.

Despite the danger (or perhaps because of it), rodeo competition seems to offer satisfactions that make all the broken bones and bruises worthwhile. One of these satisfactions is undoubtedly monetary. A Champion rodeo cowboy can earn quite a tidy sum during the year, particularly if his name happens to be Jim Shoulders (holder of sixteen world titles, four of them consecutive All-Around Cowboy Championships), Casey Tibbs (a nine-time World Champion and idol of all aspiring Saddle and Bareback Bronc riders), Bill Linderman (whose record lifetime winnings of almost half a million dollars earned him the nickname "The King"), Joe Alexander (the best Bareback Bronc rider in history, who was World Champion from 1971 through 1977), or Larry

Mahan (winner of no fewer than six All-Around Championships). These are some of the legendary figures of Rodeo.

The current crop of champions tends to come from a rodeo or ranching background. Some hold regular jobs as working cowhands between arena appearances. Some are university students. The top professionals, however, generally devote all of their time to the sport. For example, Tom Ferguson, a Champion All-Around Cowboy specializing in Calf Roping, Team Roping and Steer Roping (with a fling at Steer Wrestling from time to time), competed in 100 rodeos the year he set his $100,000 earnings record. Don Gay, a Bull Riding student of Jim Shoulders, whose father is a rodeo performer turned rodeo producer and who has dominated Bull Riding in recent years, flies from one rodeo to another in his private plane. Guy Allen, World Champion Steer Roper at the age of nineteen, is the son and grandson of champion steer ropers, while the Team Roping Champions, David and Dennis Motes, learned the ropes from their father Glen, a good team roper himself. Nowadays, a cowboy has to begin his training young. Roy Cooper, 1978 Champion Calf Roper, started at the age of nine and had won three Junior World titles by the time he was eleven; Larry Ferguson won his first Steer Wrestling contest in a junior event when he was fifteen; and Jerold Camarillo won his first Team Roping prize (the first of many) at the tender age of seven.

Incidentally, rodeo championships in the various events used to be awarded to the top money-winning rider for the year. But since 1976, the fifteen leading money-winners meet at the National Finals Rodeo, and it is this competition alone that decides the World Championship titles.

Richly endowed rodeos, such as the Cheyenne Frontier Days, the Pendleton Round-up, and the Calgary Stampede, attract the top professionals as well as the cream of the local talent. But for the more casual amateur there are numerous high-school, college, county- and state-fair, and riding-club rodeos, by no means limited to the Western states. In a number of horse-minded regions schools and colleges form rodeo teams and compete among themselves as keenly as the college-football Ivy League. In these amateur rodeos the emphasis is placed on events such as Roping, Barrel Racing, and Gymkhana, omitting the wilder contests that deal with Brahma bulls and bucking horses.

While any group can get together to put on an informal rodeo, the major ones are organized by professional rodeo producers who provide the scorers, mounted arena officials, and pickup men (to aid the cowboys in getting off the bucking broncs at the end of their round), as well as the chutes and other necessary equipment. The broncs and bulls are furnished by stock contractors, who breed and select the stock most likely to provide a fair test for rodeo contestants and thrills for the spectators. Some of the wild horses and steers become almost as famous as the cowboys who attempt to match their brains and brawn with them, and a contestant considers himself lucky to draw the worst bucker or the toughest bull. In order to make these animals even harder to handle during competition, a sheepskin-lined "bucking strap" or cinch is pulled tight around their loins just as they are released from the chute. The strap is removed by the arena pickup men when the round is over.

A good bucking horse is as hard to find as a good Hunter or Jumper. Some of them are spoiled saddle or work horses; others are wild, unbroken range-bred animals that have revealed a talent for bucking. Auctions of bucking horses are held periodically, and the stock contractors bid on them just as at any other horse sale—except that the meanest, wildest horses bring the highest prices—sometimes as high as $3,000. They seem to suffer no ill effects from the work they are asked to do, and a bucking horse may enjoy as long a career as the cowboys who attempt to ride him. Since the rider must stay on for ten seconds in order to score, a very clever bucking horse can earn his keep by doing less than thirty minutes of work a year. One famous little brown Mustang called Hell-to-Set was bucked for at least twenty years, remaining perfectly sound to the very end, and there have been many others like him. War Paint, for example, a pinto gelding who was the very first winner of the Bucking Horse of the Year title, was still unsaddling cowboys with his famed high leap from the chute at the age of twenty.

A cowboy may compete in any number of rodeo events, but the tendency among the pros is to specialize in one or two, since each contest requires an entry fee which may run as high as $200. There is a varying number of go-rounds in each event, from one to as many as seven, depending upon the duration of the rodeo and the amount of stock available. Prize money is awarded to the winner of each go-round as well as to the top scorer in each event, the best average in two or more events, and so forth, and a rodeo cowboy's standing is based on the amount of prize money he has earned rather than on the number of events he has won.

There are five standard rodeo contests:

SADDLE BRONC RIDING is practically synonymous with rodeo. It consists of riding (or rather, attempting to ride) a saddled bucking

Bobby Berger, 1977 PRCA Champion in Saddle Bronc riding aboard Old Shep at Cheyenne, Wyoming. (*PRCA photo by Jerry Gustafson*)

bronc by means of a plain halter with a single braided rope rein. Wearing a leather glove on his rein-hand, colorful leather chaps, and loosely fitted, dull-roweled spurs, the rider lowers himself into the saddle while the horse is in a chute, spurring him into the arena as the bucking strap is tightened and the gate opened. In order to qualify, the rider must have his spurs over the break of the horse's shoulders and touching the horse when the animal's front feet hit the ground on its first jump out of the chute. Now the cowboy is on his own, and he must attempt to stay in the saddle until the bell rings, marking the end of an eight- or ten-second test period. Quality as well as quantity is measured by the judges. The rougher the ride, the more the rider uses his spurs, and the more he induces the horse to buck, the higher will be his score. But he can be disqualified for touching the saddle, rein, or horse with his free hand, for losing a stirrup, for wrapping the rein around his hand or changing the rein from one hand to the other. Very often the leading saddle-bronc riders are slender and of medium height, since the winning technique is more a matter of timing, rhythm, and rapid reflexes than of strength.

BAREBACK BRONC RIDING. Again, the cowboy wears leather chaps, loose, dull-roweled spurs, and a leather glove, which is often

Joe Alexander, five times World Champion Bareback Bronc Rider and 1977 PRCA Champion, riding Pawnee Bill at Phoenix, Arizona. (*PRCA photo by Foxie*)

dipped in rosin in order to give him a better grip on the regulation one-hand rigging. The other hand remains free in the air and the rider's feet must be constantly in motion, spurring the horse in the shoulder from the moment he leaves the chute, in order to make the eight- or ten-second ride as spectacular as possible. The higher and more often the cowboy uses his spurs, the higher will be his score, for the judges award top points to the competitor who has made the most daring ride in the most skillful manner. Needless to say, a terrific strain is placed on the riding hand and arm, and since the rider's feet are sometimes as high as his head, a Bareback Bronc Champion must possess a superb sense of balance.

CALF ROPING is a contest to determine which cowboy can rope and tie a lively young calf in the shortest time. Derived from the actual ranch work of roping calves for branding, vaccination, or shipping to market, it requires speed, agility, and superior horsemanship, in addition

Roy Cooper, reigning PRCA Calf Roper, makes a fast dismount at the 1977 National Finals Rodeo. (*PRCA photo by James Fain*)

to roping skill. Perhaps that is why it attracts the most entries and is considered to be the epitome of the rodeo arts.

After a 250- to 350-pound calf has been released from the chute and the starting flag is lowered, the cowboy sprints across the starting line and attempts to rope the running calf. His horse must stop dead when the loop of the twenty-five-foot rope is thrown, and hold the rope taut as the cowboy leaps to the ground, races to the calf, throws it by hand, and then crosses and ties three feet together, finally throwing his hands up in the air to signal that the knot is made and ready for inspection by the judges. Should he miss the calf with the first throw of the rope, he has the right to throw a second one. In this case he loses a great deal of time, of course, as well as any probability of winning the go-round, but it may still keep him in the running for the over-all average.

In Calf-Roping contests the skill of the horse is just as important as that of the rider and the most successful are Quarter Horses. They are trained by their owners to work together as a team and are seldom loaned to other contestants, as is customary with the bulldoggers.

BULLDOGGING (STEER WRESTLING). In this event a wild longhorn steer is released in the arena from a chute; when a flag is lowered, the cowboy, aided by a second mounted cowboy called the "hazer,"

Tom Ferguson, World Champion All-Around Cowboy and World Champion Steer Wrestler, makes a quick catch. (*PRCA photo by Dusty Allison*)

sprints across the starting-line and races alongside the running steer. The hazing horse tries to keep the animal running straight while the bull-dogger, riding on the other side of the steer, leans from his fast-moving mount to grasp the bull by the horns, swing out of the saddle onto its back, and twist its head around in order to throw it on the side with all feet out and the head straight. It is the shortest time that wins.

A bulldogger needs a lot of strength, and a bit of weight helps too, because the steer may tip the scales at 900 pounds. He also needs the assistance of a good hazer and an excellent pair of horses if he is to mark up a good score, for the steer must be caught from the horse and not after the cowboy is on the ground. The best bulldogging horses are of the Quarter Horse breed, and they are usually trained to be used exclusively for steer wrestling. Like the legendary Baby Doll, they are often rented out by their owners to fellow contestants in return for a percentage of the winnings, and an outstanding bulldogging horse can earn more prize money than do his owner's own arena efforts.

BULL RIDING is usually the final rodeo event and the most exciting. It is the most dangerous contest of all, especially when Brahma bulls are used, for these beasts are wild, quick, and sometimes vicious. Bigger than bullfight bulls, some of them weigh as much as a ton, and transport-

Bull Riding. (*Photo by De Vere, courtesy of the Rodeo Information Commission, Inc.*)

ing them from one rodeo to another poses considerable problems for the stock contractor. Other suitable bull-riding breeds are the Brangus (an Angus-Brahma cross) and the Santa Gertrudis, which is probably the most common of all.

The cowboy, wearing a leather glove on his reining hand and dull spurs on his heels, lowers himself onto the animal's back as the chute is opened, grasping with just one hand the braided hand-hold at the end of a rope that encircles the bull's neck, leaving his other hand free in the air. Since the rules require that the rope fall off the bull after the rider has dismounted (accidentally or on purpose), a bell is attached under the animal's belly so that its weight will pull off the rope at the end of the ride. The cowboy is not required to use his spurs, although it will earn him extra points. So will his ability to sit straight on the bull's back

Dennis and David Motes, World Champion Team Roping Team, display their skill at the National Finals. (*PRCA photo by James Fain*)

—which is easier said than done. The bull may buck, kick, and attempt to throw the rider by making swerving turns, charging at the arena sideboards, or indulging in the most unexpected maneuvers. The most difficult to ride are the "spinners," who whirl about at a tremendous speed, often throwing the cowboy to the inside, where he runs the greatest risk of being stepped upon.

Some bulls, especially the Brahmas, are not at all averse to charging a cowboy once he is thrown, which is why there are not only pickup men in the arena but also two rodeo clowns, usually experienced young rodeo veterans with nerves of steel, whose job is to distract the angry bull from fallen contestants. The eight seconds during which the cowboy tries to remain on the animal's back must seem like an eternity! It is not surprising that Bull Riding attracts the younger, daredevil cowboys, while the older ones excel in Roping and Saddle Broncs, which are comparatively safer (but only comparatively).

In addition to these five standard rodeo events, there are many others that are popular in different parts of the country; for example, trick-roping contests, team roping (now one of the most popular events and growing fast), and single steer-tying, in which the steer is roped around the horns by the cowboy but thrown by the horse.

A Barrel Race. (*Photo courtesy of the American Quarter Horse Association*)

Another very widespread rodeo feature, and a point-winning Performance Contest of American Quarter Horse shows, is

BARREL RACING. This contest takes place over a cloverleaf course which is set up by placing three barrels in the arena at distances of forty, forty, and thirty-five yards, to form a triangle pattern. Each horse must race through the starting line to the first barrel, make a 360 degree turn around it to the right, a full turn around the next two to the left, and then sprint straight back across the finish line without knocking over a barrel or taking a wrong turn. The rider must hold the reins in one hand and avoid changing hands or touching the horse with his free hand.

A horse must be carefully schooled for Barrel Racing, which is a test of maneuverability as well as speed. First he is trained to make very sharp turns on his haunches and to ride the cloverleaf pattern at a moderate pace. Then the speed is gradually increased. Quarter Horses, because of their sprinting and turning ability, are hard to beat in this event, especially when there is a clever girl or woman rider in the saddle.

POLE-BENDING RACES are another exciting contest in which the girls are frequently victorious. Like the Barrel Race, it has long been a popular rodeo attraction and is also now recognized as a Performance Event of the American Quarter Horse Association, which means that winning points are counted toward qualification for the Annual AQHA Register of Merit as well as the Championship title.

The race is run around a series of five upright poles set in a straight line twenty-one feet apart. A horse may start either to the right or to the left of the first pole, but he must be consistent in his pattern, weaving in and out between the poles, making a half-turn around the last pole, and repeating the pattern back to the finish line. Knocking over a pole, touching the pole with the hand, or failure to follow the course are all causes for disqualification, and it is the fastest horse that wins. Perhaps Pole-Bending might best be described as an abbreviated equestrian version of the skier's slalom. It requires a fast and handy horse and a clever rider with an excellent sense of balance—for both of them, in order to make the best time, must literally "bend" themselves around the poles.

DRIVING AND COACHING

The sport of driving has never completely died out since its zenith in the early twentieth century, when it was a favorite leisure activity of millionaires, and its subsequent decline during the Depression. Many horse shows, particularly in the East and Midwest, continued to schedule Driving classes adapted to the confines of a show arena. But it is only more recently, and particularly since the formation of the American Driving Society in 1975, that there has been a genuine revival of this ancient equestrian sport. Competitive events now include not only horse show classes but also entire Driving shows and cross-country Driving Marathons, featuring various combinations of horses or ponies and a variety of vehicles.

Driving utilizes one or several horses. A single horse is usually harnessed to a two-wheel vehicle. Two horses can be driven side by side (a pair) or one in front of the other (a tandem). A tandem driven to a two-wheeled carriage is considered the most sporting turnout as well as one of the most difficult to drive, principally because if the leading horse

A pair. (*Photo by Budd*)

A tandem. (*Photo by Budd*)

is not perfectly under control, he can easily turn around and face the driver. Three horses can be harnessed three abreast (a trandem), or three in a line (a randem, which is rare), or as a unicorn (with a pair at the wheel and the odd horse alone in front). A four-in-hand with two pairs of horses, one in front of the other, harnessed to a road coach is the most spectacular, especially when the horses are perfectly matched. But most driving in the United States is done with singles and pairs.

In traditional driving techniques, the left hand holds all of the reins while the right hand holds the whip and makes the loops in the reins that enable the driver to turn the lead horses. Discreet voice aids are also used, and in carriage driving a brake is applied by the right hand and released by the right elbow. With big hitches of six, eight, or twelve horses, one or more assistants may share the reins. Driving any formal turnout, including a tandem, requires the collaboration of a groom, who should be an excellent horseman; driving a four-in-hand requires two grooms. There may also be a guard who blows the coaching horn.

Obviously, driving requires varied skills. The driver must acquire a thorough knowledge of harnessing, of the various vehicles involved, of driving technique, and of horse psychology. He must also know a lot about feeding, grooming, and conditioning in order to keep his horses very fit. Training programs usually include much groundwork out of harness, dressage-type exercises with bending and flexing under saddle or on the longe line, as well as lessons in responding to the whip and daily road work to build up stamina.

Competitive driving is an aesthetic as well as a sporting endeavor, because judges consider the over-all impression created by the driver, his groom and assistants, his horse or horses, his vehicle and its appointments, as well as their performance. Simple carriages are easy enough to obtain, but more elaborate, artistic carriage-making is practically a lost art, surviving mostly in Holland and in the Pennsylvania Dutch country. Driving devotees therefore go to great pains and expense in order to

A unicorn. (*Photo by Budd*)

A four-in-hand. (*Photo by Budd*)

unearth and restore fine old vehicles most appropriate to the perfectly matched horses they also try to acquire. Many economize in a time-consuming but pleasurable way by doing their own restoring. If they discover an old vehicle bearing the name of "Brewster," their labor should be worthwhile, since this New York firm was considered the Rolls-Royce of American coachmakers. Fancy trappings score no higher than an impeccable simple turnout in competitions where "suitability" is the criterion, but a stylish turnout is necessary in order to win against top competition.

Driving shows consist of various classes for different turnouts, including Pleasure Driving classes, judged on appearance and performance, and Time classes, which are more of a test of driving skill in negotiating an intricate course dotted with traffic cones which often leave a passage less than a foot wider than the width of the vehicle. Other obstacle courses present such "hazards" as bridges to be crossed, water to be forded, serpentines, and Figure Ts (which require backing up) to be maneuvered.

The most impressive competition of all is the Three-Day Driving

Competition, recently formulated by the FEI as an official international equestrian sport. Patterned after the Combined Training test for mounted horsemen, there are three phases: Presentation and Arena Dressage, in which a test pattern must be performed with changes of pace (walk, trot, trot-on, which is a faster extended gait, and backing) at specific spots; Cross-Country over an obstacle course ranging from 5 miles in elementary events to 26 miles in major competitions, including as many as six hazards, with specific time limits for each of the five sections of the drive, excess speed being penalized as well as overtime; and finally, an arena obstacle driving test.

International driving is dominated at the moment by the Hungarians, followed by the Poles, West Germans, and the Swiss. It is so popular in Holland that this small nation can muster ten international teams. Prince Philip's active participation may not yet have added much silver plate to the Royal collection, but it has certainly attracted worldwide attention to this fascinating and spectacular equestrian sport.

15.   Riding Pleasures

No other animal in history has made itself so useful and often indispensable to man as has the horse. For centuries, his sturdy back and fleet limbs provided the most satisfactory means of transportation, communication, cultivation, and national security. Then, as machines began to perform these functions more efficiently than he, his traditional role in life was radically changed until today, for the first time in history, the majority of horses in America are kept primarily for sport and pleasure.

Horse-lovers may deplore the rapid decline of the horse population. (There are about 8½ million horses in the United States today, compared to several times that number at the beginning of the century.) But the truth is that the modern horse is probably a happier creature, certainly better cared for and leading a far more pleasant life than his hardworking ancestors. He has also gained in quality what he may lack in quantity, for he is undeniably better bred.

At any rate, never before have so many horses been raised, trained, sold, and ridden purely for pleasure. Never has so much money been spent on horses—some $13 billion a year, according to a recent estimate.

And never has there been so great a variety of recreational activities available to the pleasure horseman.

ASSOCIATIONS AND CLUBS

In order to be informed of the organized activities in your own area, the first thing you might do is to subscribe to one of the horse publications dealing with the riding subjects of interest to you, and secondly, to join a club. A great number of national and local clubs bring together horsemen sharing the same breed, the same riding activity, or merely the same enthusiasm for horses in general. In the Appendix you will find a list of some of the most important nationwide organizations. A letter to the Secretary should bring you a reply with the address of the nearest affiliated group in your vicinity.

First of all, there are the general associations such as the American Horse Shows Association, which you will certainly want to join if you intend to do any showing.

You cannot join the United States Olympic Team merely by filling out a membership application and sending in a fee! But all horse-lovers are heartily welcomed by its supporting organization, the United States Equestrian Team, Inc., which raises the funds that make it possible for us to be represented in international equestrian competitions. A modest membership fee will associate you with this fine endeavor, which is important to our prestige abroad and influential in promoting interest in equestrian sport at home. Aside from the satisfaction of helping their sport and their country, members receive, among other things, a regular USET news bulletin.

Another particularly worthy group is the Professional Horsemen's Association, basically a charitable organization, to which most of the leading professional horsemen, as well as many amateurs, belong. PHA Chapters throughout the country prepare many interesting projects for Senior and Junior members, such as educational forums, social events, and a newspaper, in addition to sponsoring PHA trophy events in many horse shows.

In urban as well as rural areas, the 4-H Clubs, directed by the U. S. Department of Agriculture, sponsor light-horse projects for Junior members ten to thirteen years of age and for Seniors fourteen and over, with a triple program: horsemanship, horse management, and breeding.

Some of the individual clubs feature such additional diversions as field days, square-dancing on horseback, and mounted drills. A somewhat similar work, with special emphasis on breeding, is directed to a slightly older age group by the Future Farmers of America (FFA), most of whom are university students majoring in agriculture. Your county agricultural agent or state college of agriculture can no doubt give you information about the activities of both of these organizations in your own region.

An outstanding effort is being made to interest young people in good riding and horse management by the United States Pony Clubs, Inc., which has grown by leaps and bounds since it was founded in 1953. Since then more than 300 individual Pony Clubs have been formed throughout the country. Many of them are affiliated with a Hunt club, since one of the original purposes was to develop an interest in fox-hunting among the younger generation and at the same time to teach them to train and take complete care of their own horses or ponies. In recent years, however, the program has placed an ever greater emphasis on all-round horsemanship in the English style, and competition of the Combined Training type. A more recent Pony Club specialty is the Tetrathlon, which is a variation of the Olympic sport of Pentathlon, comprising riding, shooting, swimming, and running. As a matter of fact, Pony Clubs are perhaps the best greenhouse for fostering the talents of future Olympic Three-Day Event team members. World Champion Eventer Bruce Davidson started out as a Pony Clubber and so did his teammate Tad Coffin. Melanie Smith and Buddy Brown of the USET Jumping team were also Pony Clubbers, and Tommy Skiffington graduated from the Pony Club to become the top steeplechase jockey in America in 1977.

The Pony Club movement originated in England in 1929 as a junior division of the British Horse Society. Although the American organization is not officially connected with its overseas cousin, the same program, standards, and training methods have been adopted and the two groups maintain very close and friendly relations. Despite the name, which has been retained in honor of its British counterpart, the U. S. Pony Clubs are by no means concerned solely with ponies. As a matter of fact, most of the mounts that are owned by the young members (or, as is often the case, loaned to a member Club by generous supporters) are not ponies at all but horses. And so the word *Pony* in the title really refers more to the age of the riders than to the size of their mounts.

Children are eligible for membership until they reach the age of seventeen, at which point they may become associate members until they are twenty-one, and thereafter sustaining members. (Don't forget that adult volunteers are needed to supervise and instruct the youngsters.)

Pony Clubs sponsor many different projects in addition to instruction, including Hunter trials, point-to-points, riding camps, trail rides, overnight rides and camping trips, horsemanship clinics, fox-hunting and beagling, polo, mounted games, field trips to breeding farms and training stables, an International Exchange program, and, during the winter, indoor, unmounted meetings featuring talks by leading horsemen and movies from the Pony Clubs' unique film library, and "Knowdown" question games. Periodically throughout the country there are special Pony Club clinics in teaching, training, and judging for the more advanced, as well as Pony Club instructors' courses. Pony Club riders are rated according to a series of qualifying tests from "D" to "A," and an "A" rating represents a very fine level of horsemanship indeed. Every year a series of local and regional rallies takes place during the school holidays, culminating in a huge National Rally where youthful teams from all over the country compete in the finals that test the different phases of Pony Club training: dressage, cross-country riding, stadium jumping, stable management, veterinary science, fox-hunting, and horsemastership. As you see, this very complete program provides young riders with first-class, all-around training—as well as wonderful fun!

The rapidly growing United States Combined Training Association is the principal medium for providing promotional, instructional and technical assistance for the sport of Three-Day Eventing in the United States. As such, it provides an invaluable link between the Pony Club, USET and AHSA, by providing the wide range of services that lie outside of their respective areas of responsibility.

In numerous communities you will find informal riding clubs composed of enthusiastic equestrians who have joined forces to create and maintain local bridle paths and to practice together various group activities on horseback. Of special interest to Western riders are the amateur rodeo clubs, which are similar to Eastern riding clubs except that they are principally devoted to amateur rodeo sports, modified versions of the cowboy's daredevil arena exploits. The roster of the National Cutting Horse Association includes affiliated clubs in most states, which organize local training classes, cutting clinics, and contests. In many Western towns and cities there are sheriff's posses, parade clubs, and fiestas to provide fun for you and your horse.

All over the nation trail-ride associations organize group rides, picnic excursions, and pack trips over the magnificent natural trails in our national parks and forest preserves.

Then there are the organizations whose purpose is to promote a certain breed, such as the American Saddle Bred Horse, the Tennessee Walking Horse, the Palomino, the Morgan, or the Shetland pony.

Inspired by the unusual versatility of their respective equine favorites, the Morgan Horse Club and the Arabian Horse Club propose to their members such varied activities as cutting and dressage classes, endurance rides, parades, and breeding and training clinics. Appaloosa clubs attract attention to their colorful breed by organizing horse shows that feature Indian-type games and races run in the manner of the Nez Percé Indians, in which one horse is matched against another around a triangular course until all the horses have been eliminated except the winner. One of the most enterprising of all the breed clubs is the American Quarter Horse Association, which provides its members with every possible help in planning programs, including films that demonstrate the training and performance of the Quarter Horse on the ranch, at the race track, and in the contest arena. A special AQHA program organizes and promotes Youth Activities for young Quarter Horse fanciers in their teens. Occasionally, what starts out as a friendly pastime will develop into a full-fledged sport, like the pony trotting races which were informally organized among a few neighboring pony-lovers in Virginia several years ago and have since become an increasingly popular activity throughout the state and even further afield.

As you come in contact with fellow horsemen, you will probably be astonished by the number of equestrian activities that exist right in your own neighborhood. And even if the group to which you finally adhere does no more than meet from time to time in a member's home to talk over mutual horse plans and problems, you are sure to pass many pleasurable moments in the company of those who share your particular equestrian interests.

Should you live in an area so isolated or in a community so unhorse-minded that there is no riding club for you to join, don't forget the ever available friendship offered by books. Through books you can watch the top trainers and riders at work and learn how horsemen of today and yesterday have analyzed and solved their riding and training problems. Through books you can learn to understand your own horse better by increasing your knowledge of all horses.

Horse literature is particularly rich. There are books that cover almost every phase of equestrian activity. Books that offer the benefit of a lifetime's experience with horses to anyone who cares to open them; books that are works of art; books that are scientific treatises; and, of course, there are the delightful books of entertainment value that combine humor or adventure with an equestrian background.

To compile a distinguished library of horse books is not within the means of everyone, for some of the rare items, when they occasionally appear for sale at auction, bring fabulous prices. It is not suprising that most of the great sporting libraries were compiled by extremely wealthy men, for example, Alfred B. Maclay, or C. F. G. R. Schwerdt. (The four-volume catalogue of Schwerdt's hunting, hawking, and shooting books is an extraordinary book in itself!) However, many of the horse subjects that interest today's reader are of fairly recent origin, and apart from the early literature of classical equitation and the original editions of the more famous nineteenth-century English sporting novels, there are not so many truly *rare* horse books, and quite a few of these are available in modern reprints. All in all, a good nucleus of books about those aspects of the horse that most interest you should not take either much time or money to acquire, and it can afford rich rewards in pleasures derived and errors avoided.

If there is a single book which should surely be on the shelves of every horseman, it is a sound, modern veterinary text. Your own veterinarian is the best person to recommend the book that would be most suitable for your particular needs. However, for those whose interest in horses and reading is more extensive, there are several ways to go about forming a library.

A HORSEMAN'S LIBRARY

The broad field of equestrian literature can be broken down into innumerable smaller categories. You may choose to concentrate on one special area (such as a particular breed, or form of riding), or decide instead to make a selection from several related areas. But assuming that your own areas of interest are already defined, the first step in collecting will consist of learning what literature exists for you to collect.

The logical starting places are your local public library, your own bookseller, and perhaps the shelves of riding friends who share your interests. A careful perusal of the books they possess should give you a fair idea of the titles you would like to start with. No doubt some of these books will lead you in turn to others, either through references in the text or a bibliography at the end of the book. Should the author's comments, or the title itself, succeed in whetting your interest, ask your librarian or book dealer to check the current *Books in Print* to see if it is readily available. If it is, your only problem is a financial one (and just keeping abreast of the interesting current books in some areas of equestrian literature can be quite enough to keep your pin money at work!).

Should your growing "want list" begin to include some of the scarce or rare books, you will have the problem of locating the books as well as paying for them. Since many collectors feel that book-hunting is at least half the fun, this is a problem you may learn to cherish, and it must be admitted that few things compare to the thrill the collector feels when he spots a desirable title hidden away on a dusty top shelf. As a practical matter, however, the specialist dealer can usually save you both time and money in acquiring the rarer titles you want. Most specialist dealers take pains to advertise in the periodicals read by their potential clientele, and the pages of your favorite horse magazines will probably give you the names of bookshops which are prepared to supply or search for the titles you want. Many specialist dealers also issue catalogues of both new and out-of-print books; these make interesting reading in themselves, and can do much to expand your knowledge of the literature and develop your sense of market values.

If your interest should finally flower into the "bibliomania" that makes rare books irresistibly fascinating, you will find it very helpful to consult the handful of specialized bibliographies and books about horse books. The more important of these are listed below:

F. H. Huth, *A Bibliographical Record of Hippology* (London, 1887). A very useful list of books relating to the horse, indexed according to their dates of appearance and cross-indexed according to subject matter.

Felton, W. S. *Masters of Equitation*, London, J. A. Allen, 1962

Littauer, V. S., *Horseman's Progress*, Princeton, Van Nostrand, 1962

A. Henry Higginson, *British and American Sporting Authors* (London, 1951). Includes short biographies of the major authors, and a bibliography of sporting literature compiled by the late Sydney Smith.

R. Toole-Stott, *Circus and Allied Arts: A World Bibliography*, Vol. II (Derby, 1960). Items 1729 to 2481 constitute an excellent selected bibliography of the literature of Equitation.

THE HORSE IN ART

When one thinks of a sportsman's library, one imagines also the pictures that adorn the walls, for one collection often leads to another. As a matter of fact, some of the most attractive prints displayed in picture galleries originally appeared as illustrative plates in sporting books.

Next to man himself, no other living creature has been so often represented in the fine arts as the horse. Long before the birth of Christ, horses were sculptured by the Chinese and represented in friezes and statuary by the Greeks and Romans. Modern reproductions of these ancient masterpieces beautify many a horseman's den.

The Old Masters of the Renaissance were fascinated by the beauty of the horse, even though the Thoroughbred was yet to be developed and their most handsome models were cold-blooded war chargers. Leonardo da Vinci, an equestrian himself, filled his notebooks with horse sketches and wrote a scholarly treatise on equine anatomy. Uccello, Verrocchio, and Titian were other Italian masters noted for their skill in painting horses. Among the northern artists there were Rubens and Van Dyke, and among the Spanish, El Greco and Velázquez, one of whose most famous portraits shows the infant Don Carlos, son of Philip IV and Queen Isabella, mounted on a lively Andalusian pony.

But the Golden Age of sporting art ran from the middle of the eighteenth century to the middle of the nineteenth, and its center of activity was England. There were at the same time some famous equine artists at work on the Continent, such as Carle Vernet, who specialized in hunting and battle scenes, while his son Horace preferred military subjects, especially those glorifying the exploits of his successive royal patrons: Charles X, Louis Philippe, and Napoleon III. Their compatriot, Jean Louis Géricault, was a painter of remarkably realistic racing and cavalry scenes, whose passion for horses led him to enlist in the Musketeers and to come to an untimely end in a riding accident. However, by far the majority of the sporting artists were Englishmen, and most of the prints that bear French titles were merely Paris copies of original English works.

The most popular pictures were reprinted in dozens of editions. The original editions are classified today as "rare sporting prints" and are true collectors' items; next in value are subsequent issues from the original plates, and lastly, the copies. Not all of the sporting artists did their own engraving. In fact, some engravers, such as John Scott Sutherland and Dean Wolstenholme, Jr., were such fine interpreters of pictures by en-

"The Glasgow and London Royal Mail," by John F. Herring, Sr. (*Photo courtesy of E. J. Rousuck*)

graving that they improved upon the original works. When you see underneath a print the words "By Hacker after J. F. Herring," for example, it means that Hacker made the engraving from the original painting by Herring. Sometimes you will find it noted that one artist painted the figures and a second one the landscape background.

Most of the sporting artists were riding, hunting, and sometimes coaching men themselves. Few of the later horse painters equaled their intimate knowledge of horses, nor were they able to imbue their works with the same wealth of quaint detail, humor, and vivacity. Another reason for the sudden decline of sporting art after the middle of the nineteenth century was that modern processes of reproduction were invented and the painstaking craftsmanship of the hand engraver began to disappear. While mechanical reproduction has been highly perfected, its effect is not the same, nor is its intrinsic value. Printed color is still less beautiful than the aquatint and mezzotint that were the nineteenth-century techniques.

During this span of barely one hundred years there were dozens of major and minor sporting artists, perhaps because, as Benjamin Marshall said when he gave up portrait painting to apply his oils and brushes to hunting and racing subjects, "An English gentleman is ready to give Fifty Guineas for a portrait of his horse, and a mere Ten Guineas for one of his wife!" To mention some of the most prominent artists whose work you are most likely to come across today, we might start with:

George Stubbs, the most fashionable horse painter of his day, whom many modern critics call the greatest. He was the first to seek inspiration directly from nature after a study of the horse's anatomy and muscular system; in fact, perhaps his greatest achievement was a work on *The Anatomy of the Horse,* published in 1766. Among his sixteen portraits of English race horses is an almost life-size one of Hambletonian and others of Eclipse, Mambrino, and the venerable Godolphin Arabian, accompanied by his famous cat. Stubbs painted people just as well as he painted horses, and a number of his pictures show Sam Chifney in the saddle, riding to a fast finish with a slack rein, to illustrate this peerless jockey's controversial technique of "throwing the reins" at his horse during the last few strides before the finish line.

From James Seymour, who became a professional horse painter as a rather logical consequence of losing his fortune by gambling on the races, we have two famous paintings of the race horse Flying Childers.

"Full Cry," by John N. Sartorius. (*Photo courtesy of E. J. Rousuck*)

In 1752 Thomas Gooch published a superb set of six colored sporting prints entitled *The Life and Death of a Racehorse*.

There were no less than five painters in the Sartorius family. All of them revealed their German background in a meticulous attention to anatomical detail, but the most successful of the clan was John N., whose racing and hunting pictures include several familiar portraits of Hambletonian.

The Dean Wolstenholmes, father and son, were of an aristocratic background, both of them fine sportsmen and fox-hunters. But the son was the superior artist, excelling as a painter, engraver, and colorist. Collectors distinguish between the works of the father and son, whose signatures are identical, by the nature of the sky: the elder Wolstenholme painted gloomy clouds, while the younger one preferred bright and sunny backgrounds.

The equine portraits and racing scenes of Sawrey Gilpin have been copied countless times. What horseman is not familiar with his picture of the chestnut colt by Eclipse that was christened POTOOOOOOOO (POT8Os, for short!) and considered by many to be the best horse of the eighteenth century?

Generations of horse-lovers have been delighted by the charming Leicestershire hunting scenes and expert racing portraits of John Ferneley, Sr., whose success was never equaled by his artist sons, John, Jr., and Claude Loraine.

While rummaging through old-print and secondhand shops, you will probably notice other well-known signatures of the day, such as Ben Marshall, Harry Hall, Samuel Howitt, Abraham Cooper, Charles Hancock, Sir Francis Grant (an elegant gentleman-artist who specialized in painting aristocratic huntsmen with their hounds), James Ward (famed for his portrait of Napoleon's charger Marengo, a pony-sized white Arabian who was imported to England after being wounded during the Battle of Waterloo), and Charles Cooper Henderson (a wealthy sportsman who turned to painting coaching and road scenes after being disinherited by his family because of a surprise elopement).

The most impressive portfolio of racing portraits ever produced is that of J. F. Herring, a self-taught painter of American parentage, whose series depicting no less than thirty-three winners of the St. Leger and eighteen Derby winners constitutes a veritable history of the British turf.

Samuel Alken enjoyed an honorable reputation as an illustrator of sporting books, but the family name was given lasting fame by his nephew, Henry Alken, one of the most popular and prolific sporting art-

"Sir John Ramsden's Favorite Hunter and His Groom, Jonathan Johnson, in the Park at Byram," by George Stubbs. (*Photo courtesy of E. J. Rousuck*)

ists of all time, who produced literally thousands of paintings, drawings, prints, and book illustrations. An enthusiastic hunter, he signed his early work "Ben Tally O," and his sense of wit and humor is evident in his hunting, steeplechase, shooting, flat-racing, and coaching scenes. In the latter he so often pictured coaches rolling through snow-laden countryside, that deep snowdrifts are considered to be practically an Alken trademark. His son, Henry Gordon Alken, also signed his work "H. Alken." In fact, there were four H. Alkens in all, which provides confusion and some intriguing detective work for sporting-print collectors.

The greatest of the coaching artists was James Pollard, who, along with his father, Robert Pollard, was responsible for at least 80 per cent of the coaching prints of the period. They are vivid and attractive, full of accurate detail sometimes veering toward caricature, as the artist could not suppress a sharp sense of humor. Of special interest to racing historians are Pollard's pictures of the Newmarket Sales, which include the portraits of most of the leading contemporary personalities in racing.

The advent of the railroad in 1838 put an end to coaching as a subject for the artist. And the invention of photography at about the same

"But Late for the Kill," by Henry Alken, Sr. (*Photo courtesy of E. J. Rousuck*)

time revolutionized the field of sporting illustration. Nevertheless, artists continued to paint the horse.

The favorite of the Victorians was Sir Edwin Landseer, while we owe to the talents of W. Huggins many of the portraits of the late-nine-teenth-century race horses. A few French painters continued to frequent the race track too, and some of the impressionistic racing scenes of Degas and Dufy are recognized as modern masterpieces. Rosa Bonheur preferred to paint the Norman draft horse, while Alfred de Dreux carried on the tradition of elegant equestrian portraiture. And for the first time, American artists began to appear on the international scene, the most outstanding being Frederic Remington, whose sketches and sculpture of cowboys and Indians have been widely reproduced all over the world.

Then in 1882 a photographer, Eadweard Muybridge, published a slim volume entitled *The Horse in Motion,* which was to influence dramatically every branch of equestrian art. It all started when Leland Stanford, the California railroad magnate and sportsman, hired Muybridge to make a study of the horse's gaits, a subject that had long intrigued him, especially the question of whether there is a moment when a galloping horse has all four legs above the ground. By setting up an ingenious battery of synchronized cameras, Muybridge succeeded in taking a series of action photographs of the horse, the first in history—which, by the way, proved Stanford's theory to be correct (and paved the way for the devel-

"Why Weren't You Out Yesterday," by Sir Alfred J. Munnings. (*Photo courtesy of E. J. Rousuck*)

opment of motion pictures). For the first time, artists as well as horse-men could see the horse's movements as they really are, and since the end of the nineteenth century, the horse in action has been painted with greater accuracy than ever before.

But the Golden Age of sporting art was over. There were still to come a few remarkable equine artists, such as the late Sir Alfred Munnings, whose racing scenes and other works earned him knighthood as well as the presidency of the British Royal Academy; Lionel Edwards, who hunted and painted horses until the very last day of his life at the age of eighty-seven; Cecil Aldin; the fine American sculptor Herbert Haseltine; our Western artists Charles M. Russell and Will James; Paul Brown, a master of the horse in action; and Franklin Voss, a horseman-artist in the tradition of his illustrious predecessors. But most of these outstanding figures have already disappeared, and today there are rela-tively few fine artists in the sporting field at a time when equine art—especially the works of the old British masters—is enjoying an unprece-

Thessaly, c. 400–344 B.C.

Austrian Tyrol crown, 1484.

Carthage, 410–310 B.C.

Corinth, c. 388–300 B.C.

Syracuse, 412 B.C.

Ireland, half crown, 1939.

Italy, 10 lire, 1946

Great Britain festival crown, 1951.

U. S. Lafayette dollar, 1900.

Equestrian coins. (*Photo courtesy of the Chase Manhattan Bank*)

Elizabeth II crown, 1953.

Italian 20 lire, 1936.

Mexican peso, 1910.

dented boom. Among the most fashionable American equine portrait painters today are Richard Stone Reeves and Jean Bowman, while Randy Steffen is one of the most successful Western artists. Among the most famous contemporary horse sculptors are John Skeaping, an Englishman who is also a painter, whose statue of Secretariat stands in the paddock at Belmont Park; June Harrah; and Marilyn Newmark, who works in porcelain as well as in bronze.

Horsemen born with a collecting bent can find many other attractive items aside from books and pictures that combine their principal enthusiasms. For example, have you ever noticed the number of coins and medals that bear a horse's effigy? Some of them are very beautifully engraved. Particularly apt for the rider are those that bear the image of St. George, the patron saint of horses and horsemen (and also of England, which is one of the richest hunting-grounds for equestrian medallions of all kinds). His counterpart in the folklore of Latin cultures is Santiago, who is pictured on horseback in the coat of arms of the city of Guatemala, and whose legend is the subject of a lovely set of stained-glass windows in the Chartres Cathedral in France. Fox-hunting enthusiasts should be especially attracted to St. Hubert, for he is the patron saint of hunters. According to legend, he was hunting on horseback one Good Friday when a magnificent stag appeared before him, bearing a radiant cross between his horns. This miraculous encounter, so often depicted in pictures, sculpture, and engraving, marked St. Hubert's conversion to Christianity.

Equestrian stamps. (*Courtesy of William Steinkraus*)

Then there are horse or coaching stamp albums to tempt the equestrian collector, with a vast array of postage stamps from which to choose. The fabulous and short-lived Pony Express may have been a financial failure during its eighteen months of existence, but its artistic influence on the mails still persists, for one of the most recent issues of equestrian stamps portrays the hardy ponies of this courageous enterprise.

You might consider building up a collection of finely-wrought examples of the blacksmith's and the farrier's art, picked up in country secondhand shops and perhaps in a corner of your own old barn. Some of the old horseshoes, stirrup irons, spurs, and bits were forged with loving care and remarkable craftsmanship.

Many a nonhorseman has succumbed to the decorative appeal of horse brasses, originally a part of draft harness, and numerous other items of equestrian equipment can be adapted to decorative use. An in-

Horse brasses. (*Courtesy of Miller's*)

genious and artistic example is the extraordinary chandelier in the tack room of the former C. V. Whitney estate on Long Island, which is entirely composed of antique driving bits.

EQUESTRIAN EVENTS, AT HOME AND ABROAD

The confirmed horse-lover can become so absorbed in his interest that he is led far away from his own home and stable. During the year there are a number of exceptional horse events that every horseman will want to witness at least once in his lifetime.

The rodeo year is ushered in by the Pike's Peak Or Bust Rodeo, held in January in Colorado Springs. One of the summer highlights is the Cheyenne Frontier Days Rodeo in Wyoming, which has been growing bigger and better ever since its founding in 1897. The Pendleton Round-up and Canada's week-long Calgary Stampede are other unforgettable Western events held in a fiesta atmosphere, while the season reaches its climax in November, when San Francisco's Cow Palace is the scene of the gigantic Grand National Livestock Exposition, Horse Show, and Championship Rodeo. Another spectacular West Coast event is the Southern California Exposition National Horse Show in Del Mar, which offers classes for practically every AHSA division during the three weeks preceding its climactic Finals on the Fourth of July. The outstanding Pacific Coast indoor winter show is the Grand National, held in San Francisco's famed Cow Palace.

In the eyes of most Hunter and Jumper horsemen, the event of the year is the National Horse Show. Held in New York's Madison Square Garden during the first week in November, it features international jumping teams who come from many lands to compete in the Washington International, then at New York City, and finally at the Royal Winter Fair in Toronto, Canada, where there is a complete agricultural fair in addition to the wide variety of horse show events.

Some of our own shows combine agriculture with horses too. Among the important horse shows that take place side by side with livestock judging are the Fort Worth Southwestern Exposition and Fat Stock Show, the Houston Horse Show and Livestock Show, the Pacific International in North Portland, Oregon, the National Western Livestock Show in Denver, the American Royal Live Stock Horse Show and Rodeo in Kansas, and the Kentucky State Fair. The latter event is the occasion for

The National Horse Show at Madison Square Garden. (*Photo by "The News"*)

the most important Saddle Horse gathering of the year, for it is here that the National Saddle Horse World Champions are crowned.

Perhaps the most unique site of equestrian activities in the world is the beautiful Kentucky Horse Park in Lexington, with its lavish facilities for a varied calendar of events which included the 1978 Three-Day World Championship, and an International Museum of the Horse. This is, incidentally, the newest but not the only museum in America devoted to the horse. Among others, there are the National Museum of Racing at Saratoga Springs, the Kentucky Derby Museum at Churchill Downs, the American Saddle Horse Museum in Louisville, Kentucky, and the Hall of Fame of the Trotter at Goshen, New York.

Every racing fan must dream of witnessing for himself the three great American races that make up the Triple Crown: the Kentucky Derby, the Preakness (at Pimlico, Maryland), and the Belmont Stakes (New York). It is also the dream of every race-horse owner and trainer to equal the achievement of the eleven great three-year-old Thoroughbreds who have won all three races: Sir Barton (1919), Gallant Fox (1930), Omaha (1935), War Admiral (1937), Whirlaway (1941), Count

The Kentucky Derby of 1973 as Secretariat, ridden by Ron Turcotte, gallops toward his first victory in the Triple Crown. (*Wide World photo*)

Fleet (1943), Assault (1946), Citation (1948), Secretariat (1973), Seattle Slew (1977), and Affirmed (1978). You can, by the way, visit a fascinating exhibit in honor of these and other turf immortals at the National Museum of Racing in Saratoga Springs.

Harness racing, not to be outdone, has not only one, but two Triple Crowns. For trotters there are the Hambletonian, the Kentucky Futurity, and the Yonkers Futurity. The pacers' trio consists of the Little Brown Jug Trial (named after a nineteenth-century World Champion pacer and held at Delaware, Ohio), the William H. Cane Futurity (at Yonkers, New York), and the Messenger Stake (at Roosevelt Raceway, New York). To date, the harness world has feted six Triple Crown winners in the trotting division, the most recent being Super Bowl in 1972; and there have been four Triple-Crown-winning pacers: Adios Butler, Romeo Hanover, Bret Hanover, and Most Happy Fella.

While the most important steeplechase events of the year are the Temple Gwathemy Memorial, the Colonial Cup International, and the American Grand National, the jumping race that is surrounded by the most fashionable crowds, the most traditional aura, and the most colorful festivities is the historic Maryland Hunt Cup.

Globe-trotting horse-lovers find it pleasant and simple to combine rewarding moments of equestrian tourism with their holiday itinerary abroad. Some enterprising travel agents plan European trips especially for horsemen, taking in most of the horsy high spots—and there are many to choose from.

Ireland has the Irish Derby, Italy the Italian Derby, and Germany the Hamburg Derby, but in England Thoroughbred racing is literally the Sport of Kings—and of the Queen, who frequently races her horses under the royal colors. The outstanding events on the British racing calendar include the Epsom Derby, a supreme test of speed and stamina that has been raced the first week in June by three-year-old colts and fillies ever since 1780. Its famous Tattenham Corner, a treacherous sharp bend near the end of the one-and-a-half-mile uphill and downhill course, often decides the eventual winner. After the running of the Aintree Grand National Steeplechase at Liverpool, anybody can walk the 4½ mile course and see for himself the thirty fences, including the notorious Becher's Brook that has been the cause of so many mishaps. The Ascot Gold Cup marks the climax of the London social season, and you may very likely see the Queen and her entourage in the Royal Enclosure. You needn't be disappointed if your travel schedule does not permit you to attend such famous stakes races as the St. Leger and the Epsom Oaks. These classics have been run for almost two hundred years and will undoubtedly persist for many more. But one day, try to visit the Newmarket Sales; it is the meeting place for Thoroughbred fanciers from all over the world.

Across the Channel in France the most important races of the year are the Grand Prix de Paris that inaugurates the racing season in June, and the Arc de Triomphe that ends it in October, both of them run at the elegant Longchamps race track, where the atmosphere is far more Parisian than on a sight-seeing bus. Just a few hours from Paris on the Normandy Coast is Deauville, the Saratoga Springs of the Continent, with its own racing season, yearling sales, and polo matches which, along with its marvelous beach, yacht basin, and luxury hotels, attract the cream of international turf society.

American horse-show exhibitors cannot fail to be impressed by the prestige their sport enjoys abroad, the beauty of the show rings, and the size and enthusiasm of the crowds that gather around them. The Royal International Horse Show is held in London at the beginning of July, with its hotly disputed King George V Cup for international Jumpers. Americans can take pride in the fact that this event, one of the most coveted "wins" in jumping, has been awarded five times in recent years to members of the United States Equestrian Team: twice to Hugh Wiley, who rode Master William and Nautical to victory in 1958 and 1959; in 1956 to Bill Steinkraus, who tied with himself for first place riding Night Owl and First Boy, and then returned in 1964 to win it again with Sinjon; and to Frank Chapot, riding Main Spring, in 1974.

Another outstanding London event is the Horse of the Year Show in October (indoors), while a short train ride will take you to the Hickstead Derby at the All-England Jumping Course in Hickstead, which is organized each August by Douglas Bunn, who used to be one of Britain's leading amateur show-jumping riders. Three-Day enthusiasts will not want to miss the famous Badminton Horse Trials, held on the beautiful estates of the Duke of Beaufort, Queen Elizabeth's "Master of the Horse," or the competition held later in the year at Burghley. (For specific dates, contact the British Horse Society, 16 Bedford Square, London W.C. 1.)

The Dublin Horse Show lasts an entire well-filled (and often rainy)

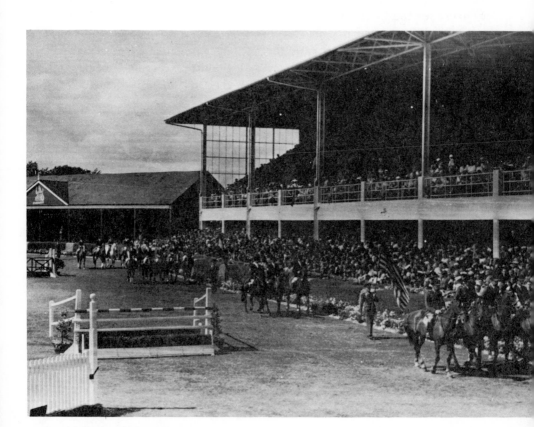

At the Dublin Horse Show.

The Italian Caribinieri performing in the Piazza di Siena, scene of the Rome Horse Show. (*L'Année Hippique photo*)

week in August, during which the fortunate visitors find that twenty-four hours a day simply isn't enough time for taking in all the show events, horse sales, and exhibits in the attractive permanent horse-show installations in the suburb of Ballsbridge, not to mention the nightly balls. For those who can manage to tear themselves away from all of this excitement, there are some interesting excursions to be made nearby. Not far from Dublin is the Irish National Stud and the Curragh, Ireland's famous racing center. Ireland is, in fact, the horseman's paradise. Horses are everywhere—to try, to buy, or merely to admire and to talk about. You can easily rent a horse for a day's hunting with one of the numerous and hospitable Hunts, where half the Field is frequently composed of visitors riding rented or borrowed mounts.

For sheer beauty, the Rome Horse Show, held every May in the Borghese Gardens right in the heart of the Eternal City, reigns supreme. But for size, the prize must certainly go to Aachen (Aix-la-Chapelle) near the Belgian-German-French border, where the largest international European horse show is held in July. Here the jumping classes often present more than one hundred entries from many different nations who are faced with a most varied and formidable array of obstacles, including banks and water. Every day for a week forty or fifty thousand spectators

The "Auf Wiedersehen" ceremony at the conclusion of the Aachen Horse Show. (*L'Année Hippique* photo)

fill the huge stadium. At the end of the show, as the riders make one final tour of the ring, the Aachen tradition is for the entire audience to stand up and wave their handkerchiefs while singing a hearty "Auf Wiederse-hen."

No horseman traveling through Austria should fail to visit the cele-brated Spanish Riding School in Vienna, with its crystal-chandeliered in-door arena where the amazing Lippizaner horses train and perform. Founded in the seventeenth century as a cavalry training school for the sons of the Court nobles, it has been maintained by the Austrian state since the fall of the monarchy in 1938. But there still hangs a portrait of Emperor Charles VI at the back of the royal box, which is still saluted by the riders as they enter the arena clad in traditional Imperial uniforms. The Lippizaners are specially bred and trained from birth to perform the highest degree of *haute école* dressage. At the end of their schooling, these equine ballerinas are able to execute six different controlled jumps, to which the Spanish Riding School owes its worldwide celebrity: the *levade, mézair, courbette, croupade, ballotade,* and *capriole.* The last is the most difficult of all, for the horse leaps upward and at the same time stretches out his hind legs almost horizontally.

Three Lippizaner horses of the Spanish Riding School in Vienna performing a "pas de trois." (*Photo courtesy of the Austrian State Tourist Department*)

While you're in Austria, you might consider doing your sight-seeing on horseback. The countryside lends itself particularly well to this sporting form of travel, and horse or pony treks are organized almost as widely as in the British Isles. A few specialized American travel agencies are experienced in planning this original kind of a European holiday in England, Ireland, France, Spain, Austria, Norway, and even in Iceland.

The serious horseman with an observing eye and curiosity concerning equestrian training techniques would learn a great deal by visiting one of the European Olympic training centers. (Be sure to write first and introduce yourself.) The French team trains at Fontainebleau, with the dressage training taking place at Saumur, home of the French Cavalry, right in the heart of the Loire château country. Saumur, in fact, has a

The headquarters of the United States Equestrian Team at Gladstone, New Jersey. (*Photo courtesy of the USET*)

castle of its own which today houses a fascinating equestrian museum that displays, among numerous other exhibits, an unusual collection of bits, spurs, and other tack dating back to the most ancient times. Germany has a magnificently equipped training center at Warendorf (Westphalen). The Italian Army Team's headquarters are not far from Rome at Passo Corese.

Since the spring of 1961, the United States Equestrian Team has at last found a permanent headquarters of its own on the magnificent former Brady estate at Gladstone, New Jersey, now owned by the Beneficial Corporation. There, a program has been developed to train riders and horses for international competitions, just as other nations of the world have done. Nation-wide screening tests are held every four years all over the country, and advanced young riders over sixteen years of age compete in a series of tests on the flat and over fences before a special jury. The leading riders are then invited to Gladstone for an intensive training program. The USET Dressage training and team selection program also takes place at Gladstone.

The USET Combined Training Event program is established separately at Hamilton, Massachusetts, on a splendid property that was donated to the town of Hamilton by Forrester Clark, and loaned by the town to the Team. Under the direction of Jack Le Goff, there is the same system of nation-wide trials every four years, the intensive training of team prospects, and final selection.

Every four years the Mecca of all international horsemen is the city that has been selected as host for the Olympic Games. Proud of the fact that an equestrian event was chosen as the climactic final competition, horse-lovers gather from all over the globe to watch the world's most accomplished riders and some of the world's finest horses compete in the most exacting equestrian tests.

There are four Olympic equestrian events: (1) Grand Dressage; (2) the Three-Day Event, a Combined-Training Test with the same horses and the same riders competing in a Dressage Test the first day, a Steeplechase and Cross-country Endurance Test the second, and Stadium Jumping the third; (3) Individual Grand Prix Jumping; and (4)

William Steinkraus and Snowbound, Individual Gold Medal winners in the 1968 Olympic Games. (*Photo by Keystone*)

Michael Matz and Grande, Individual Bronze Medal winners at the 1975 Pan American Games. (*Photo courtesy of the USET*)

the Grand Prix des Nations (the Nation's Cup), international team jumping taking place in two rounds during the morning and afternoon of the final day of the Games. In recent years, the most formidable Nation's Cup teams have been the German, American, and British, although there are outstanding individual riders from many other countries. International dressage competition was long the specialty of the Scandinavians and the Swiss, but now Germany dominates the field, with Russia and Switzerland close behind and the United States within striking distance. As for the Three-Day Event, it is often full of surprises, but it is safe to say that horses and riders from the United States, Great Britain, Germany, and Australia will be well placed at the finish.

The Pan American Games, held every four years in the year preceding the Olympics, feature the same equestrian events. Because they are held in a North or South American city, and periodically in the United States, they may be more easily accessible to visiting American horsemen than the Olympic Games.

World Championships in each of these three disciplines are held every four years at the midpoint in the Olympic cycle, normally in the homeland of the current title-holder. These competitions are very exciting but quite different from the Olympic events; first of all, because they are open to professionals as well as to amateurs, and also because the rules are not necessarily the same. In the Jumping World Championship, for example, the final, deciding test requires the four top-placed riders to jump a short course on each of the four final horses.

Bruce Davidson, two-time winner of the Three-Day Event World Championship, riding Might Tango.

The Bronze Medal winning American Dressage Team at the 1976 Olympic Games: Dorothy Morkis, Edith Master, and Hilda Gurney. (*Photo courtesy of the AHSA*)

Tad Coffin and Bally Cor, winners of the Individual as well as the Team Gold Medal in the Three-Day Event of the 1976 Olympic Games. (*Photo courtesy of the USET*)

These are the red-letter occasions and the four-star sites of the equestrian scene. But wherever a horseman travels, whether it is merely into the next county or to another hemisphere, he will discover that his love of horses is a passport to a world of pleasure.

16.   Parting with Your Horse

Human life seems short enough, but the life span of the horse is only about a third of ours. Despite some noted exceptions such as the famed English draft horse Old Billy, who was born in 1759 and passed away in 1822 at the ripe age of sixty-three, or the American race horse Old Romp, who was foaled in 1824 and respectfully interred in 1878, the working years of an average horse total between fifteen and twenty. Very often this normal expectancy is abbreviated by accident, injury, or premature unsoundness. Therefore, every horseman, when he acquires a mount of his own, should be aware of the fact that his riding years will probably outnumber those of his faithful four-legged comrade.

However, there is no ceremony that binds a rider to his horse "until death do us part," and in actual practice the relationship is most often dissolved long before then by a friendly divorce, the most common grounds for complaint being incompatibility. Perhaps a young rider has simply outgrown the pony that taught him how to ride; later on, he may have transferred his interests from pleasure hacking to jumping, for example, or from trail riding to competitive cutting, only to realize that his horse is unsuited to this new activity. Perhaps a rider has been able to make greater progress than his horse and will be happier with a mount whose capabilities more nearly match his own ambitions. Occasionally the situation is reversed, and a horse proves to possess really outstanding ability, far greater than that of his owner. It is a temptation to revel in the pleasure of owning such an exceptional creature and to satisfy one-self with a few blue ribbons, awarded from time to time in tribute to the horse's talent and in spite of the rider's personal limitations. But consci-entious horsemen would consider it fairer to such a horse to place him in the hands of an expert who is qualified to guide him to the full develop-ment of his native gifts.

Whatever the grounds for separation, if you decide to sell your horse you will proceed in just the same way as his previous owner who origi-nally sold him to you: by contacting other horsemen, advertising in the horse publications, or by placing him with a reliable dealer.

You will probably be amazed by your change of attitude once the roles are reversed! Old-timers say that two distinctly different languages are used when speaking of horses: the buyer's and the seller's. So don't be surprised to find yourself describing as "spirited and willing to go" the horse you formerly complained of as being "completely crazy," or using the phrase "well-mannered" to express the quality you used to consider just plain "sluggish."

Naturally, you should try to make the best deal you can when you are engaged in selling your horse. But at the same time, if you evaluate his strong points and his weaknesses objectively and make an honest effort to find for him a home where his qualities correspond to the re-quirements of his new owner, everybody will be happier—and most of all your horse.

It is simple enough to part with a horse who has proved to be an un-satisfactory partner. But what about the one who has served you faith-fully and well for years and who, because of old age or unsoundness, finds it increasingly difficult to fill the role he has held so long in your riding career?

Until the Fountain of Youth is at last discovered, the only sure way of prolonging the working life of a horse is to exercise foresight at the moment you buy him. Don't let a fast-growing child make the mistake of undermounting himself. Anticipate whenever possible the future orienta-tion of your riding activities and choose a horse who has already had ex-perience in the field you ultimately wish to enter. You will also gain years of riding satisfaction by seeking soundness at the time you choose your horse and by preserving it afterward with proper care and good stable management. Sometimes you may be able to increase your horse's working life span by giving him progressively less strenuous jobs to perform. One example is Mrs. Ogden Phipps's outstanding steeplechase race horse Neji, who dethroned the long-reigning title-holder Elkridge as all-time money winner in the sport and was three times winner of the Belmont Grand National. After retiring from the track, where he won Stakes carrying as much as 173 pounds, Neji competed in the Working Hunter division with considerable success, and later on served as a school horse for Mrs. Phipps's daughter Cynthia. Before returning to Australia after the Rome Olympics, owner-rider Laurie Morgan presented his Three-Day Event Gold Medal winner Salad Days II to the Duchess of Beaufort, and the horse became her favorite Hunter. And do you remember Mandarin, the French steeplechaser who made world headlines when, ridden by Fred Winter (now a leading steeplechase trainer in England, where his charges once included Jay Trump), he won the Grand Steeplechase of Paris despite the fact that his bridle broke at the fourth fence of the 26-fence figure-eight Auteuil course? It seems that the once fiery steeplechaser became the most docile of hacks. As for Jay Trump, who retired from steeplechasing after an unprecedented third-time victory in the Maryland Hunt Cup, he kept in condition by riding to hounds with his owner, Mrs. Mary C. Stephenson, in the saddle.

Notwithstanding all our efforts, the sad fact is that as the years roll by, equine as well as human mechanisms run down, and the day will inevitably arrive when your horse is no longer able to bear in comfort a normal work load. If he is reasonably sound and not extremely old, you can in some cases still find a buyer for him. The wise and aged horse who taught you how to hunt and jump may be the ideal mount for another young beginner who is just learning how to ride. But it is always painful to part with a faithful friend, and especially to deliver him to a strange home where you are not certain of the treatment he will be given. And so, whenever possible, most owners prefer to see their aged horses finish their days in dignified retirement.

Retirement does not mean neglect. You aren't expected to maintain your mount in the luxurious leisure of such great old horses as Democrat, the courageous international Jumper, who finished his life in the green pastures of the Morven Stud Farm as an honored guest of U. S. Equestrian Team Chairman Whitney Stone, or of Man O' War, who received in palatial quarters on the Faraway Farm in Kentucky more than a million

Man O' War in retirement with his faithful groom, Will Harbut. (*Photo by Skeets Meadors*)

Sinjon, after a glorious career in international jumping competitions with the United States Equestrian Team, lives in contented retirement with a seventeen-year-old pony, Mighty Moose, to keep him company. (*Photo by James Deutschmann*)

and a half admiring visitors (and, perhaps with more enthusiasm, several hundred mares in heat). But neither should you simply turn an old horse out to pasture and let him fend for himself. Old horses, like young ones, require an appropriate diet, plenty of water, and periodic attention to their feet and teeth. Human or animal companionship is especially welcome when there is no longer any regular activity to break the monotony of a veteran's waning days.

As a matter of fact, retirement does not agree with all horses, particularly those who have led a very active life and become accustomed to the excitement of the race track or the show ring. The venerable British race horse Creggmore Boy, retired because of old age, began to lose condition so rapidly that he was re-entered in steeplechase events at twenty-one, not because his owner expected to win, but simply to keep the gallant old campaigner healthy and happy. A famous English pony Jumper, Doxy, seemed to enjoy the show ring so much that his retirement was postponed time and again, until he was finally withdrawn from competition at the age of twenty-five. But even then, Doxy so hated the idea of remaining idle that when the van was being loaded to go to a show, he would dash in from his field, run up the loading ramp, and slip into his old traveling place, from which he stubbornly refused to budge. The wondrous Kelso became so restless after only a few months of retirement that he returned to racing at the age of eight and continued to outdistance all rivals as the top money-winning race horse of all time. (But when he was nine he agreed to settle down and to accompany his owner, Mrs. Richard du Pont, on her morning canters around her Maryland farm just as if he were any well-bred hack, instead of a multimillionaire.)

Even when the very best of care is given, time eventually takes its toll. With horses, the legs are often the first part of the body mechanism to break down. When a faithful old animal is no longer able to move about, or if for any other reason he is unable to maintain himself in a reasonably sound condition, one must face the bitter truth that it may be kinder to have him put down than to allow him to waste away gradually in silent suffering. It sometimes takes courage to be kind. But in our day, when modern methods of equine euthanasia have made the procedure swift and painless to the horse, you can be sure that it is far more humanitarian to have a competent veterinarian put an end to the agony of an ailing animal than to prolong it selfishly in order to avoid ruffling your own sensibilities.

Whether or not good horses are reunited with their masters in heaven is a matter of abstract speculation. But there is in certain cases a means of perpetuating on earth at least some of the qualities of a well-loved riding comrade, and that is by breeding and bringing up its offspring.

If your horse is a gelding, there is of course no such possibility. If he is a stallion, you can allow him to be used as a stud by other owners' mares; if he is a superior example of his breed and shows ability to pass on his qualities to his get, he may provide you with some incidental income—but not necessarily with a son or daughter, because the foal remains the property of the owner of the mare. Besides, most stallions who serve as riding horses are rarely used for breeding, since many horsemen believe that stud activity is detrimental to their disposition. However, if you own a mare, if you are willing to dispense with her services for twelve months, and if you are sure that her physical, temperamental, and genetic qualities are worth reproducing, you may be tempted to consider the appealing idea of breeding her. Even if your mare appears to be a marvelous breeding prospect, there is another important question you should ask yourself: Are you properly equipped to raise a foal? Foals raised in a box stall rarely attain the substance and size of free-running foals reared on a breeding farm. While early human handling is important for all domesticated animals, a foal also needs equine playmates and freedom in a natural environment in order to develop the instincts that are necessary to his well-being and survival. All things considered, the one-horse breeder's prospects are seldom brilliant (although many suc-

A newborn foal. (*Photo by Bert Clark Thayer*)

cessful experiences could be cited to refute this statement). On the other hand, it can be stated categorically that breeding your mare is not a sure and easy way to get a second good horse cheaply; it will involve considerable expense, as well as much time and care.

Breeding horses is a science requiring special equipment, qualified personnel, veterinary supervision, knowledge, experience and, in order to be really successful, an indefinable breeding talent. It may be true that wild horses have no difficulty procreating in their natural state, but the result has always been a gradual degeneration of the breed. The indigenous wild ponies that once roamed the American plains had become entirely extinct long before the conquistadors arrived to repopulate our prairies with their Spanish stock.

On Thoroughbred stud farms it has been estimated that an average of only six or seven out of every ten breeding attempts result in actual conception. An amateur's chances are even slimmer, with the ever-present risk of infection or injury either to the stallion or mare from inept handling. Statistically, range-breeding (turning a stallion out to pasture with a group of mares) is far more apt to result in conception—90 per cent of the time, according to a recent survey. But range-bred animals conceive in the late spring or early summer, whereas "handbreeding" is done earlier in order to produce early spring foals. There is also an infinitely greater chance of injury with pasture breeding, which is nowadays considered impractical and is seldom practiced deliberately. It is therefore much more sensible to make your breeding arrangements with a stud farm than to attempt to take matters into your own inexperienced hands or to leave everything to nature.

Breeding by artificial insemination may be practiced with certain breeds (including the American Quarter Horse, Saddle Bred, Appaloosa, Palomino, and Pinto) within certain strictly enforced limitations, but it is not permissible under any conditions for registered Arabians, Morgans, Hackneys, and Tennessee Walking Horses. Thoroughbreds, too, are ineligible for registry unless they are the result of a natural breeding—which may, however, be reinforced by subsequent artificial insemination. On the other hand, artificial insemination is permitted with Standardbreds, which is why a top Harness Racing sire has a far greater number of progeny than a comparable Thoroughbred.

Some mares have been able to conceive at remarkably advanced ages, for example, the Arabian brood mare *Ferda 596, who produced Ferseyn when she was twenty-four years old and lived to see the handsome colt become one of the leading sires of Arabian show winners in America. The fabulous trotting champion of the last century, Goldsmith Maid, who held four World's Records when she was nineteen and continued racing until she was twenty-one, gave birth to her first foal the following year at the age of twenty-two, and foaled two others later. Galopin, the great race horse and sire of many champions, was by an eighteen-year-old stallion out of a nineteen-year-old mare.

Mares start to come in heat when they are twelve to fifteen months old and the heat periods return thereafter at approximately twenty-one-day intervals, with ovulation usually occurring two days before the end of the two- to six-day period. Spring is the traditional breeding season for horses, because the spring heats are more evident and often longer, and the mares are more likely to conceive. It is also in the spring that the sperm in the stallion's semen is believed to be most concentrated. Furthermore, because the average gestation period for horses is about 340 days (although it can range from 300 to 385 days), a foal conceived in May will be born the following April, when the pastures are green and succulent and the weather mild.

A male horse reaches puberty at the age of eighteen to twenty-four months, but he reaches full sexual maturity only at the age of three or four years, when successful race horses are generally bred for the first time, but only to a limited number of carefully selected mares. Thereafter, they may "cover" as many as forty or fifty broodmares each season, tapering off when they start to age.

In choosing a mate for your mare, you must weigh many factors. If she is registered in a stud book, you should by all means breed her to another registered animal in order to qualify the offspring for registration too. On the other hand, if your mare is of nondescript or unknown origin, you should try to "upgrade" her by selecting a well-bred mate of the same general type who will reinforce her good qualities and counteract her weaknesses.

There are four methods of breeding: crossbreeding (between two horses of different breeds), outcrossing (between two completely unrelated families of the same breed), inbreeding (between two closely related horses, such as mother to son, niece to uncle, or granddaughter to grandsire), and line-breeding (a mild form of inbreeding where one ancestor appears a number of times in the same pedigree).

In general, inbreeding leads to refinement and accentuates or "fixes" certain qualities without adding any new ones. It has produced some exceptional individuals, such as the race horse Battlefield, both of whose parents had been sired by Fair Play, or the Quarter Horse King, whose dam is said to have been the result of an accidental brother and sister mating, but excessive inbreeding eventually results in degeneration. Line-breeding likewise serves to establish a type. Horses such as the Morgan, who all trace back to the same ancestor, are necessarily line-bred. Occasional judicious outcrosses are practiced by expert breeders in order to preserve the vigor and fertility of a highly line-bred family. Crossbreeding is somewhat unpredictable. There are, however, certain crosses that have shown an unusually high percentage of success, such as the Quarter Horse and Thoroughbred combination that produces a half-bred Working Hunter type, the Cleveland Bay and Thoroughbred that often results in a good heavyweight Hunter, or the Welsh pony crossed with an Arabian or a small Thoroughbred to provide a superior, all-round children's pony. Arabian and Thoroughbred blood bring refinement and speed to almost any other breed. But it is risky for an inexpert breeder to mate two animals who are dissimilar in type or size, and absolutely foolhardy to select a horse as a stud for your mare simply because he happens to be stabled nearby.

Breeding for color is uncertain, the only well-established formulas being that two chestnuts always produce a chestnut, two blacks produce only black or chestnut, and at least one gray parent is required to produce a gray. There is no means of predetermining the sex of a foal, but your chances are about fifty-fifty, since fifty-one fillies are born for every forty-nine colts.

When selecting a breeding mate for your mare, you should consider not only bloodlines but also conformation and soundness. Of course, defects like ringbone and spavin are not actually inheritable. However, since they are usually the result of structural weaknesses which can very definitely be inherited, horses suffering from such infirmities are likely to pass on to their offspring a tendency to develop the same condition. Similarly, a horse's past performance is one of the major standards used in selecting a stud, not because speed or performing ability can be inherited as such, but because quality of performance is the result of conformation and temperamental attributes that are transmitted by genes from one generation to the next. That is why a Thoroughbred's breeding value is measured by the number of Stakes winners produced, and why a trotter's stud fee bears a direct relationship to his speed per mile and that of his get. It is also the reason why the Thoroughbred bloodlines of France and Italy, where the most important races are for older horses over long distances, are noted for their staying power; while the United States and Canada, where the richest purses are for two-year olds, have become the best sources of sprinting blood. British and Irish breeders try to strike a happy medium between the two extremes.

There is no such slide-rule to measure the breeding potential of a Hunter or a hack, although the stud quality of Saddle and Quarter Horse stallions may be evaluated by the show-ring or arena winnings of themselves and especially of their previous progeny. Champion Jumpers come in all shapes and spring from the most varied origins. But the records seem to show that jumping ability can be inherited to a certain extent. Coq Gaulois sired many superior Hunters and Jumpers, while Man O' War was the source of some of our greatest jumping, as well as racing talent, including Battleship, the first American horse to win the Aintree Grand National. One of the most notably consistent Jumper sires in the United States was Mrs. Cloyce Tippet's Thoroughbred Hunter Bonne Nuit, who produced at least twenty-five outstanding performers, including Hollandia, Riviera Wonder, and Night Owl, all distinguished mounts of the U. S. Olympic Team, as well as such Open Jumper Champions as Grey Aero and Ping Pong. Good Twist, Night Lark, and Catch On Fire, who also bore Bonne Nuit blood, were good jumpers themselves and, in turn, produced good jumpers. Major Allhusen's great Event mare

Laurien, who was a brilliant natural jumper, produced several fine Eventers, including a son, Laureston, who won the individual Gold Medal at the Munich Olympic Games.

Although some indifferent performers have been excellent breeders, the greatest sires have possessed performing ability as well as the ability to pass their qualities on to their progeny. Some famous racing sires have been so prepotent that their foals tended to resemble them no matter what they were bred to. Whenever possible, you should study the previous get of the stallion you are considering as a mate for your mare.

You can seek a suitable mate by studying the stallion advertisements in the annual breeding issues of the horse publications and the breeding classes at horse shows, and by inquiring of the breed associations or among your own riding friends and acquaintances. Stud fees range from $100 to $500 up. They reach astronomical sums for the leading Thoroughbred racing sires, whose services are often reserved for members of the owning syndicate, in which a share may be worth $150,000. A service to Secretariat costs $60,000 if you can get it, and $40,000 for the top-ranking racing sire Roberto. A little further down on the list, it would cost "only" $7,500 or less. On a much more modest scale, the 4-H Club breeding program arranges for some first-class stallions to stand at stud for its young members at a very small fee, and sometimes none at all.

Every era has its fashionable breeding bloodlines. A particularly successful combination, incidentally, is referred to as a "nick." Certain family names add prestige to a pedigree and dollars to a stud fee, as in the case of the Quarter Horse lines of Three Bars, King and his son Poco Bueno, or the Quarter Horse race horse Go Man Go (who was actually three-fourths Thoroughbred); the Saddle Horse families of Rex Peavine, Bourbon King, and the incomparable Wing Commander, who was the World Champion Five-Gaited Saddle Horse from 1948 through 1954.

The late Aga Khan used to refuse to inspect the horses selected for breeding on his stud farms. Placing his entire faith in the horses' bloodlines and performance records, he was afraid he would allow himself to be influenced by an attractive appearance. But most owners prefer to observe personally the horses they intend to mate, and whenever possible they pay a visit to several likely breeding farms and study the stallions offered at stud.

When the choice has been made and all the arrangements completed, the mare is sent to the stud farm a week before her heat period is due, where she remains in boarding for at least ten weeks. Sometimes it is advisable to leave her there throughout her entire pregnancy, foaling, and weaning period, bringing her home only when the foal is five or six months old. If you wish to have the foaling take place in your own stable, you should consult your veterinarian as soon as your mare returns from being bred, for she will require special feed and care, and preparations for foaling must be made well in advance of the expected date. The vet can tell if the mare is pregnant by rectal palpation of the uterus thirty or forty days after the mating, and by a blood test one month later. A mare who misses two successive heat cycles is almost certainly pregnant.

The immediate signs of foaling are unmistakable. Two days or so before the event, the mammary glands fill up, then a waxy substance forms at the end of the teats. When milk begins to drip, foaling should occur some twenty-four hours later. The mare also seeks isolation and is rather irritable. She is restless, paws the ground, and holds her tail slightly elevated. Her muscles seem flabby and the croup area sinks. Uterine contractions occur four to twenty-four hours before the foal appears, as nature attempts to position it properly in the uterus. This is the moment to clean the future mother's genital area and to notify the vet.

Horses are never born but "foaled" or "dropped." The actual obstetrical process, like the process of mating, should be supervised by an experienced person. Most of the time a mare needs no help during parturition (delivery) and the foal presents itself normally, front feet first, with the nose and head tucked between the forelegs, followed by the shoulders, hips, and hind legs and feet, with the back upward. But should the presentation be abnormal, veterinary attention is required immediately, and in any case, both dam and foal require assistance in order to avoid infection and to complete the parturition safely. This is not always a simple matter to organize in your own barn, particularly since mares like to give birth during the night and only when they believe themselves to be alone. Nevertheless, the process is generally accomplished in about half an hour and complications are rare.

It is important to see that the placenta is expulsed, which normally occurs thirty to sixty minutes after parturition. If it is retained for as long as eight hours, there is danger of infection and the vet should be summoned at once. He can give the mare an injection to clear the uterus. It is also vital to make sure that the foal's head is freed from the fetal envelope so that normal breathing can begin. It is unnecessary, however, to cut the umbilical cord. Most breeders prefer to let it break off naturally and then to disinfect the stump. Supervision is useful at this point in order to ensure that the mare, when rising, does not step on her newborn foal. The little creature should be on his own feet within thirty or sixty minutes, and within a few hours will attempt to nurse. Make sure that he does so, because this first milk offers him the vital protection of antibodies as well as nutrients. Many breeding farms take the precaution of administering antibiotic and tetanus antitoxins to newborn foals. An early bowel movement is important too. Twenty-four hours after foaling, the dam and foal can be placed together in a small field or paddock. A rather confined area is better than a pasture, in which the foal might become exhausted trying to keep up with his roving mother.

Your veterinarian will plan a program of postnatal care and feeding for the dam and foal through the next few months. Foals start eating on their own when they are ten to fourteen days old, but they continue to nurse for three months, at which point the mare's milk starts to decrease. By six months, they have attained almost half of their adult body weight, are already gobbling four or five pounds of grain a day, and are ready to be weaned. During this maximum growth period, their feet must be trimmed and worming administered as necessary; the usual program is a worming at two months of age, then every other month until they are one year old. Halter training is begun as soon as possible. By the age of eighteen months, they have almost attained their adult height and girth measurements, and by the age of two years, almost their adult body weight.

You should refrain from riding your mare while the foal is still suckling, because strenuous exercise will affect the mother's milk. But after the foal has been weaned, the mare can be brought back into riding condition with a progressively increased amount of daily work. Meanwhile, you can already start to work with her foal and in a few years (three, at least) you may experience the joy of riding a horse whom you have bred and trained yourself, and who possesses some of the qualities that have endeared its parent to you.

While the idea is undeniably appealing, the truth is that very few independent horse-owners find it practicable to indulge in any breeding activity. In order to undertake a project involving such considerable expense, time, and effort, a horseman's fondness for his mare must be very great indeed.

Is a horse capable of feeling for its master a similar degree of affection? Objective observers are obliged to answer "No," maintaining that the horse's attachment to his owner is based more on self-interest, habit, and familiarity than on sentiment. Some add that it may even be entirely imaginary. And yet, it must be admitted that there have been instances

Little Squire ridden by Mickey Walsh, for whom he accomplished such exploits as this.

in which some kind of a mysterious bond has existed between a rider and his horse. Because the occurrence is rare, it is all the more precious.

Hundreds of bystanders at Ascot some years ago were convinced of witnessing an example of equine affection on the part of the great racing sire Hyperion toward his first trainer, the Hon. George Lambton. After preparing the phenomenal colt for his two-year-old season on the turf, Lambton became seriously ill and had to abandon his job. Two years later, as Hyperion was being led into the parade ring just before the Gold Cup Race in which he was to run, he caught sight of his old friend sitting in a wheel chair by the rail. Pulling away from his lad, he sped to Lambton's side with joyful recognition and displayed obvious reluctance to turn away and return to the ring.

Is it entirely imaginary that some horses seem to attach themselves

Snowman ridden by his owner, Harry de Leyer. (*Photo by Budd*)

to one particular rider and never do their best for anybody else? Mickey Walsh's famous Jumper Little Squire was ridden by other horsemen smaller and lighter than he, far better suited to the diminutive pony's size, but only with Walsh in the saddle did he achieve his greatest successes. A similar case was that of a legendary British show Jumper, Little Jim, who, despite his mere 13.2½ hands, scored victories over the keenest competition for almost twenty years when he was ridden by his 170-pound owner, G. F. Bowser. But whenever Bowser attempted to lighten the aging pony's burden by having him mounted by a smaller rider, Little Jim was never inspired to put forth his best efforts.

Equine sporting history is studded with the names of memorable "one-man horses," for example, Colonel Harry Llewellyn's Foxhunter, Hans Winkler's Halla, Wilf White's Nizefela, Harry de Leyer's Snow-

A foal on a breeding farm. (*Photo by Bert Clark Thayer*)

man, and the Chevalier d'Orgeix's Sucre de Pomme. The fabulous Tetrarch would only allow himself to be ridden by the jockey Steve Donoghue and succeeded in unseating, sometimes with rare violence, every other rider who attempted to mount him.

Some horses, through years of devoted service to an illustrious master, have earned themselves a place in history. No chronicle of the Revolutionary War period would be complete without the name of General Washington's war charger Nelson, who was his companion on many historic occasions. After surviving the dreadful winter in Valley Forge, Nelson took part in the victorious Battle of Yorktown, and when Washington became the first President of the United States, he too returned to Mount Vernon, where they often rode to hounds together.

When two great adversaries confronted each other at the Battle of Waterloo, there were two great horses to aid them in the crucial combat. Napoleon was mounted on his favorite white Arabian Marengo, while the Duke of Wellington's charger was the courageous and indefatigable Copenhagen. A grandson of Eclipse, the powerful chestnut carried his soldier master during eighteen straight hours, until the French defeat was certain. Retired afterward to the seven-thousand-acre estate in England that was the British government's victory reward to Wellington, he

Napoleon and Marengo. (*Photo courtesy of the Musées Nationaux*)

so endeared himself to the entire Wellington family that the Duchess often wore among her priceless jewels a modest bracelet made from a braid of Copenhagen's hair.

Historians have recorded the courage and devotion of countless other equine heroes, such as General Grant's beautiful dark bay Cincinnati, General Sheridan's gallant black Winchester, and General Sherman's Thoroughbred Lexington and his half-bred with the simple name of Sam. Is there a horse-lover who has remained unmoved by the friend-

General Robert E. Lee and Traveller. (*U. S. Army photograph*)

ship of General Robert E. Lee and his faithful Traveller? The Confederate leader was a superb horseman and a fine soldier, hardly prone to sentimentality. And yet his affection for his high-spirited horse was so great that from the close of the war until his death, he took Traveller riding every day and even insisted upon feeding him himself.

Most of these horses disappeared into retirement or passed away, while their riders continued their equestrian careers on other mounts. So it is with every horse-owner, and so it will be with you. Like these eminent equestrians, you can expect to experience not only the sorrow of one day parting with your horse, but also the joy of forming new friendships with his successors. Throughout a horseman's lifetime there may figure many different riding partners, each one adding something new to his knowledge and understanding of horses and horsemanship.

The adventure of developing a harmonious relationship with a new horse need never dull the glowing memory of his predecessors. In fact, if you are like most horsemen, you will find that deep in your heart there always remains a special warm spot for the unforgettable creature who was the very first horse of your own.

George Washington and Nelson. (*Engraved by F. Halpin from an original painting by A. Chappel*)

(*Photo by Bert Clark Thayer*)

APPENDIXES

Appendix A

Sources of Information

American Horse Council, Inc.
    1700 K Street N.W., Washington, DC   20006
    (Research and statistical information on the horse industry)
USDA Animal and Plant Health Inspection Service
    Federal Center Building, Hyattsville, MD   20782
    (Information on equine diseases and horse protection)
National Agricultural Library
    Beltsville, MD   20705
    (Horse literature about horsemanship and the horse industry)
Bureau of Outdoor Recreation
    U. S. Department of the Interior, Washington, DC   20240
    (Information on the National Trails System)
U. S. Forest Service, Recreation Management
    U. S. Department of Agriculture, Washington, DC   20250
    (Information on trails within National Forests)
National Park Service
    U. S. Department of the Interior, Washington, DC   20240
    (Information on activities within National Parks)
University of California
    Animal Science Extension, Davis, CA   95616
    (Publisher of a brochure on "Obtaining Horse Information")

Appendix B

American ALBINO Association, Inc.
Box 79, Crabtree, OR 97335
ANDALUSIAN Horse Registry of America, Inc.
P. O. Box 1290, Silver City, NM 88061
APPALOOSA Horse Club, Inc.
P. O. Box 8403, Moscow, ID 83843
National APPALOOSA Pony, Inc.
P. O. Box 206, Gaston, IN 47342
ARABIAN Horse Registry of America, Inc.
3435 S. Yosemite Street, Denver, CO 80231
International ARABIAN Horse Association
P. O. Box 4502, Burbank, CA 91503
American BUCKSKIN Registry Association
P. O. Box 1125, Anderson, CA 96007
International BUCKSKIN Horse Association
P. O. Box 357, St. John, IN 46373
CLEVELAND BAY Society of America
Berryville, VA 22611
American CONNEMARA Pony Society
HoshieKon Farm, Goshen, CT 06756
American HACKNEY Horse Society
P. O. Box 174, Pittsfield, IL 62363
HORSE OF THE AMERICAS Registry
248 N. Main Street, Porterville, CA 93257
American MORGAN Horse Association, Inc.
P. O. Box 1, Westmoreland, NY 13490
American MUSTANG Association
P. O. Box 338, Yucaipa, CA 92399
American PAINT HORSE Association
P. O. Box 13486, Fort Worth, TX 76118
The PALOMINO Horse Association, Inc.
P. O. Box 324, Jefferson City, MO 65101
PALOMINO Horse Breeders of America
P. O. Box 249, Mineral Wells, TX 76067
PART-THOROUGHBRED Stud Book
11783 North Ranch Lane, Scottsdale, AR 85260
PASO FINO Owners and Breeders Association
P. O. Box 1579, Tryon, NC 28782

The PINTO Horse Association of America, Inc.
    P. O. Box 3984, San Diego, CA   92103
PONY OF THE AMERICAS Club
    1452 N. Federal, Box 1447, Mason City, IA   50401
American QUARTER HORSE Association
    P. O. Box 200, Amarillo, TX   79168
American SADDLE HORSE Breeders Association
    929 S. Fourth Street, Louisville, KY   40203
American SHETLAND PONY Registry
    P. O. Box 435, Fowler, IN   47944
The SPANISH MUSTANG Registry, Inc.
    Route 2, Box 80, Marshall, TX   75670
The United States Trotting Association (STANDARDBRED)
    750 Michigan Avenue, Columbus, OH   43215
TENNESSEE WALKING HORSE Breeders' and Exhibitors' Association
    P. O. Box 286, Lewisburg, TN   37091
The Jockey Club (THOROUGHBRED)
    380 Madison Avenue, New York, NY   10017
American TRAKEHNER Association
    P. O. Box 268, Norman, OK   73069
North American TRAKEHNER Association
    Box 100, Bath, OH   44210
WELSH PONY Society of America
    P. O. Box 2977, Winchester, VA   22601

Appendix C

Equestrian Organizations

American Association of Equine Practitioners
    Route 5, 14 Hillcrest Circle, Golden, CO 80401
American Driving Society
    339 Warburton Avenue, Hastings-on-Hudson, NY 10706
American Endurance Ride Conference
    6222 Thornton Avenue, Newark, CA 94560
American Farriers Association
    P. O. Box 695, Albuquerque, NM 87103
American Horse Shows Association
    527 Madison Avenue, New York, NY 10022
American Masters of Foxhounds Association
    112 Water Street, Boston, MA 02109
Eastern Competitive Trail Ride Association
    P. O. Box 57, Oran, NY 13125
Eastern States Trail Ride Association
    P. O. Box 142, Douglasville, GA 30133
Equestrian Trails, Inc.
    10723 Riverside Drive, P. O. Box 2086, North Hollywood, CA 91602
F.E.I. (Federation Equestre Internationale)
    Schosshaldenstrasse 32, 3006 Berne, Switzerland
Future Farmers of America
    P. O. Box 15160, Alexandria, VA 22309
Girls Rodeo Association
    8909 N.E. 25th Street, Spencer, OK 73084
International Rodeo Association
    P. O. Box 615, Pauls Valley, OK 73075
International Side-Saddle Association
    R. D. 2, Box 2096, Mount Holly, NJ 08060
National Cutting Horse Association
    P. O. Box 12155, Fort Worth, TX 76116
National 4-H Service Committee
    150 N. Wacker Drive, Chicago, IL 60606
National High School Rodeo Association
    P. O. Box 35, Edgar, MT 59026
National Intercollegiate Rodeo Association
    P. O. Box 2088, Huntsville, TX 77340
National Steeplechase and Hunt Association
    P. O. Box 308, Elmont, NY 11003

National Trails Council
    7120 Ridge Road, Frederick, MD 21701
North American Trail Ride Conference
    1505 E. San Martin Avenue, San Martin, CA 95046
Professional Horsemen's Association of America
    Fox Hill Farm, Old Sleepy Hollow Road, Pleasantville, NY 10570
Professional Rodeo Cowboys Association
    101 Pro Rodeo Drive, Colorado Springs, CO 80919
United States Pony Clubs
    303 S. High Street, West Chester, PA 19380
U. S. Combined Training Association
    One Winthrop Square, Boston, MA 02110
U. S. Dressage Federation, Inc.
    Box 80668, Lincoln, NB 68501
U. S. Equestrian Team, Inc.
    Gladstone, NJ 07934
U. S. Polo Association
    1301 W. 22nd Street, Suite 706, Oak Brook, IL 60521
U. S. Trotting Association
    750 Michigan Avenue, Columbus, OH 43215

Appendix D

There are numerous publications, abroad as well as in the United States, of particular interest to horsemen. The following selection includes many of the more important ones. Ken Kimbel (P. O. Box KK, Plant City, FL 33566) and The Book Stable (5326 Tomahawk Trail, Fort Wayne, IN 46804) are among the firms that specialize in handling subscription orders for equestrian magazines in America. Breed clubs and associations also edit publications that range from a few mimeographed sheets to full-color magazines such as *The Voice of the Tennessee Walking Horse, The Morgan Horse Magazine, The Quarter Horse Journal, Palomino Horses,* and *The Maryland Horse* (Thoroughbreds). The leading agent for foreign publications—and, incidentally, one of the foremost dealers in horse literature in the world—is J. A. Allen & Company (One Lower Grosvenor Place, Buckingham Palace Road, London, England).

American Horseman (general interest)
> 257 Park Avenue South, New York, NY   10010

The Blood Horse (Thoroughbred racing)
> P. O. Box 4038, Lexington, KY   40504

California Horse Review (general interest)
> 2796 E. Acampo Road, Acampo, CA   95220

The Chronicle of the Horse (Thoroughbred sports, covering racing, hunting, horse shows, steeplechase, polo, Junior activities, etc. Official publication of the United States Pony Clubs, the MFH Association of America, the U. S. Equestrian Team, and the U. S. Combined Training Association)

Classic (a luxurious publication of general interest to horsemen)
> 551 Fifth Avenue, New York, NY   10017

Dressage & Combined Training (educational and show)
> P. O. Box 2460, Cleveland, OH   44112

Equus (Horse health and management by renowned specialists, luxuriously presented, highly informative)
> P. O. Box 968, Farmingdale, NY   11747

Hoof & Horn (rodeo and ranching)
> P. O. Box C, Englewood, CO   80110

Hoof Beats (Standardbred racing)
> 750 Michigan Avenue, Columbus, OH   43215

Horse and Horseman (general interest)
> P. O. Box HH, Capistrano Beach, CA   92624

Horse & Rider (general interest)
> Box 555, Temecula, CA   92390

Horse Illustrated (general interest, Western)
> Box A, Lake Elsinore, CA   92330

Horse Lovers' National Magazine (general interest)
   P. O. Box 3003, Menlo Park, CA 94025
Horseman, The Magazine of Western Riding
   5314 Bingle Road, Houston, TX 77092
Horsemen's Yankee Pedlar (general interest)
   Box 897, Wilbraham, MA 01095
Horse, Of Course! (general interest)
   Derbyshire Building, Temple, NH 03084
Polo News
   P. O. Box 267, Middleburg, VA 22117
Practical Horseman (Thoroughbred sports)
   19 Wilmont Mews, West Chester, PA 19380
Rodeo Sports News
   2929 W. 19th Avenue, Denver, CO 80204
Saddle and Bridle Magazine (showing)
   2333 Brentwood Boulevard, St. Louis, MO 63144
The Thoroughbred Record (Thoroughbred racing)
   P. O. Box 11788, Lexington, KY 40511
Trail Blazer Magazine (competitive trail riding)
   P. O. Box 1855, Paso Robles, CA 93446
Turf and Sport Digest (Thoroughbred Racing)
   511 Oakland Avenue, Baltimore, MD 21212
The Western Horseman (general interest)
   3850 N. Nevada Avenue, Colorado Springs, CO 80901

FOREIGN

L'Année Hippique (in French, German, and English)
   Published in Switzerland, the most luxurious and complete equestrian annual in the world, recording the international horse show scene.
Chevaux et Cavaliers (in French)
   An illustrated monthly newspaper
L'Eperon (in French)
   Quarterly. The leading equestrian magazine of France.
Horse and Hound (in English)
   British, general interest and fox-hunting.
L'Information Hippique (in French)
   Horse shows and racing.
Kavalkade (in German)
   An annual illustrated record of the year's horse shows in Germany.
The Light Horse (in English)
   A monthly, incorporating *Show Jumping* and *Horse News*.
Pony (in English)
   Monthly British magazine for children.
Reiter und Fahrer (in German)
   Illustrated monthly.
Sankt Georg (in German)
   Bimonthly. The leading German equestrian magazine.
Sankt Georg Almanach (in German)
   An illustrated annual of the riding sports in Germany, especially show jumping and horse shows.

INDEX

Index